Register for Free Membership to

solutions@syngress.com

Over the last few years, Syngress has published many best-selling and critically acclaimed books, including Tom Shinder's *Configuring ISA Server 2000*, Brian Caswell and Jay Beale's *Snort 2.0 Intrusion Detection*, and Angela Orebaugh and Gilbert Ramirez's *Ethereal Packet Sniffing*. One of the reasons for the success of these books has been our unique **solutions@syngress.com** program. Through this site, we've been able to provide readers a real time extension to the printed book.

As a registered owner of this book, you will qualify for free access to our members-only solutions@syngress.com program. Once you have registered, you will enjoy several benefits, including:

- Four downloadable e-booklets on topics related to the book. Each booklet is approximately 20-30 pages in Adobe PDF format. They have been selected by our editors from other best-selling Syngress books as providing topic coverage that is directly related to the coverage in this book.

- A comprehensive FAQ page that consolidates all of the key points of this book into an easy to search web page, providing you with the concise, easy to access data you need to perform your job.

- A "From the Author" Forum that allows the authors of this book to post timely updates links to related sites, or additional topic coverage that may have been requested by readers.

Just visit us at **www.syngress.com/solutions** and follow the simple registration process. You will need to have this book with you when you register.

Thank you for giving us the opportunity to serve your needs. And be sure to let us know if there is anything ~~~~~~ ~~ ~~~~~ your job easier.

D1303806   S ®

SYNGRESS®

Microsoft®
Log
Parser Toolkit

Gabriele Giuseppini
Mark Burnett

KEY	SERIAL NUMBER
001	HJIRTCV764
002	PO9873D5FG
003	829KM8NJH2
004	PLBBB569NM
005	CVPLQ6WQ23
006	VBP965T5T5
007	HJJJ863WD3E
008	2987GVTWMK
009	629MP5SDJT
010	IMWQ295T6T

PUBLISHED BY
Syngress Publishing, Inc.
800 Hingham Street
Rockland, MA 02370

Microsoft Log Parser Toolkit

Printed in the United States of America
1 2 3 4 5 6 7 8 9 0
ISBN: 1-932266-52-6

Publisher: Andrew Williams   Page Layout and Art: Patricia Lupien
Acquisitions Editor: Christine Kloiber   Copy Editor: Amy Thomson
Technical Editor: Mark Burnett   Indexer: Nara Wood
Cover Designer: Michael Kavish

Distributed by O'Reilly Media, Inc. in the United States and Canada.
For information on rights and translations, contact Matt Pedersen, Director of Sales and Rights, at Syngress Publishing; email matt@syngress.com or fax to 781-681-3585.

Acknowledgments

Syngress would like to acknowledge the following people for their kindness and support in making this book possible.

Syngress books are now distributed in the United States and Canada by O'Reilly Media, Inc. The enthusiasm and work ethic at O'Reilly is incredible and we would like to thank everyone there for their time and efforts to bring Syngress books to market: Tim O'Reilly, Laura Baldwin, Mark Brokering, Mike Leonard, Donna Selenko, Bonnie Sheehan, Cindy Davis, Grant Kikkert, Opol Matsutaro, Steve Hazelwood, Mark Wilson, Rick Brown, Leslie Becker, Jill Lothrop, Tim Hinton, Kyle Hart, Sara Winge, C. J. Rayhill, Peter Pardo, Leslie Crandell, Valerie Dow, Regina Aggio, Pascal Honscher, Preston Paull, Susan Thompson, Bruce Stewart, Laura Schmier, Sue Willing, Mark Jacobsen, Betsy Waliszewski, Dawn Mann, Kathryn Barrett, John Chodacki, and Rob Bullington.

The incredibly hard working team at Elsevier Science, including Jonathan Bunkell, Ian Seager, Duncan Enright, David Burton, Rosanna Ramacciotti, Robert Fairbrother, Miguel Sanchez, Klaus Beran, Emma Wyatt, Rosie Moss, Chris Hossack, Mark Hunt, and Krista Leppiko, for making certain that our vision remains worldwide in scope.

David Buckland, Marie Chieng, Lucy Chong, Leslie Lim, Audrey Gan, Pang Ai Hua, and Joseph Chan of STP Distributors for the enthusiasm with which they receive our books.

Kwon Sung June at Acorn Publishing for his support.

David Scott, Tricia Wilden, Marilla Burgess, Annette Scott, Andrew Swaffer, Stephen O'Donoghue, Bec Lowe, and Mark Langley of Woodslane for distributing our books throughout Australia, New Zealand, Papua New Guinea, Fiji Tonga, Solomon Islands, and the Cook Islands.

Winston Lim of Global Publishing for his help and support with distribution of Syngress books in the Philippines.

Technical Editor

Mark Burnett is an independent researcher, consultant, and writer specializing in Windows security. Mark is author of *Hacking the Code: ASP.NET Web Application Security* (Syngress Publishing, ISBN: 1-932266-65-8), co-author of *Maximum Windows 2000 Security* (SAMS Publishing, ISBN: 0-672319-65-9), co-author of *Stealing The Network: How to Own the Box* (Syngress Publishing, ISBN: 1-931836-87-6), and is a contributor to *Dr. Tom Shinder's ISA Server and Beyond: Real World Security Solutions for Microsoft Enterprise Networks* (Syngress Publishing, ISBN: 1-931836-66-3). He is a contributor and technical editor for Syngress Publishing's *Special Ops: Host and Network Security for Microsoft, UNIX, and Oracle* (ISBN: 1-931836-69-8). Mark speaks at various security conferences and has published articles in Windows IT Pro Magazine (formerly Windows & .NET Magazine), Redmond Magazine, Information Security, Windows Web Solutions, Security Administrator, SecurityFocus.com, and various other print and online publications. Mark is a Microsoft Windows Server Most Valued Professional (MVP) for Internet Information Services (IIS).

Lead Author

Gabriele Giuseppini is a Software Design Engineer at Microsoft Corporation in the Security Business Unit, where he developed Microsoft Log Parser to analyze log files.

Originally from Rome, Italy, after working for years in the digital signal processing field, he moved to the United States with his family in 1999, and joined Microsoft Corporation as a Software Design Engineer working on Microsoft Internet Information Services.

Contributing Authors

Edward Brothers works as a software development consultant in the Seattle area. With over 16 years in this field, he has a broad range of experience spanning building complete test organizations and developing test automation to writing database conversion tools and honing creative troubleshooting skills doing product support for Microsoft in the late 80s. Ed has instructed and developed material for new hire training programs and is very active with Boy Scout and Cub Scout camping programs. Many of his recent consulting activities have entailed conducting detailed analysis of existing test procedures then evaluating where different types of test automation can be employed to achieve the greatest ROI.

Bernard Cheah (MCP+I, MCSE, MCDBA, CCSE) is a Microsoft Most Valuable Professional (MVP) specializing in IIS Server. He is currently a contract solution consultant working on Internet solutions analysis, design, and consultancy as well as implementation. His primary focus includes online ecommerce system security and high availability features. He is pursuing his masters in IT business strategy at the University of Portsmouth, UK.

Jeremy Faircloth (Security+, CCNA, MCSE, MCP+I, A+, etc.) is an IT Manager for EchoStar Satellite L.L.C., where he and his team architect and maintain enterprise-wide client/server and Web-based technologies. He also acts as a technical resource for other IT professionals, using his expertise to help others expand their knowledge. As a systems engineer with over 13 years of real world IT experience, he has become an expert in many areas including web development, database administration, enterprise security, network design, and project management. Jeremy has contributed to several Syngress books including *Managing and Securing a Cisco SWAN*

(ISBN: 1-932266-91-7), *C# for Java Programmers* (ISBN: 1-931836-54-X), *Snort 2.0 Intrusion Detection* (ISBN: 1-931836-74-4), and *Security+ Study Guide & DVD Training System* (ISBN: 1-931836-72-8).

Andrew Galloway is an Internet Systems Engineer specializing in low-level monitoring, debugging and troubleshooting in the enterprise space. He is currently involved in system engineering at MSN, playing a Lead Problem Management role in one of the largest enterprise deployments of Microsoft NT technology, SQL server and Internet Information Server in the world.

An online veteran, he started his online presence in the early 1980's by using his Apple II computer to interconnect with multiple local BBS's, buying his first Hayes Microcoupler 300 baud modem at the age of 12. He is constantly trying to automate his life, writing code in many languages, including C#, VB, Perl and others. When he isn't trying to automate anything in sight, he is trying to find newer and better ways to monitor network traffic, server performance and end user experience at MSN. He holds a Microsoft MCSE, the Cisco CCNA and works in close tandem with many hardware and software vendors to distribute Web applications and create load balancing devices that improve networking performance for client server applications.

Mike Gunderloy (MCSE, MCSD) is an independent software developer and journalist who has written dozens of books and hundreds of articles. He also maintains the Unofficial LogParser Support Site at www.logparser.com . He's contributed code to several Microsoft products and has done extensive work with Microsoft .NET. When he's not in front of the computer, Mike raises chickens, ducks, and garlic on his farm in Washington state.

Laura E. Hunter (CISSP, MCSE: Security, MCDBA) is a Senior IT Specialist with the University of Pennsylvania, where she provides network planning, implementation, and troubleshooting services for various business units and schools within the university. Her specialties include Microsoft Windows 2000 and 2003 design and implementation, troubleshooting, and security topics. Laura's previous experience includes a position as the Director of Computer Services for the Salvation Army and as the LAN administrator for a medical supply firm. She is a regular contributor to the TechTarget family of Web sites, and to Microsoft Certified Professional Magazine.

Laura has previously contributed to Syngress Publishing's *Configuring Symantec Antivirus, Corporate Edition*, as well as the *Syngress Windows Server 2003 MCSE/MCSA DVD Guide & Training System* series as a DVD presenter, contributing author, and technical reviewer. Laura was recently awarded the prestigious MVP award as a Microsoft "Most Valued Professional." Laura holds a bachelor's degree from the University of Pennsylvania and is a member of the Network of Women in Computer Technology, the Information Systems Security Association, and InfraGard, a cooperative undertaking between the U.S. Government and other participants dedicated to increasing the security of United States critical infrastructures.

Dan Kahler (MCSD, MCSE, MCDBA) is a Senior Operations Engineer with MCI Enterprise Hosting, a Digex Service, which helps enable organizations to quickly, safely and cost-effectively deploy on-line commerce, Web-enabled business applications or business-to-business Web Services. With over 7 years experience developing and administering Windows and Web-based solutions, he specializes in using Microsoft technologies to simplify and automate day-to-day system administration tasks. Dan contributed to the *Microsoft Internet Information Services (IIS) 6.0 Resource Kit* (Microsoft Press, ISBN: 0735614202) as a technical reviewer and tester, and is active in the Baltimore .NET user group (www.baltomsdn.com). Dan currently resides in Eldersburg, Maryland with his wife Shannon and children Nicole and Ethan.

David A Kleiman (CISSP, CIFI, CISM, MCSE) has worked in the information technology sector since 1983. He began his first IT security company, Hackers, Inc. a Florida corporation in 1991.

Currently he is the owner of SecurityBreachResponse.com and is the Chief Information Security Officer for Securit-e-Doc, Inc. Prior to this, he was Vice President of Technical Operations with Intelliswitch, Inc. a Florida Corporation supervising an international telecommunications and Internet Service Provider network. David is a recognized security expert; he specializes in computer forensic investigations, incident response, intrusion analysis, security audits, and secure network infrastructures. He has written several Microsoft technologies secure installation and configuration guides for use by network professionals. He has developed a Windows operating system lockdown tool, Securit-e-Lok—www.s-doc.com/products/slok.asp, that surpasses NSA (National Security Agency), NIST (National Institute of Standards and Technology), and Microsoft Common Criteria Guidelines. This tool is currently in use at NASA, U.S. Department of Treasury, Office of the Inspector General and the US Marshals Office. He is a regular contributor to many security-related newsletters, web sites, and Internet Security Forums.

David is a member of: The FBI's InfraGard, the Information Systems Audit and Control Association (ISACA), the International Information Systems Forensics Association (IISFA), the International Information System Security Certification Consortium (ISC2), and the International Association of Counter Terrorism and Security Professionals (IACSP).

Contents

**Visit www.syngress.com/solutions to download all
of the scripts from this book!**

Foreword

In 2000, when I first wrote Log Parser at Microsoft as an internal test tool, the two or three people that knew about it would tease me saying that it was "yet another log parser" tool, and that was so true. The first version, in fact, was just a simple "log dumper" that printed all of the fields of a single Microsoft Internet Information Services (IIS) log file to the console window. The tool was completing its testing job fairly, but its usefulness was dwarfed by other internal tools that I knew product support analysts were using at the time; tools that had their own cool user interfaces but had limited filtering and sorting capabilities. For these reasons, I decided to see what operations users needed to perform most frequently when processing log files: advanced filtering capabilities and arbitrary sorting were a must while data aggregation and statistical calculations were a plus. This looked so much like SQL language that most processing tools required a back-end SQL database to perform these operations. So I started playing around with the idea of enhancing my little tool with a *built-in* SQL processor, to give users a way to achieve results quickly and easily without the need for a back-end database. Armed with the ubiquitous "dragon" book, the wonderful lessons on parsing techniques learned from Professor Daniele Nardi at my alma mater in Rome, and with the voice recorder that my wife Monica gave me as a gift to stop me from scribbling notes all the time, I set myself up to build a SQL engine at the core of my "yet another log parser" tool. After a few months, the Log Parser core SQL engine was capable of executing complex queries, and the Log Parser architecture allowed plug-in input processors and output formatters.

I guess that the power of this tool rests in the simplicity of its design. These three powerful pieces—the input formats, the output formats, and the SQL engine core in the middle—allow users to mix and match input parsers with output formatters. With Log Parser, you create the data processing pipeline that best fits your needs; at the same time, however, the endless possibilities allowed by this flexible design have proven to be Log Parser's curse, making the tool very difficult to be understood and employed effectively by first-time and seasoned users alike. During the interactions with users on public newsgroups and forums I have realized that even though the tool documentation does provide a complete reference, what users really need are real-world examples of what they can achieve with Log Parser.

This book is aimed at filling this gap. Here you will find working tools and techniques developed by some of those early users that creatively fought against the poor usability and little documentation of the initial versions of the tool. Among these brave pioneers is Mark Burnett, whose article entitled *Forensic Log Parsing with Microsoft's Log Parser* helped fuel the widespread adoption of the tool among security-aware IT administrators. The authors in this book have developed usages of Log Parser that I had never thought were possible, and you will find that you do not need to be a SQL expert to leverage the capabilities of the tool that they reveal while guiding you through their arsenal of queries and commands.

I hope that after reading this book you will see that Log Parser can help you implement and optimize a number of those projects that you have been working on for some time, be it log consolidation systems, system monitoring applications, reporting facilities, or whatever you'll find out that Log Parser can help you with. And if you ever need to ask a question or want to simply show your queries to the rest of the World, don't hesitate to log on to Mike Gunderloy's www.logparser.com, where I, and hundreds of other Log Parser users, will gladly address your problems and appreciate your suggestions.

Hope to see you there soon.

— *Gabriele Giuseppini*
Software Design Engineer,
Microsoft Corporation

Chapter 1

Introducing Log Parser

Scripts and Samples in this Chapter:

- Retrieving fields from the Event Log
- Searching for Information
- Ordering the Output
- Top-Ten Lists
- Parsing Text Files
- Querying System Information
- Parsing NetMon Files
- Implementing Custom Input Formats
- Using the DATAGRID Output Format
- Creating Custom Text Files
- Creating Charts
- Uploading Query Results to a SQL Database
- Converting Log File Formats

In This Toolbox

Log files—records of events that have occurred in a system—often contain information deemed crucial to a business. However, most times log files can be so large that it becomes almost impossible to extract useful data or find meaningful patterns in the amount of information that they provide. The Log Parser tool allows users to treat log files and other information as SQL tables, the rows of which can be queried, processed, and formatted in different ways. The power of the SQL language, together with the variety of data that can be processed by Log Parser, make it possible to extract specific information, calculate statistics, and generate reports from large amounts of data.

A Brief Background

The Log Parser tool was born around 2000 as a utility to test the logging mechanisms of Microsoft's Internet Information Services (IIS). The first inception of the tool allowed users to retrieve and display all the fields from a single log file in any of the three text-logging formats supported by IIS.

As tests became more complicated, the need arose for more specialized tasks, including the possibility to filter log entries matching specific criteria and to sort the resulting entries according to values of specific fields. To provide a succinct and well-established way to specify these operations from a command-line shell, the tool underwent its first major makeover and began to support a very limited dialect of the SQL language. Log Parser 1.0 was born, and its use began spreading among internal Microsoft users and product support analysts.

After some time, the SQL language dialect processor was completely redesigned, enriched with functions, aggregate functions, and the *GROUP BY* clause, and with improved performance characteristics; at the same time, the tool underwent a second major architectural makeover, which separated the log file parsers and the console output formatter from the core SQL engine, making it possible for generic "input formats" and "output formats" to easily plug in with the new architecture. Just for fun, the first non-IIS input formats made their appearance, including the Event Log (EVT) input format and the File System (FS) input format, together with the first nonconsole output format, the SQL output format. It didn't take long for IIS program managers to notice that the tool's capabilities could be leveraged by end users as well, greatly simplifying most of the tasks related to processing of log files. In fact, in November 2001 Log Parser 2.0 made its public debut as a freely downloadable tool from the pages of www.microsoft.com.

The user response was so favorable that the new 2.1 version of the tool, which included many new input and output formats, was included in the IIS 6.0 Resource Kit Tools, published in April 2002.

The tool has been continuously improved since then, thanks especially to the feedback and suggestions of its many users; new input and output formats have been added, and the core SQL engine has been improved with new functions and better-performing algorithms.

This 2.2 version marks the latest release of the Log Parser tool, designed and engineered with the vision of helping users achieve their data-processing goals in a simple, fast, and powerful way.

Building Queries

With the Log Parser tool, users can run queries written in a dialect of the Structured Query Language (SQL) on data coming from different sources. The data processed by the queries is provided by *input formats*; these are data processors that enumerate information from different sources and provide the data as *input records* on which the queries operate. Once a query is executed, it generates *output records*, which are handed to *output formats*—data processors that consume output records, format data, and send them to different *targets*.

Retrieving Fields from the Event Log

For our first example of a Log Parser command, we'll start with a simple, basic task: retrieving some fields from the Event Log.

To run this command, start a command-line shell, navigate to the folder where the LogParser.exe command-line executable has been copied or make sure that the folder is in the system path, and type the following command:

```
C:\>LogParser -i:EVT -o:NAT "SELECT TimeGenerated, SourceName FROM System"
```

The output will look like this:

```
TimeGenerated          SourceName
-------------------    -----------------------
2004-04-18 18:48:04    EventLog
2004-04-18 18:48:04    EventLog
2004-04-18 18:48:27    Service Control Manager
2004-04-18 18:48:27    Service Control Manager
2004-04-18 18:48:27    Service Control Manager
2004-04-18 18:48:27    Service Control Manager
2004-04-18 18:48:27    Service Control Manager
2004-04-18 18:48:27    Service Control Manager
2004-04-18 18:48:27    Service Control Manager
2004-04-18 18:48:27    Service Control Manager
Press a key...
```

Let's analyze this command in detail. The first argument is *-i:EVT*, which tells Log Parser that we want to use the EVT *input format*—that is, the input format that enumerates the events in the Windows Event Log. In fact, the *-i* parameter is used to indicate which input format we want our query to operate on.

The second argument is *-o:NAT*, which tells Log Parser that we want to use the NAT *output format*—that is, the output format that displays the query results in a readable, nicely formatted way. In fact, the *-o* parameter is used to indicate which output format we want our query results processed by.

The third argument is our SQL query. In this example, the query is a very simple one: The *SELECT* clause specifies which of the input record fields we want to be handed to the output format, and the *FROM* clause specifies where we want to retrieve the input records from.

In our example, we have specified that we want to retrieve two fields: the *TimeGenerated* field and the *SourceName* field. These are just two fields out of the 15 fields exported by the EVT input format. We can see what fields are exported by the EVT input format by typing the following help command:

```
C:\>LogParser -h -i:EVT
```

The output of this help command displays some useful information on the EVT input format, which includes a list of the exported fields:

```
Fields:
   EventLog (S)          RecordNumber (I)      TimeGenerated (T)
   TimeWritten (T)       EventID (I)           EventType (I)
   EventTypeName (S)     EventCategory (I)     EventCategoryName (S)
   SourceName (S)        Strings (S)           ComputerName (S)
   SID (S)               Message (S)           Data (S)
```

The *FROM* clause that we have used specifies *System* as the data source that we want the EVT input format to retrieve records from. This means that we want to retrieve records from the System Event Log; if we wanted to retrieve records from the Security Event Log, we could have specified *Security* in the *FROM* clause. If we wanted to retrieve events from both the System and Security Event Logs, we could have specified both in our *FROM* clause, using a comma character as a separator, this way:

```
C:\>LogParser -i:EVT -o:NAT "SELECT TimeGenerated, SourceName FROM System, Security"
```

TIP

It is possible to parse Event Logs from another computer by specifying the Event Log names in UNC notation, as in the following example:

```
C:\>LogParser -i:EVT -o:NAT "SELECT TimeGenerated, SourceName FROM \\MYCOM-
PUTER1\System, \\MYCOMPUTER2\Security"
```

When we execute commands using the NAT output format, we can see that the format displays 10 lines and then prompts the user to press a key before displaying the next 10 lines. This behavior can be overridden by specifying a value for the *rtp* parameter of the NAT output format.

Most of the Log Parser input and output formats accept *parameters* that are used to fine-tune their behaviors to match our needs. The *rtp* parameter of the NAT output format specifies the number of rows to print before prompting the user to press a key. If we want to change the value of this parameter to 5, for example, we would type the following command:

```
C:\>LogParser -i:EVT -o:NAT -rtp:5 "SELECT TimeGenerated, SourceName FROM System"
```

Specifying *-1* for this parameter disables the prompt altogether and causes the NAT output format to display all the output records without interruption.

We can see a description of all the parameters supported by an input format by typing the input format help command that we have used before:

```
C:\>LogParser -h -i:EVT
```

We now have a command that displays selected fields from the Event Log to the console output. What if we want to write this output to a file instead?

Well, forget command-line redirection. In the Log Parser SQL-centric world, this can be accomplished using the *INTO* clause of the SQL language:

```
C:\>LogParser -i:EVT -o:NAT "SELECT TimeGenerated, SourceName INTO myoutput.txt FROM
System"
```

This command causes the NAT output format to write its output to the myoutput.txt file instead of the console output. When an *INTO* clause is used, the NAT output format disables the user prompt between output records and writes all the output records to the file without interruption. When a query does not include an *INTO* clause, the NAT output formats assumes a default *INTO* clause with a value of *STDOUT*—that is, the console output.

The commands that we have used in these examples can be simplified by leveraging a couple of shortcuts. When the *FROM* clause in a query specifies a well-known value, Log Parser is able to automatically recognize the input format that should handle the *FROM* clause. This is true for the *System* or *Security* values we have used so far in our examples: Log Parser recognizes that *System* or *Security* are commonly used names of Event Logs and automatically selects the EVT input format for us.

The same applies for output formats: If a query does not include an *INTO* clause, Log Parser automatically selects the NAT output format. This means that we could rewrite our example command as follows:

```
logparser.exe file: "SELECT TimeGenerated, SourceName FROM System"
```

Thus we obtain the same effect as the fully specified command in our first example.

Retrieving Fields from IIS Logs

The simple command that we have used to display Event Log fields can be easily modified to display fields from an IIS Web log file. To do so, we need to first change the input format to the input format responsible for parsing the IIS logs in their currently configured format. Assuming that our IIS Web server is configured to log using the W3C Extended Log File Format, we need to pick the IISW3C input format.

Then we need to decide which of the IISW3C fields we want to retrieve. Again, we can see what fields are exported by this input format using the following help command:

```
logparser.exe file: -h -i:IISW3C
```

Let's assume that we are interested in the *date*, *time*, and *cs-uri-stem* fields.

Finally, we need to change our *FROM* clause to specify the IIS log files that we are interested in parsing. We can do so in two ways: by specifying the paths to the log files or by specifying the ID number of a virtual IIS site whose logs we want to parse. Assuming that we want to parse the log files of the site with ID *1* (the default Web site), our command looks like the following:

```
C:\>LogParser -i:IISW3C -o:NAT "SELECT date, time, cs-uri-stem FROM <1>"
```

The output will look like this:

```
date       time     cs-uri-stem
---------- -------- --------------------
2003-11-18 00:28:33 /Default.htm
2003-11-18 00:28:33 /style.css
2003-11-18 00:28:33 /images/address.gif
2003-11-18 00:28:33 /cgi-bin/counts.exe
2003-11-18 00:28:42 /gorice/rulesinfo.nsf
2003-11-18 00:28:42 /gorice/rulesinfo.nsf
2003-11-18 00:28:42 /gorice/rulesinfo.nsf
2003-11-18 00:28:42 /gorice/rulesinfo.nsf
2003-11-18 00:28:42 /gorice/rulesinfo.nsf
2003-11-18 00:28:42 /gorice/rulesinfo.nsf
Press a key...
```

TIP

We can parse IIS logs from multiple Web sites by specifying a comma-separated list of site identifiers, as in the following example:

```
logparser.exe file: -i:IISW3C -o:NAT "SELECT date, time, cs-uri-stem
FROM <1>, <2>, <3>"
```

In addition, we can parse remote IIS logs by specifying a full IIS metabase path that includes the remote computer name:

```
logparser.exe file: -i:IISW3C -o:NAT "SELECT date, time, cs-uri-stem
FROM </MYSERVER2/W3SVC/1>, </MYSERVER3/W3SVC/1>"
```

Searching for Information

We have just seen how easy it is to retrieve a listing of *all* the events in the Windows Event Log and *all* the log entries in a set of IIS log files. However, we are often interested in retrieving *selected* events or log entries—that is, events or log entries that satisfy particular search conditions. For example, we might be interested in retrieving those events generated by a specific event source, or log entries corresponding to requests coming from a particular IP address. How do we accomplish these tasks? Enter the *WHERE* clause of the SQL language. This clause is used to specify a condition that input records must satisfy for the input records to be further processed by a query. The condition can be as simple as specifying a value for a field or as complex as specifying a set of conditions joined by the *AND* and *OR* logical operators.

The following Log Parser command displays fields from the System Event Log events that are generated by the *Service Control Manager* source:

```
logparser.exe file: "SELECT TimeGenerated, SourceName FROM System WHERE SourceName =
'Service Control Manager'"
```

The output will look like this:

```
TimeGenerated           SourceName
------------------      ----------------------
2004-04-18 18:48:27 Service Control Manager
2004-04-18 18:48:27 Service Control Manager
2004-04-18 18:48:27 Service Control Manager
2004-04-18 18:48:27 Service Control Manager
2004-04-18 18:48:27 Service Control Manager
2004-04-18 18:48:27 Service Control Manager
2004-04-18 18:48:27 Service Control Manager
2004-04-18 18:48:27 Service Control Manager
2004-04-18 18:48:27 Service Control Manager
2004-04-18 18:48:27 Service Control Manager
Press a key...
```

We can specify additional conditions on the events by using the *AND* and *OR* logical operators. For example, the following Log Parser command displays fields from the System Event Log events that are generated by the *Service Control Manager* source and for which the event ID is 7024 (indicating that a service terminated with an error):

```
logparser.exe file: "SELECT TimeGenerated, SourceName FROM System WHERE SourceName =
'Service Control Manager' AND EventID = 7024"
```

User Logons

The following command returns the account names that logged on the MYSERVER2 computer, together with the times at which the logons occurred:

```
logparser.exe file: "SELECT TimeGenerated, SID FROM Security WHERE EventID = 528" -i:EVT
-resolveSIDs:ON
```

This query selects the *TimeGenerated* and *SID* fields of the Security events for which the ID is 528—that is, events signaling a user logon. By setting the *resolveSIDs* parameter to ON, we tell the EVT input format that we want the *SID* field returned as a full account name rather than as the alphanumerical representation of the account identifier.

Long-Running Pages

The following command parses W3C Extended IIS log files matching the specified file search pattern and returns the date, time, and the URI-stem of the requests that took more than 30 seconds to execute:

```
logparser.exe file: "SELECT TO_TIMESTAMP(date, time) AS Timestamp, cs-uri-stem FROM
W3SVC2\ex0402*.log WHERE time-taken >= 30000" -i:IISW3C
```

This query introduces us to a powerful element of the Log Parser SQL language: functions. The Log Parser SQL language includes more than 80 functions that can be used to manipulate the content of fields. These functions include string manipulation functions, arithmetical functions, system information functions, and so on.

In this query we have used the *TO_TIMESTAMP* function, which takes a date and a time as arguments, merges the values into a single date and time field (called a *timestamp* field in the Log Parser SQL language), and returns the new value. For convenience, this new field is renamed *Timestamp* using the *AS* keyword.

Error Responses

The following query returns the timestamp and the URI-stem of the requests that generated HTTP errors:

```
---Ch01ErrorResponses.sql---
SELECT  TO_TIMESTAMP(date, time) AS Timestamp,
        cs-uri-stem
FROM    W3SVC2\ex0402*.log
WHERE   sc-status BETWEEN 400 AND 599
---Ch01ErrorResponses.sql---
```

The *WHERE* clause in this query uses the *BETWEEN* operator, which tests a value for inclusion in an interval of values. The same *WHERE* clause could have been written as follows:

```
WHERE sc-status >= 400 AND sc-status <= 599
```

Events in the Past Two Days

The following query returns the source name, timestamp, and ID of the System events that have been generated in the past two days:

```
---Ch01EventsInPast2Days.sql---
SELECT  SourceName,
        TimeGenerated,
        EventID
FROM    System
WHERE   TimeGenerated >
        SUB( TO_LOCALTIME(SYSTEM_TIMESTAMP()),
             TIMESTAMP('0000-01-03 00:00:00', 'yyyy-MM-dd hh:mm:ss')
```

```
      )
---Ch01EventsInPast2Days.sql---
```

Since the task of retrieving data that happened *X* time ago is quite common, it's worth spending some time analyzing in detail the *WHERE* clause of this query.

The *WHERE* clause in this query specifies that we only want events whose *TimeGenerated* field is greater than the current date and time minus two days. We can specify the current date and time using the *SYSTEM_TIMESTAMP()* function; this function takes no arguments and returns the current system date and time, in Universal Time Coordinates (UTC) time. Since the *TimeGenerated* field contains the date and time of the event using the *local* time, we need to convert the current system time from UTC time to local time, and we do so with the *TO_LOCAL-TIME()* function, which takes a timestamp as argument, subtracts or adds the current time zone and daylight saving time bias, and returns a new timestamp in local time.

Now that we have the current timestamp in local time, we need to subtract two days from it. We can use the *SUB()* function, which takes two arguments and returns their difference. We use the current local timestamp as the first argument, and we need to specify a two-day interval for the second argument.

The Log Parser SQL language does not have an "interval" data type; however, we can specify a two-day interval using the value of the timestamp corresponding to two days after the *origin of time*. The origin of time in the Log Parser date arithmetic, also called *time zero*, is January 1 on year 0, at 00:00:00 o'clock; this means that the timestamp corresponding to a two-day interval is January 3 on year 0—in other words, two days after the origin of time.

Timestamp values are entered with the *TIMESTAMP* keyword in the Log Parser SQL language. The *TIMESTAMP* keyword takes two arguments: the timestamp itself in a format of choice and a string of *format specifiers* that describes how the timestamp is formatted. In our example, we have formatted our timestamp as *yyyy-MM-dd hh:mm:ss*—that it, as a four-digit year value, followed by a dash, followed by a two-digit month value, followed by a dash, and so on.

Putting it all together, our two-day interval is written as:

```
TIMESTAMP('0000-01-03 00:00:00', 'yyyy-MM-dd hh:mm:ss')
```

And the timestamp corresponding to "two days ago" is then:

```
SUB( TO_LOCALTIME(SYSTEM_TIMESTAMP()),
     TIMESTAMP('0000-01-03 00:00:00', 'yyyy-MM-dd hh:mm:ss')
)
```

We can write a more concise two-day interval by noting that the time portion of the interval is not needed, since we only need to subtract two days and leave the time portion as is. Our interval can therefore be written as follows:

```
TIMESTAMP('0000-01-03', 'yyyy-MM-dd')
```

Events in the Past Thirty Minutes

The previous *WHERE* clause can be easily modified to specify a 30-minute interval in the following way:

```
WHERE TimeGenerated >
      SUB( TO_LOCALTIME(SYSTEM_TIMESTAMP()),
          TIMESTAMP('00:30:00', 'hh:mm:ss')
      )
```

Requests from IP Addresses

The following query parses the W3C Extended IIS log files for the specified site and returns all the fields of the log entries corresponding to requests made by clients with the specified IP addresses:

```
---Ch01RequestsFromIPAddresses.sql---
SELECT *
FROM   <1>
WHERE  c-ip IN ('192.168.1.100'; '192.168.2.100'; '192.168.2.101')
---Ch01RequestsFromIPAddresses.sql---
```

The * keyword used in the *SELECT* clause of this query means *all the fields*, and even though it is often a useful shortcut, when used with the NAT output format it generates an output that is often quite unreadable, due to the fact that each output record has so many fields that the lines printed to the console output overflow the console window width and span multiple rows.

The *WHERE* clause in this query uses the *IN* operator, which tests a value for inclusion in a list of values. The same *WHERE* clause could have been written as follows:

```
WHERE  c-ip = '192.168.1.100' OR
       c-ip = '192.168.2.100' OR
       c-ip = '192.168.2.101'
```

Swiss Army Knife

Reusing a Query with Parameters

As an alternative to specifying the text of the query as argument of a Log Parser command, it is possible to save the query in a separate text file and invoke the Log Parser command-line tool, specifying the file itself as an argument. When saved in a text file, the query can also be formatted on multiple lines, thus improving its readability. For example, the previous query can be saved in a query.sql text file as follows:

Continued

```
SELECT *
FROM   <1>
WHERE c-ip IN ('192.168.1.100'; '192.168.2.100'; '192.168.2.101')
```

And executed with the following command:

```
logparser.exe file:query.sql -o:NAT -i:IISW3C
```

Another advantage of using query files is that a query in a text file can use *parameters*. Parameters are custom "variables" enclosed within percent (%) characters, and they can appear anywhere in a query. When we execute a query file, we can specify values for the parameters, and the specified values will replace the parameters verbatim.

For example, the following query is saved in the Ch01RequestsFromIPAddressParameter.sql text file:

```
---Ch01RequestsFromIPAddressParameter.sql---
SELECT *
FROM   %INPUT_FILE%
WHERE c-ip = '%FILTER_IP%'
---Ch01RequestsFromIPAddressParameter.sql---
```

We can execute the query as follows:

```
logparser.exe file: Ch01RequestsFromIPAddressParameter.sql?INPUT_FILE=<4>+FILTER_IP=
192.168.10.20
```

This command would substitute the specified values for the parameters in the text file, resulting in the following query being executed:

```
SELECT *
FROM   <4>
WHERE c-ip = '192.168.10.20'
```

Summarizing Data

The queries we have seen in the past examples return specific fields from the data being parsed. However, in many situations, we might be interested in *calculating summaries* of the data being parsed, rather than in the *raw* data itself. For example, given a W3C Extended IIS log file, we might be interested in the *number* of requests that the server received for each page or in the *average* time it took for each page to execute. With the SQL language, this can be accomplished with the *GROUP BY* clause and with *aggregate functions*.

For example, the following query parses IIS log files and returns the number of requests received by the server for each page:

```
---Ch01HitsPerPage.sql---
SELECT cs-uri-stem, COUNT(*)
FROM <1>
GROUP BY cs-uri-stem
---Ch01HitsPerPage.sql---
```

The output of this query would look like the following:

```
cs-uri-stem            COUNT(ALL *)
--------------------   ------------
/Default.htm           13
/FAA.css               13
/images/address.gif    21
/cgi-bin/counts.exe    25
/gorice/rulesinfo.nsf  28
/maindefault.htm       12
/top2.htm              11
/990136.swf            11
/top.htm               10
/left3.htm             11
Press a key...
```

The *GROUP BY* clause is used to divide all the input records into *groups* using the specified field(s) as the grouping criteria. In this example, we are dividing all the log entries into groups based on the values of the *cs-uri-stem* field. This means that we will end up having as many groups as the number of *different* pages logged in the log files, and each log entry will belong to the group of entries having the same value for the *cs-uri-stem* field.

After all the log entries are divided into groups, the entries in each group are aggregated into a single record. During this phase, *aggregate functions* in the *SELECT* clause are calculated on all the entries in the group, returning a single, summarizing value. Different from the "normal" functions we have seen so far, which calculate their result value on the values of a *single* record, aggregate functions calculate their values across *multiple* records—in other words, the records that belong to the same group.

The *COUNT* aggregate function is used to calculate the number of records belonging to each group; given that in our example each group contains all the requests for the same page, the *COUNT(*)* function will return the total number of requests for each page.

Average Request Time Per Extension

The Log Parser SQL language supports eight aggregate functions, including *SUM, AVG, MAX,* and *MIN*. In the following example query, we group together IIS log entries using the page extension as the grouping criteria, and we summarize all the entries with the same page extension using the *AVG* aggregate function to calculate the average time-taken value across all the requests in the same group:

```
---Ch01AvgRequestTimePerPageType.sql---
SELECT EXTRACT_EXTENSION(cs-uri-stem) AS PageType,
       AVG(time-taken)
FROM <1>
GROUP BY PageType
---Ch01AvgRequestTimePerPageType.sql---
```

The output of this query would look like the following:

```
PageType AVG(ALL time-taken)
-------- ------------------
htm      430
css      81
gif      203
exe      156
nsf      12372
swf      14458
jpg      512
html     78
dll      3
asp      14675
Press a key...
```

Average Total Request Time

The following query returns the global average request time across *all* the entries in the IIS log files for the specified site:

```
---Ch01AvgRequestTimeTotal.sql---
SELECT AVG(time-taken)
FROM <1>
---Ch01AvgRequestTimeTotal.sql---
```

This query shows a special usage of the *GROUP BY* clause and aggregate functions: When a query uses aggregate functions and no *GROUP BY* clause, *all* the entries are grouped into a single group, and aggregate functions are thus calculated across *all* the entries. The output of this query would look like the following:

```
AVG(ALL time-taken)
------------------
2224
```

Total Bytes Sent Per Day

The following query uses the *SUM* aggregate function to calculate the total number of bytes sent back to clients each day:

```
---Ch01BytesSentPerDay.sql---
SELECT date, SUM(sc-bytes)
FROM <1>
GROUP BY date
---Ch01BytesSentPerDay.sql---
```

Total Bytes Received Per Hour Per Client

The following query returns the total bytes received by the server each hour from each client IP address:

```
---Ch01BytesRecvdPerHourPerClient.sql---
SELECT TO_STRING(time, 'hh') AS Hour,
       c-ip,
       SUM(cs-bytes)
FROM <1>
GROUP BY Hour, c-ip
---Ch01BytesRecvdPerHourPerClient.sql---
```

In this example, groups are created on two different fields: the hour at which the request was made and the IP address of the client that made the request. The output of this query will consist of as many records as the number of different *<hour, client address>* pairs existing in the log. Given the magnitude of records generated by this query, we might only be interested in seeing those records showing clients that sent, for example, at least 100K of data in their requests. To do this, we need to specify a filtering condition on the value of the *SUM* aggregate function. We can't use the *WHERE* clause for this purpose, since the *WHERE* clause can only be used for conditions on values of the *input* records of a query, whereas our condition is on a value calculated after the groups are aggregated into an *output* record.

The *HAVING* clause is exactly what we need. The *HAVING* clause behaves just like a *WHERE* clause, except that we can use values of aggregate functions in it.

Our filtered query will look like the following example:

```
---Ch01BytesRecvdPerHourPerClientFiltered.sql---
SELECT TO_STRING(time, 'hh') AS Hour,
       c-ip,
       SUM(cs-bytes)
FROM <1>
GROUP BY Hour, c-ip
HAVING SUM(cs-bytes) >= 100000
---Ch01BytesRecvdPerHourPerClientFiltered.sql---
```

Ordering the Output

Let's reconsider our previous example in which we calculated the total number of requests for each page in an IIS log:

```
SELECT cs-uri-stem, COUNT(*)
FROM <1>
GROUP BY cs-uri-stem
```

The output of this query would look like follows:

```
cs-uri-stem                COUNT(ALL *)
--------------------       ------------
/Default.htm               13
/FAA.css                   13
/images/address.gif        21
/cgi-bin/counts.exe        25
/gorice/rulesinfo.nsf      28
/maindefault.htm           12
/top2.htm                  11
/990136.swf                11
/top.htm                   10
/left3.htm                 11
Press a key...
```

If we want to identify the pages responsible for the largest number of requests, we'll have to scroll through all the results of this query to find the largest values of the *COUNT(*)* aggregate function.

It would be really handy if we could sort the output according to the number of requests for each page, having the pages responsible for the largest number of requests appear at the top of the output records. In the SQL language, this is accomplished with the *ORDER BY* clause. The *ORDER BY* clause specifies which output record fields we want the output records to be sorted on and in which direction. The *DESC* keyword specifies that we want to sort the output records in descending order, whereas the ASC keyword specifies that we want to sort the output records in ascending order.

The following query sorts the results of the previous example according to the values of the *COUNT(*)* aggregate function, in descending order:

```
---Ch01HitsPerPageOrdered.sql---
SELECT cs-uri-stem, COUNT(*)
FROM <1>
GROUP BY cs-uri-stem
ORDER BY COUNT(*) DESC
---Ch01HitsPerPageOrdered.sql---
```

This query behaves exactly like the previous one, with the exception that output records are now sorted:

```
cs-uri-stem                      COUNT(ALL *)
----------------------------     ------------
/gorice/laws.nsf                 108
/gorice/rulesinfo.nsf            28
/cgi-bin/counts.exe              25
/images/address.gif              21
/image/top.jpg                   19
/FAA.css                         13
/Default.htm                     13
```

```
/maindefault.htm              12
/images/tail.gif              12
/startarea/startarea980102.htm  11
Press a key...
```

File and Directory Listings

The following command returns a list of the files in a folder and in its subfolders, ordering the files by their size in descending order:

```
LogParser "SELECT Name, Size FROM C:\Windows\*.* ORDER BY Size DESC" -i:FS
```

This command introduces us to the FS input format. Different from the input formats we have seen so far, the FS input format does not parse any log file. In fact, this input format enumerates files and directories, returning an input record for each file or directory with information such as the file or directory name, its size, its attributes, and so on.

Here is a sample output of this command:

```
Name                                            Size
----------------------------------------------- --------
driver.cab                                      76699621
dotnetfx.exe                                    24265736
software                                        18612224
Data1.cab                                       16342961
netfx1.cab                                      14638644
hwxjpn.dll                                      13463552
Microsoft Office 2003 Setup(0001)_Task(0001).txt  13243970
oembios.bin                                     13107200
oembios.bin                                     13107200
HCdata.edb                                      12591104
Press a key...
```

Top-Ten Lists

The previous examples can be modified to generate "top-10" lists using the *TOP* keyword. The *TOP* keyword is used in the *SELECT* clause with a number *n* to specify that we are only interested in the first *n* output records. Once *n* output records have been returned, the query execution is completed and the remaining output records are simply discarded. Combined with the *ORDER BY* clause, the *TOP* keyword makes sure that only the topmost *n* records are returned.

The following query returns the top 10 requested URLs in the specified logs:

```
---Ch01Top10RequestedPages.sql---
SELECT TOP 10 cs-uri-stem, COUNT(*)
FROM <1>
GROUP BY cs-uri-stem
ORDER BY COUNT(*) DESC
```

```
---Ch01Top10RequestedPages.sql---
```

By changing the direction of the *ORDER BY* operation, we can retrieve the "bottom 10" requested URLs in the specified logs:

```
---Ch01Bottom10RequestedPages.sql---
SELECT TOP 10 cs-uri-stem, COUNT(*)
FROM <1>
GROUP BY cs-uri-stem
ORDER BY COUNT(*) ASC
---Ch01Bottom10RequestedPages.sql---
```

Top-Ten Long-Running Pages

The following query returns the top 10 longest-running pages in the specified logs:

```
---Ch01Top10LongRunningPages.sql---
SELECT TOP 10 cs-uri-stem, AVG(time-taken)
FROM <1>
GROUP BY cs-uri-stem
ORDER BY AVG(time-taken) DESC
---Ch01Top10LongRunningPages.sql---
```

Top-Twenty Largest Files

The following query uses the FS input format to return the top 20 largest files in the specified directory and in its subfolders:

```
---Ch01Top20LargestFiles.sql---
SELECT TOP 10 Name, Size
FROM C:\Windows\*.*
ORDER BY Size DESC
---Ch01Top20LargestFiles.sql---
```

Gathering Input

Log Parser offers a number of input formats so varied that it can be thought of as more a SQL engine operating on heterogeneous data than a parser of log files. In fact, especially with the latest 2.2 release, not only can Log Parser be used to retrieve data from a wide variety of text file formats (all the IIS log file formats, generic NCSA log files, CSV, TSV, and XML text files), but it can also be used to parse specialized binary files (NetMon files, ETW trace files), to retrieve system information (Event Log, files and directories, registry keys, and Active Directory objects), and to process custom data through the use of user-implemented input format plug-ins.

Parsing Text Files

The majority of the input formats supported by Log Parser 2.2 can be used to parse text files in a number of popular formats. The text file input formats in Log Parser 2.2 are:

- **IISW3C and IIS** These input formats parse IIS log files in the W3C Extended Log File Format and in the Microsoft IIS Log File Format, respectively.

- **NCSA** Parses log files in the NCSA Common, Combined, and Extended Log File Formats.

- **HTTPERR** Parses the new HTTP Error log files generated by the Http.sys driver.

- **URLSCAN** Parses log files generated by the UrlScan IIS Filter.

- **W3C** Parses generic log files in the W3C Extended Log File Format, such as Personal Firewall log files, Exchange Tracking log files, and Windows Media Server log files.

- **CSV** Parses generic comma-separated text files, such as those generated by PerfMon or Excel.

- **TSV** Parses generic "tabular" text files—space-separated and tab-separated data.

- **XML** Parses XML documents.

- **TEXTLINE** Parses generic text files, returning each line in a file.

- **TEXTWORD** Parses generic text files, returning each word in a file (i.e., each string separated by spaces).

PerfMon CSV Files

The performance data gathered by the PerfMon utility can be saved to a CSV file, thus making it available for consumption by Log Parser through the CSV input format.

The field names in a CSV file generated by PerfMon can be quite long, as shown by the following example:

```
"(PDH-CSV 4.0) (Pacific Daylight
Time)(420)","\\GAB1\System\Processes","\\GAB1M\System\Threads"
"09/22/2004 08:50:17.184","32","365"
"09/22/2004 08:50:22.191","32","364"
"09/22/2004 08:50:27.198","32","362"
"09/22/2004 08:50:32.205","32","362"
"09/22/2004 08:50:37.213","32","362"
"09/22/2004 08:50:42.220","32","362"
"09/22/2004 08:50:47.227","32","363"
"09/22/2004 08:50:52.234","33","378"
"09/22/2004 08:50:57.241","35","396"
"09/22/2004 08:51:02.249","34","397"
"09/22/2004 08:51:07.256","33","380"
```

```
"09/22/2004 08:51:12.263","32","368"
```

Moreover, each field value in a CSV text file generated by PerfMon is enclosed within double-quote characters.

However, this log file is perfectly suitable to be parsed by Log Parser. Working with CSV, TSV, W3C, or XML text files, Log Parser detects automatically the data type of each field, making it simpler to execute queries against the logged data. In fact, these input formats work with a two-staged approach: During the *inspection stage*, the input formats inspect a fixed number of initial lines to determine the number of fields, the field types, and the field names. This process can be fine-tuned by a number of parameters, which are commonly used when the files being parsed have a variable number of fields in each row, or when the files being parsed do not have a header line. After the number of fields, their types, and their names has been determined, the real *parsing stage* begins, in which the files are parsed again from beginning to end and input records are generated to be processed by the query.

Swiss Army Knife

Detecting Data Types Automatically

During the initial inspection stage, the CSV, TSV, W3C, and XML input formats determine the data types of the columns and fields in the input data by parsing a fixed number of entries and checking whether or not all the values in a field are formatted as integers, decimal numbers, or timestamps. If at least one value is not formatted as any of these, the field is assumed to be of the *STRING* data type.

For example, when parsing the previous PerfMon sample file, the CSV input format automatically detects that the values in the second and third column are integers, making it possible to use these fields' values as arguments of arithmetical and aggregate functions that operate on integer values. We can view the results of the inspection stage by issuing the following command:

```
logparser.exe file: -h -i:CSV Test_000001.csv
```

This help command shows the field names and types detected by the CSV input format when parsing the specified CSV file generated by PerfMon:

```
Fields:
  Filename (S)
  RowNumber (I)
  (PDH-CSV 4.0) (Pacific Daylight Time)(420) (S)
  \\GAB1\System\Processes (I)
  \\GAB1\System\Threads (I)
```

The first two fields generated by the CSV input format are always *Filename* and *RowNumber*, which indicate the file and the line number being parsed.

Continued

Following these fields are the fields extracted by the CSV input format from the input files. As we can see, the second and third columns in the CSV file are detected as being of the integer type. However, the first column, containing a date, has been detected as a string type. This is because the CSV input format (together with the TSV, XML, and W3C input formats) by default expects dates to be formatted with the *yyyy-MM-dd hh:mm:ss* format. We can change this expectation setting the *-iTsFormat* parameter to the format of the timestamp fields contained in the file:

```
logparser.exe file: -h -i:CSV Test_000001.csv -iTsFormat:"MM/dd/yyyy hh:mm:ss.ll"
```

This time we obtain the following output:

```
Fields:
  Filename (S)
  RowNumber (I)
  (PDH-CSV 4.0) (Pacific Daylight Time)(420) (T)
  \\GAB1\System\Processes (I)
  \\GAB1\System\Threads (I)
```

As we can see, the first column has been detected of the timestamp type, and we can therefore use date and time functions on its values.

The following query can be used to calculate the average, maximum, and minimum number of processes and threads in each minute:

```
---Ch01PerfMonAverages.sql---
SELECT TO_STRING(Minute, 'hh:mm') AS MinuteStr,
       AVG(\\GAB1\System\Processes) AS AvgProc,
       MAX(\\GAB1\System\Processes) AS MaxProc,
       MIN(\\GAB1\System\Processes) AS MinProc,
       AVG(\\GAB1\System\Threads) AS AvgThread,
       MAX(\\GAB1\System\Threads) AS MaxThread,
       MIN(\\GAB1\System\Threads) AS MinThread
USING  QUANTIZE([(PDH-CSV 4.0) (Pacific Daylight Time)(420)], 60) AS Minute
FROM   Test_000001.csv
GROUP BY Minute
---Ch01PerfMonAverages.sql---
```

Assuming that this query has been saved in the Ch01PerfMonAverages.sql file, we can execute it with the following command:

```
logparser.exe file:Ch01PerfMonAverages.sql -i:CSV -iTsFormat:"MM/dd/yyyy hh:mm:ss.ll"
```

And obtain the following output:

```
MinuteStr AvgProc MaxProc MinProc AvgThread MaxThread MinThread
--------- ------- ------- ------- --------- --------- ---------
08:50     32      35      32      368       396       362
08:51     33      34      32      381       397       368
```

This query introduces us to a novel element of the Log Parser SQL language.

If you look closely at the query, you can see a *USING* clause. This clause is not part of the SQL language specification, but it is implemented by the Log Parser SQL language to make queries more readable. In the *USING* clause, we can create new values and give them names so that we can refer to those names anywhere else in the query. Values declared in the *USING* clause are not output, they are only declared for some other clause to use them. In this example, we have declared a new *Minute* value as the first column's timestamp rounded off to a minute. This way, our *GROUP BY* clause and our *SELECT* clause can refer to the new *Minute* value concisely, instead of repeating the *QUANTIZE* function twice.

NetStat Output

Thanks to the TSV input format, Log Parser can be used to parse the output of those tools that generate a tabular text output.

For example, the output of the NetStat utility consists of values separated by spaces:

```
C:\LogParser>netstat -a

Active Connections

  Proto    Local Address    Foreign Address       State
  TCP      GAB1:1025          GAB1.mydomain.com:0  LISTENING
  TCP      GAB1:1036          GAB1.mydomain.com:0  LISTENING
  TCP      GAB1:netbios-ssn  GAB1.mydomain.com:0   LISTENING
  UDP      GAB1:netbios-ns    *:*
  UDP      GAB1:netbios-dgm   *:*
  UDP      GAB1:1900          *:*
  UDP      GAB1:42508         *:*
```

The TSV input format can be used to parse the output of this utility, as well as the output of many other tools that generate tabular output.

Before parsing this text, we have to analyze its characteristics:

- The separator character in this output is a space character.

- Fields are separated by more than one space. (The *Local Address* string contains a single space character, but it belongs to a single column.)

- Fields are separated by a variable number of spaces rather than by a fixed number of spaces.

- The data that we want to parse starts at the third line. (We want to skip the *Active Connections* line and the following blank line.)

All these characteristics translate into values for the parameter of the TSV input format.

Putting this all together, we can query the output of the NetStat utility with the following command:

```
Netstat -a | LogParser -i:TSV "SELECT [Local Address] FROM STDIN WHERE State =
'LISTENING'" -iSeparator:space -nSep:2 -fixedSep:OFF -nSkipLines:2
```

And obtain:

```
Local Address
---------------
GAB1:1025
GAB1:1036
GAB1:netbios-ssn
```

Note that we have used *STDIN* as the *from-entity* in this query. *STDIN* is a special keyword that can be used with most text input formats, indicating that we want the input format to read data from the standard input stream. This allows us to "pipe" the output of a command into a Log Parser command.

Also note that the TSV input format, together with the CSV input format, parses by default the first line of the input data as a header containing the names of the input fields. The field names extracted from the header become the names of the input record fields, allowing our queries to refer to column values by their names.

When the files being parsed do not contain a header, we need to set the *headerRow* parameter to *OFF*, to avoid having the input format parse the first line of data as the header line. When *headerRow* is set to *OFF*, the input record fields are automatically named *Field1*, *Field2*, and so on.

Live Stocks

Not only can most input formats read from the standard input—some of them can also read data from Internet URLs, as long as the downloaded data matches the specified input format.

For example, the following command retrieves stock ratings from the specified Yahoo! page:

```
logparser.exe file: "SELECT Date, Open, High, Low FROM
http://ichart.finance.yahoo.com/table.csv?s=MSFT&d=1&e=1&f=2004" -i:CSV
```

This URL returns stock ratings in CSV format, which can then be parsed by the CSV input format.

RSS Feeds

Another commonly used Log Parser input format is the XML input format. This input format uses internally the MSXML parser to parse XML documents, and it returns the values of the nodes and attributes found in the documents.

The XML input format supports three different ways to parse XML documents, called *field modes* and selectable through the *fMode* parameter. These are different ways that the document tree can be traversed, and each way is reflected in the structure of the records generated by the input format. A comprehensive explanation of the three different field modes can be found in the Log Parser documentation.

The following command uses the *tree* field mode to parse the RSS XML document at the specified www.logparser.com URL:

```
logparser.exe file: "SELECT title, dc:creator FROM
http://www.logparser.com/instantforum33/rssfeed.aspx?id=1&Task=ForumRSS" -i:XML
-fmode:Tree
```

Querying System Information

Log Parser 2.2 supports four input formats that do not parse files but rather return information retrieved from different Windows system components. These input formats are:

- **EVT** Returns events from the Windows Event Log.
- **FS** Returns information on files and directories.
- **REG** Returns information on registry keys and values.
- **ADS** Returns properties of Active Directory objects.

Registry Entries Written to in the Past Twenty-Four Hours

The following query uses the REG input format to return the path and name of the registry values under the HKEY_LOCAL_MACHINE\SOFTWARE registry key that have been modified in the past 24 hours:

```
---Ch01RegValuesModifdPast24Hours.sql---
SELECT    Path,
          ValueName
FROM      HKLM\SOFTWARE
WHERE     LastWriteTime >= SUB(
            SYSTEM_TIMESTAMP(),
            TIMESTAMP('0000-01-02', 'yyyy-MM-dd')
          )
---Ch01RegValuesModifdPast24Hours.sql---
```

Files Modified in the Past Twenty-Four Hours

The following query uses the FS input format to return the full path of the files in the System32 directory and in its subfolders that have been modified in the past 24 hours:

```
---Ch01FilesModifdPast24Hours.sql---
SELECT    Path
FROM      C:\Windows\System32\*.*
WHERE     LastWriteTime >= SUB(
            SYSTEM_TIMESTAMP(),
            TIMESTAMP('0000-01-02', 'yyyy-MM-dd')
```

```
    )
---Ch01FilesModifdPast24Hours.sql---
```

Assuming that the query is saved to the Ch01FilesModifdPast24Hours.sql file, the command is executed as follows:

```
logparser.exe file:Ch01FilesModifdPast24Hours.sql -i:FS -useLocalTime:OFF
```

Master Craftsman

Monitoring File Changes

The FS input format can be used to implement a simple file-change monitor that can be run periodically to detect changes, including new files, deleted files, and changes to existing files, in a directory of interest.

To effectively detect a change in the content of a file, we will use the HASHMD5_FILE() Log Parser function, which takes the full path of a file as argument and returns a string containing the MD5 hash of the file content.

Our first step consists of creating a *baseline*—that is, a CSV text file containing a snapshot of the current files. This can be accomplished with the following command:

```
logparser.exe file: "SELECT Path, HASHMD5_FILE(Path) AS Hash INTO BaseLine.csv FROM C:\
Test\*.* WHERE Attributes NOT LIKE '%D%'" -i:FS -o:CSV
```

The BaseLine.csv file will look like the following:

```
Path,Hash
C:\Test\count.asp,14BF344117DC03536291490E85ACB6A3
C:\Test\important.dll,6DD4566EB245627B49F3ABB7E4502DD6
C:\Test\index.htm,099C87AAA19AC2642D9B80A3E66634DC
```

Once the baseline file has been generated, we can periodically query the same directory to detect changes in its files. This is accomplished by first executing the same command, saving the results to a different CSV file:

```
logparser.exe file: "SELECT Path, HASHMD5_FILE(Path) AS Hash INTO Latest.csv FROM
C:\Test\*.* WHERE Attributes NOT LIKE '%D%'" -i:FS -o:CSV
```

Once the latest.csv file has been created, we can compare this file with the BaseLine.csv file to detect which files have changed.

An easy way to compare the two CSV files is to query both of them using the CSV input format, aggregating on the *Path, Hash* pair of fields and returning only the entries that appear once in both files. Unchanged files, in fact, will have identical hashes, and their *Path* and *Hash* values will appear in both files. On the other hand, modified, deleted, or created files will have unique *Path, Hash* pairs.

Continued

The following query returns the paths of the files that have been changed, deleted, or created since the baseline creation:

```
---Ch01FilesModifdHash.sql---
SELECT DISTINCT Path,
               REPLACE_IF_NOT_NULL(Hash, '') AS Dummy,
               COUNT(*)
FROM    BaseLine.csv, Latest.csv
GROUP BY Path, Hash
HAVING COUNT(*) <> 2
---Ch01FilesModifdHash.sql---
```

Chapter 8, "Security Auditing," offers more detailed information on how to use the FS input format to monitor file changes in a system.

Computers Owned by a Domain Account

The ADS input format queries Active Directory objects and returns their properties. By default, the ADS input format enumerates all the objects found under the Active Directory path or LDAP path specified in the *FROM* clause, and it returns an input record for each property of each object. In this case input records have a fixed structure, and they include a *PropertyName* field and a *PropertyValue* field with the names and values of the objects' properties. The default mode of operation is useful when we want to query different types of objects across our Active Directory tree and we need to reference specific properties owned by different object types.

However, if we specify the name of an Active Directory object class for the *objClass* parameter, the ADS input format enumerates only objects of that type, and it returns an input record for each object found; in this case, input records contain a field for each property of the object. This mode of querying Active Directory objects is useful when we are interested in objects of a specific type only and we want our queries to reference multiple properties of the same object.

For example, the following query uses the latter mode to enumerate all the *computer* Active Directory objects and return the *cn* property (the computer name) of those objects whose security descriptor lists the specified account name as the owner:

```
---Ch01ComputersOwnedByAccount.sql---
SELECT cn
FROM
'LDAP://mydomain.corp.mycompany.com/CN=Computers,DC=mydomain,DC=corp,DC=mycompany,DC=com'
WHERE EXTRACT_TOKEN(nTSecurityDescriptor, 0, '|')
      LIKE '%\gabriele'
---Ch01ComputersOwnedByAccount.sql---
```

This query can be executed with the following command:

```
logparser.exe file:Ch01ComputersOwnedByAccount.sql -i:ADS -objClass:computer
```

www.syngress.com

Parsing NetMon Files

The NETMON input format parses capture files generated by the NetMon application. NetMon capture files contain a binary dump of the network packets sent and received on a network interface, and they are usually employed in troubleshooting networking issues.

The NETMON input format can be used to return packet information in two different ways. When the *fMode* parameter is set to *TCPIP*, the NETMON input format returns an input record for each TCP/IP *packet* in the capture file. In this mode, it is possible to query for single packets and retrieve packet properties, such as the TCP flags, the IP time-to-live field, and so on. When the *fMode* parameter is set to *TCPConn*, the NETMON input format returns an input record for each TCP/IP *connection* in the capture file. In this mode, data across multiple packets belonging to the same connection is aggregated into a single input record, which contains fields such as the whole payload exchanged between the source and destination endpoints, the total number of frames used in the connection, and so on.

Chapter 4, "Examining Other Logs," provides in-depth tools that leverage the NETMON input format to extract useful information from NetMon capture files. In this chapter, we explore a few simple yet effective queries that will give us a glimpse of NETMON input format usage.

Raw Network Usage

Given a NetMon capture file, we can query the file in *TCPIP* mode to calculate the "raw" network usage—that is, the real number of bytes exchanged between the TCP/IP endpoints in the captured network traffic. This number of bytes includes the Ethernet frame bytes, the IP header bytes, and the TCP header and payload bytes, and it is definitely larger and more comprehensive than the number of bytes that can be calculated from IIS log files, which include only the TCP payloads of HTTP connections.

The following query uses the *TCPIP* mode to return the number of bytes exchanged every 30 seconds:

```
---Ch01RawBytesPer30Seconds.sql---
SELECT QUANTIZE(DateTime, 30) AS HalfMinute,
       SUM(FrameBytes)
FROM   mycapture.cap
GROUP BY HalfMinute
---Ch01RawBytesPer30Seconds.sql---
```

This query is executed with the following command:

```
logparser.exe file:Ch01RawBytesPer30Seconds.sql -i:NETMON -fMode:TCPIP
```

Here is a sample output:

```
HalfMinute              SUM(ALL FrameBytes)
--------------------    --------------------
2004-03-01 12:17:00.0 120
```

```
2004-03-01 12:17:30.0 8804
2004-03-01 12:18:30.0 2990
2004-03-01 12:19:00.0 16462
2004-03-01 12:19:30.0 8766
```

Connections by IP Addresses

The following query uses the *TCPConn* mode to return the total number of connections established by each IP address:

```
---Ch01ConnectionsPerIPAddress.sql---
SELECT SrcIP,
       COUNT(*) AS Connections
FROM   FTPSSL2.cap
GROUP BY SrcIP
---Ch01ConnectionsPerIPAddress.sql---
```

This query is executed with the following command:

```
logParser.exe file:Ch01ConnectionsPerIPAddress.sql -i:NETMON -fMode:TCPConn
```

Here is a sample output:

```
SrcIP         Connections
------------- -----------
192.168.1.100 1
192.168.1.103 9
192.168.1.101 1
```

Implementing Custom Input Formats

Log Parser 2.2 offers the possibility for users to implement their own input formats and use them with both the command-line Log Parser executable and the Log Parser scriptable COM components.

Custom input formats (also referred to as *input format plug-ins*) are implemented as COM objects exposing the methods of the *ILogParserInputContext* interface. This interface includes methods that describe the input records generated by the custom input format and methods that return the input records themselves. Since the interface is based on OLE automation, custom input formats can be implemented in a variety of programming languages, ranging from C++ to Visual Basic, scripting languages (VBScript/Jscript), and .NET languages.

Once implemented and registered with the COM infrastructure, a custom input format can be used with the command-line Log Parser executable through the COM input format. This input format "encapsulates" the custom input format COM object and provides a way for users to interact with it through the command line.

The topic of creating and using input format plug-ins is covered in detail in Chapter 9, "Enhancing Log Parser."

Producing Output

Together with the variety of input formats we have seen so far, Log Parser supports a number of output formats that can be used to send query results to different targets. The output formats supported by Log Parser can save query results as text files (in CSV, TSV, W3C, XML, and custom formats), send results to a SQL table, display results in a dialog window, create chart images, and send data to a Syslog server.

The topics covered in this section are expanded in Chapter 10, "Formatting, Reporting, and Charting."

Using the DATAGRID Output Format

The DATAGRID output format behaves pretty much like the NAT output format we have been using so far—the only difference being that the query results are displayed in a Windows dialog in a graphical fashion, rather than being displayed to the console output.

To use the DATAGRID output format, we can either specify *DATAGRID* as the output format name with the *-o* switch or we can simply specify an *INTO* clause with the value of *DATAGRID*, as shown by the following example:

```
logparser,exe: file "SELECT EventID, COUNT(*) INTO DATAGRID FROM System GROUP BY EventID"
```

This command returns the total number of events logged for each event ID in the System Event Log. This time, different from the examples we have seen so far, the results are displayed to a window like the one shown in Figure 1.1.

Figure 1.1 The DATAGRID Window

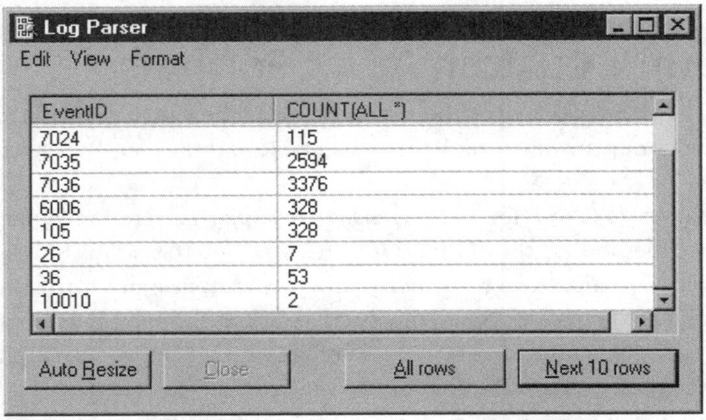

Similarly to the NAT output format, the DATAGRID output format displays 10 lines before waiting for the user to push a button to display the next 10 rows; also in this case, the number or rows can be overridden through the *rtp* parameter.

By default, the DATAGRID output format automatically scrolls the grid list when new rows are output. This behavior can be overridden through the **View | AutoScroll** menu item.

Creating Custom Text Files

The text output formats supported by Log Parser can be used to generate files compatible with most of the applications that we might need to post-process our query results. For example, we can create CSV files that can be post-processed by Microsoft Excel.

However, in some cases we might need to format the output data in a way that is not supported by any of the Log Parser output formats. For example, we might want to output data as HTML pages formatted according to our preferences. For this reason, Log Parser supports the TPL (template) output format. This output format requires users to specify a template file that describes how the query results should be formatted. Template files contain three sections: a header, a body, and a footer. The header section contains the text that we want to be output once at the beginning of the output file; the footer section contains the text that we want to be output once at the end of the output file. These sections can contain special variables that act as placeholders for the names of the output record fields; when the output file is generated, these variables are replaced with the specified field names.

The body section of the template file contains the text that we want output for each output record. Here we can specify variables that act as placeholders for field *values*; when an output record is generated, these variables are replaced with the values of the corresponding output record fields, and the entire body section is written to the output file.

Event Log Monitor HTML Page

One of the most common applications of the TPL output format is to generate HTML files containing our query results.

In this example, we want to create an HTML page containing the last 50 error events from the System Event Log. Once we have constructed the example, the code presented here can be scheduled to run at frequent intervals to create an HTML page that can be accessed remotely to monitor the Event Log.

We start with our query:

```
---Ch01Top50ErrorEvents.sql---
SELECT TOP 50 SourceName,
              Message,
              TimeGenerated
INTO   EventMonitor.html
FROM   System
WHERE  EventType = 1
---Ch01Top50ErrorEvents.sql---
```

Executed with the EVT input format *direction* parameter set to *BW*, this query returns the selected fields from the last 50 error events logged in the System Event Log.

Next we create our template file. The template file should represent the HTML page as we want it to be formatted, broken down into the three sections—the header, the body, and the footer.

An example of such a page is the following:

```
<LPHEADER>
<HTML>

<HEAD>
<TITLE>Last 50 Error Events</TITLE>
</HEAD>

<BODY BGCOLOR="#F0F0F0">

<CENTER><H2>Last 50 Error Events</H1></CENTER>
<TABLE WIDTH="100%" BORDER="0" BGCOLOR="#C0C0C0"
        CELLPADDING="4" CELLSPACING="2">

<TR>
  <TH ALIGN="LEFT" BGCOLOR="#B0B0B0">%FIELDNAME_1%</TH>
  <TH ALIGN="LEFT" BGCOLOR="#B0B0B0">%FIELDNAME_2%</TH>
  <TH ALIGN="LEFT" BGCOLOR="#B0B0B0">%FIELDNAME_3%</TH>
</TR>
</LPHEADER>

<LPBODY>
<TR>
  <TD ALIGN="LEFT" BGCOLOR="#E0E0C0">
    <NOBR><TT><B>%FIELD_1%</B></TT></NOBR>
  </TD>
  <TD ALIGN="LEFT" BGCOLOR="#E0E0C0">
    <TT>%FIELD_2%</TT>
  </TD>
  <TD ALIGN="LEFT" BGCOLOR="#E0E0C0">
    <TT>%FIELD_3%</TT>
  </TD>
</TR>
</LPBODY>

<LPFOOTER>
</TABLE>

</BODY>

</HTML>
```

```
</LPFOOTER>
```

This page, which we'll assume is saved in the EventMonitor.tpl text file, contains three special tags delimiting the three TPL sections: *<LPHEADER>, <LPBODY>,* and *<LPFOOTER>.* The header section contains the *header* of the HTML page—that is, the portion of the page that should be written out only once at the beginning of the output file. This section references three variables: *%FIELDNAME_1%, %FIELDNAME_2%,* and *%FIELDNAME_3%.* These variables are substituted at runtime with the names of the corresponding output record fields (in our case, *SourceName, Message,* and *TimeGenerated*).

Following the header section is the body section, containing the HTML text that we want to be written out for each output record. In our example, this section consists of an HTML table row that formats the output record. The body section references three variables: *%FIELD_1%, %FIELD_2%,* and *%FIELD_3%.* These variables are substituted at runtime with the values of the corresponding output record fields.

Finally, the footer section contains the portion of the HTML page that should be written once at the end of the output file.

Putting it all together, we can execute the query and generate an HTML file with the following command:

```
logParser.exe file:Ch01Top50ErrorEvents.sql -o:TPL -tpl:EventMonitor.tpl -direction:BW
```

This command executes our query using the TPL output format with the template file specified as the value of the *tpl* parameter and generates a file named EventMonitor.html that will look like the example shown in Figure 1.2.

Figure 1.2 HTML Page Created by the TPL Output Format

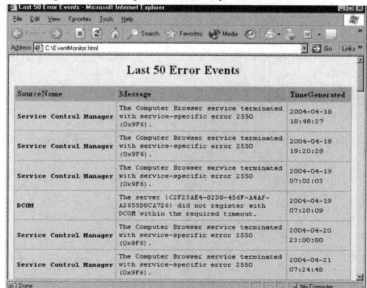

Swiss Army Knife

Writing to Multiple Output Files

We can extend the previous example to create three different HTML pages containing Error, Warning, and Informational events.

Instead of executing the same command three times to create the three pages, we can take advantage of a little-known Log Parser feature called Multiplex. This feature allows us to execute a single command and have the results of the command written to multiple output files.

Not all the Log Parser output formats support the Multiplex feature, but the TPL output format certainly does. To use the Multiplex feature, all we have to do is specify a * wildcard in the output filename specified for the *INTO* clause. When the output filename contains a wildcard, the output format substitutes the wildcard with the first field value of each output record and writes the data to the resulting filename. The output record field used in the filename substitution is then discarded, meaning that it will not appear in the output data.

To take advantage of the Multiplex feature, we can modify our query as follows:

```
---Ch01Top50ErrorEventsMultiplex.sql---
SELECT TOP 150 MyEventTypeName,
            SourceName,
            Message,
            TimeGenerated
USING EXTRACT_TOKEN( EventTypeName, 0, ' ') AS MyEventTypeName
INTO   EventMonitor_*.html
FROM   System
---Ch01Top50ErrorEventsMultiplex.sql---
```

Notice that we have modified our *SELECT* clause to include the name of the event type as its first field, and we have specified a * wildcard in the output filename. When an Error event is processed, its output will be written to the EventMonitor_Error.html file; the same will happen with Warning and Information events.

We can execute this query with the following command:

```
logparser.exe file:Ch01Top50ErrorEventsMultiplex.sql -o:TPL -tpl:EventMonitor.tpl
-direction:BW
```

After the command has run, we can verify that there are now three HTML files in our directory:

```
09/28/2004  08:09 AM            14,176 EventMonitor_Error.html
09/28/2004  08:09 AM            32,335 EventMonitor_Information.html
09/28/2004  08:09 AM            11,588 EventMonitor_Warning.html
```

Creating Charts

When we worked previously on top-10 lists, many of us might have thought that the output records of those queries would have been perfectly suited to be displayed in a chart. In fact, with the previous releases of Log Parser, one of the most common applications of the CSV output format was to generate CSV files containing top-10 lists, which would then be imported into Microsoft Excel to generate charts.

Log Parser 2.2 makes it simple to generate charts by skipping the CSV step altogether and providing a new *CHART* output format that directly generates image files with the results of our queries. Since the *CHART* output format uses the Microsoft Office Web Components, we need a licensed Microsoft Office (either 2000, XP, or 2003) installed on our computer.

The rules for using the *CHART* output format are simple: All the fields in our query output records have to be numeric, with a single exception—the first field only can be a string field, in which case its values are used as the *category* (X-axis) labels displayed on the chart.

The following query returns the top 10 requested URLs in the specified logs:

```
---Ch01Top10RequestedPagesChart.sql---
SELECT TOP 10 cs-uri-stem, COUNT(*) AS Hits
INTO    MyChart.gif
FROM    <1>
GROUP BY cs-uri-stem
ORDER BY Hits DESC
---Ch01Top10RequestedPagesChart.sql---
```

To generate a chart, we can execute the following command:

```
logparser.exe file:Ch01Top10RequestedPagesChart.sql -o:CHART -chartType:Bar3D
```

The *chartType* parameter lets us specify the type of chart we want to generate. The number of chart types available depends on the Microsoft Office version we have installed, but in any case we can choose among a large variety of chart types.

This command creates a MyChart.gif image similar to the example shown in Figure 1.3.

Figure 1.3 Top-10 URLs Chart

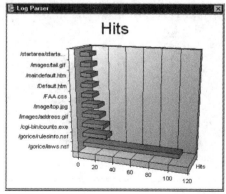

Bytes Per Extension

The following query returns the distribution of the number of bytes sent by the server for each page type:

```
---Ch01BytesSentPerPageTypeChart.sql---
SELECT    TO_LOWERCASE(EXTRACT_EXTENSION(cs-uri-stem)) AS PageType,
          MUL(PROPSUM(sc-bytes), 100.0) AS PercentBytes
INTO      Chart.gif
FROM      <1>
GROUP BY  PageType
HAVING    PercentBytes >= 1.0
ORDER BY  PercentBytes DESC
---Ch01BytesSentPerPageTypeChart.sql---
```

This query introduces us to the new *PROPSUM* aggregate function. In this example, *PROPSUM* calculates the *ratio* of the *SUM* aggregate function calculated on the groups specified by the *GROUP BY* clause to the *SUM* aggregate function calculated on *all* the input records—that is, the total number of bytes sent. When multiplied by 100, this value gives us the percentage of bytes sent for each page type.

Since we are talking about percentages, we can have the results of this query written to a pie chart. This is accomplished by the following command, which generates a chart similar to the one shown in Figure 1.4:

```
logparser.exe file:Ch01BytesSentPerPageTypeChart.sql -o:chart -chartType:Pie
```

Figure 1.4 Bytes Per Extension Chart

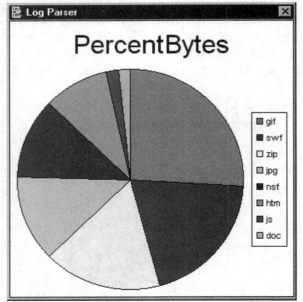

Hits Per hour

Another commonly charted query is the one that returns the hourly number of hits to a Web site:

```
---Ch01HitsPerHourChart.sql---
SELECT    QUANTIZE(time, 3600) AS Hour,
          COUNT(*) AS Hits
INTO      Chart.gif
FROM      <1>
GROUP BY Hour
ORDER BY Hour ASC
---Ch01HitsPerHourChart.sql---
```

Executed with the following command, this query creates a chart similar to the one shown in Figure 1.5:

```
logparser.exe file:Ch01HitsPerHourChart.sql -o:chart -chartType:ColumnStacked -
chartTitle:"Hits Per Hour"
```

Figure 1.5 Hits-Per-Hour Chart

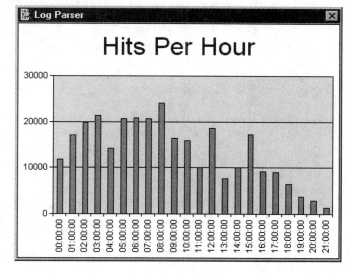

This query can be easily modified to show daily or monthly Web usage. For example, the following query calculates the Web site monthly usage:

```
---Ch01HitsPerMonthChart.sql---
SELECT    TO_STRING(date, 'yyyy-MM') AS Month,
          COUNT(*) AS Hits
INTO      Chart.gif
FROM      <1>
```

```
GROUP BY Month
ORDER BY Month ASC
---Ch01HitsPerMonthChart.sql---
```

Master Craftsman

Simple Live Web Statistics

The *CHART* output format finds its ideal application in creating an almost real-time Web statistics system. Such a system can be implemented by executing a set of queries on IIS log files at predefined intervals; each query extracts specific aggregated data, such as the top 10 requested URLs, distribution of HTTP status codes, monthly and hourly hits, and so on, and generates a chart image file as output.

To implement an effective Web statistics system, we will use the checkpoint feature, which, supported by many input formats, allows users to parse log files incrementally. In other words, every time we execute a query on log files, we tell the input format to remember the position of the last log entry parsed from each file. This state information is persisted in a separate checkpoint file. The next time that we execute a query, the input format reads the previous checkpoint file, finds which log files have been updated with new entries since the last query execution, and parses only the new log entries, updating the checkpoint file with the new state. The checkpoint feature is enabled by using the *iCheckPoint* parameter with the name of a checkpoint file.

The system that we are implementing works in two stages. In the first stage, we update a single CSV database file containing aggregated IIS log file data from all the log files. This data is a compressed view of all the log file entries, and it contains all and only the information necessary to calculate the statistics that we are interested in. During the first stage, we use the checkpoint feature to parse only new log entries, and we merge this new data with the "old" data currently in the database file. In the second stage, we parse the database CSV file multiple times with different queries that extract the statistics and create chart images.

The first stage is a single query that uses the IISW3C input format with the checkpoint feature to parse only new IIS log file entries, returning aggregated data that we save to a temporary CSV file. This first-stage query calculates the total number of requests per hour, URL, and HTTP status code:

```
---Ch01WebStatsQuery1.sql---
SELECT      QUANTIZE(TO_TIMESTAMP(date, time), 3600) AS Hour,
            cs-uri-stem,
            sc-status,
            COUNT(*) AS Hits
INTO        Temp1.csv
FROM        <1>
GROUP BY Hour,
            cs-uri-stem,
```

Continued

```
                sc-status
---Ch01WebStatsQuery1.sql---
```

The query is executed with the following command:

```
logparser.exe file:Ch01WebStatsQuery1.sql -i:IISW3C -iCheckPoint:WebStats.lpc -o:CSV
-headers:OFF
```

When the first stage is completed, we'll have a Temp1.csv CSV file containing the total number of new requests per hour, URL, and HTTP status code.

The very first time that we execute this query, the Temp1.csv file contains information from *all* the log files, and we can simply rename this file Database.csv.

On the other hand, if this is not the first time we execute the query, we need to merge the temporary CSV file with the previous Database.csv CSV file containing the data we have extracted so far from all the log files. This can be accomplished by a simple query that uses the CSV input format to parse both the temporary CSV file and the database CSV file, merges the entries, and generates a third "updated database" CSV file:

```
---Ch01WebStatsMerge.sql---
SELECT       Field1,
             Field2,
             Field3,
             SUM(Field4)
INTO         UpdatedDatabase.csv
FROM         Database.csv, Temp1.csv
GROUP BY Field1,
                     Field2,
                     Field3
---Ch01WebStatsMerge.sql---
```

This query is executed as follows:

```
logParser.exe file:Ch01WebStatsMerge.sql -i:CSV -headerRow:OFF -o:CSV -headers:OFF
```

In the final step of the first stage, we replace the "old" database CSV file with the new updated database CSV file, using the following shell commands:

```
copy /Y UpdatedDatabase.csv Database.csv
del Temp1.csv
del UpdatedDatabase.csv
```

In the second stage, we can query the Database.csv file multiple times with different queries to generate the charts we are interested in. Our first query extracts the top 10 requested URLs from the Database.csv file:

```
---Ch01WebStatsTop10Requests.sql---
SELECT TOP 10 Field2 AS URL,
             SUM(Field4) AS Hits
INTO         Top10Urls.gif
FROM         Database.csv
GROUP BY URL
```

Continued

```
ORDER BY Hits DESC
---Ch01WebStatsTop10Requests.sql---
```

Our second query extracts the hourly distribution of hits:

```
---Ch01WebStatsHitsPerHour.sql---
SELECT TO_STRING(Field1, 'hh') AS Hour,
       SUM(Field4) AS Hits
INTO   HourlyHits.gif
FROM   Database.csv
GROUP BY Hour
ORDER BY Hour ASC
---Ch01WebStatsHitsPerHour.sql---
```

Our third query extracts the status code distribution:

```
---Ch01WebStatsStatusCodes.sql---
SELECT Field3 AS Status,
       SUM(Field4) AS Hits
INTO   StatusCodes.gif
FROM   Database.csv
GROUP BY Status
ORDER BY Hits DESC
---Ch01WebStatsStatusCodes.sql---
```

Putting it all together, our Web statistics system is implemented by the following batch file, which can be scheduled to run at 10-minute intervals:

```
REM
REM First stage
REM

REM
REM Parse the latest log file entries and write aggregated data
REM into the Temp1.csv temporary CSV file
REM
logparser.exe file:Ch01WebStatsQuery1.sql -i:IISW3C -
iCheckPoint:WebStats.lpc -o:CSV -headers:OFF

REM
REM If it's the first time we parse the log files, then the temporary
REM CSV file is our database CSV file; otherwise, we need to merge the
REM temporary file with the database file
REM
IF EXIST Database.csv {
logparser.exe file:Ch01WebStatsMerge.sql -i:CSV -headerRow:OFF -o:CSV
-headers:OFF
copy /Y UpdatedDatabase.csv Database.csv
del Temp1.csv
```

Continued

```
    del UpdatedDatabase.csv
) else (
    ren Temp1.csv Database.csv
)


REM
REM Second stage
REM


REM
REM Generate the Top 10 requested URL's chart
REM
logparser.exe file:Ch01WebStatsTop10Requests.sql -i:CSV -headerRow:OFF
-o:CHART -chartType:Bar3D


REM
REM Generate the Status Code distribution chart
REM
logparser.exe file:Ch01WebStatsStatusCodes.sql -i:CSV -headerRow:OFF -
o:CHART -chartType:Pie


REM
REM Generate the Hourly Hits chart
REM
logparser.exe file:Ch01WebStatsHitsPerHour.sql -i:CSV -headerRow:OFF -o:CHART -
chartType:RadarLineFilled
```

Uploading Query Results to a SQL Database

Another commonly used Log Parser output format is the SQL output format, which can be used to upload query results into a table in any ODBC-compliant database, including Microsoft SQL Server databases and Access databases.

The SQL output format can be used to either create the target table and upload the query results to it or to append the query results to an existing table. In the latter case, it's important to remember that the number of fields and the type of each field in our query results must match the number of fields and the type of each field in the target table, as explained in the Log Parser documentation.

The SQL output format has a number of parameters that are used to specify the target database. We can either specify a full connection string with the *oConnString* parameter, or we can specify separately the server name, the database name, the ODBC driver, the username and password for the connection, and so on.

Consolidating IIS Logs

The SQL output format is often used to upload entries from IIS log files into a SQL database for further analysis. For these tasks, the checkpoint feature is commonly used to build scheduled systems that parse the IIS log files at predefined intervals and upload only the newest log entries.

These log consolidation systems usually filter out "uninteresting" entries, such as requests to image files and 404 responses, before uploading the log files.

The following query uploads the interesting entries from the specified Web sites' log files into the specified SQL table:

```
---Ch01ConsolidateLogs.sql---
SELECT TO_TIMESTAMP(date, time),
       c-ip,
       cs-method,
       cs-uri-stem,
       cs-uri-query,
       sc-status,
       sc-bytes,
       cs-bytes,
       time-taken
INTO    IISTABLE
FROM    <1>, <2>, <3>
WHERE   cs-uri-stem NOT LIKE '%.gif' AND
        sc-status NOT IN (404; 301; 302; 304)
---Ch01ConsolidateLogs.sql---
```

This query can be executed with the following command:

```
logparser.exe file:Ch01ConsolidateLogs.sql -i:IISW3C -iCheckPoint:Consolidate.lpc -o:SQL
-server:MYSQLSERVER -database:IISLOGS -username:IISLogsUser -password:XXXXXX
```

The topic of consolidating and archiving log files is covered in greater detail in Chapter 6, "Managing Log Files."

Converting Log File Formats

With Log Parser, converting a log file from a source format to a target format is a matter of executing a simple *SELECT* query using an input format matching the source format and an output format matching the target format and eventually using some simple functions to "fix" fields that have slightly different values in the two formats.

For example, to convert an IIS log file in the W3C Extended Log File Format to a log file in the Microsoft IIS Log File Format, we just need to execute a simple query using the IISW3C input format and the IIS output format. In our query, we need to make sure that the *date* and *time* fields are converted from UTC coordinates (used in the W3C format) into local time coordinates (used in the IIS format). Other that this, the *SELECT* clause just shuffles around some fields to match the positions of the fields in the IIS format:

```
---Ch01W3CToIIS.sql---
SELECT c-ip,
       cs-username,
       TO_DATE(TO_LOCALTIME(TO_TIMESTAMP(date, time))),
       TO_TIME(TO_LOCALTIME(TO_TIMESTAMP(date, time))),
       s-sitename,
       s-computername,
       s-ip,
       time-taken,
       sc-bytes,
       cs-bytes,
       sc-status,
       sc-win32-status,
       cs-method,
       cs-uri-stem,
       cs-uri-query
INTO   inetsv1.log
FROM   extend1.log
---Ch01W3CToIIS.sql---
```

The Log Parser command-line executable has some built-in conversion queries that can be executed when conversion mode is enabled with the *-c* command-line switch. These queries convert IIS log files from and to the most popular IIS log file formats, including the new Binary log format.

A detailed list of the Log Parser built-in conversion queries is displayed when we type the following help command:

```
LogParser -h -c
```

Chapter 6, "Managing Log Files," provides additional examples of ways to convert log files between different formats.

Final Touches

In this chapter we have seen how we can use simple SQL-like queries on a variety of input data to search for specific information and to calculate statistics. The queries that we have seen can be easily adapted to work on data coming from different sources, including IIS log files, the Windows Event Log, system information, and generic text files. Finally, the results of these queries can be formatted and presented in different ways, leveraging the variety of output formats supported by Log Parser.

The next chapters expand the topics that we have covered in this overview, providing real-world, usable tools that will make our data-mining tasks easier and powerful.

Chapter 2, "Monitoring IIS," and Chapter 3, "Exploring the Windows Event Log," show how IIS log files and the Windows Event Log can be queried to obtain useful information on performance, stability, and security of a system.

Chapter 4, "Examining Other Logs," and Chapter 5, "Watching Firewall, IDS, and Router Logs," investigate the use of less-known Log Parser input formats to extract useful information from different types of log files, including NetMon capture files, ISA Server logs, and DNS logs.

Chapter 6, "Managing Log Files," shows how Log Parser can be also useful in the log management problem space, including examples of ways to convert, archive, and separate log files.

Chapter 7, "Investigating Intrusions," and Chapter 8, "Security Auditing," put Log Parser to work in the forensic analysis and security auditing world. The tools in Chapter 7 show how to find and correlate the hidden traces left by intruders in our systems; the tools in Chapter 8 give us effective ways to monitor our systems to help us detect intrusions.

Chapter 9, "Enhancing Log Parser," and Chapter 10, "Formatting, Reporting, and Charting," explore advanced uses of Log Parser features that enable us to make the most of the input and output formats, showing us also how to write scripts using the Log Parser scriptable COM components and how to write custom input format plug-ins.

Finally, Chapter 11, "Handling Complex Data," shows how to push Log Parser to its limits, with tools that use the Log Parser SQL language and the Log Parser command-line executable in "creative" ways to perform tasks that at first glance might seem impossible to achieve with the Log Parser tool.

Chapter 2

Monitoring IIS

Scripts and Samples in this Chapter:

- Analyzing Request Details
- Analyzing Error Requests
- Analyzing Illegal Requests

In This Toolbox

IIS 6.0 is the latest version of the Internet Information Services (IIS) offered by Microsoft. It includes a variety of well-known services including Hyper Text Transfer Protocol (HTTP), File Transfer Protocol (FTP), Simple Mail Transfer Protocol (SMTP), and Network News Transfer Protocol (NNTP). Although each of these services handles its own site access activity logging, there are no built-in tools that are able to parse from these plain text log files in order to extract useful information.

With additional log sources such as the HTTP error log (HTTPERR) and URL filtering log (URLSCAN, if installed), it is a tedious task to analyze these different log sources and try to understand the activities taking place in the IIS server. This chapter will showcase the magic of Microsoft's Log parser tool in trying to make any system administrator's life easier with many creative parsing queries.

Monitoring Performance and Usage

One of the major advantages of monitoring the site access activity logging is that the log file helps you to keep track of all the details when a particular request is sent to your IIS server. It provides you with who, when, where, and how contents are being accessed.

Site access details are vital to understanding the usage and health performance of your IIS server. Information that is logged includes a visitor's IP address, user account accessing the contents, timestamp of when requests were made, server status reply about the request, the requested resource location, the amount of bytes used in the request, and more. Table 2.1 shows the types of IIS services and supported log formats.

Table 2.1 IIS Services and Logging Formats

Type of Service	IIS	NCSA	ODBC	W3C Extended	Centralized Binary
FTP	Yes	No	Yes	Yes	No
Web	Yes	Yes	Yes	Yes	Yes
SMTP	Yes	Yes	Yes	Yes	No
NNTP	Yes	Yes	Yes	Yes	No

NOTE

It is recommended that you configure logs using the World Wide Web Consortium (W3C) extended format. This is the most comprehensive log format in IIS and it allows you to customize different logging property fields. The queries shown in this chapter are based on W3C extended format.

Analyzing Request Details

Let's start with some basic information about the IIS site logging feature. By default, the World Wide Web service (w3svc) and Microsoft FTP service (msftpsvc) are configured with W3C extended format. However, not all fields are enabled. SMTP service (smtpsvc) uses the same W3C extended format, but is not enabled by default. For the NNTP service (nntpsvc), logging is not enabled with Microsoft IIS log format as the default.

It is recommended that you use the W3C extended format and enable all extended log fields for the maximum amount of access details. With such details, you are able to analyze the requests pattern in a more precise manner. Table 2.2 exhibits the available log fields supported in W3C extended format.

Table 2.2 W3C Extended Log Fields

Property	Field	Description
Client IP Address	c-ip	Client IP address that accessed the IIS server
User Name	cs-username	User name that accessed the IIS server
Service Name	s-sitename	Site name serving the request, for example, W3Svc1
Server Name	s-computername	IIS server name
Server IP Address	s-ip	IIS server IP address serving the request
Server Port	s-port	IIS server port number serving the request
Method	cs-method	Client action request, for example, GET, POST
URI Stem	cs-uri-stem	Request content name, for example, html, asp page
URI Query	cs-uri-query	Query action along with client request
Protocol Status	sc-status	Status code of the request
Protocol Substatus	sc-substatus	Substatus code of the request
Win32 Status	sc-win32-status	Status code in Windows terms
Bytes Sent	sc-bytes	Number of bytes sent by server
Bytes Received	cs-bytes	Number of bytes received by server
Time Taken	time-taken	Amount of time to process the request
Protocol Version	cs-version	Client protocol version, for example, HTTP, FTP
Host	cs-host	Client computer name
User Agent	cs(User-Agent)	Application used by client, for example, browser
Cookie	cs(Cookie)	Content of cookies send or received
Referer	cs(Referer)	Previous URL that directed client to current site

Even though W3C extended log format provides many extended log fields, some fields do not provide useful meaning to certain IIS services. For example, *cs-host, cs(User-Agent) cs(Referer) cs(Cookie)* will be a *NULL* value and show as '-' in the Microsoft FTP service log file, as those fields are not related to the service.

The default log path for IIS is located at %Windir%/system32/Logfiles/. Each service has its own logging directory using the service name (w3svc, msftpsvc) followed by site ID X. The following lists the default log folder names of IIS services:

- **FTP** MSFTPSVCX
- **W3C** W3SVCX
- **SMTP** SMTPSVCX
- **NNTP** NNTPSVCX

The *X* represents the service site ID. For example, a default website site ID is 1, and the w3svc1 will be the default log path. This site ID is the identification number generated by IIS when you create a new service site. In previous versions of IIS, the identification numbers are incremental, but with IIS 6.0, the site ID is randomly created by IIS based on the website's name. It is recommended that you relocate this default log path to a dedicated disk volume and secure it with proper NTFS permissions listed here:

- **Administrators** Full Control
- **System** Full Control
- **Backup Operator** Read

If you need to grant access to a user or user's application to access the log file, you should only grant *read* permission, as the log file should not be modified at all. When relocating the default log path, you can either place it on a dedicated disk partition or you can configure remote logging; this is another way to help you secure the log file from being modified by attackers.

It is important to note that time logged in W3C extended format uses Greenwich Mean Time (GMT) per W3C specification. For more information on how to enable W3C extended log fields, please refer to www.microsoft.com/resources/documentation/WindowsServ/2003/standard/proddocs/en-us/log_customw3c.asp.

In this section, we will focus on the following log fields used to diagnose performance information for different IIS requests:

- **Bytes Sent and Received (sc-bytes, cs-bytes)** The number of bytes IIS uses to accept and reply to a request. This can give you bandwidth usage information about IIS server, allowing you to plan for future network bandwidth upgrades. It can also tell you when something is wrong with your server. For example, if there is a sudden increase in bytes sent or received by the FTP server, you might want to check if there are users uploading or downloading a huge file that could be compromising disk and bandwidth resources.

- **Status Code (sc-status)** IIS reply status code tells you whether the request was successfully fulfilled by IIS or why the request failed. Again, this not only helps you in troubleshooting IIS server, but it also give you clues as to whether someone is trying to gain unauthorized access to your IIS server.

- **Time Taken (time-taken)** The amount of time IIS took to fulfill the request. This is helpful in determining how long a request was served. For example, if an active server page (ASP) query took more than 2 minutes to complete, you might want to review the coding to determine if there is a problem with the logic flow.

- **Request Content (cs-uri-stem)** The requested resource filename, particularly useful in locating most and least popular content in your IIS server. Coupled with other fields, you will be able to identify what content page take a long time to process and the bandwidth occupied by the content.

Obtaining Long Running Web Requests

The Ch02Top10WebRequests.sql query returns the top 10 long-running web requests from a particular web log source. It includes details about the requested filename, the number of times it was called, the maximum time spent for the request, and the average bytes sent. The output result is grouped by the requested filename in order of the maximum time taken followed by the number of hits.

```
---Ch02Top10WebRequests.sql---
SELECT
    TOP 10
    STRCAT(EXTRACT_PATH(cs-uri-stem),'/') AS RequestPath,
    EXTRACT_FILENAME(cs-uri-stem) AS RequestedFile,
    COUNT(*) AS Hits,
    MAX(time-taken) AS MaxTime,
    AVG(time-taken) AS AvgTime,
    AVG(sc-bytes) AS AvgBytesSent
FROM %source% TO %destination%
GROUP BY cs-uri-stem
ORDER BY MaxTime, TotalHits DESC
---Ch02Top10WebRequests.sql---
```

This query is particularly useful in identifying problematic web requests. For example, if there is an ASP query listed in the result, you need to check the code and figure out why it took such a long time to process. A long running request might affect the server's entire performance, as the application is taking CPU processing cycles from other requests.

The *%source%* at *FROM* clause is the log source parameter. It could be '*ex*.log*', meaning the query will traverse down from the current query directory looking for W3C extended log files, You can also specify the website ID as <*//localhost/w3svc/1*> to parse the log files located in w3svc1 log directory.

The *%destination%* at *TO* clause lets you specify the output filename for storing the result. In order to get the correct output you need to specify *-o:(output)* format when running the query. If omitted, *NATIVE* mode or *−o:NAT* will be the default output format.

To run the query, access a command prompt, navigate to the directory where you installed the query samples, and enter the following:

```
logparser.exe file:Ch02Top10WebRequests.sql?source="<//localhost/w3svc/1>"
+destination="Top10WebRequests.txt" -o:NAT
```

> **TIP**
>
> Since IIS 6.0 no longer applies incremental site ID as it did in previous versions, to quickly identify which site ID associated with different websites, you can use the built-in Active Directory Services Interfaces (ADSI) query, **iisweb.vbs /query**, at the command prompt. This will list all websites registered locally with site name, site id, status, IP, port, and host header name.

The query instructs Log parser to read Ch02Top10WebRequests.sql with the log source (local machine website ID 1) and generate output in *NATIVE* format to the Top10WebRequests.txt text file. If you do not want to see the process statistics, you can specify *-stats:OFF* at the end of the command syntax. The following shows the sample output of Top10WebRequests.txt:

RequestedPath	RequestedFile	Hits	MaxTime	AvgTime	AvgBytesSent
/reg/	reg.asp	821	80212	40212	1200
/expand/	incoming.asp	4095	39322	29322	20322
/processing/	cust_up.asp	3900	33293	30233	2932
/kiv/	stock.html	8032	32002	31922	370921
/expand/	detail.asp	6293	30092	29392	39223
/processing/	cust_add.asp	200	15082	13978	2011
/processing/	inv_tune.asp	2099	13021	12911	8232
/kiv/	elite.aspx	5822	11929	9218	932
/	news.asp	10003	8922	6832	2111
/html/	abs.html	4022	7990	5820	29201

The output shows that the potential problematic query includes reg.asp, which took a maximum of 80 seconds to process with an average of 1.2 kilobytes sent. This information indicates that you should ask the developer to revise the query and try to optimize the code. Another example, stock.html, which took a maximum of 32 seconds processing time for IIS to serve the 370 kilobytes static content, should be reorganized to a smaller content page.

This useful query helps to identify long-running web requests in your IIS server. You are advised to run this query routinely or customize it to your needs in order to get the latest health status of the applications running on IIS server.

WARNING

It is important to note that the queries presented in this chapter are assumed to be running on a healthy IIS server. This means that there are no hardware bottlenecks such as CPU, memory, network bandwidth, etc.

Swiss Army Knife

Scanning Big Images

Huge image file will incur longer processing time and consume additional network bandwidth. By applying the following example query, you will be able to identify the top 10 largest image files:

```
---Ch02Top10Images.sql---
SELECT
    TOP 10
    STRCAT(EXTRACT_PATH(TO_LOWERCASE(cs-uri-stem)),'/') AS RequestedPath,
    EXTRACT_FILENAME(TO_LOWERCASE(cs-uri-stem)) AS RequestedFile,
    COUNT(*) AS Hits,
    MAX(time-taken) AS MaxTime,
    AVG(time-taken) AS AvgTime,
    MAX(sc-bytes) AS BytesSent
FROM %source% TO %destination%
WHERE
    (EXTRACT_EXTENSION(TO_LOWERCASE(cs-uri-stem)) IN ('gif';'jpg'))
    AND
    (sc-status = 200)
GROUP BY TO_LOWERCASE(cs-uri-stem)
ORDER BY BytesSent, Hits, MaxTime DESC
---Ch02Top10Images.sql---
```

Continued

> The modified query will look for the top 10 image files based on size of bytes transferred; the output also includes the maximum and average time taken by IIS to send the images to the client end. As shown in the query, it will scan images with the file extensions .gif and .jpg and a 200 *sc-status*, which indicates a successful request. *TO_LOWERCASE* is use to ensure request filenames are converted to lowercase before being compared with the query parameter and the *GROUP BY* clause. For example, if requests were made to an image file with the names of ipp0002.gif and ipp0002.Gif, though both are the same file, Log parser will output two different names.
>
> Again, you can freely modify the query to suit your needs. For example, if your website contains bitmap files (BMP) or Portable Network Graphic (PNG) files, you can simply add in bmp or png in the *WHERE* clause.

Obtaining The Most Popular FTP Downloads

The Ch02Top10FtpDownloads.sql query returns the most popular FTP downloads from a particular FTP log source. It includes details of the requested filename, the number of times it was downloaded, the average time spent for the request, and the average kilobytes sent. The output is grouped by requested filename total downloads.

```
---Ch02Top10FtpDownloads.sql---
SELECT
    TOP 10
    TO_LOWERCASE(cs-uri-stem) AS RequestedFile,
    COUNT(*) AS TotalDownloads,
    DIV(AVG(sc-bytes),1024) AS AvgBytesSent(k)
FROM %source% TO %destination%
WHERE
    (cs-method LIKE '%sent')
    AND
    (sc-status = 226)
GROUP BY RequestedFile
ORDER BY TotalDownloads, AvgBytesSent(k) DESC
---Ch02Top10FtpDownloads.sql---
```

This query is particularly useful in identifying the most popular FTP downloads. As shown in the query, you will notice how we can apply built-in functions of Log parser to convert the number of bytes sent by the server to kilobytes format. First, the query averages out the *sc-bytes*; this derives the actual file size of the content. This value is then divided by 1024, which returns the kilobytes of the file size.

The *WHERE* clause is the key in this query. It determines the download request by comparing *cs-method* to the command *sent*. Typical IIS FTP log file shows *[232]sent* followed by the filename in the *cs-uri-stem* field. The [223] indicates the 223rd connection to the FTP service since it was started, where '*sent*' represent the server sent the file to client. The status code 226 indicates the request has been successfully fulfilled.

To run the query, access a command prompt, navigate to the directory where you installed the query samples, and enter the following:

```
C:\Log parser>LogParser.exe file:Ch02Top10FtpDownloads.sql?source="ex*.log"
+destination="Top10FtpDownloads.txt" -stats:OFF -o:NAT
```

This instructs Log parser to read *Ch02Top10FtpDownloads.sql* with the log source ex*.log, meaning all extended log files in the current directory matching input mask. Output is generated in *NATIVE* format to the *Top10FtpDownloads.txt* text file, This query also uses *-stats:OFF* to hide Log parser processing statistics. The following shows the sample result of the query:

RequestedFile	TotalDownloads	AvgBytesSent(K)
/download/avreport.zip	2822	20656
/download/pro2k.exe	2193	9832
/susan/holiday.zip	1902	13230
/download/basic.zip	802	8781
/faq.pdf	792	1292
/download/released.zip	502	2003
/susan/games.zip	390	1829
/arron/networkv2.vsd	102	5921
/location/map.gif	99	121
/download/update.txt	23	188

TIP

You can easily change the query to find the Top 10 least popular downloads by removing the *DESC* syntax. In other words, *DESC* instructs Log parser to list in descending order, where the highest number of downloads will be at the top. By removing the *DESC*, the default order is ascending, which will display the results from the lowest number to highest number of downloads.

Another simple modification is to find the top 10 uploads. To do so, change the selection criteria to *cs-method LIKE '%created'*, and replace the *sc-bytes* (server sent bytes) to *cs-bytes* (client sent bytes). The method name *created* represents upload and *cs-bytes* indicates file size sent from client side.

Monitoring Entry Points

The Ch02Top10EntryPoints.sql query returns the entry points of your website. An entry point is defined as the first content requested by clients. A hyphen '-' in the *cs(Refer)* field can be treated as an entry point, as the request was made without any referrer information. The query generates results that include the entry point path, requested content, average time taken, and total number of hits. The output is grouped by requested content details in the order of total hits.

```
---Ch02Top10EntryPoints.sql---
SELECT
    Top 10
```

```
    STRCAT(EXTRACT_PATH(TO_LOWERCASE(cs-uri-stem)),'/') AS RequestedPath,
    EXTRACT_FILENAME(TO_LOWERCASE(cs-uri-stem)) AS EntryPoint,
    AVG(time-taken) AS AvgTime,
    COUNT(*) AS Hits
FROM %source% TO %destination%
WHERE
    (cs(Referer) IS NULL)
    AND
    (sc-status BETWEEN 200 AND 307)
GROUP BY cs-uri-stem, cs(Referer)
ORDER BY Hits DESC
---Ch02Top10EntryPoints.sql---
```

Running this query enables you to understand the most popular entry Uniform Resource Locator (URL) from a particular website. This information is useful in website design planning; when you notice the average time taken for a particular entry point is high, you will need to look at the requested content, and fine-tune it to provide better user experience.

To run the query, access a command prompt, navigate to the directory where you installed the query samples, and enter the following:

```
C:\Log parser>LogParser.exe
file:Ch02Top10EntryPoints.sql?source="<//webhost/w3svc/example.com>"
+destination="Ch02Top10EntryPoints.txt" -stats:OFF -o:NAT
```

The query starts off by extracting the requested content path and the content name, and then calculates the average time spent by IIS on fulfilling the request. Notice that the log source is reading from a Web server called *Webhost* with the website description *example.com*.

The *WHERE* clause in the query instructs Log parser to check if the *cs(Referer)* value is equal to *NULL*. Although you will notice the '-' in the W3C extended log file, during actual parsing the Log parser will treat it as a *NULL* value. Hence, checking this *NULL* value will indicate that this is the first request the client is requesting. In short, this is an entry point. The last part of the query checks for *sc-status* code, which indicates whether the request made has been successful or not. A non-error status code falls between 200 to 307 according to HTTP Request For Comment (RFC) specification. 200 indicates a successful reply, while 3XX indicates a redirection. For example, if the request is made to */mydir/*, by default IIS will redirect to the configured default page, hence a 301 response is made. The reason for 307 as the last in the range is because that is the last valid non-error HTTP status code per RFC specification.

TIP

For more information about HTTP status code definitions, please refer to the Microsoft Knowledge article: IIS Status Codes at support.microsoft.com/?id=318380 or visit www.w3.org/Protocols/rfc2616/rfc2616-sec10.html#sec10 for the RFC specification.

The following shows the sample result of the query:

RequestedPath	EntryPoint	AvgTime	Hits
/	index.aspx	1843	92142
/main/		4329	79210
/main/	index.aspx	2983	67092
/support/	mainkb.aspx	3984	47382
/support/	kbsearch.aspx	19320	37798
/support/	faq.aspx	8920	29012
/customer/	login.aspx	3981	13944
/customer/	lastchanged.html	2930	9382
/	topnews.aspx	8221	8321
/main/	newsfeed.aspx	7292	3023

From the query results, you will get a better picture about how often IIS content is being accessed. This information also illustrates user behavior and preferences. For example, certain users like to access the latest news directly (*topnews.aspx*). Take note on the second listing that the *EntryPoint* is blank. In this case, the entry points were made on the specific path only, whereby IIS will return the default document page.

TIP

Now, you can find valid entry points with *Ch02Top10EntryPoints.sql*, but how about invalid or error entry points? You can change the *WHERE* clause *sc-status* checking from successful replies to unsuccessful. Changing it to *sc-status BETWEEN 400 AND 505* will allow you to track down invalid or error entry points.

Monitoring Web Referrers

The Ch02Top10Referrer.sql query returns the top 10 referrers to your website. We define a referrer as requests that do not originate from the website. It is easy to identify, as the cs(Referer) field should contains URLs other than the current website. The query generates results including: the successful requested content, total number of hits, remote host name, and referrer's URL. The output is grouped by requested content, remote host name, referrer's URL and is ordered by total hits.

NOTE

The following query assumes a request was made by a client browser and will include referrer field information. However, certain browsers can be configured not to send this detail, hence, IIS may log '-' as the data for the *cs(Refer)* field.

---

www.syngress.com

```
---Ch02Top10WebReferrer.sql---
SELECT
    Top 10
    EXTRACT_FILENAME(TO_LOWERCASE(cs-uri-stem)) AS RequestedFile,
    count(*) AS Hits,
    REVERSEDNS(EXTRACT_TOKEN(cs(Referer), 2, '/')) AS HostName,
    TO_LOWERCASE(EXTRACT_TOKEN(cs(Referer), 0, '?')) AS ReferrerURL
FROM %selection%
WHERE
    (HostName <> '%domainname%')
    AND
    (cs(Referer) IS NOT NULL)
    AND
    (EXTRACT_EXTENSION(TO_LOWERCASE(cs-uri-stem)) IN ('asp';'aspx';'html';'html'))
    AND
    (sc-status BETWEEN 200 AND 307)
GROUP BY RequestedFile, HostName, ReferrerURL
ORDER BY Hits DESC
---Ch02Top10WebReferrer.sql---
```

This query is particularly useful in understanding referrers that are bringing traffic to your website. It is also a good starting point to understand how well your affiliate partners are doing if you are running affiliated programs to attract traffic.

Let's look at the some of the actions performed in the query. First, it extracts the content filename, then resolves the remote host IP address to a host name using the *REVERSEDNS* function, and finally extracts the full request path without any query string from the referrer's URL.

> **NOTE**
>
> It is important to note that *REVERSEDNS* requires Domain Name Service (DNS) server access. It will take a longer processing time if there are many IP addresses to be resolved. When Log parser is unable to resolve the host name, remote IP address will be shown instead.

Notice that in the *FROM* clause, we specify *%selection%* rather than *%source%* and *%destination%*, as in the previous query. This a more flexible query, as we can control the output directive at the command-line level. For example, when executing the query at a command line, you could enter the following:

```
LogParser.exe
file:Ch02Top10WebReferrer.sql?selection="<1> TO output.csv"+domainname="www.mysite.com"
-o:CSV
```

This syntax will pass in the value *<1> TO output.csv* into the query, while the *-o:CSV* instructs Log parser to generate the result in Comma Separated Values (CSV) format

Or, you can do it the following way:

```
logparser.exe file:Ch02Top10WebReferrer.sql?selection="<1>"+domainname="www.mysite.com"
```

This syntax will pass in the value *<1>* into the query, and use the default *NATIVE* format to generate output, since we did not specify the *-o* directive.

The *WHERE* clause in the query instructs Log parser to check if the referrer is from its own site. This is done by checking the *%domainname%* parameter. It then makes sure that the referrer field is not empty. The current query focuses on the filenames that have .asp, .aspx, .html or .htm in the file extension, and successful responses with status codes between 200 and 307.

To run the query, access a command prompt, navigate to the directory where you installed the query samples, and enter the following:

```
logparser.exe file:Ch02Top10WebReferrer.sql?selection="<1> TO
output.csv"+domainname="www.mysite.com" -o:CSV
```

With this, Log parser parses the log files from website ID 1, with *www.mysite.com* as the *%domainname%*, since we want to filter the local referrer. The query will generate the result in a file named *output.csv* using comma-separated value (CSV) format.

The following shows the sample result of the query:

```
RequestedFile,Hits,HostName,ReferrerURL
default.aspx,18323,,www.google.com, http://www.google.com/search
11966.aspx,13299,search.yahoo.com,http:// http://search.yahoo.com/search
rss.aspx,9921,blog.joycode.com,http://blog.joycode.com/sync/refresh.asp
faq.html,7212,netsvr,http://netsvr/printers/ipp_0001.asp
testtree.aspx,5723,192.168.10.2,http://192.168.10.2/loadtest.aspx
hostheader.asp,2332,www.baidu.com, http://www.baidu.com/baidu
nlbsetup.htm,1993,www.networkfaq.com,http://www.networkfaq.com/nlb/link.html
8213.aspx,921,rd.3exp.com,http://rd.3exp.com/news.asp
redirect.asp,722,freelink.com,http://freelink.com/42/923/921/link
redirect.asp,125,link.mysite.com,http://link.mysite.com/cust/3023/track.asp
```

TIP

This example query looks for successful requests. You can simply modify the *sc-status* parameter in the *WHERE* clause to look for 404 errors, which indicate "page not found". With this information, if you are looking for broken URLs referred by the remote host, you can inform related parties to correct the error and reflect the latest URL for the desired content.

Master Craftsman

Identify Image Leaching

Image leaching is defined as hot-linking or borrowing images directly from your Web server. This causes additional bandwidth due to these unwanted requests. By modifying the example query, you will be able to identify these leaching activities.

```
---Ch02Top10ImageLeaching.sql---
SELECT
    Top 10
    TO_LOWERCASE(cs-uri-stem) AS RequestedFile,
    count(*) AS Hits,
    STRCAT(TO_STRING(DIV(SUM(sc-bytes),1024)),'k') AS TotalBytesSent,
    TO_LOWERCASE(EXTRACT_TOKEN(cs(Referer), 0, '?')) AS ReferrerURL
FROM %selection%
WHERE
    (EXTRACT_TOKEN(cs(Referer), 2, '/') <> '%domainname%')
    AND
    (cs(Referer) IS NOT NULL)
    AND
    (EXTRACT_EXTENSION(TO_LOWERCASE(cs-uri-stem)) IN ('gif';'jpg';'bmp'))
    AND
    (sc-status IN (200;304))
GROUP BY RequestedFile, ReferrerURL
ORDER BY Hits, TotalBytesSent DESC
---Ch02Top10ImageLeaching.sql---
```

The modified query will list the top 10 image leaching activities outside the website's Fully Qualify Domain Name (FQDN), specifically looking for images with .gif, .jpg and .bmp extensions. The result will include requested image names, total hits with total number of kilobytes of those illegal requests, and the referrer's URL.

In this particular query, we only check for a HTTP status code of either 200 or 304. Status code 304 represents that the data was not modified; meaning a previous request was made on the same image, but there were no changes since that request. However, you will see minor bandwidth usage in *sc-bytes*; this is due to the status code and HTTP headers sent to remote machines.

Using the results, you will be able to take further action in dealing with these illegal requests. For example, you can either block access or report the activity to the referrer host webmaster.

Monitoring Bandwidth Usage

The Ch02DailyBandwidth.sql query produces a daily report from a particular log source. The calculation of bandwidth usage is based on total incoming and outgoing bytes from IIS server. Since this query only utilizes *cs-bytes* for incoming traffic and *sc-bytes* for outgoing traffic, this query can be apply to any IIS service, such as SMTP or NNTP. The query summarizes bandwidth on a daily basis together with the total incoming and outgoing bandwidth usage in kilobyte format.

```
---Ch02DailyBandwidth.sql---
SELECT
    TO_STRING(TO_TIMESTAMP(date, time), 'MM-dd') AS Day,
    DIV(Sum(cs-bytes),1024) AS Incoming(K),
    DIV(Sum(sc-bytes),1024) AS Outgoing(K)
INTO %chartname%
FROM %source%
GROUP BY Day
---Ch02DailyBandwidth.sql---
```

It is important to collect bandwidth usage information, as it provides the overall performance of traffic occurring in your IIS service. For example, if there is a sudden surge in FTP bandwidth usage, you might want to parse the log file to see the recent activities that caused the sudden increase in bandwidth usage. It could be that your FTP server has been *tagged*, and become a public host for illegal software and movie file distribution. You could also utilize these usage details to plan for your network bandwidth requirements.

This query is simple and neat; first it uses the *TO_TIMESTAMP* function to consolidate the *date* and *time* field into month/month – day/day format. After that, it totals up the daily usage from bytes received by the server (*cs-bytes*) and bytes sent from the server (*sc-bytes*). The figures are then divided by 1024 to generate a kilobytes unit.

The *SELECT* part of the query produces the following output:

```
Day     Incoming(K) Outgoing(K)
----    ----------- ---------------
08-11   33243        203923
08-12   69023        582830
08-13   58328        458391
......
```

This type of output is perfect for a chart display. Notice the *INTO* clause in the query; we will use this clause and specify the output image file using the *%chartname%* parameter. Next, as you might already be aware, the *%source%* is where you specific the log source.

NOTE

The example shown in this section only uses one chart type (ColumnStacked3d). To learn more about different chart types supported, you can refer to the appendices in the back of this book, or access the help document using the following command:

```
C:\ Log parser>LogParser.exe -h -o:chart | more
```

This will show you available chart type details as well as parameters you can specify when using the -o:chart method. However, it is important to take note that chart diagram outputs require Microsoft Office XP or later to be installed. This is because chart diagram outputs use the Office application library when generating the output.

To run the query, access a command prompt, navigate to the directory where you installed the query samples, and enter the following:

```
logparser.exe
file:Ch02DailyBandwidth.sql?chartname="daily.gif"+source="<
//localhost/smtpsvc/1>" -o:chart -chartType:ColumnStacked3d    -chartTitle:"Daily SMTP
Bandwidth Report"
-view -groupSize:800x600
```

First, *daily.gif* is specified as the output filename, and since we are interested in visualizing bandwidth usage for the SMTP service, we point the log source to the default SMTP site. To output as a chart, use the *-o:chart* option. Specify the chart type using *-chartType*; this example uses a Column Stacked chart with 3D effect. The *-chartTitle* specifies the chart title, and finally, the *-view* instructs Log parser view the image file at the end of the process and *-groupSize* specifiesthe image resolution size. See Figure 2.1 for the sample chart diagram.

Figure 2.1 Sample Chart Diagram – Daily SMTP Bandwidth Report

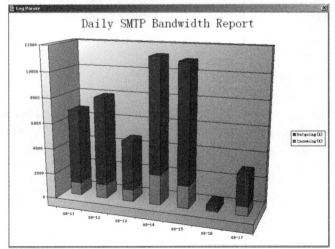

TIP

Removing the -*view* parameter saves the chart diagram image directly to disk without viewing it after parsing. Combine this with a simple batch file and task scheduler, and you can create an HTML file to display an automatically updated chart image.

Master Craftsman

More Bandwidth Usage Analysis

With a few small changes to the existing query, you can monitor hourly or monthly bandwidth usage for a specific range of dates. The key is in the *SELECT* clause. For example, to obtain hourly bandwidth usage, instead of selecting per day grouping, change it to hourly.

```
---Ch02HourlyBandwidth.sql---
SELECT
    QUANTIZE(TO_TIMESTAMP(date, time), 3600) AS Hour,
    DIV(Sum(cs-bytes),1024) AS Incoming(K),
    DIV(Sum(sc-bytes),1024) AS Outgoing(K)
INTO %chartname%
FROM %source%
GROUP BY Hour
---Ch02HourlyBandwidth.sql---
```

The query first quantizes the date and time to the nearest hour, which results in an hourly grouping of the results. Take note that now the log source should be a daily log file, such as ex080104.log

To make it more interesting, what if you would like to know the bandwidth usage for a specific date range? The answer:

```
---Ch02DateBandwidth.sql---
SELECT
    TO_STRING(TO_TIMESTAMP(date, time), 'MM-dd') AS Day,
    DIV(Sum(cs-bytes),1024) AS Incoming(K),
    DIV(Sum(sc-bytes),1024) AS Outgoing(K)
INTO %chartname%
FROM %source%
Where (Day BETWEEN '%from%' AND '%to%')
GROUP BY Day
---Ch02DateBandwidth.sql---
```

Continued

> Notice that a *WHERE* clause is added to apply the date range condition, and two additional variables are used. To run the query, you will enter:
>
> ```
> logparser.exe
> file:Ch02DateBandwidth.sql?chartname="daterange.gif"+source="<//localhost/msftpsvc/1>"
> +from="08-01"+to="08-07" -o:chart -chartTitle:"FTP Bandwidth Usage" -view
> -chartType:ColumnStacked3d
> ```
>
> This command instructs Log parser to parse default FTP website log files from August 1st to August 7th.
>
> Next, to gather monthly information, simply change it to the following:
>
> ```
> ---Ch02MonthlyBandwidth.sql---
> SELECT
>     TO_STRING(TO_TIMESTAMP(date, time), 'MMMM') AS Month,
>     DIV(Sum(cs-bytes),1024) AS Incoming(K),
>     DIV(Sum(sc-bytes),1024) AS Outgoing(K)
> INTO %chartname%
> FROM %source%
> GROUP BY Month
> ---Ch02MonthlyBandwidth.sql---
> ```
>
> As you may have noticed, simple modifications to the SELECT statement and adding a WHERE clause will help you to obtain useful information. This makes Log parser a very powerful and flexible parsing tool.

Ensuring Stability

Besides providing performance and usage information, periodically analyzing W3C extended log files gives you the inside view of server health status. HTTPERR and URLSCAN log files provide further details that are not captured in the W3C extended log file. Analyzing these different log files helps to ensure the stability of your IIS server. Key capabilities include identifying ASP errors with the request details, error codes, and messages; understanding the difference between client side versus service side errors; translating HTTP status code to meaningful error messages; and analyzing URLSCAN log files.

Analyzing Request Errors

By analyzing error requests, you can determine the health of your IIS applications, find clues for troubleshooting, and identify potential risks associated with the request.

Besides the key IIS log fields introduced in previous section, you will learn more about the following new and useful log fields:

- **User name (cs–username)** This field captures the username making the request. If anonymous access is allowed, the default IUSR_<COMPUTERNAME> account will be the request identity and it is logged as '-' in the IIS log file. If the site is configured to use user authentication, users will be required to provide a valid username and password, and IIS will log the username in the log file.

- **Procotol Substatus (sc–substatus)** This is a new property field for W3C extended log format introduced in IIS 6.0. In previous versions of IIS, only status codes are captured in IIS logs, making troubleshooting more troublesome, as some general status codes contain substatuses. For example, 404.2 and 404.3 both are generic "file not found" errors. However, in IIS 6.0, 404.2 indicates that the dynamic content extension was not allowed, while 404.3 tell you that the required Multipurpose Internet Mail Exchange (MIME) type is not registered with IIS server.

- **Win32 Status (sc–win32–status)** This field holds theWin32 programming error code. This status code gives you more information about the request status, and helps you troubleshoot further when the HTTP status and substatus do not provide enough information.

In addition, HTTPERR and URLSCAN log files can assist you in analyzing error requests. IIS 6.0 introduces the HTTP.SYS kernel mode driver. This driver keeps its own log files and it is an important source for identifying error requests and understanding server health status. The default log path for HTTPERR is *%windir%/system32/Logfiles/HTTPERR* . Table 2.3 exhibits the available log fields supported in HTTPERR.

Table 2.3 HTTP Error Log Fields

Property	Field	Description
Date	date	The date when the request was made
Time	time	The time when the request was made
Server Name	s-computername	IIS server name
Client IP Address	c-ip	Client IP address that accessed the IIS server
Client Port	c-port	Client source port number
Server IP Address	s-ip	IIS server IP address serving the request
Server Port	s-port	IIS server port number serving the request
Protocol Version	cs-version	Client protocol version, for example, HTTP 1.0 / 1.1
Method	cs-method	Client action request, for example GET, POST
URI	cs-uri	Requested content and query string (if any)
User Agent	cs(User-Agent)	Application used by client, for example, browser
Referer	cs(Referer)	Previous URL that directed client to current site
Cookie	cs(Cookie)	Content of cookies send or received
Host	cs-host	Client computer name
Protocol Status	sc-status	Status code of the request
Bytes Sent	sc-bytes	Number of bytes sent by server

Continued

Table 2.3 HTTP Error Log Fields

Property	Field	Description
Bytes Received	cs-bytes	Number of bytes received by server
Time Taken	time-taken	Amount of time to process the request
Service Name	s-siteid	Site ID serving the request, for example, W3Svc1
Reason Phrase	s-reason	Short error description
Queue Name	s-queuename	Name of the application pool

TIP

To learn more about HTTPERR logging, please refer to: *INF: Http.sys Registry Settings for IIS* at http://support.microsoft.com/?id=820129 and *INFO: Error Logging in HTTP API* at http://support.microsoft.com/?id=820729.

Although IIS 6.0 has advanced security features that are part of Windows Server 2003, you can deploy the URLSCAN Internet Server API (ISAPI) filter to further restrict HTTP requests. URLSCAN monitors incoming HTTP requests based on a set of rules. If requests do not comply with the URLSCAN rule sets, IIS replies with a "404 File Not Found" error to the client and writes an entry in the URLSCAN log file.

By default, URLScan creates daily log files for each worker process. These log files are created in the *%windir%/system32/inetsrv/urlscan/logs/* folder. Table 2.4 exhibits the available log fields supported in URLSCAN.

Table 2.4 URLSCAN Log Fields

Property	Field	Description
Date	date	The date when the request was blocked
Time	time	The time when the request was blocked
Client IP Address	clientip	Client IP address that accessed the IIS server
Reason	comment	Reason detail of blocked request
Service Name	siteinstance	Site ID serving the request, for example, W3Svc1
URL	url	Requested content name and query string

NOTE

Most of the features included in URLSCAN are built into IIS 6.0. Hence, you need to analyze your particular environment to determine whether you actually need to deploy URLScan. For more information about IIS 6.0 built-in security features and differences with URLScan, please refer to www.microsoft.com/technet/ security/tools/urlscan.mspx?#XSLTsection123121120120.

Identifying Request Errors

The Ch02ClientErrors.sql query provides a list of the error requests that occurred due to invalid client requests. For example, if the client IP address is prohibited from visiting the content, IIS returns a 403.6 HTTP status code. The result generated includes the requested content filename, the error code, and the actual interpreted error message.

```
---Ch02ClientErrors.sql---
SELECT
    RequestedFile, ErrCode, Total, ClientDesc, ErrDesc, Win32Desc
    USING sc-win32-status AS WinCode,
    REPLACE_IF_NULL(TO_LOWERCASE(cs-username),'Anonymous') AS UserName,
    STRCAT(STRCAT(' (',REVERSEDNS(c-ip)),')') AS ClientIP,
    TO_LOWERCASE(cs-uri-stem) AS RequestedFile,
    STRCAT(TO_STRING(sc-status), STRCAT('.',TO_STRING(sc-substatus))) AS ErrCode,
    Count(*) AS Total,
    STRCAT(Username,ClientIP) AS ClientDesc,
    CASE ErrCode
        WHEN '400.0' THEN 'Bad Request.'
        --Access Error--
        WHEN '401.1' THEN 'Access Denied - Login failed.'
        WHEN '401.2' THEN 'Access Denied - Logon failed due to server config.'
        WHEN '401.3' THEN 'Access Denied - ACL checking failed.'
        WHEN '401.4' THEN 'Access Denied - Authorization failed by filter.'
        WHEN '401.5' THEN 'Access Denied - Authorization failed by ISAPI/CGI
application.'
        WHEN '401.7' THEN 'Access Denied - Access denied by URL authorization policy on
the Web server.'
        --Forbidden Error--
        WHEN '403.1' THEN 'Forbidden - Execute access.'
        WHEN '403.2' THEN 'Forbidden - Read access.'
        WHEN '403.3' THEN 'Forbidden - Write access.'
        WHEN '403.4' THEN 'Forbidden - SSL required.'
        WHEN '403.5' THEN 'Forbidden - SSL 128 required.'
        WHEN '403.6' THEN 'Forbidden - IP address rejected.'
        WHEN '403.7' THEN 'Forbidden - Client certificate required.'
        WHEN '403.8' THEN 'Forbidden - Site access denied.'
        WHEN '403.9' THEN 'Forbidden - Too many users.'
        WHEN '403.10' THEN 'Forbidden - Invalid configuration.'
        WHEN '403.11' THEN 'Forbidden - Password change.'
        WHEN '403.12' THEN 'Forbidden - Mapper denied access.'
```

```
        WHEN '403.13' THEN 'Forbidden - Client certificate revoked.'
        WHEN '403.14' THEN 'Forbidden - Directory listing denied.'
        WHEN '403.15' THEN 'Forbidden - Client Access Licenses exceeded.'
        WHEN '403.16' THEN 'Forbidden - Client certificate is untrusted or invalid.'
        WHEN '403.17' THEN 'Forbidden - Client certificate has expired or is not yet valid.'
        WHEN '403.18' THEN 'Forbidden - Cannot execute requested URL in the current
application pool.'
        WHEN '403.19' THEN 'Forbidden - Cannot execute CGIs for the client in this
application pool.'
        WHEN '403.20' THEN 'Forbidden - Passport logon failed.'
        --Not Found Error--
        WHEN '404.0' THEN 'Not Found - File or directory not found.'
        WHEN '404.1' THEN 'Not Found - Web site not accessible on the requested port.'
        WHEN '404.2' THEN 'Not Found - Web service extension lockdown policy prevents
this request.'
        WHEN '404.3' THEN 'Not Found - MIME map policy prevents this request.'
        --Non-Common Error--
        WHEN '405.0' THEN 'HTTP verb used to access this page is not allowed.'
        WHEN '406.0' THEN 'Client browser does not accept the MIME type of the requested
page.'
        WHEN '407.0' THEN 'Proxy authentication required.'
        WHEN '412.0' THEN 'Precondition failed.'
        WHEN '413.0' THEN 'Request entity too large.'
        WHEN '414.0' THEN 'Request-URI too long.'
        WHEN '415.0' THEN 'Unsupported media type.'
        WHEN '416.0' THEN 'Requested range not satisfiable.'
        WHEN '417.0' THEN 'Execution failed.'
        WHEN '423.0' THEN 'Locked error.'
        WHEN '424.0' THEN 'Failed Dependency.'
        ELSE 'Unknown error'
    END AS ErrDesc,
    WIN32_ERROR_DESCRIPTION(WinCode) AS Win32Desc
FROM %source%
WHERE (sc-status BETWEEN 400 AND 424)
GROUP BY RequestedFile, ErrCode, ClientDesc, ErrDesc, Win32Desc
ORDER BY Total DESC
---Ch02ClientErrors.sql---
```

Though it looks complicated, this query is actually straight-forward. The *USING* clause defines three variables referenced by other columns in the query. The SQL statement first declares the *sc-win32-status* as *WinCode*, then it gathers the user name for the requests, placing the content *Anonymous* in that field if an anonymous user makes the request. The SQL statement then formats the *c-ip* field as a standard IP address. Finally, the *STRCAT* function concatenates *UserName* and *ClientIP* variables to *ClientDesc*.

The *CASE* clause is used to determine the actual message from the *ErrCode*. The *WHERE* clause filters the request to only include those status codes related to client side requests, which, according to RFC specification, ranges from 400 to 424. Additional substatus codes are defined per IIS status code documentation. One of the output fields, *Win32Desc*, is actually the Win32 error message obtained using the *WIN32_ERROR_DESCRIPTION* function.

To run the query, access a command prompt, navigate to the directory where you installed the query samples, and enter the following:

```
C:\Log parser>LogParser.exe
file:Ch02ClientErrors.sql?source="<1>" -o:NAT -rtp:-1 > ClientErrors.txt
```

This command instructs Log parser to read the default website log files, output all rows in *NATIVE* format, and redirect output to the *ClientErrors.txt* text file.

```
RequestedFile                   ErrCode   Total    ClientDesc
-----------------------------   -------   -----    -------------------------
/printers/ipp_0002.asp          401.1     322      Anonymous (192.168.10.18)
/printers/ipp_0002.asp          401.2     322      Anonymous (192.168.10.18)
/printers/hplaser/.printer/     404.0     61       indev\susan (susan.indev)
/certsrv/default.asp            404.2     28       indev\administrator (indev)
/secure/syscheck.aspx           401.3     24       indev\viewer (192.168.10.21)
/certenroll/                    403.14    3        indev\susan (susan.indev)
/printers/ipp_0004.asp          401.5     2        Anonymous (192.168.10.93)


ErrDesc
--------------
Access Denied - Login failed.
Access Denied - Logon failed due to server config.
Not Found - File or directory not found.
Not Found - Web service extension lockdown policy prevents this request.
Access Denied - ACL checking failed.
Forbidden - Directory listing denied.
Access Denied - Authorization failed by ISAPI/CGI application.


Win32Desc
------------------------
The operation completed successfully.
No credentials are available in the security package.
The system cannot find the file specified.
Windows cannot open this program because it has been prevented by a software
    restriction policy.
   For more information, open Event Viewer or contact your system
   administrator.
Logon failure: unknown user name or bad password.
Access is denied.
The operation completed successfully.
```

```
Statistics:
-----------
Elements processed: 32121
Elements output:      15
Execution time:       8.18 seconds
```

TIP

When you experience huge amounts of client side errors, you can modify the *WHERE* clause condition to isolate errors base on more specific code ranges. For example, if you would like to focus on access related errors, simply change the ending status code to 401.

To quickly summarize client side errors, you can simplify the query to the following:

```
---Ch02ClientErrorsSummary.sql---
SELECT
     STRCAT(TO_STRING(sc-status), STRCAT('.',TO_STRING(sc-substatus))) AS
ErrCode,
     Count(*) AS Total
FROM %source%
WHERE
     (sc-status BETWEEN 400 AND 424)
GROUP BY ErrCode
ORDER BY Total DESC
---Ch02ClientErrorsSummary.sql---
```

Swiss Army Knife

Analyzing Server Side Errors

Modifying the last query to the following will provide you with details of server-side errors:

```
---Ch02ServerErrors.sql---
SELECT
     RequestedFile, ErrCode, Total, ErrDesc, Win32Desc
     USING sc-win32-status AS WinCode,
     TO_LOWERCASE(cs-uri-stem) AS RequestedFile,
     STRCAT(TO_STRING(sc-status), STRCAT('.',TO_STRING(sc-substatus))) AS ErrCode,
     Count(*) AS Total,
```

Continued

```
    CASE ErrCode
        WHEN '500.0' THEN 'Internal server error.'
        WHEN '500.12' THEN 'Server Error - Application is busy restarting on
the Web server.'
        WHEN '500.13' THEN 'Server Error - Web server is too busy.'
        WHEN '500.15' THEN 'Server Error - Direct requests for Global.asa are not
allowed.'
        WHEN '500.16' THEN 'Server Error - UNC authorization credentials incorrect.'
        WHEN '500.18' THEN 'Server Error - URL authorization store cannot be
opened.'
        WHEN '500.100' THEN 'Server Error - Internal ASP error.'
        WHEN '501.0' THEN 'Header values specify a configuration that is not
implemented.'
        WHEN '502.1' THEN 'Web server received an invalid response while acting
as a gateway or proxy.'
        WHEN '502.2' THEN 'Error in CGI application.'
        WHEN '503.0' THEN 'Service unavailable'
        WHEN '504.0' THEN 'Gateway timeout.'
        WHEN '505.0' THEN 'HTTP version not supported.'
        ELSE 'Unknown error'
    END AS ErrDesc,
    WIN32_ERROR_DESCRIPTION(WinCode) AS Win32Desc
FROM %source%
WHERE (sc-status BETWEEN 500 AND 505)
GROUP BY RequestedFile, ErrCode, ErrDesc, Win32Desc
ORDER BY Total DESC
---Ch02ServerErrors.sql---
```

The modified query only parses error requests with HTTP status codes ranging from 500 to 505, which are server side error codes.

Understanding ASP Errors

To further understand what is causing server side errors, the Ch02AspErrors.sql query generates a list of the server side errors that occurred in your ASP application. Under normal circumstances, these type of errors are often caused by coding errors in the server side query, for example, |12|800a0009| Subquery_out_of_range:_'arrayA(...)'. This error indicates that the *arrayA* variable defined in a server side query is out of range. The format normally starts with a pipe character followed by a line number, another pipe separator, the error code, and finally one last pipe separator with an ASP error message.

In some special error instances, IIS may only capture the first two separator values, such as |32|8004005| This type of error might not be caused by an ASP query, but rather another problem such as an incorrect IIS configuration. The query results include the error ASP page name, the query string submitted if any, the error detail, message, and the line number in the ASP page that caused the error. This query lists the most frequent to least frequent ASP pages that had errors.

```
---Ch02AspErrors.sql---
SELECT
    Uri, Errorcode, ErrorMsg, LineNo, Total
    USING STRCAT(cs-uri-stem, REPLACE_IF_NOT_NULL(cs-uri-query, STRCAT('?', cs-uri-
query))) AS QryStr,
    TO_LOWERCASE(EXTRACT_TOKEN(QryStr, 0, '|')) AS Uri,
    EXTRACT_TOKEN(cs-uri-query, 2, '|') AS ErrorCode,
    EXTRACT_TOKEN(cs-uri-query, -1, '|') AS ErrorMsg,
    EXTRACT_TOKEN(cs-uri-query, 1, '|') AS LineNo,
    COUNT(*) AS Total
FROM %source%
WHERE
    (cs-uri-stem LIKE '%.asp')
    AND
    (sc-status = 500)
GROUP BY Uri, ErrorCode, ErrorMsg, LineNo
ORDER BY Total DESC
---Ch02AspErrors.sql---
```

With the result, you can quickly identify which ASP query is experiencing the most errors during processing and the type of errors. The line number comes in handy when you need to pinpoint which line of the code breaks.

This query is simplified in Log parser version 2.2, as the new *EXTRACT_TOKEN* function makes it easier to obtain the desired value in the *cs-uri-query* field. First, the query extracts the ASP content requested along with the query string, if any. The *USING* clause declares aliased field-expressions that are not part of the output columns, but can be referenced anywhere in the query. This is particularly useful for improving readability of the query. After that, the error string in the field is extracted into 3 different columns, namely, error code, message, and the query line number.

The condition in the *WHERE* clause looks for ASP requests using the *LIKE* operator to locate any requests containing the string *.asp*. The request HTTP status must be equal to 500. Log parser will only return requests matching both conditions. To run the query, access a command prompt, navigate to the directory where you installed the query samples, and enter the following:

```
C:\Log parser>LogParser.exe
file:Ch02AspErrors.sql?source="ex*.log" -o:NAT -rtp:-1 > AspErrors.txt
```

The command syntax tells Log Parser to parse all extended log files in the current directory, and output it in *NATIVE* format, which is a default screen listing. The *-rtp* stands for rows to print. The default rows to print are 10, hence after 10 rows, the query pauses for user interaction. To avoid this, we specify *-1* to instruct Log parser to output all rows without any pause. The result is then redirected to a text file named *AspErrors.txt*:

```
Uri                                                ErrorCode
-------------------------------------------------- ---------
/asp/doorwaytop.asp?                               800a01a8
```

```
/asp/depositcheck.asp?                                    800a0401
/asp/leftmenu.asp?                                        ASP_0147
/asp/login.asp?                                           80004005
/certenroll/nsrev_netsvr2.asp                             80070005
/asp/cust_postupdate.asp?custid=134&sel_id=454647         800a0009
/asp/reportsearch.asp?id=29&format=2&style=lightdesc      ASP_0113
/print/pdfview.asp                                        800a01a8
/submit.asp                                               800a01b6
. . . . . . . . . . . . .
```

```
ErrorMsg                                                  LineNo      Total
-------------------------------------------------------- ------     -----
Object_required:_'objRst'                                 326         320
Expected_end_of_statement                                 7           182
500_Server_Error                                          -           153
Keyword_xsl:call-template_may_not_be_used_here.__         99          93
CCertAdmin::IsValidCertificate_Access_is_denied._         6           33
     0x80070005_(WIN32:_5)
Subscript_out_of_range:_'arrayA(...)'                     820         29
Script_timed_out                                          -           16
Object_required:_'ACEpdfObj'                              7           8
Object_doesn't_support_this_property_or_method:_'SetAccountID'  29    4
```

```
Statistics:
-----------
Elements processed: 27649
Elements output:     20
Execution time:      12.32 seconds
```

In the sample output, *leftmenu.asp* is producing a general 500_Server_Error, hence no *LineNo* was given. This type of error might be caused by the code itself and no full error message is being captured by IIS; it could also be that the ASP engine crashed. Normally, you need to check the Windows Event Viewer to see if there is an additional event log entry that provides more information.

Analyzing HTTPERR Errors

The HTTP Application Programming Interface (API) error logs are generated by HTTP.SYS. This new kernel mode driver handles HTTP requests and routes them to the related application pool. Errors that occur in this driver will trigger a log entry in the HTTP API error logs. By default, HTTP API error logging is enabled; you can monitor this log file to troubleshoot client HTTP request errors. For example, a 503 status code indicates that the application is not available. This log file also captures illegal requests sent to IIS including bad request, forbidden access, and more.

NOTE

Brief descriptions of HTTP.SYS roles:

- Keeping track of client connections established to the server.
- Accept HTTP requests and route it to respective application pool request queue.
- Facilitate Quality of Service (QoS) features, including connection limits, timeouts, request queue length, and throttling bandwidth usage.
- Send responses back to client and implement kernel mode caching.

New log fields are supported when software updates are installed.
Additional properties are now available for logging in the Httperr#.log file in IIS 6.0. Visit support.microsoft.com/?id=832975 for additional information.

The Ch02AppPoolErrors.sql query scans the HTTP API error log and produces a list of failed requests related to application pool errors. The query focuses on the famous 503 service unavailable error that results from a variety of conditions. Output includes the server and the client IP address, website detail, the number of errors, the name of the application pool, and the error message.

```
---Ch02AppPoolErrors.sql---
SELECT
    REVERSEDNS(c-ip) AS ClientIP,
    TO_LOWERCASE(cs-uri) AS ClientRequest,
    STRCAT(STRCAT('SiteID:',To_STRING(s-siteid)),STRCAT(STRCAT('(',s-ip),')')) AS
WebSite,
    COUNT(*) AS Total,
    s-queuename AS AppPool,
    CASE s-reason
        WHEN 'AppOffline' THEN 'Application error, AppPool taken offline.'
        WHEN 'AppPoolTimer' THEN 'AppPool too busy.'
        WHEN 'AppShutdown' THEN 'AppPool being shutdown.'
        WHEN 'ConnLimit' THEN 'Site level connection limit reached.'
        WHEN 'Disabled' THEN 'AppPool disabled and offline.'
        WHEN 'N/A' THEN 'Internal error. E.g. memory allocation failed.'
```

```
        WHEN 'QueueFull' THEN 'AppPool request queue is full.'
        ELSE 'Unknown error'
    END AS ErrDesc
FROM HTTPERR
WHERE (sc-status = 503)
GROUP BY ClientIP, ClientRequest, WebSite, AppPool, ErrDesc
ORDER BY Total DESC
---Ch02AppPoolErrors.sql---
```

This query is particularly useful when performing a full scan of the entire history of web application errors. If you notice many errors such as those indicating an application shuts down, you might want to do a filter on specific websites depending on the application pool to minimize the impact of downtime.

The *STRCAT* function for the *WebSite* column is defined as '*Site ID:YY (X.X.X.X)*' format, where *YY* represents the website ID and *X.X.X.X* is the site IP address. Notice that in the *FROM* clause, the *HTTPERR* directive instructs Log parser to parse all *HTTPERR#* log files. You can change it to *httperr2.log* if you wish to only scan the log file. Take note that you must specify the *httperr2.log* path or it must located at the same path as the query.

To run the query, access a command prompt, navigate to the directory where you installed the query samples, and enter the following:

```
logparser.exe
file:Ch02AppPoolErrors.sql -o:NAT -rtp:-1 > AppPoolErrors.txt
```

This instructs Log parser to output the result as *NATIVE* format with all rows at once, and redirect it to the *AppPoolErrors.txt* text file:

```
ClientIP          ClientRequest        WebSite                        Total
-------------     -----------------    -------------------            -----
192.168.10.112    /                    SiteID:2(192.168.10.18)        24
192.168.10.99     /crm/index.aspx      SiteID:832483(192.168.10.18)   18
susan.indev       /deploy/upload.asp   SiteID:2912(192.168.10.19)     9
wastest           /loadtest.aspx       SiteID:2(192.168.10.18)        3


AppPool              ErrDesc
-------------        ----------------------------
DefaultAppPool       AppPool disabled and offline.
CRMv2                AppPool too busy.
InHousePool          Internal error. E.g. memory allocation failed.
TestPool             Site level connection limit reached.


Statistics:
-----------
Elements processed: 1135
Elements output:    4
Execution time:     0.09 seconds
```

Swiss Army Knife

Understanding Invalid Requests

While the sample query focuses on application pool-related errors, the following modified query scans for invalid requests. These error requests are not yet reaching the actual website and application pool, rather, they are dropped at the HTTP.SYS driver level; hence there is no website ID or application pool name. Typical causes will be unknown host name, access forbidden due to restriction rules, and others.

```
---Ch02HTTPErrors.sql---
SELECT
    TO_STRING(TO_TIMESTAMP(date, time), 'MM-dd') AS Day,
    REVERSEDNS(c-ip) AS ClientIP,
    TO_LOWERCASE(cs-uri) AS ClientRequest,
    s-ip AS WebServerIP,
    COUNT(*) AS Total,
    s-reason AS ErrDesc
FROM HTTPERR
WHERE
    (sc-status <> 503)
    AND
    (sc-status IS NOT NULL)
GROUP BY Day, ClientIP, ClientRequest, WebServerIP, ErrDesc
ORDER BY Day DESC
---Ch02HTTPErrors.sql---
```

This query groups results by day, starting from the most recent errors. It searches for invalid requests with sc-status not equal to 503 or NULL. The *s-reason* field provides the error detail of the request. For detailed information on these messages, please refer to *INFO: Error Logging in HTTP API* at http://support.microsoft.com/?id=820729.

Analyzing URLSCAN Errors

Monitoring URLSCAN log files allows you to detect rejected requests or malicious attacks against your server. If you suspect your application requests were blocked by URLSCAN, you can analyze the log entries to fine-tune URLSCAN.ini to suit your application needs.

NOTE

Before analyzing URLSCAN errors, you must install URLSCAN. For information on how to install URLSCAN, please refer to:
Using URLSCAN on IIS at http://support.microsoft.com/?id=307608.

The Ch02UrlscanErrors.sql query scans the URLSCAN logs and produces a list of rejected requests that failed to comply with URLSCAN.ini rule sets. This query extracts critical information from the log files, summarizes it, and makes it easier to understand. The result includes the client IP address, the targeted requests, the website ID, the number of time requests got rejected, and the reason for rejection.

```
---Ch02UrlscanErrors.sql---
SELECT
    REVERSEDNS(clientip) AS ClientIP,
    TO_LOWERCASE(url) AS ClientRequest,
    siteinstance AS WebSiteID,
    COUNT(*) AS Total,
    EXTRACT_TOKEN(EXTRACT_TOKEN(comment,0,', '),0, 'Request') AS ErrDesc
FROM URLSCAN
GROUP BY ClientIP, ClientRequest, WebSiteID, ErrDesc
ORDER BY Total DESC
---Ch02UrlscanErrors.sql---
```

The query scans every URLSCAN log file in the default path *%windir%/system32/inetsrv/urlscan/logs/*. Notice that the URLSCAN log format field name is quite different from the rest of IIS-related logs. For more information, please refer to Appendix C for URLSCAN input format. The error message from the log files is simplified and extracted as the *ErrDesc* column. The result is ordered by the number of rejected requests.

To run the query, access a command prompt, navigate to the directory where you installed the query samples, and enter the following:

```
logparser.exe
file:Ch02UrlscanErrors.sql -o:NAT -rtp:-1 > UrlscanErrors.txt
```

This instructs Log parser to output the result in *NATIVE* format with all rows at once, and redirect it to the *UrlscanErrors.txt* text file:

```
ClientIP          ClientRequest
-------------     -----------------------------------------------------------------
192.168.10.43     /printers/hplaser/.printer/
192.168.10.43     /rettest.idq
192.168.10.243    /asp/doorway.asplanguageid=2&gmtoffset=480
192.168.10.212    //cgi-bin/..%255c..%255c..%255c..%255cwinnt/system32/cmd.exe
192.168.10.212    //adsamples/..%c0%af..%c0%af..%c0%af..%c0%af../winnt/system32/cmd.exe
192.168.10.212    /iisadmpwd/aexp2b.htr
192.168.10.249    -
192.168.10.249    -
192.168.10.212    //iisadmpwd/..%f0%80%80%af..//..%f0%80%80%af../winnt/system32/cmd.exe
192.168.10.212    //_vti_adm/..%252f..%252f..%252f..%252fwinnt/system32/cmd.exe
192.168.10.243    /asp/eventindex.files/eventselection.htm
192.168.10.243    /asp/..\images\neteller.gif
```

```
192.168.10.212   /scripts/iisadmin/bdir.htr
192.168.10.249   -
192.168.10.249   -
192.168.10.249   -
192.168.10.40    /printers/hplaser/.printer/


WebSiteID       Total      ErrDesc
---------       -----      --------------------------------------------------
1               354        URL contains '.' in the path.
1               332        URL contains extension '.idq'
1923490         294        URL contains sequence '&'
73223           103        URL normalization was not complete after one pass.
73223           102        URL contains extension '.exe'
1               85         URL contains extension '.htr'
-               78         Sent verb '/GET'
-               78         Sent verb 'TRACE'
73223           69         URL contains high bit character.
73223           56         URL contains disallowed header 'transfer-encoding:'
1923490         53         URL contains '.' in the path.
1923490         31         URL contains sequence '\'
73223           12         URL contains extension '.htr'
-               9          Sent verb 'OPTIONS'
-               4          Sent verb 'pGET'
-               1          Sent verb '=POST'
1               3          URL contains '.' in the path.


Statistics:
-----------
Elements processed: 924
Elements output:     19
Execution time:      23.08 seconds
```

From the sample output, the request rejected the most is */printers/hplaser/.printer/*. To solve this error, simply change the value for *AllowDotInPath* from 0 to 1 in URLSCAN.ini, and restart IIS services for the changes to take effect. Next in the sample, you will notice a number of rejected requests with weird characters in the request column. These are general attempts to exploit IIS server, and of course none of those requests are successful, as they are blocked by URLSCAN. In the next section we will explore these exploits more.

Scanning for Security Breaches

Log files are an important and useful troubleshooting channel to resolve failure or error requests, as well as the monitor usage status of the IIS server. The other key factor in why log files are so important is that they are also a valuable source of information for identifying potential attack behavior and intrusion patterns.

By understanding these attack requests, not only are you able to tell whether the attacks have been successful or not, you also can plan the next course of action against these failed requests. These requests could be anything, including information disclosure, unauthorized access, and more.

Analyzing Illegal Requests

An illegal request is any request that a user should not send to the server under normal circumstances, but would send in the case of an attack. For example, a hacker trying to gain remote access might try exploiting a known vulnerability via IIS. Hence, it is vital to be aware of illegal requests made to the server and ensure the server is running with the latest service packs and hot fixes.

This section analyzes all IIS-related log sources, ranging from W3C extended logs to HTTPERR and URLSCAN log files. For more information, please refer to:

- Table 2.2 W3C Extended Log Fields
- Table 2.3 HTTPERR Log Fields
- Table 2.4 URLSCAN Log Fields

Scanning For Failed Authentication and Unauthorized Access

Failed authentication occurs when a user accessing protected content fails to properly authenticate with the server, while unauthorized access indicates that a user failed the Access Control List (ACL) checking on the requested content. Such information provides you with detail about users or attackers who are trying to access certain content that they should not access.

The Ch02AuthAclFailure.sql query scans the W3C extended log files, searching for requests that fail authentication or are denied due to NTFS permissions. This query is similar to the Identify Error Requests sample query presented earlier in this chapter, however, this focuses only on authentication and authorization failures.

```
---Ch02AuthAclFailures.sql---
SELECT
    RequestedFile, ClientDesc, Total, ErrDesc, ErrDate
    USING TO_LOWERCASE(cs-username) AS UserName,
    STRCAT(STRCAT(' (',REVERSEDNS(c-ip)),')') AS ClientIP,
    STRCAT(TO_STRING(sc-status), STRCAT('.',TO_STRING(sc-substatus))) AS ErrCode,
    TO_LOWERCASE(cs-uri-stem) AS RequestedFile,
    STRCAT(Username,ClientIP) AS ClientDesc,
    Count(*) AS Total,
    CASE ErrCode
```

```
        --Access Error--
        WHEN '401.1' THEN 'Access Denied - Login failed.'
        WHEN '401.2' THEN 'Access Denied - Logon failed due to server config.'
        WHEN '401.3' THEN 'Access Denied - ACL checking failed.'
        WHEN '401.4' THEN 'Access Denied - Authorization failed by filter.'
        WHEN '401.5' THEN 'Access Denied - Authorization failed by ISAPI/CGI
application.'
        WHEN '401.7' THEN 'Access Denied - Access denied by URL authorization policy on
the Web server.'
        --Forbidden Error--
        WHEN '403.1' THEN 'Forbidden - Execute access.'
        WHEN '403.2' THEN 'Forbidden - Read access.'
        WHEN '403.3' THEN 'Forbidden - Write access.'
        WHEN '403.4' THEN 'Forbidden - SSL required.'
        WHEN '403.5' THEN 'Forbidden - SSL 128 required.'
        WHEN '403.6' THEN 'Forbidden - IP address rejected.'
        WHEN '403.7' THEN 'Forbidden - Client certificate required.'
        WHEN '403.8' THEN 'Forbidden - Site access denied.'
        WHEN '403.9' THEN 'Forbidden - Too many users.'
        WHEN '403.10' THEN 'Forbidden - Invalid configuration.'
        WHEN '403.11' THEN 'Forbidden - Password change.'
        WHEN '403.12' THEN 'Forbidden - Mapper denied access.'
        WHEN '403.13' THEN 'Forbidden - Client certificate revoked.'
        WHEN '403.14' THEN 'Forbidden - Directory listing denied.'
        WHEN '403.15' THEN 'Forbidden - Client Access Licenses exceeded.'
        WHEN '403.16' THEN 'Forbidden - Client certificate is untrusted or invalid.'
        WHEN '403.17' THEN 'Forbidden - Client certificate has expired or is not yet
valid.'
        WHEN '403.18' THEN 'Forbidden - Cannot execute requested URL in the current
application pool.'
        WHEN '403.19' THEN 'Forbidden - Cannot execute CGIs for the client in this
application pool.'
        WHEN '403.20' THEN 'Forbidden - Passport logon failed.'
        ELSE STRCAT('Unknown error, status:',ErrCode)
    END AS ErrDesc,
    date AS ErrDate,
FROM %source%
WHERE
    (sc-status BETWEEN 401 AND 403)
    AND
    (cs-username IS NOT NULL)
    AND
    (date >= SUB(SYSTEM_TIMESTAMP(), TIMESTAMP('%day%', 'd')))
GROUP BY RequestedFile, ClientDesc, ErrDesc, ErrDate
ORDER BY Total DESC
---Ch02AuthAclFailures.sql---
```

The *USING* clause defines the *UserName* and *ClientIP* variables referenced by the *ClientDesc* column in the query. We use the *CASE* clause to derive the actual message based on the *ErrCode*. The *WHERE* clause specifies the status code related to either authentication or access errors, which, according to RFC specification, ranges from 401 to 403. The second condition checks for non-anonymous login, and the last condition determines the number of days of log files to scan.

To run the query, access a command prompt, navigate to the directory where you installed the query samples, and enter the following:

```
logparser.exe
file:Ch02AuthAclFailures.sql?source="<1>"+day="1" -o:NAT -rtp:1 > AuthAclFailures.txt
```

The syntax instructs Log parser to read the current day of the default website log files, output it in *NATIVE* format with all rows at once, and redirect it to *AuthAclFailures.txt*. The *+day* parameter specifies the number of days. The number *1* indicates today. To specify ten days before, use the value *11*, for example, *+day="11"*. Note that the maximum number of days that you can specify is 31, which is equivalent to one month. To facilitate scanning of all log files, simply remove the last checking condition.

```
RequestedFile          ClientDesc                            Total
--------------------   -----------------------------------   -----

/secure/syscheck.aspx  indev\viewer (192.168.10.21)           84
/secure/               indev\administrator (netsvr)           72
/printers/ipp_0004.asp indev\bernard (192.168.10.43)          50
/printers              indev\ali (netsvr)                     21
/internal/             indev\administrator (192.168.18.19)    14
/devfolder/            myadmin                                 7
/passport/             guest (192.168.10.122)                  3


ErrDesc                                                       ErrDate
----------------------------------------------------------   ----------

Access Denied - ACL checking failed.                         2004-09-01
Forbidden - Directory listing denied.                        2004-09-01
Access Denied - Authorization failed by ISAPI/CGI application. 2004-09-01
Access Denied - Login failed.                                2004-09-01
Forbidden - IP address rejected.                             2004-09-01
Access Denied - ACL checking failed.                         2004-09-01
Forbidden - Site access denied.                              2004-09-01


Statistics:
-----------

Elements processed: 27655
Elements output:    21
Execution time:     10.62 seconds
```

Master Craftsman

Monitoring Other IIS services

Analyzing authentication failures in FTP services are as follows:

```
---Ch02FtpSecurity.sql---
SELECT
    TO_LOWERCASE(cs-username) AS UserName,
    REVERSEDNS(c-ip) AS ClientIP,
    date AS LogDate,
    COUNT(*) AS Total
FROM %source%
WHERE
    (cs-method LIKE '%PASS')
    AND
    (sc-status = 503)
GROUP BY UserName, ClientIP, LogDate
ORDER BY Total DESC
---Ch02FtpSecurity.sql---
```

To identify authentication failures in the FTP service, the query analyzes requests with the client method *PASS*, which represents the authentication process. Status code 503 indicates that the authentication failed due to invalid user credentials or that the security policy prohibited such logon requests. For more information about FTP status codes, please refer to: www.w3.org/Protocols/rfc959/4_FileTransfer.html.

For FTP access-related errors, the following query focuses on error code 550, which indicates requested action not taken, either due to the file requested not being available, insufficient permissions, or some other reason.

```
---Ch02FtpAccess.sql---
SELECT
    TO_LOWERCASE(cs-username) AS UserName,
    REVERSEDNS(c-ip) AS ClientIP,
    date AS LogDate,
    STRCAT(EXTRACT_TOKEN(cs-method,-1,']'),STRCAT(' ',cs-uri-stem)) AS FtpRequest,
    COUNT(*) AS Total
FROM %source%
WHERE sc-status = 550
GROUP BY UserName, ClientIP, LogDate, FtpRequest
ORDER BY Total DESC
---Ch02FtpAccess.sql---
```

Continued

The core part of this query is the *FtpRequest field*, where Log parser extracts the actual actions performed that FTP services could not fulfill. A typical example of this would be *RMD mydir*, which indicates a failed attempt to remove the *mydir* directory, or *sent mydata.zip*, which tells you that client failed to download the file *mydata.zip*.

Analyzing SMTP authentication and relay failures:

```
---Ch02SmtpSecurity.sql---
SELECT
    REVERSEDNS(c-ip) AS ClientIP,
    date AS LogDate,
    CASE cs-method
        WHEN 'AUTH' THEN 'Authentication failed'
        WHEN 'RCPT' THEN STRCAT('Unable to Relay - ', cs-uri-query)
        ELSE STRCAT('Unknown error, method:',cs-method)
    END AS ErrDesc,
    COUNT(*) AS Total
From %source%
WHERE (sc-status IN (535;550))
GROUP BY ClientIP, LogDate, ErrDesc
ORDER BY Total DESC
---Ch02SmtpSecurity.sql---
```

Notice that this query is similar to the Ch02Ftpsecurity.sql query. The difference is the condition checking in the *WHERE* clause. In the IIS SMTP protocol, status code 535 defines authentication failures, where the *AUTH* is the authentication action requested by clients. For relay error, the status code is defined as 550 and *RCPT* is the action requested by clients. The *RCPT* action represents *'Received to'* the recipient of the e-mail, and it is captured in this format *+TO:+<username@domain-name.com>*. Notice that the query did not capture *cs-username* as in IIS SMTP. This field normally contains the client computer name when authentication fails. For more information about SMTP verbs and reply codes, please refer to: www.w3.org/Protocols/rfc822/rfc822.txt.

Analyzing NNTP error requests:

```
---Ch02NntpSecurity.sql---
SELECT
    CASE TO_LOWERCASE(cs-username)
        WHEN '<user>' THEN 'Anonymous'
        ELSE TO_LOWERCASE(cs-username)
    END AS UserName,
    REVERSEDNS(c-ip) AS ClientIP,
    STRCAT(cs-method,STRCAT(' ',cs-uri-stem)) AS NNTPRequest,
    Count(*) AS Total,
    CASE sc-status
        WHEN 400 THEN 'NNTP service discontinue.'
        WHEN 411 THEN 'Newsgroup not found.'
        WHEN 412 THEN 'No newsgroups selected.'
        WHEN 420 THEN 'No current article selected.'
        WHEN 421 THEN 'No next article in newsgroup.'
```

Continued

```
        WHEN 422 THEN 'No previous article in newsgroup.'
        WHEN 423 THEN 'No such article number in newsgroup.'
        WHEN 430 THEN 'No such article in newsgroup.'
        WHEN 435 THEN 'Article not wanted - do not send it.'
        WHEN 436 THEN 'Transfer failed - try again later.'
        WHEN 437 THEN 'Article rejected - do not try again.'
        WHEN 440 THEN 'Article posting not allowed.'
        WHEN 441 THEN 'Article posting failed'
        WHEN 480 THEN 'Logon required.'
        ELSE STRCAT('Unknown error - Request:', NNTPRequest)
    END AS ErrDesc
FROM %source%
WHERE (sc-status BETWEEN 400 AND 480)
GROUP BY Username, ClientIP, NNTPRequest, ErrDesc
ORDER BY Total DESC
---Ch02NntpSecurity.sql---
```

This query focuses on errors occurring during retrieval and posting of news articles. When a newsgroup allows anonymous posting, NNTP writes *<user>* as the anonymous *cs-username*, hence the *CASE* clause at the beginning of the query instructs Log parser to replace this string with the value *Anonymous*. The error code range 400 to 480 indicates negative responses by IIS NNTP. For more information about NNTP reply status code, please refer to: www.w3.org/Protocols/rfc977/rfc977.html.

Scanning Malformed HTTP Requests

As discussed earlier, HTTP.SYS is the new kernel mode driver that handles HTTP requests, placing them into each application pool's request queue. This kernel mode driver captures invalid and malformed requests to the HTTPERR log file. If a request fails at this level, request detail will not get logged in the W3C extended log file, as the request never reaches the website. On the other hand, if a request gets past this HTTP.SYS checking, URLSCAN, if installed, will check the request again to see if it matches the URLSCAN rule sets. Finally, the request then reaches the application processing filter hosted on the IIS server.

The Ch02MalformedHTTP.sql query parses the HTTPERR log file searching for invalid requests. This query focuses on requests with status codes of 400, 403, and 411. Note that the HTTPERR log does not record a substatus code. Error 400 is categorized as "Bad Request", which may include requests with an invalid verb, host header name, or some other malformed HTTP header. 403 errors mean the request was forbidden, which may include attempts to access protected content or invalid URL references. 411 errors are mainly related to HTTP PUT requests where content length is not specified.

The query groups result on a daily basis and sorts by the number of invalid requests. Columns generated include the client IP address, the HTTP verb used, the targeted web server IP address, the number of invalid requests, and the detailed error message.

```
---Ch02MalformedHttp.sql---
SELECT
```

```
        TO_STRING(TO_TIMESTAMP(date, time), 'MM-dd') AS Day,
        REVERSEDNS(c-ip) AS ClientIP,
        cs-method AS ClientMethod,
        s-ip AS WebServerIP,
        COUNT(*) AS Total,
        CASE s-reason
            WHEN 'BadRequest' THEN 'Bad and Invalid Request.'
            WHEN 'Verb' THEN 'Invalid HTTP verb.'
            WHEN 'Hostname' THEN 'Hostname not found.'
            WHEN 'Header' THEN 'Invalid Header during parsing.'
            WHEN 'URL' THEN 'Invalid URL detected.'
            WHEN 'Forbidden' THEN 'Request denied'
            WHEN 'LengthRequired' THEN 'HTTP PUT length missing.'
            ELSE STRCAT('Unknown error, Err:',cs-uri)
        END AS ErrDesc
FROM HTTPERR
WHERE (sc-status IN (400;403;411))
GROUP BY Day, ClientIP, ClientMethod, WebServerIP, ErrDesc
ORDER BY Day, Total DESC
---Ch02MalformedHttp.sql---
```

This query is very useful for identifying potential attacks, though it also provides you with important details for troubleshooting. For example, a forbidden access captured by HTTP.SYS might indicate that a user is trying to access certain content that is not allowed. To further protect IIS, system administrators can further restrict access by blocking the client IP address at the firewall level, preventing such malformed requests from hitting the IIS server.

To run the query, access a command prompt, navigate to the directory where you installed the query samples, and enter the following:

```
C:\Log parser>LogParser.exe
file:Ch02MalformedHttp.sql -o:NAT -rtp:-1 > MalformedHttp.txt
```

This instructs Log parser to output the results in *NATIVE* format with all rows at once, and redirect it to *MalformedHttp.txt*. The following shows the sample result of the query:

```
Day       ClientIP        ClientMethod   WebServerIP     Total  ErrDesc
----      --------        ------------   -------------   -----  -----------
08-31     susan           PUT            192.168.10.18   15     HTTP PUT length
                                                                missing.
08-31     devsvr2         GET            192.168.10.18   9      Request denied
08-29     testlabpc2      GET            192.168.10.18   21     Hostname not found
08-29     192.168.10.21   GET            192.168.10.43   16     Bad and Invalid
                                                                Request.
08-29     testlabpc2      POST           192.168.10.43   7      Request denied
08-29     susan           GET            192.168.10.18   1      Invalid Header during
                                                                parsing.
```

```
08-27      192.168.10.21   GET        192.168.10.43   25   Invalid URL detected.
08-27      192.168.10.22   GET        192.168.10.43   8    Bad and Invalid
                                                           Request.
08-27      192.168.10.23   Unparsed   192.168.10.43   7    Bad and Invalid
                                                           Request.
08-27      192.168.10.21   GET        192.168.10.43   2    Invalid Header during
                                                           parsing.
08-18      devsvr2         Invalid    192.168.10.18   4    Invalid HTTP verb.


Statistics:
-----------

Elements processed: 232
Elements output:     18
Execution time:      21.61 seconds
```

Swiss Army Knife

Detecting Code Red and Nimda

Back in 2001, the famous Code Red worm bombarded the IIS world. It exploited vulnerabilities in IIS 5.0 and IIS 4.0. Though IIS 6.0 is not vulnerable to this particular attack, it is sometimes helpful to know more about this notorious worm to learn how to deal with future worms. Code Red uses a known buffer overflow vulnerability that exists in Microsoft Indexing Service. By default, this service is enabled on an IIS 4.0 or IIS 5.0 server. It replicates itself by attacking more IIS servers from the infected machine.

Nimda, another IIS 'killer' worm, was first released back in 2001 utilizing a Web server folder traversal vulnerability. It allows malicious users to execute arbitrary code on the affected server, and spreads by using the same techniques as the Code Red variants, whereby it scans vulnerable machines and tries to inject its code.

Although Microsoft had released patches for the vulnerability long before these worms were released, sadly, many un-patched infected IIS servers existed that began attacking other servers on the Internet.

By modifying the sample query to the following, you can view details regarding symptoms of these worms' attacks.

```
---Ch02Nimda.sql---
SELECT
    REVERSEDNS(c-ip) AS ClientIP,
    s-ip AS WebServerIP,
    COUNT(*) AS Total
FROM HTTPERR
WHERE
```

```
        (sc-status = 400)
    AND
    ((s-reason = 'URL') OR (s-reason = 'BadRequest'))
    AND
((cs-uri LIKE '%cmd.exe%') OR (cs-uri LIKE '%root.exe%'))
GROUP BY ClientIP, WebServerIP
ORDER BY Total DESC
---Ch02Nimda.sql---
```

For the Nimda worm, the footprint can be identified by checking the *cs-uri* field, where it is trying to access *cmd.exe* or *root.exe*. IIS 6.0 is not vulnerable to this web folder traversal attack and requests to certain command-line executables are strictly restricted to admin users only. Notice that the query checks for two different reasons: *URL* or *BadRequest*, as attackers might use different request queries and HTTP verbs when trying to exploit the server.

Next, to detect Code Red worm, try the following:

```
---Ch02CodeRed.sql---
SELECT
    REVERSEDNS(c-ip) AS ClientIP,
    s-ip AS WebServerIP,
    COUNT(*) AS Total
FROM HTTPERR
WHERE
    ((s-reason = 'URL') OR (s-reason = 'BadRequest'))
    AND
((cs-uri LIKE '%default.id_%') OR (cs-uri LIKE '%null.id_%'))
GROUP BY ClientIP, WebServerIP
ORDER BY Total DESC
---Ch02CodeRed.sql---
```

This query assumes that requests against *default.id_* and *null.id_* with s-reason belong to *URL* or *BadRequest* are mostly due to Code Red worm attacks. The *LIKE* clause checking the *.id_* represents the file extension, which can be *ida,* or *idq.* The underscore '_' matches any single character. Notice that the condition checking does not check for status code 400, as the buffer overflow request strings might mess up the status code field in HTTPERR log.

By running both queries, you can detect Code Red and Nimda worms, though these exploits do not harm IIS 6.0 server. However, using the results and filtering those attacking IP addresses at firewall level will reduce unwanted requests reaching the IIS server.

Scanning HTTP Verbs in Client Requests

Under most conditions, the common HTTP verbs used to make web requests are POST and GET. However, there are scenarios when other verbs are used. For example, Web Distributed Authoring and Versioning (WebDav) uses other verbs including OPTIONS, PROFIND, and others. The presence of these uncommon verbs in different log sources might indicate potential attacks if such services or components are not installed on IIS.

NOTE

To learn about WebDav, please refer to:

- HOW TO: Create a Secure WebDAV Publishing Directory at support.microsoft.com/?id=323470
- HTTP Extensions for Distributed Authoring – WEBDAV at ftp.isi.edu/in-notes/rfc2518.txt

---

The Ch02Httpverbs.sql query scans for uncommon verbs in W3C extended log files. The result includes the client IP address, the HTTP verbs used, the requested content, and status code, as well as the total number of requests.

```
---Ch02HttpVerbs.sql---
SELECT
    REVERSEDNS(c-ip) AS ClientIP,
    cs-method AS Verb,
    cs-uri-stem AS RequestedFile,
    STRCAT(TO_STRING(sc-status), STRCAT('.',TO_STRING(sc-substatus))) AS StatusCode,
    COUNT(*) AS Total
FROM %source%
WHERE (cs-method NOT IN ('POST';'GET'))
GROUP BY ClientIP, Verb, RequestedFile, StatusCode
ORDER BY Total DESC
---Ch02HttpVerbs.sql---
```

This query scans for HTTP verbs other than *POST* or *GET*. Any requests using HTTP verbs other than POST or GET might be suspicious and might require further investigation.

To run the query, access a command prompt, navigate to the directory where you installed the query samples, and enter the following:

```
logparser.exe
file:Ch02HttpVerbs.sql -o:NAT -rtp:-1 > HttpVerbs.txt
```

This instructs Log parser to output the results in *NATIVE* format with all rows at once, and redirect it to *HttpVerbs.txt*. The following shows the sample result of the query:

```
ClientIP        Verb       RequestedFile StatusCode Total
-------------   --------   ------------- ---------- -----
washost2        HEAD       /index.aspx   200.0      192
192.168.10.21   OPTIONS    /devtest/     404.0      93
192.168.10.36   PROPFIND   /Download/    404.0      69
192.168.10.36   OPTIONS    /devtest/     404.0      21
testlabpc2      TRACE      /             501.0      11
```

From the sample output, it is clear that WebDav-related requests failed with 404 replies, and the *TRACE* verb is not implemented based on the 501 status code. The result is not only helpful to assist in troubleshooting, but it also provides clues as to which HTTP verbs clients use in their requests. For example, if you do not need the *TRACE* verb for the functionality of your website, you can install URLSCAN to restrict the HTTP verb.

Swiss Army Knife

More HTTP Verbs Scanning

Let's recap the flow when a client makes an HTTP request. The request first reaches the HTTP kernel mode driver and, after limited parsing, the request is placed in an application pool request queue (assuming the application pool is healthy). Before the application process (ISAPI) takes over, URLSCAN (if installed) verifies the request against its configured rule sets. If the request passes the URLSCAN checking, the application ISAPI filter receives and processes the request.

Hence, there are two additional log sources that might contain suspicious HTTP verbs. The HTTPERR captures non-supported HTTP verbs:

```
---Ch02HttpErrVerbs.sql---
SELECT
    REVERSEDNS(c-ip) AS ClientIP,
    cs-method AS Verb,
    COUNT(*) AS Total
FROM HTTPERR
WHERE
    (sc-status = 400)
    AND
    (s-reason = 'Verb')
GROUP BY ClientIP, Verb
ORDER BY Total DESC
---Ch02HttpErrVerbs.sql---
```

This query looks for requests with status code 400 and with the *reason phrase* containing the string "verb." Normally, the verb will be "Invalid", as HTTP.SYS failed to parse the request.

Next, if URLSCAN is installed, the URLSCAN log files will capture all illegal HTTP verbs. By default, *GET*, *HEAD*, and *POST* are the only allowed HTTP verbs defined in URLSCAN.ini. To scan for rejected HTTP verbs in URLSCAN, try the following:

```
---Ch02UrlscanVerbs.sql---
SELECT
    REVERSEDNS(clientip) AS ClientIP,
    EXTRACT_TOKEN(comment,1,'\'') AS Verb,
```

Continued

```
     COUNT(*) AS Total
FROM URLSCAN
WHERE (comment LIKE '%Sent Verb%')
GROUP BY ClientIP, Verb
ORDER BY Total DESC
---Ch02UrlscanVerbs.sql---
```

Essentially, this query checks for URLSCAN comments that contain of the string "Sent Verb". The *EXTRACT_TOKEN* function extracts the value of the HTTP verb; the separator used in this example is a single quote ', the backslash \ is used to escape the single quote.

Scanning for ASP Attacks

There many possible forms of ASP application attacks, including continuous requests that put a heavy process load on the server and SQL injections for abusing ASP forms. While there are no fixed patterns to detect actual attack procedures, it is possible to parse the W3C extended log files to determine possible attacks that might have taken place.

The Ch02AspAttacks.sql query is similar to Ch02AspErrors.sql. While the ASP error query focuses on generic ASP application errors caused by the query, this query detects possible attack behavior, for example if the error occurred many times in a day and originated from the same client IP address.

```
---Ch02AspAttacks.sql---
SELECT
    DISTINCT
    REVERSEDNS(c-ip) AS ClientIP,
    TO_LOWERCASE(cs-uri-stem) AS RequestedFile,
    TO_LOWERCASE(cs-uri-query) AS QryStr,
    COUNT(*) AS Total
FROM %source%
WHERE
    (TO_LOWERCASE(EXTRACT_EXTENSION(cs-uri-stem)) = 'asp')
    AND
    (sc-status = 500)
GROUP BY ClientIP, RequestedFile, QryStr
HAVING (Total > 100)
ORDER BY Total DESC
---Ch02AspAttacks.sql---
```

By looking at the requested content and query string (if any), you might be able to determine if those requests were legitimate or part of a malicious attack. The next course of action will be to verify the actual ASP script itself, correct code flaws, if discovered, and further protect the server by filtering out the requested client's IP address.

The condition checking in the *WHERE* clause looks for requests with status code 500 and the asp file that encountered the errors more than 100 times.

The difference between *HAVING* and *WHERE* is that *HAVING* is able to apply condition checks on aggregate functions. Adding a *HAVING clause* between the *GROUP BY* and *ORDER BY* clause allows you to specify additional checking.

To run the query, access a command prompt, navigate to the directory where you installed the query samples, and enter the following:

```
C:\Log parser>LogParser.exe
file:Ch02AspAttacks.sql?source="<2>" -o:NAT -rtp:-1 > AspAttacks.txt
```

The command syntax tells Log parser to parse all extended log files for website ID 2, output it in *NATIVE* format, and redirect the output to a text file named *AspAttacks.tx:*

```
ClientIP        RequestedFile          QryStr                                        Total
------------    --------------------   ------------------------------------------    -----
susan.indev     /cust_update.asp       |28|800a01a8|Object_required:_'objRst'        364
192.168.10.30   /asp/db_process.asp    -                                             213
testlabpc2      /default.asp           view=q&id=921&section=230                      209
devsvr2         /asp/sport.asp         ASP_0147|500_Server_Error                     166
192.168.10.21   /db/remove.asp         |6|80004005|                                  138

Statistics:
-----------
Elements processed: 47531
Elements output:    5
Execution time:     19.94 seconds
```

Final Touches

In this chapter we have covered different IIS log sources for understanding performance, reliability, and security in IIS server. Besides understanding the IIS logging structure, the general request processing flows, and running the sample queries, the core values delivered here are to help you realize what data is available in different log files and inspire creative thinking to derive meaningful information from this data. Microsoft Log parser is a free-form tool; it is up to system administrators like you to create useful queries and discover its true value.

Chapter 3

Exploring the Windows Event Log

- Viewing Logon/Logoff Activity

- Tracking Authentication Failures

- Differentiating Between Benign and Warning Events

- Identifying Brute Force Attacks

- Tracking Security Policy Violations

- Auditing Successful and Unsuccessful File Access Attempts

- Identifying Benign System Events

- Tracking System Failures

- Trending

- Creating System Error Reports

- Identifying Application Errors

- Working with Served Application Security

In This Toolbox

A critical aspect of ensuring system stability is the ongoing monitoring and analysis of System event logs. Like UNIX systems, Microsoft Windows operating systems (OSs) have logging features that can aid you in diagnosing system problems and ensuring that your system is optimized and secure. Most administrators don't make full use of these features, however, due to the extensive amount of time it takes to read through thousands upon thousands of log file entries. This makes it difficult for administrators to take a proactive approach to systems administration by eliminating problems before they become critical. Throughout this chapter, we will be discussing how Log Parser can help with this task and make a tedious task not only easy, but fun as well.

Monitoring User Activity

When analyzing the overall performance and functionality of servers, you should always keep user activity in mind. Unusual user activity can be an indicator of system problems or security issues. By analyzing the user activity reported in your system logs, you can determine trends in logon/logoff activity, potential authentication problems, and hacking activity.

Monitoring user access to the system will allow you to trend out system usage and determine peak usage times as well as identify problem areas for users authenticating with the server. We will be going over a few techniques you can use to easily view and analyze this data using Log Parser.

Another important aspect in determining relevant events in your system logs is determining which behavior is benign and which behavior indicates trouble. For example, if a user fails to authenticate one time in a week span, you can be pretty certain that the user simply mistyped his or her password and is not trying to hack into your system. Alternatively, if a user has two failed authentication attempts hourly for an extended period you should look more deeply into the problem. We will be covering these types of events and going over how to make the critical determination as to whether a behavior is benign or a warning sign. Of course, we'll also examine how Log Parser can simplify this task for you.

Security is, and always should be, a top priority for anyone working on key infrastructure systems. Log Parser can help you identify events that could indicate a potential hack attempt or even just a user attempting to look at something they shouldn't be looking at. By enabling file access auditing and using Log Parser to examine the results, you can even track down potential security issues at the file level. Digging through these same log files to track down this data manually is both tedious and unnecessary with the advanced capabilities of Microsoft's Log Parser utility.

Viewing Logon/Logoff Activity

As we've mentioned, monitoring of system logon and logoff activity can help you in trending system utilization and peak usage times. The converse of this is determining the time that the system is least utilized, which in turn allows you to pick the best possible time to perform maintenance on the system.

Detailing User Logins

A useful view of system logon activity is to detail out the number of successful logons over a 24 hour period. That should give us some useful information about peak times for authentication on any given date. This requires a fairly simple query through Log Parser to not only gather, but also view this information.

Run this query with the following command:

```
logparser.exe file:Ch03DetailingUserLogins.sql -i:EVT -o:datagrid
--- Ch03DetailingUserLogins.sql ---

SELECT
    to_date(timegenerated) AS Date,
    quantize(to_time(timegenerated), 3600) AS Hour,
    Count(*) AS Number_of_Events
FROM Security
WHERE EventID=528
    AND date='2004-09-01 00:00:00'
GROUP BY date,
    hour


--- Ch03DetailingUserLogins.sql ---
```

This query gathers all security log entries where the EventID is 528 (a successful logon). Log Parser then groups these entries by the hour and does a count to determine the number of successful logons per hour. We limit our query to a specific date and receive the result shown in Figure 3.1.

Figure 3.1 Hourly Successful Logons

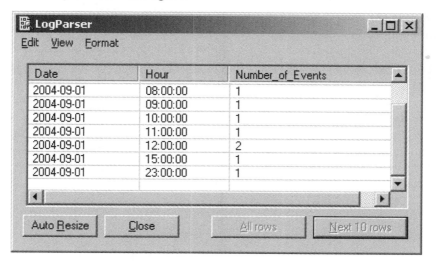

Let's break this query down and go over exactly what we're doing to generate these results. First, we build our SELECT statement. The first thing we want to display is the date that we're working with, so we use the TO_DATE function on the *TimeGenerated* field. This simplifies the timestamp into a simple date value, which we then rename to *Date* using the syntax *as Date*.

Generating the next column is a little more difficult than usual because we don't want to know the actual time value; we simply want to know what hour range it is in. To obtain this data, we use the QUANTIZE function. QUANTIZE rounds values based on a quantization value. In this case, we are taking the *TimeGenerated* timestamp from the Security event log and converting it using the TO_TIME function into a simple time value. Then we quantize the time value using 3600 seconds (one hour) as our quantization value. This rounds the time value into one-hour segments. So, for example, an event that occurs at 2004-09-01 15:14:13 is changed to 15:14:13 with the TO_TIME function, then to 15:00:00 with the QUANTIZE function. Finally we add *as Hour* to the syntax to specify *Hour* as our value name.

Since we don't want the specific logon information, just the number of logons, the next statement provides a count of the number of events matching our criteria. Using the term COUNT(*) we generate a record count for each grouping as our next column. Later in the query, we place a GROUP BY statement, which isolates this count to the specific group of data that we're interested in. We name this event count *Number_of_Events* using the usual *as Number_of_Events* syntax.

For our data source we are using the Security event log, so we specify this in our FROM statement. Also, we want to limit our date to a specific event and date, so we specify these values in a WHERE clause. Specifically, we limit the results of our query to events where *EventID*=517 and *date*=2004-09-01 00:00:00. The time value of 00:00:00 must be in the clause, as the *Date* column is still processed as a timestamp even though it only contains date values.

Finally, as I mentioned previously, we need to specify the grouping to use for our count of events. We do this using a GROUP BY statement and specifying the columns we're interested in. In this case, we use the *date* column as well as the *hour* column. Both must be defined to get the data into the right order.

That ends our SELECT statement. We finish up our command line by specifying the input and output formats. The input format could be automatically determined by Log Parser, however it's a good habit to go ahead and specify the format regardless just so no unexpected errors occur in other queries. For our purposes, a datagrid would probably be the best format to output this data in just so we can easily view the results. To output in a datagrid format, you simply add **-o:datagrid** to the end of the command line.

Using this query makes determining the number of logons per hour very easy to do. Expanding the query slightly could allow you to view the data in other ways such as average daily/weekly logon traffic or peak logon utilization times throughout a month.

Swiss Army Knife

Modifying User Logon Data for Charting

Sometimes looking at a datagrid view of user logon data doesn't clearly identify the information that you're looking for. It's a proven fact that humans respond best to analog data rather than digital data, therefore pictures make more sense to us than text data points. You can easily modify the code given for detailing user logon data into a chart to make the data more usable. The code below shows one way that this could be done:

```
logparser.exe file:Ch03ChartingUserLogins.sql -i:EVT -charttype:column3d -legend
off -chartTitle "Hourly Logons" -view -o:chart


--- Ch03ChartingUserLogins.sql ---


SELECT
    quantize(to_time(timegenerated), 3600) AS Hour,
    Count(*) AS Number_of_Events
INTO logons.gif
FROM Security
WHERE EventID=528
GROUP BY hour
ORDER BY Number_of_Events


--- Ch03ChartingUserLogins.sql ---
```

Determining Active Users

Another important task for a system administrator is to determine which users are actively using the system compared to those who have accounts and don't use them. Typically you can find information like this by checking the last logon date for the users and determining those users who have not logged on within a specified time period.

However, this does not really help in determining true system usage. The user may authenticate on the network, but never actually connect to a specific application server that you are running. By reviewing the logs on the application server for successful authentications, we can more accurately determine how often specific users are accessing a specific system. Log Parser can help with this and chart out the frequency at which various users have authenticated with the server. Run this query with the following command:

```
logparser.exe file:Ch03DeterminingActiveUsers.sql -i:EVT -o:datagrid
```

```
--- Ch03DeterminingActiveUsers.sql ---

SELECT
    SID,
    resolve_sid(sid) AS UserName,
    count(*) AS Number_of_Logons
FROM Security
WHERE EventID='528'
    AND to_string(timegenerated,'yyyy-MM-dd HH:mm:ss') like '2004-09%'
GROUP BY SID
--- Ch03DeterminingActiveUsers.sql ---
```

The above code performs a query to determine a count of the number of successful logon attempts per user over a one-month timeframe. Based on this information, you can determine which users are frequent or infrequent users of the system. By comparing this list with your full user list, you can also determine which users are completely inactive on this specific server. Figure 3.2 shows the results of our query.

Figure 3.2 Number of Logon Events per User

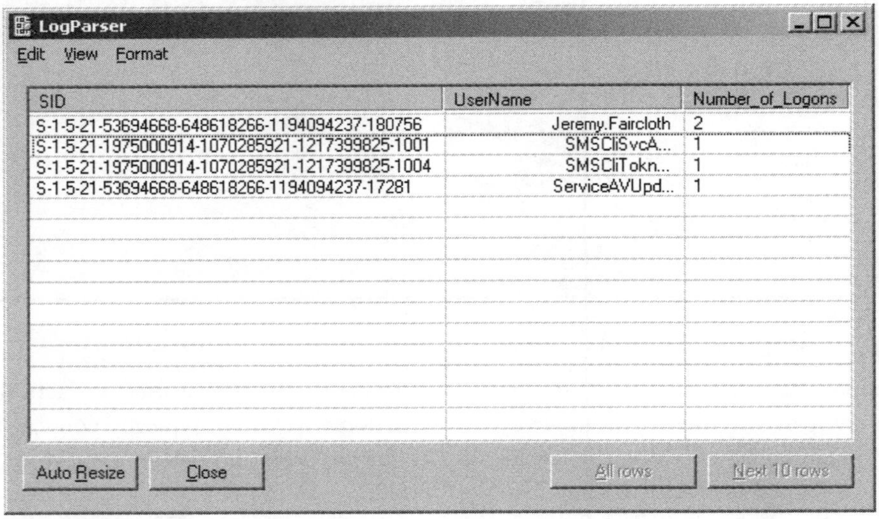

Let's go over how this query works. First, we need to specify which data values we need for our SELECT statement. We need to know who the users are, so we specify the value of *SID* and also use the function RESOLVE_SID in order to get the data in a more readable format. Next, we need to know how many logon events have been generated for each SID, so we add the COUNT(*) syntax to the statement.

Next we specify that we are pulling this data from the Security event log and limit our data with a WHERE clause. The WHERE clause starts out being very simple as we use it to limit the *EventID* field to the value of 528 in order to view successful logon attempt events. The clause then becomes more complex as we limit the date in which the events occurred to a specific month. To do so, we need to convert the *timegenerated* value to a string and use a LIKE statement to limit the results. The syntax **to_string(timegenerated, 'yyyy-MM-dd HH:mm:ss')** converts the *timegenerated* timestamp to a string in the format year–month–day hour:minute:second. We then use a LIKE statement that queries for the string **2004-09** at the beginning of the timestamp string.

Finally, we group our data by the *SID* value so we can perform a count of the number of occurrences per SID. We also need to specify the input and output format, so we add this to the end of the command line using the syntax **-i:EVT −o:datagrid**.

Tracking Authentication Failures

When performing regular security audits of your servers, it is always important to know how many failed authentication attempts have occurred. This helps you in several ways. First, you are able to determine specific users who may have forgotten their password and failed to request a new one. Second, and more importantly, you may be able to detect potential hacking attempts against your server by analyzing the results and noting an increase in failed logon attempts either for a single user or for multiple users. Finally, you may be able to determine problems with the system that are causing authentication failures by multiple users at a specific time. These problems could relate to network connectivity, system utilization, or a failure of an authentication server.

Listing Failed Logons

Log Parser can easily use your event logs to detail out the failed logons over a specific timeframe. The following command and query can be used to list all failed logons on a specific date:

```
logparser.exe file:Ch03ListingFailedLogons.sql -i:EVT -o:datagrid


--- Ch03ListingFailedLogons.sql ---

SELECT
    timegenerated AS LogonTime,
    extract_token(strings, 0, '|') AS UserName
FROM Security
WHERE EventID IN (529;
    530;
    531;
    532;
    533;
    534;
    535;
    537;
    539)
    AND to_string(timegenerated, 'yyyy-MM-dd HH:mm:ss') like '2004-09%'
--- Ch03ListingFailedLogons.sql ---
```

By running the query above, you are able to see how many authentication failures have occurred on the date you specified, as well as which user IDs experienced failures. The output you receive should be similar to that shown in Figure 3.3.

Figure 3.3 Failed Logons

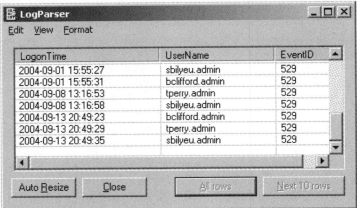

In this query, we begin by specifying that we want to obtain the timestamp for the event from the *timegenerated* field. From there, the query gets a little trickier than usual. For failed logon events, the UserID for the event itself is always **SYSTEM**. In order to get the actual ID that the logon was attempted with, we need to parse out some data from the description or *Strings* field. To do so, we use the EXTRACT_TOKEN function to tokenize the string using the pipe (|) character and specify that we want the first or 0 token which is the UserName.

Next we specify that we wish to pull this data from the current Security log. Our WHERE clause specifies a specific range of security events that indicate logon failures and we use this to limit our data to those specific events. A description of each of these events is detailed in Table 3.1. In the WHERE clause, we also specify the date stamp that we're looking for in the same manner as the previous query. We also need to specify the input and output format so we add this to the end of the command line using the syntax **–i:EVT –o:datagrid**.

Table 3.1 Failed Logon EventIDs

EventID	Description
529	The logon attempt was made with an unknown username or a known username with a bad password.
530	The user account tried to log on outside the allowed time.
531	A logon attempt was made by using a disabled account.
532	A logon attempt was made by using an expired account.

Continued

Table 3.1 Failed Logon EventIDs

EventID	Description
533	The user is not allowed to log on at this computer.
534	The user attempted to log on with a logon type that is not allowed, such as network, interactive, batch, service, or remote interactive.
535	The password for the specified account has expired.
537	The logon attempt failed for other reasons.
539	The account was locked out at the time the logon attempt was made. This event is logged when a user or computer attempts to authenticate with an account that has been previously locked out.

Identifying Single Versus Multiple Failed Logons

When working with failed logons, it sometimes helps to be able to quickly determine how prevalent logon failures are over a specific time period. In the section above, we went over how to list failed logons, but using this query requires us to manually determine how frequently a specific user ID is experiencing problems.

You can use Log Parser to automatically tally up the number of failed logons for each user by utilizing a slightly different query. The following command and query is one example of how this can be accomplished:

```
logparser.exe file:Ch03SingleVsMltplFailedLogons.sql -i:EVT -o:datagrid


--- Ch03SingleVsMltplFailedLogons.sql ---


SELECT
    extract_token(strings, 0, '|') AS UserName,
    count(*) AS Number_of_Events
FROM Security
WHERE EventID IN (529;
    530;
    531;
    532;
    533;
    534;
    535;
    537;
    539)
    AND to_string(timegenerated, 'yyyy-MM-dd HH:mm:ss') like '2004-09%'
GROUP BY UserName
HAVING Number_of_Events>2


--- Ch03SingleVsMltplFailedLogons.sql ---
```

Our output is shown in Figure 3.4.

Figure 3.4 Multiple Failed Logon Events (>2 Occurrences)

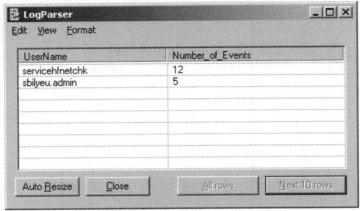

In this query, we are doing a bit more work up front, but minimizing the manual effort required to identify multiple login failures. We start out with the EXTRACT_TOKEN function parsing out the actual userid with the failed logon. Next, we perform a count of the number of events and display that value as *Number_of_Events*. We then identify the Security event log as our data source and add in a WHERE clause specifying the events that we want to watch for, as well as the specific date that we want the data from.

Finally, we add a GROUP BY statement to organize our results and also add in a HAVING statement. To limit the data to only show us data from events that occur multiple times, we specify **Number_of_Events>2** in the HAVING statement. If we were to change that value to >5, we would end up with the result shown in Figure 3.5.

Figure 3.5 Multiple Failed Logon Events (>5 Occurrences)

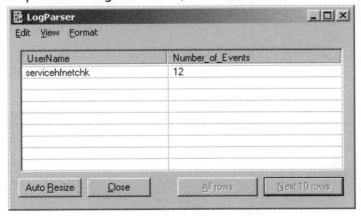

Differentiating Between Benign and Warning Events

As an administrator, you are often required to look over a great deal of log data and attempt to determine which data is important and what can be ignored. When systems add information to logs, they will typically create entries for crucial events right next to those for informational events. Most operating systems provide some method for logging a severity level with an event, but there is no way to guarantee that the severity level that was logged is accurate.

Windows is no different in that it blindly adds all security events to the security log and only differentiates between benign and warning events by the type of entry (Information, Warning, Error, Success Audit, Failure Audit, etc). These types can help identify which items the logging system thinks are important, but the system only adds logs in the way it is instructed to do so by the code that it is running. If the code is written in such a way that critical events are logged with the *Information* type, there is no way to tell at a quick glance whether or not those events are really critical.

To determine which events are benign and which are warning events, you have to rely on your skills and experience as an administrator. What Log Parser can do to help you is to make it easier to parse through your Windows event logs to find the events that you are looking for or ignore those that you know are benign.

Ignoring Successful Entries

A very basic way of weeding out what are typically benign events is to ignore any entries in your security log that are of the *Success Audit* type. One way of doing this is to search your security event log for any items that are of the *Failure Audit* type, however there is always the possibility that somehow something got logged that is neither of the Success Audit nor the Failure Audit type. Using the following command and query, you can easily perform this type of search using Log Parser:

```
logparser.exe file:Ch03IgnoringSuccessfulEntries.sql -i:EVT -o:datagrid


--- Ch03IgnoringSuccessfulEntries.sql ---

SELECT
    *
FROM Security
WHERE eventtype<>8
--- Ch03IgnoringSuccessfulEntries.sql ---
```

This query selects all columns from the security event log and displays them if they have any event type other than 8. Event type 8 is the equivalent of Success Audit Event and is the criteria that we wanted to ignore in this search.

Correlating Events Around Failures

In the previous query, we simply ignored all successful events and focused on those events that were identified as failures or anything other than successful. When performing systems administration, however, you might want to see what other events occurred around a failure event. Determining this information is typically quite difficult, but as usual, Log Parser can make that job a little easier for you.

For an example, let's say that you want to know every event that occurred within the same ten-minute timeframe as every failure event. To determine this, we'll first need to determine when the failures occurred, then gather the additional data around those timeframes. The following command and query show how this can be done:

```
logparser.exe file:Ch03FailureEventCorrelation.sql -i:EVT -o:datagrid


--- Ch03FailureEventCorrelation.sql ---


SELECT
    quantize(timegenerated, 600) AS TimeFrame,
    timegenerated,
    eventtype,
    eventtypename,
    message
FROM Security
WHERE timeframe=
    (
    SELECT
        quantize(timegenerated, 600)
    FROM Security
    WHERE eventtype<>8
    )


--- Ch03FailureEventCorrelation.sql ---
```

This query is a little more complex than the previous one, but it certainly helps a great deal when analyzing long log files! In order to create this query, you first have to think backwards a little bit. The first piece of information that you need to gather is the timeframe in which the non-successful events occurred. To do this, we use the SELECT statement:

```
SELECT
        quantize(timegenerated, 600)
    FROM Security
    WHERE eventtype<>8
    )
```

However, this query alone will certainly not provide all of the information we are looking for. Now that we have the query to determine the non-successful event timeframe, we need to wrap that query inside another query to find the other events around that timeframe. This process is known as an *embedded select* or a *multiple select* statement. The query to determine specific values around a pre-determined timeframe is:

```
SELECT
    quantize(timegenerated, 600) AS TimeFrame,
    timegenerated,
    eventtype,
    eventtypename,
    message
FROM Security
WHERE timeframe=<TIMEFRAME>
```

The trick here is to replace the <TIMEFRAME> marker in the above query with the data that we gathered from our original query for timeframes of the failure events. By doing so, the full query gathers any event with a ten minute (600 second) quantized timeframe around the ten minute quantized timeframe of the non-successful event. Using this query and modifying it to fit your needs will allow you to quickly and easily determine not only what failed, but also what events may have led up to the failure.

Swiss Army Knife

Modifying Event Correlation

The event correlation code that we've gone over can be modified to work in many different ways. Obviously you can change the timeframe for the events to gather, but you can also further refine the query to only give you specific events that occurred during that timeframe. For example, if you only want to know about logon failures that occurred during the timeframe in which you're experiencing system event failures, you might use the following query:

```
logparser.exe file:Ch03CorrelatingLogonFailures.sql -i:EVT -o:datagrid


--- Ch03CorrelatingLogonFailures.sql ---


SELECT
    quantize(timegenerated, 600) AS TimeFrame,
    timegenerated,
    eventtype,
    eventtypename,
    message
FROM Security
WHERE timeframe=
```

Continued

```
        (
        SELECT
              quantize(timegenerated, 600)
        FROM System
        WHERE eventtype<>8
        )
AND
EventID IN (529;
        530;
        531;
        532;
        533;
        534;
        535;
        537;
        539)

--- Ch03CorrelatingLogonFailures.sql ---
```

Identifying Brute Force Attacks

When dealing with system security, a major concern is the possibility of a *brute force* attack on your system. The determining factor as to whether or not an attack is a brute force attack is the manner in which the attack occurs. When attempt after attempt after attempt is made to perform a specific attack action, the overall event is considered a brute force attack because the attacker is trying to break into the system using brute force.

Log Parser can help you quickly analyze your security event logs and determine whether or not one of these brute force attacks is potentially occurring. By creating queries that watch for the behavior of a brute force attack, you may be able to stop an attack before it is successful.

Identifying a Brute Force Authentication Attack

A great example of a brute force attack is one in which someone is trying to guess the password for one of your users. Let's say that the attacker knows from previous experience that you have a policy in place that disables an account if three unsuccessful logon attempts are made within a one-hour window by the same UserID. With this in mind, the attacker is not going to risk locking out the account that he is trying to hack. However, the attacker will want to maximize his or her available time and attempt the maximum number of attacks that he or she can within a specific time period.

A quick way to check for this type of activity is to use the same query listed above for identifying multiple failed logons. With a little modification, this query can perform an intelligent scan for brute force logon attempt behavior. The original query is listed on the following page:

```
logparser.exe file:Ch03SingleVsMltplFailedLogons.sql -i:EVT -o:datagrid
```

```
--- Ch03SingleVsMltplFailedLogons.sql ---

SELECT
     extract_token(strings, 0, '|') AS UserName,
     count(*) AS Number_of_Events
FROM Security
WHERE EventID IN (529;
     530;
     531;
     532;
     533;
     534;
     535;
     537;
     539)
     AND to_string(timegenerated,'yyyy-MM-dd HH:mm:ss') like '2004-09%'
GROUP BY UserName
HAVING Number_of_Events>2
```

```
--- Ch03SingleVsMltplFailedLogons.sql ---
```

As is, this query works great for determining multiple failed logon events on the same day. However, that behavior in and of itself does not signify that a brute force attack is occurring. In order to make this query more effective, we need to add in the behavior signature of a brute force attack and get a little more detail.

The best way to add that behavior search into our query is to go back to what the attacker has determined your security policy is. The account will be locked out if more than two logon attempts fail within a one-hour time period by the same UserID. So, to maximize his or her potential attack time, the attacker will probably try to perform two logon attempts, determine whether or not they fail, then wait an hour and try twice more. So what we would look for is three or more failed logon events throughout the day and obtain the timeframe in which those events occurred.

To query based on this information, we need to modify our original query as follows:

```
logparser.exe file:Ch03BruteForceAttack.sql -i:EVT -o:datagrid
--- Ch03BruteForceAttack.sql ---

SELECT
     extract_token(strings , 0, '|') AS UserName,
     quantize(timegenerated, 3600) AS TimeFrame,
     count(*) AS Number_of_Events
FROM new_security.evt
WHERE EventID IN (529;
```

```
        530;
        531;
        532;
        533;
        534;
        535;
        537;
        539)
GROUP BY UserName,
     timeframe
HAVING Number_of_Events>2
--- Ch03BruteForceAttack.sql ---
```

The only real changes in this query were the removal of the date search and the addition of a *TimeFrame* value based on the quantized *timegenerated* field. When running this query, we will be presented with a datagrid showing the number of failure events for each username within a one-hour timeframe. A quick glance at the output shown in Figure 3.6 shows you the accounts that could be experiencing a brute force attack. Following up with the user to find out more detail on what is going on would be a worthwhile practice when this type of activity is found.

Figure 3.6 Brute Force Activity

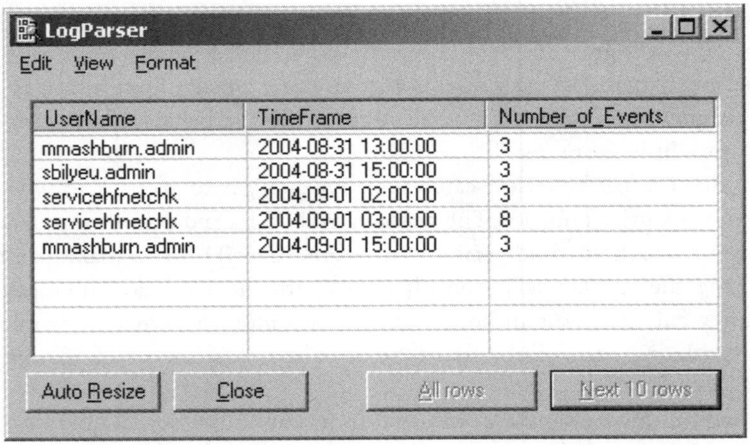

Tracking Security Policy Violations

Most companies have developed some form of security policy that addresses concerns around account and password security, permissible system access, unacceptable behavior, etc. These policies dictate the specific rules that each user must follow when accessing information technology (IT) systems.

A useful activity that admins typically perform is a regular audit to ensure that corporate security policies are being adhered to. Some of the information useful for an audit of this nature can be found in the Windows event logs. A great example is tracking user logons for desktop systems. By correlating all of your event log data from multiple systems and digging through them with Log Parser, you can determine whether or not users are violating a policy restricting them to log on to only one machine at a time.

Determining Logon/Logoff Behavior

Another example that requires no log correlation is determining whether users are typically logging off after their work day or leaving their systems logged in. Some companies do have this behavior documented as a violation of their corporate security policy.

To gather this data with Log Parser, we'll need to first determine all of the logoff events, then check to see if there is a logon event for the same day that does not have an associated logoff event for the same SID. The following command and query can help us determine this behavior:

```
logparser.exe file:Ch03LogonLogoffBehavior.sql -i:EVT -o:datagrid
```

```
--- Ch03LogonLogoffBehavior.sql ---

SELECT
    resolve_sid(sid) AS UserName,
    eventid,
    timegenerated
FROM Security
WHERE eventid='528'
    AND to_date(timegenerated)='2004-09-06 00:00:00'
    AND sid not in
    (
    SELECT DISTINCT
        sid
    FROM Security
    WHERE eventid='538'
        AND to_date(timegenerated)='2004-09-06 00:00:00'
    )

--- Ch03LogonLogoffBehavior.sql ---
```

In this query, we need to work backwards a little bit to get the information we need. First, we determine which data we want in our report. In this case, we should gather the userID, the eventID that we're working with, and the time the event occurred. Next, we'll specify the security event log as our data source.

Our creation of the WHERE clause is the more difficult part of this query. The first two items are fairly simple; the *eventID* has to be **528** for a successful logon and the date that we want information about has to be specified. Also, we'll need to do a *select within a select* to limit our incoming data. Specifically, we want data where the SID with the 528 event does not exist in a query of the 538 events for the same date. You should see results similar to those shown in Figure 3.7.

Figure 3.7 Logon Events with No Logoff Event

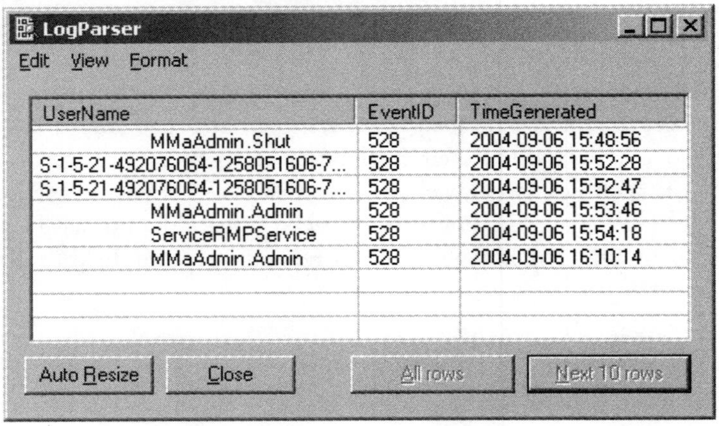

By performing our query in this manner, we are able to isolate those users who have logged on at some point during a specific day, but do not have an associated logoff event for the same day. This will not catch all users who log on without logging off, as it does not take into account the possibility of multiple logon/logoff events for each user in a single day. However, it can help minimize the number of security policy violations of this type.

Auditing Successful and Unsuccessful File Access Attempts

Another important dataset to examine when looking at overall system security is the audit log for successful and unsuccessful file access attempts. Using NTFS (NT file system), you can enable auditing at the file system level for individual files or directories. This allows you, as an administrator, to determine whether or not someone has accessed or attempted to access critical data.

Often, file access auditing is disabled because so much data is generated out of the audit logs that it is almost impossible to sort through the information available and extract events that are important to be aware of. This is where Log Parser can help in your efforts to ensure that your systems are well secured.

Auditing Unsuccessful File Access Attempts

When auditing is enabled for NTFS objects, Windows adds events to the Security event log to indicate the objects that are accessed. As part of this event entry, information is recorded as to the object that was accessed, the user accessing the object, and the date/time that the object was accessed. You can use Log Parser to quickly collect the events around these object access attempts.

Obviously the area more administrators are interested in is the objects that a user tries to access when they're not supposed to. With a good security implementation, this typically results in an unsuccessful file access attempt. Using Log Parser to scan through the security logs, you can quickly identify these events and export them for analysis. The command and query shown below will identify all of the unsuccessful file access events in your security log:

```
logparser.exe file:Ch03UnsuccessfulFileAccess.sql -i:EVT -o:datagrid
```

```
--- Ch03UnsuccessfulFileAccess.sql ---


SELECT
    timegenerated AS EventTime,
    extract_token(strings, 8, '|') AS UserName,
    extract_token(strings, 2, '|') AS File
FROM Security
WHERE EventID = '560'
    AND EventTypeName = 'Failure Audit event'
    AND extract_token(strings, 1, '|') like 'File'
--- Ch03UnsuccessfulFileAccess.sql ---
```

When this query runs, it looks for any events in the security log with an eventID of 560 (Success Audit), but further refines that data to events with a type of Failure Audit event. It also parses through the associated event description to ensure that we only look at files, not directories. From that subset, Log Parser extracts the time of the event, the username associated with the event, and the filename. All of this data is then displayed in a datagrid format. You can take this further by having Log Parser export the data into an XML file or some other format for evidence gathering needs.

Auditing Successful File Access Attempts

Many administrators often fail to monitor successful file access attempts in addition to the unsuccessful attempts. While the most important events to watch for are indeed failures, it is also important not to lose sight of the auditing capabilities available for successful file access attempts.

A scenario where this can be used will help. For example, let's say that you are an administrator for a large corporation with a legal department. The department is currently engaged in putting together some information around a very important case and is storing this information in the department's shared drive. In the course of events, word reaches the legal department that somehow the legal department for the other side of the case has gotten a hold of the strategy that your company's legal department was going to use and is putting together a rebuttal. The only people who should have had access to the files containing this information are the members of the legal department. They ask you to track down who has accessed those files.

If you have planned ahead for this eventuality, you have already enabled successful file access auditing for the legal department's shared drive. Using Log Parser, you can easily extract the information that the legal department needs and provide it to them quickly. The script below illustrates how this is done:

```
logparser.exe file:Ch03SuccessfulFileAccess.sql -i:EVT -o:datagrid


--- Ch03SuccessfulFileAccess.sql ---

SELECT
    timegenerated AS EventTime,
    extract_token(strings, 8, '|') AS UserName,
    extract_token(strings, 2, '|') AS File
FROM Security
WHERE EventID = '560'
    AND EventTypeName = 'Success Audit event'
    AND extract_token(strings, 1, '|') like 'File'
--- Ch03SuccessfulFileAccess.sql ---
```

If you look closely at this code, you'll see that this is almost the same as the previous script you saw on auditing unsuccessful file access attempts. The only real difference is the change in the event type name. Instead of "Failure Audit event" we're now looking for "Success Audit event". Running this script will extract all of the successful file access events from your security log. You could further refine this to search for events that occur with a specific directory path or filename to make the amount of data to look through smaller.

Tracking System Health

Overall system health is always a primary concern for systems administrators. Most of the time, an administrator is stuck in a reactive role trying to fix problems, but whenever possible a proactive role should be taken to eliminate potential problems in advance.

Log Parser can help make taking a proactive role toward system health much easier. By being able to quickly extract important system data and ignore unimportant events, you can change the chore of reading through event logs from a full day task to a few minute exercises. In this section, we'll be going over how to identify benign events in your system log and how to discriminate between a benign event that only occurs once and benign events that occur multiple times signifying an actual problem. We'll also touch on tracking system failures and crashes and extracting that data from the System event log. Finally, we'll go over trending and reporting based on System event logs.

As we go through this, always keep in mind ways you can use these scripts in your own systems administration work to save yourself time and help yourself work more efficiently. Obviously we can't show every script that would be useful to a systems administrator here, but this should give you a good foundation for modifying these for your own use as well as creating your own scripts.

Identifying Benign System Events

Benign system events are those events that by themselves are innocuous or unimportant. As a system is constantly logging information from all of the subsystems, a lot of data being logged is not really necessary for diagnosing a problem or proactively checking on a system's health. When you are working with event logs, you typically do it by eye. Any administrator who has been working with Microsoft event logs for a while has picked up through experience which events they need to watch for and which events can be safely ignored.

We've already defined benign events as those events that by themselves are innocuous or unimportant. You should keep in mind that with log data, beauty is in the eye of the beholder. What may not be important to one administrator might be critical to another. As you read through this section, be aware that some of the events listed as benign may be events that some administrators must watch for as part of their job function. This all depends on the specific needs of you and your system.

However, problems come into play when a new administrator is just learning how to work with Microsoft operating system logging or an experienced administrator is under a time crunch. In both of these cases, digging through all of the benign events in the system log takes time and effort that can be better spent elsewhere.

Another important area where this comes into play is in log file storage or retention. When you have a lot of events in your system logs that are unnecessary, they take up additional space. While this typically isn't a big deal for a single system with normal logging, it can quickly turn into a major issue when working with log files from many systems or on systems with a very high logging level enabled. In cases such as this, it could certainly help save on system resources if you didn't save all of log data that is useless to you, such as informational events or known errors.

In order to mitigate these problems, you can use Log Parser to go through your existing event logs and create a new log that ignores the events that you know are unnecessary. This saves on space and makes it easier for new administrators or administrators in a hurry to look through a log and only see what is important for them. It also presents an additional benefit in that processing time can be shortened when using Log Parser in the future to go through these files looking for specific information. Less data simply means less work that Log Parser and the system have to go through to find what you're looking for.

The following script illustrates a method of using Log Parser to go through a System event log and create a new XML log file that eliminates all of the data that an administrator might deem unnecessary:

```
logparser.exe file:Ch03ExcludeBenignEvents.sql -i:EVT -o:datagrid

--- Ch03ExcludeBenignEvents.sql ---

SELECT
    timegenerated AS EventTime,
    EventId AS ID,
```

```
        sourcename AS Name,
        Message
INTO sysenv.xml
FROM system
WHERE sourcename not in
        ('Print';
        'MRxSmb';
        'w32time';
        'TermServDevices')
--- Ch03ExcludeBenignEvents.sql ---
```

Running this script will cause Log Parser to go through your System event log and export all of the data in the log to a file called sysenv.xml. The WHERE clause in this statement causes Log Parser to ignore any events from the example sources "Print", "MRxSmb", "w32time", and "TermServDevices," therefore the new XML file will contain all but those events.

This can be easily modified to work with the specific events that you want to ignore from your files, but these serve as good examples. A very important thing to keep in mind here is that when you make the decision that one of these events can be ignored, that decision should not be taken lightly. In the event that you are saving the exported files for historical purposes or doing further Log Parser parsing on those files, remember that if you exclude something it's gone forever. Use caution when choosing the data you want to leave out of these files and make sure that if you are operating under any legal requirements (such as a security investigation) that you protect yourself. A good practice to use in a situation like this is to back up the original event logs on tape and keep your extracted copies on disk for future use.

Identifying Single vs. Multiple Events

Some events may be benign in and of themselves, but when they start occurring very frequently or very profusely they may indicate larger issues. In order to watch for these, you can use Log Parser to filter your System event log to only display events that have occurred multiple times over a specified period. For example, if you want to show all events that have occurred more than once over the last thirty days, you could use the following code:

```
logparser.exe file:Ch03SingleVsMltplEvents.sql -i:EVT -o:datagrid


--- Ch03SingleVsMltplEvents.sql ---


SELECT
        EventId AS ID,
        count(*) AS number_of_events
FROM system
WHERE SUB(to_int(TimeGenerated), to_int(system_timestamp())) < -2592000
GROUP BY ID
ORDER BY number_of_events desc
--- Ch03SingleVsMltplEvents.sql ---
```

This script will use Log Parser to go through your System event log and extract all data for events that have occurred multiple times within the last thirty days. This is similar to the code segment listed previously in the chapter for identifying multiple failed logon attempts, but it has a unique difference. You should note the code used to specify the date range for events. In this case, we use Log Parser's SUB function to subtract the current system timestamp from the timestamp for the event. The result is then evaluated to ensure that it is less than –2592000, or thirty days. This can be modified to select the specific timeframe that you're interested in using units of one second. The result is shown in Figure 3.8.

Figure 3.8 Single Versus Multiple System Events

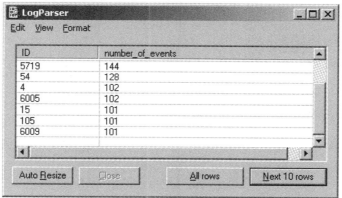

Master Craftsman

Using Time to Help You

Working with units of time in log files has always been a tricky operation. Many times you know exactly how many days worth of data you need, but sometimes you receive requests for "anything after 1pm" or "somewhere between four days ago and now." The function code listed below can help you limit your log file data in a WHERE clause to any time X number of seconds ago.

```
WHERE SUB(to_int(TimeGenerated), to_int(system_timestamp())) < -2592000
```

This code can help you create incredibly useful queries that answer the tough questions such as, "A breach recently occurred, but we don't know when. Can you get everything from about 4 hours ago to now?"

Tracking System Failures

As always, administrators are most interested in the failures of their systems. All systems fail over time, and where an administrator earns his or her paycheck is in finding out why and trying to prevent it from occurring again in the future. Log parser can help you with this task by helping you to find the specific failure events quickly.

Auditing for Dr. Watson Errors

One of the most common failure events for a system is the dreaded Dr. Watson error. This type of error basically indicates that an application has crashed and Windows is starting the Dr. Watson debug tool to gather information around the crash event. Most administrators can't do much with the actual Dr. Watson data, but it can usually be sent to the developer of the application for analysis and a possible fix.

Using Log Parser, you can quickly scan through the System event log and gather information around any "Dr. Watson" errors that have occurred. The following code shows one method of doing so:

```
logparser.exe file:Ch03AuditingDrWatson.sql -i:EVT -o:datagrid

--- Ch03AuditingDrWatson.sql ---


SELECT
    timegenerated AS EventTime,
    extract_token(strings, 0, '|') AS Program
FROM system where sourcename= 'DrWatson'

--- Ch03AuditingDrWatson.sql ---
```

Using this code, Log Parser goes through the System event log looking for any events from the *sourcename* of DrWatson. For any event from this source, it outputs the time that the event occurred, as well as the name of the program which crashed. This is then displayed in the datagrid format for you to examine.

Auditing for System Startups

When a Windows system is rebooted, it does so in one of two ways. It is either intentionally restarted, or it has crashed and restarted. By looking through the System event log, you can manually determine when your system has been restarted, but using Log Parser makes this process much faster. The following code illustrates a quick method to determine any restart events, expected or unexpected for your system:

```
logparser.exe file:Ch03AuditingSystemStartups.sql -i:EVT -o:datagrid

--- Ch03LogonLogoffBehavior.sql ---
```

```
SELECT
    timegenerated AS EventTime,
    message AS Message
FROM system
WHERE eventid= '6005'
--- Ch03AuditingSystemStartups.sql ---
```

This is a very simple Log Parser query to find any events with an EventID of 6005. This eventID indicates that Windows has started the event log service and has therefore been restarted. The results of this query include the time that the event occurred, as well as the event message itself. Keep in mind that the timestamps for these events show when the system was started, not when it went down. Figure 3.9 shows the results for this query.

Figure 3.9 System Startup Audit Results

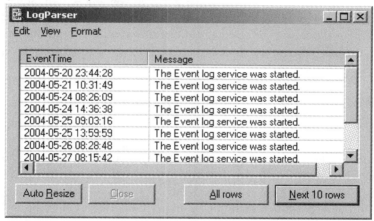

Auditing for Unexpected Shutdowns

Windows systems automatically perform several system checks when they start up. One of these system checks determines whether or not the system was cleanly shut down the last time the system was brought down. To the operating system, this information can signify whether or not it should run the chkdsk utility to ensure file integrity has been maintained, as well to perform any other necessary recovery activity.

To an administrator, an event in the event log indicating that the system was shut down improperly can indicate that the administrator should examine the system to determine what caused the improper shutdown. This could range from a power failure to an operating system crash, but regardless, the administrator should try to find out what happened. In addition, the administrator may want to do some proactive work on the system to try to prevent this from occurring again. Log Parser can help you in watching for this type of shutdown by specifically querying the system log for events that indicate that the last shutdown was not clean. The following query illustrates how this can be done:

```
logparser.exe file:Ch03AuditingUnexpectedShutdowns.sql -i:EVT -o:datagrid

--- Ch03AuditingUnexpectedShutdowns.sql ---

SELECT
    timegenerated AS EventTime,
    message AS Message
FROM system
WHERE eventid= '6008'

--- Ch03AuditingUnexpectedShutdowns.sql ---
```

This is another very simple query that can be useful to you as a systems administrator. The EventID that Log Parser is searching for in this case is 6008, which is an event logged at startup to indicate that the last shutdown was unexpected or otherwise not a clean shutdown. By watching for these events, you can try to determine the cause and proactively prevent additional system downtime.

Trending

When working with any complex system, using statistics can help you in tracking down errors in the system. This is true for everything from mathematical proofs to information technology systems. Often, a particular series of events will repeat itself on a regular basis. When this occurs and the person examining the events determines that the series of events is the same, the result is a trend.

The process of filtering through many, many events and watching for repeated events is called *trending*. It is through this process that many systems administrators are able to predict a specific behavior occurring and prevent it in advance. For example, if over a period of ten years an administrator determines that he has to replace hard drives every three years due to failure, he can proactively plan to buy a replacement drive at two and a half years and cleanly replace the potentially failing drive rather than waiting for it to fail.

The same process applies to software and operating system events. By closely monitoring what is occurring with your software, you can trend out events and try to proactively prevent problems there as well. For example, if you see, based on your trending, that a specific process causes your server to crash every thirty days, you can plan a scheduled reboot at twenty five days to cleanly restart the system. This can prevent the possibility of system corruption due to the crashes.

Most frequently, systems administrators log all of their data to be used for trending into a database or a spreadsheet, then use a charting application or function to chart out the data. A visual representation is always more understandable to the human mind than the raw data. Log Parser has built-in graphing capabilities to take your data and chart it out for you in an easy-to-use format. This capability can help you a great deal in trending your system information.

Trending System Startups

One of the most frequently trended items for systems administrators is system restarts. Everyone wants to know how frequently a system has been restarted over a specific time period, as this can help in determining the overall health of your system. Using the same EventIDs mentioned in the previous section, we can use Log Parser to parse through the System event log and trend out system startup events. The following code shows how this can be done:

```
logparser.exe file:Ch03TrendingSystemStartups.sql -i:EVT -o:chart -charttype:column3d -
legend off -chartTitle "Number of StartUp Events" -view:on

--- Ch03TrendingSystemStartups.sql ---

SELECT
    quantize(timegenerated, 3600) AS Time,
    Count(*) AS Number_of_Events
INTO Startup.gif
FROM system
WHERE EventID= '6005'
GROUP BY Time
ORDER BY Number_of_Events
--- Ch03TrendingSystemStartups.sql ---
```

In this code, we use the basics of the previous system startup query, but add a lot to it to get our trending data. First, we use the quantize function again to specify a one-hour timeframe for our chart data. You can obviously change this to trend on a daily, weekly, or even monthly basis. In addition, we simply do a COUNT of the events for the quantized period. When working with a chart in this manner, you want to minimize the amount of data that you're using. Consequently, you want to leave out unnecessary things such as the actual event message, etc.

For generating the chart, we specify that we want Log Parser to put the results of this query into a GIF file (Startup.gif) so that the chart can be saved. We also specify several chart-specific parameters such as the charttype *column3d*, which indicates a three dimensional bar chart. In this example we also turn of the legend, specify a title, and tell Log Parser that we want to view the chart immediately. Running this query results in the screen shown in Figure 3.10.

Figure 3.10 System Startup Trend Chart

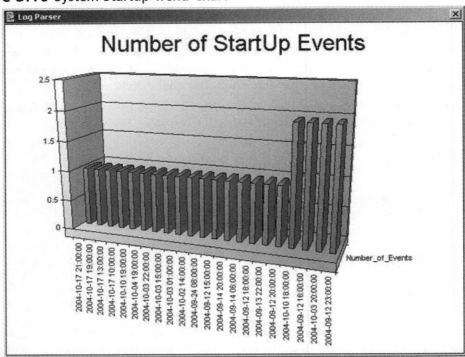

Trending Netlogon Failures

Another set of events that a systems administrator may be interested in trending is Netlogon failures. These events indicate failures of the Windows Netlogon service, which may indicate that the system is unable to communicate properly with other systems on the network to perform authentication and other tasks. Taken together, these events can tell you that your system is having trouble communicating.

Trending Netlogon failures can help you in determining whether or not the system is experiencing failures of this type at a specific time on a regular basis. If the trend shows this is true, you know that either the network itself is experiencing problems at those specific times or that the remote systems that your system is trying to communicate may be overloaded or down at those times. To determine either, you must first trend out the data you have available. The following code illustrates how to do this:

```
logparser.exe file:Ch03TrendingNetlogonFailures.sql -i:EVT -o:chart -charttype:column3d -
legend off -chartTitle "Number of Netlogon Failures" -view:on

--- Ch03TrendingNetlogonFailures.sql ---

SELECT
```

```
    quantize(TimeGenerated,3600) AS Time,
    count(*) AS number_of_events
INTO netlog.gif
FROM system
WHERE SourceName like 'netlogon'
    AND SUB(to_int(TimeGenerated), to_int(system_timestamp())) > -2592000
GROUP BY Time
--- Ch03TrendingNetlogonFailures.sql ---
```

This query is very similar to the previous trending query in that we quantize the timeframe for the event and gather a count of the events. We also add in one of the functions we used in a previous query for limiting the timeframe we're interested in for results. Finalizing our code with the chart-specific options we want Log Parser to use results in a GIF file trending out our Netlogon failures in a three dimensional bar chart.

Creating System Error Reports

Another very common task for a systems administrator is the creation of system error reports. These reports go into a lot more detail than a system downtime report and many companies require administrators to create system error reports weekly and review the errors among the IT teams.

You've already seen how Log Parser can help you in eliminating non-useful data from event logs. A system error report takes this one step further and combines some of the Log Parser features that we've covered previously.

Generating a Useful System Error Report

A problem most system error reports have is that they contain too much data. It can take hours to go through a report for a series of critical servers, no matter how few there are. In order to be more productive, it helps to minimize the amount of data that you have to analyze. We have covered this to some degree previously in the chapter. To generate a useful system error report, we'll combine a few of the features we've used before to minimize the amount of data that ends up in our final report. The following code illustrates the creation of a system error report:

```
logparser.exe file:Ch03SystemErrorReport.sql -i:evt -o:datagrid

--- Ch03SystemErrorReport.sql ---

SELECT
    SourceName AS Name,
    EventId AS ID,
    count(*) AS number_of_events
FROM system
WHERE SUB(to_int(TimeGenerated), to_int(system_timestamp())) > -2592000
    AND sourcename not in
    ('Print';
    'MRxSmb';
    'w32time';
    'TermServDevices')
GROUP BY ID,
    Name
HAVING number_of_events > 1
ORDER BY number_of_events desc

--- Ch03SystemErrorReport.sql ---
```

In this example, we have combined a lot of the Log Parser features. First, we define what we want to see in the end result. In this case, we just want to see the error source, the eventID, and the number of events that occurred over the last month. For limiting the dataset to a month, we use the same SUB function previously employed for other scripts. In addition, we want to make sure we're only dealing with serious problems here, so if an event hasn't occurred more than once, we'll ignore it. Finally, we use the same method previously described for ignoring benign events here.

Using all of these features together gives us a very good view into errors that have occurred on a specific system over the last month. Further fine-tuning of your query can make this dataset even smaller and help you to quickly identify issues that warrant special attention or analysis.

Monitoring Application Health

Along with monitoring the overall health of your systems, you need to monitor the health of the applications that run on your systems. System errors in general are fairly easy to monitor. They are typically logged in a single place (system log) and are easily researched through a single vendor.

Application errors are a little more difficult to work with. The operating system really has no idea of the intricacies of the applications running on it, so the OS must rely on the application to do its own logging. This means that it is completely up to the developers of the application to get the logging details right and to log enough information to the right places. In addition, to try to decipher the meaning of most application errors that are logged, you must refer to the documentation or technical information provided by the vendor who wrote the application. Depending on how many applications you are running on a system, this could be a very difficult task.

Quite often, application logging is done on individual text files rather than the Windows application log. This makes it a little more difficult to look at all of the applications on a system at once, but it can still be done. For the purposes of these examples, we're going to assume that we're working with applications that log to the Windows application log.

In this section, we're going to go over two main types of applications. First we'll go over applications that are local to a specific system or *local applications*. Next we'll take a look at applications that users access remotely or *served applications*. The information provided by each of these types of applications differs and you have to look at errors for each type a little differently.

Identifying Application Errors

Both local applications such as WinZip, Diskeeper, and MS Office applications, as well as served applications can log their errors to the local Application event log. By using Log Parser to go through this data, you can get a pretty good picture of how well your local or served applications are running.

Some applications will log only error messages; others log all types of informational messages. This will vary on a per application basis, so you need to have a fairly good understanding of the application before you can tune your queries to look for specific information.

Finding Events From a Specific Application

The first step toward learning how an application does its logging is to simply find all events that the application has logged. This may include error, warning, and informational events. After gathering this data, you can further tune your queries to only give you the specific information that you need.

For example, if you want to gather all Diskeeper startup entries, you will need to first determine how these entries are logged, then extract them individually. For this example, we will use a very simple query to gather all of the Application event log entries for a given application.

```
logparser.exe file:Ch03SpecificApplicationEvents.sql -i:evt -o:datagrid


--- Ch03SpecificApplicationEvents.sql ---


SELECT
    timegenerated AS Time,
    EventTypeName AS Event,
    SourceName AS Application
FROM application
WHERE Application like 'esent'
---Ch03SpecificApplicationEvents.sql ---
```

With this query we are extracting the time, event, and source name for any of the events in the application log where the source name is "esent". This will subset the Application event log data and show us all the entries available for this particular application (Microsoft Exchange) in the datagrid format. This query can be further tuned to include only error events or any other criteria that you find you need regarding an application.

Finding Error Events from a Specific Application

If an application does any logging to the Windows application log at all, it will typically log error messages at a minimum. Most developers consider this the most basic information that an administrator will need and include error logging as their default logging setting. Some applications will allow you to set a logging level in order to force the application to log informational or warning messages in addition to the error messages.

Like the last query, pulling error events from the application log for a specific application is very simple. It just requires a slight modification to the previous script to specify the type of event that we are looking for.

```
logparser.exe file:Ch03SpecificApplicationErrors.sql -i:evt -o:datagrid


--- Ch03SpecificApplicationErrors.sql ---


SELECT
    timegenerated AS Time,
    EventTypeName AS Event,
    SourceName AS Application
FROM application
WHERE Application like 'vmauthd'
    AND event like 'error event'
```

```
--- Ch03SpecificApplicationErrors ---
```

In this example, we are dealing with an application that uses a source of "vmauthd". When running this query, Log Parser will go through the application log and find any events from this source (VMWare) that have the text "error event" in the *EventTypeName* field. The resulting dataset will be displayed in the datagrid format.

Auditing for Application Dr. Watson Errors

Along with any application specific error messages, many applications will cause a Dr. Watson error to be generated when they crash. As mentioned previously, a Dr. Watson error occurs when Windows initiates a session of its debugger/crash handler. When this happens, the application itself will typically not log an error event, as it is in the process of crashing and isn't going through its event logging routines.

For capturing Dr. Watson errors, we can use a simple Log Parser query to extract these from the Application event log. Note that in the previous example we were gathering this information from the System event log. I have actually seen these logged in both places, so it would probably be a good idea to run both the previous query and this example in order to make sure that you catch all instances of the errors.

```
logparser.exe file:Ch03AuditingAppDrWatson.sql -i:evt -o:datagrid
```

```
--- Ch03AuditingAppDrWatson.sql ---


SELECT
    timegenerated AS EventTime,
    extract_token(strings, 0, '|') AS Program
FROM application where sourcename= 'DrWatson'
--- Ch03AuditingAppDrWatson.sql ---
```

Working with Served Application Security

One of the biggest areas in which application logging differs between local and served applications is in application security. Local applications don't really worry about security or authentication to a great degree. They may need to authenticate to access something on a remote system or they may deal with NTFS permissions for accessing local files, but local applications typically don't treat security in the same way that a served application does.

Working with a served application, you'll find that it will often include its own authentication routines or handle application security in its own unique way. A prime example of this is the Siebel eBusiness application in which the application offers the ability to authenticate against either a remote database or use LDAP (Lightweight Directory Access Protocol) to authenticate against a directory service. With this application, regardless of the authentication method used, it will still log a failure in the same way in its logs.

Identifying Served Application Login Failures

The most commonly logged error for served applications that use authentication is login failures. These errors will either be logged to an application-specific log file or to the Windows Application event log. You should note that in the previous sections on login failures, all of the error logging took place in the Windows security event log. Most served applications do not use the security event log but rather the Application event log for recording these events.

Any application login failure recorded in the Application event log should be logged either under the source for the application itself or a source the developers chose to use for security/authentication-specific errors. As with any of the queries for application events, familiarity with the application is required. The following script is a basic example of how this type of query can be performed, but to make it work for your applications, you must substitute application specific information into the query.

```
logparser.exe file:Ch03ServedApplicationLoginFailures.sql -i:evt -o:datagrid


--- Ch03ServedApplicationLoginFailures.sql ---


SELECT
    timegenerated AS Time,
    EventTypeName AS Event,
    SourceName AS Application
FROM application
WHERE Application like 'vmauthd failure'
    AND event like 'error event'


--- Ch03ServedApplicationLoginFailures ---
```

This code assumes that the application we're working with logs all login failure events under the *SourceName* of "vmauthd failure". Most applications will either use a unique source for login failures or include the failure as part of the message text for the standard application source.

Identifying Served Application Security Failures

When working with a served application, you may need to deal with more than just authentication problems. The application may log other security events such as an inability to access a file or a problem connecting to a remote portion of the application. If the application does log these errors to a Windows event log, it will be logging them to the Application event log instead of the Security event log in a manner similar to that used for application login failures.

Using Log Parser, it is another simple query to go through and gather any security related event log message from an application, assuming that the application has a specific way of logging the message, (that is, from a specific source). Again, this will vary with every application, so you will need to be familiar with the specific application that you're dealing with in order to be able to properly refine your query. To do this, simply use the same code listed above for login failures and modify as necessary to support other events. An example follows:

```
logparser.exe file:Ch03ServedApplicationSecurityFailures.sql -i:evt -o:datagrid

--- Ch03ServedApplicationSecurityFailures.sql ---

SELECT
     timegenerated AS Time,
     EventTypeName AS Event,
     SourceName AS Application
FROM application
WHERE Application like 'ipsec-violation'
     AND event like 'error event'

--- Ch03ServedApplicationSecurityFailures ---
```

Final Touches

In this chapter, we have gone over many of the features available in Log Parser for working with Windows event logs. Through the sections we've covered, we have looked into the Security, System, and Application event logs and used many sample Log Parser queries to pull data from these logs for analysis.

There are a few key points you should remember when working with these logs:

- Differentiating between single and multiple events is a critical feature in Log Parser for working with the Security event log.

- Differentiating between benign events and actual errors or warnings is very important for having an accurate view of your system environment.

- When working with applications and the Application event logs, it is critical that you have a thorough understanding of the specific application you are working with.

Keeping these points in mind will help you make the most of the Log Parser utility. You'll find that as you practice using this tool, it will be a very important part of your overall systems administrator toolbox. Log Parser can help you a great deal in conserving time and effort when you need to parse through large amounts of Windows event log data.

Chapter 4

Examining Network Traffic and Performance Logs with Log Parser

Scripts and Samples in this Chapter:

- Getting into the Netmon Format
- Getting Started with Log Parser's Netmon Format
- Finding Soft Errors in TCP Requests
- Log Parser, Netmon and Proxy Servers
- Using Netmon and Log Parser to Watch for Worms/Intruders
- Basic NT Performance Log Queries
- Advanced NT Performance Log Queries

In This Toolbox

Network capture files recorded by Microsoft Network Monitor (Netmon) are a great low-level way to understand what is happening inside a network application or on a network. While the user interface of this application is generally very useful, it struggles with complicated data search patterns and in understanding the relationships between multiple data packets.

Log Parser quite nicely fills this gap by giving you direct access to all the raw data in the packet and puts the SQL query capability of Log Parser to use in finding what can often be a needle in a haystack for a tester or network administrator. Additionally, in this toolbox you will learn how to take this same concept and apply it to NT performance log data and also make it more manageable and more useful.

Reading Netmon Capture Files with Log Parser

Like other types of large data sources, network trace data can be gigantic in size and its very nature can make it look very arcane, even to a well-trained eye. Even with that in mind, Log Parser can be used to reveal networking data that has previously been either unavailable to an administrator or difficult to retrieve at best. However, this data is easily reachable with Log Parser.

For example, do you run a website with an ISAPI DLL (Internet Server Application Programming Interface Dynamic Link Library) that exposes public, user-specified function calls? Do you want to reproduce the parameters that are generating a page that is not classified by IIS (Internet Information Server) as an "error," but is still not generating the expected response intended for the user? You only know what external URL (Uniform Resource Locator) the user sees and not what the actual request was since it's a server to server call and the end user cannot see the actual URL. The other server is external and you do not have access to their server's logs, so you can't look there for the referring URL. You're stuck, right? Wrong. Network captures can tell you the URL that the client asked for where an IIS/HTTP (Hypertext Transfer Protocol) log cannot, since it technically is not an error to IIS. This is often referred to by administrators as a *soft* error, which is basically defined as a suboptimal result that is not severe enough to be labeled an exception by the application. Finding soft errors is where using network captures can shine since all the raw data is available to the investigator. Network captures offer raw access to TCP (Transmission Control Protocol) packet information and Log Parser presents it in straightforward fields without missing or arcane descriptions, also providing an optional, connection-oriented view that shows all the packets in a particular connection. This connection includes all the packets in a request stream from start to finish and can be accessed by using the **–fmode:TCPCONN** switch to Log Parser.

Getting into the Netmon Format

As mentioned previously, Log Parser plainly identifies all the fields inside the TCP packet, which allows the administrator to spend his or her time investigating and not deciphering the packet's format and fields. See Tables 4.1 and 4.2 for details on all the network fields that are exposed by Log Parser's Netmon input format.

Also present in Log Parser's Netmon format are the following optional switches:

- **–fMode** TCPIP | TCPConn

  ```
  Field mode: TCPIP: each record is a single TCP/IP packet;
  ```

  ```
  TCPConn: each record is a single TCP/IP connection
  [default value=TCPIP]
  ```

- **–binaryFormat** ASC | PRINT | HEX

  ```
  Format of binary fields [default value=ASC]
  ```

Table 4.1 Netmon Capture File Fields and Properties in Raw Format

Property	Field	Description
Frame Number	Frame	Relative Ethernet frame number in the capture file starting from 1.
Time of day	DateTime	W3C Timestamp on each frame.
Frame size in bytes	FrameBytes	The size of the Ethernet frame, up to a maximum value of 1514 bytes, including all TCP and IP (Internet Protocol) data.
Source MAC address	SrcMAC	The source server's Layer 2 network or Media Access Control (MAC) address.
Source IP address	SrcIP	The IP address of the host sending the packet.
Source TCP port	SrcPort	The TCP socket that the packet is originating from.
Destination MAC address	DstMAC	The destination server's Layer 2 network or MAC address.
Destination IP address	DstIP	The IP address of the host receiving the packet.
Destination TCP port	DstPort	The TCP socket that the packet is bound for.

Continued

Table 4.1 Netmon Capture File Fields and Properties in Raw Format

Property	Field	Description
IP Protocol Version	IPVersion	IP protocol version—V4 or V6.
IP Time to live	TTL	The amount of time in seconds that the packet is allowed to live. In practice, this is used as a maximum hop count for the packet. Every router the packet crosses must decrement this counter by one. Once the counter is zero, the packet must be discarded by the router and the sender notified via ICMP (Internet Control Message Protocol) messages that the TTL (time to live) has expired in transit. This prevents erroneous or otherwise malicious packets from circulating a damaged network indefinitely.
TCP flags	TCPFlags	Flags in the TCP header designating the type of packet—URG, ACK, PSH, RST, SYN, and FIN. They are abbreviated in Log Parser by the 1st letter.
TCP Sequence number	Seq	The TCP sequence number that was chosen by the original source host to designate the TCP connection.
TCP ACK number	Ack	The TCP acknowledgement number that was chosen by the original source host for the destination server to use when responding to the TCP connection request.
TCP Window size	WindowSize	The maximum amount of TCP data in bytes that the sending server will allow to be outstanding between the two hosts without the reception of an acknowledgement.
TCP data size in bytes	PayloadBytes	The size of the TCP portion of the packet, up to a maximum value of 1460 bytes.
TCP data	Payload	The raw TCP data that is being transmitted, in ASCII or HEX format.
TCP Connection / session identifier	Connection	A relative connection number that is assigned by Log Parser to every established TCP connection in the capture file. This is done by deriving data from the TCP sequence/Acknowledgement numbers/source and destination ports and other factors.

Table 4.2 Netmon Capture File Fields and Properties in Connection Format

Property	Field	Description
Starting Frame Number of session	StartFrame	Starting Ethernet frame number in the session.
Ending Frame Number of session	EndFrame	Ending Ethernet frame number in the session.
Total frames in session	Frames	Total number of individual frames in the session.
Source MAC address	SrcMAC	The source server's Layer 2 network or MAC address
Source IP address	SrcIP	The IP address of the host sending the packet.
Source TCP port	SrcPort	The TCP socket that the packet is originating from.
Destination MAC address	DstMAC	The destination server's Layer 2 network or MAC address.
Destination IP address	DstIP	The IP address of the host receiving the packet.
Destination TCP port	DstPort	The TCP socket that the packet is bound for.
Time taken to complete session	TimeTaken	The amount of time, in seconds, that the session took to complete.
Time of day	DateTime	W3C Timestamp on each frame.
TCP data size in bytes on packet from client	SrcPayloadBytes	The size of the TCP portion of the user's packet, up to a maximum value of 1460 bytes.
TCP data included in the client's request	SrcPayload	The end user's request to the server host in ASCII.
TCP data size in bytes on packet from server	DstPayloadBytes	The size of the TCP portion of the response packet, up to a maximum value of 1460 bytes.
TCP data included in the server's response	DstPayload	The server's response to the user host in ASCII.

TIP

Full Microsoft TCP/IP implementation details can be found at www.microsoft.com/technet/itsolutions/network/deploy/depovg/tcpip2k.mspx.

Getting Started with Log Parser's Netmon Format

Let's briefly look over two basic queries in the Netmon format to give some context. These are basic IIS requests for web pages. One is shown in connection format (**-fmode:TCPConn**) and the other is shown in the standard TCPIP format, which is the default. Use command syntax like this for any Netmon query in Log Parser:

```
logparser.exe file:Ch04TCPConn.sql -fmode:TCPConn
```

```
---Ch04TCPConn.sql---
SELECT
            SrcIP,
            DstIP,
            DstPort,
            SrcPayload,
            DstPayload
FROM      FOO.cap
WHERE     DstPort = 80
OR               SrcPort = 80
AND     DstPayload like '%200%'
```

Output:

```
SrcIP           DstIP           DstPort SrcPayload
12.52.84.19    61.4.12.13        80        GET foo.gif HTTP/1.0..Accept: image/gif, image/x-
xbitmap, image/jpeg, image/pjpeg, application/x-shockwave-flash, */*..Accept-Language: en-
us..Accept-Encoding: gzip, deflate..User-Agent: Mozilla/4.0 (compatible; MSIE 6.0; Windows
98).. X-Forwarded-For: 19.24.114.2..Via: 1.1 TTCache04 (Jaguar/3.0-59)..


DstPayload
HTTP/1.1 302 Object moved..Server: Microsoft-IIS/5.0..Date: Mon, 27 Sep 2004 20:42:34
GMT..P3P:CP="BUS CUR CONo FIN IVDo ONL OUR PHY SAMo TELo"..Location:
http://foo.com/foo.gif..Content-Length: 121.. image/gif, image/x-xbitmap, image/jpeg,
image/pjpeg, application/x-shockwave-flash, */*..Cache-control:
private....<head><title>Object moved</title></head>.<body><h1>Object Moved</h1>This
object may be found <a HREF="">here</a>.</body>.
---Ch04TCPConn.sql---
---Ch04TCPIP.sql---
SELECT
            SrcIP,
            DstIP,
            DstPort,
            Payload
FROM      FOO.cap
WHERE     DstPort = 80
```

```
OR       SrcPort = 80
```

```
Output:
SrcIP          DstIP          DstPort Payload
19.175.37.8    21.21.12.13    80      GET  foo.gif HTTP/1.0..Accept: image/gif, image/x-
xbitmap, image/jpeg, image/pjpeg, application/x-shockwave-flash, */*..Accept-Language: en-
us..Accept-Encoding: gzip, deflate..User-Agent: Mozilla/4.0 (compatible; MSIE 6.0; Windows
98).. X-Forwarded-For: 19.214.114.2..Via: 1.1 TTCache04 (Jaguar/3.0-59)..Connection:
Keep-Alive....
---Ch04TCPIP.sql---
```

Finding Soft Errors in TCP Requests

Now that we have seen a little of how Log Parser displays data, let's move more into some troubleshooting. As mentioned in the introduction to this chapter, network requests using platform technologies like IIS/Java/etc. often defy common definitions of failure. This usually is the result of an application failure (for example, a custom ISAPI) being too granular for a generic host application (like IIS), hence the term *soft* failure. Regardless of the definition or the reason, the resultant problem is that the user is getting the wrong response, and the administrator and the application developer have to find out the root cause. The IIS log doesn't show anything more than a 200 [OK] response to a million or so requests and there is not any way in the IIS log to tie those requests to the responses that the client is seeing. The bad response has to be backtracked to the exact parameters that were passed to the IIS web server so that the problem can be found.

> **TIP**
>
> **Example:** `logparser.exe file:Ch04TCPConn.sql?filename=FOO.cap -fmode:TCPConn`
> Notice that the capture filename is passed to the SQL file as a parameter. This technique is reused throughout this chapter.

```
---Ch04ErrantHTTP.sql---
SELECT
        TimeTaken,
        SrcPayload,
        DstPayload
FROM    %filename%
WHERE   DstPayload like '%UseMethodX%'
ORDER   BY SrcPayload
---Ch04ErrantHTTP.sql---
```

This example shows the requests that had a response, which included **UseMethodX** in the ASCII portion of the TCP response packet to the user. While IIS logs will only show the request and the IIS/WIN32 status of the request, this output is organized around the reply that was received by the client and also shows the full data portion of the server's reply to the request. Here is an example of a reply to this query:

```
2046.875000
GET /redirect.dll?UseMethodX
HTTP/1.1 302 Object moved..Server: Microsoft-IIS/5.0..Date: Mon, 27 Sep 2004 20:42:33
GMT..P3P:CP="BUS CUR CONo FIN IVDo ONL OUR PHY SAMo TELo"..Location:
http://foo.com/OLDredirectpage.htm..Content-Length: 121..Content-Type: text/html..Set-
Cookie: FOOCOOKIE=thiscookievalue; expires=Mon, 04-Oct-2021 19:00:00 GMT;
domain=.foo.com; path=/..Cache-control: private....<head><title>Object
moved</title></head>.<body><h1>Object Moved</h1>This object may be found <a
HREF="">here</a>.</body>.
```

Perhaps you suspect that the error centers around cookies that are not being passed, or are being passed erroneously. This will retrieve the URL requested, the HTTP status code (302), and also all the headers and cookies that were sent back. We can check for cookies being set by the server and/or presented by the client. For server cookies it is:

```
---Ch04Server_Cookies.sql---
SELECT
SUBSTR(EXTRACT_TOKEN(Payload,1,'Cookie:'),0,INDEX_OF (EXTRACT_TOKEN(Payload, 1,
'Cookie:'), '..'))
AS ServerCookie
FROM %filename%
WHERE ServerCookie is not NULL
AND SrcPort = 80


output:
COOKIE1=UM=; expires=Tue, 26-Apr-2022 12:00:00 GMT; domain=.FOO.com; path=/
```

For client cookies it is:

```
SELECT
SUBSTR(EXTRACT_TOKEN(Payload,1,'Cookie:'),0,INDEX_OF (EXTRACT_TOKEN(Payload, 1,
'Cookie:'), '..'))
AS ClientCookie
FROM %filename%
WHERE ClientCookie is not NULL
AND DstPort = 80


output:
XC1=V=3&PGID=a978000eba114d48888576637e3b5729;
```

Master Craftsman

Understanding TCP Sequencing

Please note, while Log Parser can identify packets that should be grouped together by using the **–fmode:TCPConn** switch, it is useful to know how to sequence TCP packets and connections manually as well, especially when looking at network traffic behind proxies and accelerators that do not always close TCP connections like normal clients. In the proxy cases, using the **–Fmode:TCPConn** switch results in a relatively small number of unique connections with many requests appended together. To isolate specific requests in these cases, you will have to read the sequences manually with Log Parser. You may have to manually examine the network frames a few times (select * from FOO.cap) to understand your connection profiles (how many bytes are on the request/response, etc) before you can write reliable, specific queries, but it is certainly possible and useful with a little practice.

When manually looking at TCP captures, especially in captures from very busy networks, one way to follow a particular request from start to finish is to leverage the TCP sequence and acknowledgement numbers attached to each TCP packet. The following is a basic explanation of that process, but the full explanation of TCP sequencing is present in the TCP RFC, Section 3.3, located here: www.ietf.org/rfc/rfc793.txt

In a simple TCP data request, the client sends a TCP sequence number on any request to a remote server to uniquely identify that packet. This number is chosen on connection startup by the client and is 32 bits in length. The host also sets any applicable TCP flags for the packet, based upon the packet's profile. For example, on an initial request, the SYN (Synchronize) field in the TCP header will be set by the client. On the first server reply, the ACK (Acknowledge) header will be set in addition to the SYN header and so on. When data is appended to a TCP request, the PSH (Push Data) flag is set in addition to the ACK flag. When a client wants to end the connection, it will include the FIN flag in its packet to the server.

Any time that the ACK flag is set in the TCP header, a non-zero acknowledgement number is present in the packet as well. Acknowledgment numbers are generally formed when a host will "Acknowledge" another host's request by sending back the sending host's TCP sequence number in the Acknowledgement field of its response packet to "Acknowledge" the receipt of that specific packet. Additionally, any host "Acknowledging" TCP packets will increment this Acknowledgement number slightly using a few simple guidelines:

- If a client's packet only has the SYN flag present (in the case of the 1st packet in a TCP connection), the Acknowledgement number will be 0, since no data is being "acknowledged." However, the server's reply to this packet will have an Acknowledgement number of the clients initial TCP Sequence number (also known as ISN) + 1. For Example, when the Server acknowledges a packet from the client with ONLY the SYN flag set:

  Server's Acknowledgement number = ISN + 1

Continued

Server's TCP Sequence number = New 32 bit TCP sequence number that it generates.

■ If a packet is received, but no data is being sent, the host will acknowledge that packet and increment the Acknowledgment number + 1. For example, when a Server acknowledges a packet from the client with the ACK flag set, but no data:

Server's Acknowledgement number = Client's TCP Sequence number +1

Server's TCP Sequence number = Client's ACK number

■ If the client OR server is ALSO acknowledging the receipt of TCP data (the packet it is acknowledging had the PSH flag set), it will increment its Acknowledgment number by the amount of TCP data bytes it received. For example, when a Server acknowledges client's data:

Server's Acknowledgement number = Client's TCP Sequence number + data bytes

Server's TCP Sequence number = Client's ACK number

Log Parser, Netmon and Proxy Servers

If a server is behind a proxy, finding the same data as in the previous example might prove difficult since most proxies re-use TCP connections. Consequently, using Log Parser's TCPConn mode may not give us the granular data that is needed. This query, while a bit slow, will give the TCP request that was the predecessor to any response. If what you need did not occur immediately before the reply in the request stream, but rather is one or more frames back in the chain, repeat the following process or further nest the following query to get where you need.

```
--- Ch04ManualTCP.sql ---
SELECT
        Frame,
        DateTime ,
        FrameBytes,
        SrcPort,
        DstPort,
        TCPFlags,
        Seq,
        Ack,
        WindowSize,
        PayloadBytes,
        Payload
FROM    %filename%
WHERE   Payload like Payload '%UseMethodX%'
OR
```

```
     (SEQ IN(
SELECT
         Ack from %filename% where Payload like '%UseMethodX%')
)
--- Ch04ManualTCP.sql---
```

Using Netmon and Log Parser to Watch for Worms/Intruders

While there are a lot of intrusion methods out there on the market, it is still useful to look at your raw network packets to see who is doing what on your network. You will always find something going on that you did not previously know about, benign or otherwise. If you suspect some machines on your network are owned and trying to infect your servers, you might perform a quick network trace and use a query like this one, which could be easily tuned to look for the specific exploit you are worried about. This one looks for machines infected by many of the known worm entry points/exploits on the network and calls out machines that may be compromised.

```
---Ch04owned.sql---
SELECT
         DISTINCT REVERSEDNS(srcip) AS SuspiciousMachineName,
         srcip,
         dstport,
         COUNT(srcip) as SuspiciousConns
FROM     %filename%
WHERE    dstport in
(80;137;445;559;1025;1026;1027;135;1434;2745;2535;3127;3410;5000;5554;6129;27374;65506)
GROUP BY srcip,
         dstport
HAVING   SuspiciousConns > 5

output:
```

SuspiciousMachineName	SrcIP	DstPort	SuspiciousConns
Coderedworm.foo.com	24.42.23.91	80	6
joe.com	23.23.18.67	80	6
bob.hacket.ca	21.7.16.229	80	6

```
---Ch04owned.sql---
```

Deriving Data from NT Performance Logs

Ever have a colleague drop off a 1GB NT performance log and ask you to "take a look" at it to see if you find anything unusual? With Log Parser, you can actually take a quick look at a huge performance log and spot problem vectors much easier. The code in this section uses Log Parser to identify every individual performance counter in an NT performance log and output to the console the minimum, maximum, and average values for each of the counters that are in the log file. This gives the administrator a good chance of seeing something unusual and a much smaller investigative surface to explore. Once you spot a problem, you can query all the granular data with a standard Log Parser CSV query to get every individual reading for a particular NT performance counter that you think is worthy of investigation.

NOTE

The following code assumes your NT performance logs are in CSV output format. The code could be modified to accommodate TSV logs if needed.

Basic NT Performance Log Queries

Before we query the files, let's take a really quick look at gathering that data easily from the command line — by using the resource kit utility LogMan.exe, we can quickly create an NT Performance log collection and start/stop it. Use the following script (Ch04CreateLog.cmd) and the sample NT counter list which follows this code to create a log to analyze with Log Parser and output a graph of the data. It will create the log collection on the local machine and start collecting data. In the example, we just collect for 2 seconds on the local machine, but the script is easy to modify to suit any time needs and LogMan.exe can create logs on remote machines by adding the –S <servername> switch.

TIP

LogMan always inserts the computername into each NT performance counter – make sure you account for this in your queries. In the following example, we pass a parameter designating the servername to Ch04QueryMem.sql like this:

```
logparser.exe file:Ch04QueryMem.sql?filename=memory.csv+server=myServer -view:on -
charttype:Column3d
```

```
---Ch04CreateLog.cmd---
@echo off

if "%1"=="/?" goto :usage
if "%1"=="" goto :usage

REM drop the countergroup if it exists
@echo stopping and deleting any old copies of the logset...
logman stop %1>nul
logman delete %1>nul
REM create a new set
logman create counter %1 -cf %1 -rf 00:00:02 -o c:\perflogs\ -si 00:00:01 -f csv --v
REM start the set for 2 seconds and then stop
```

```
goto :eof
:usage
ECHO Ch04CreateLog.cmd {NTCounterlistFile}
ECHO Example: Ch04CreateLog.cmd Ch04taskman
goto :eof

:eof
@echo on
---Ch04CreateLog.cmd---
---Ch04taskman---
"\Memory\Commit Limit"

"\Memory\Committed Bytes"
---Ch04taskman---


---Ch04QueryMem.sql---
SELECT
        AVG([\\%servername%\Memory\Commit Limit]) as Limit,
        AVG([\\%servername%\Memory\Committed Bytes]) as Used
FROM    %filename%
TO      Memory.gif
---Ch04QueryMem.sql---
```

The output is shown in Figure 4.1.

Figure 4.1 Output of Ch04QueryMem.sql

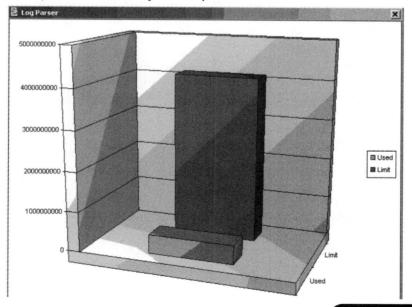

Advanced NT Performance Log Queries

While performance logs are just CSV files, anyone running in an enterprise would be quick to point out that no two NT performance logs are the same—people are always measuring something different with a different number of columns. Astute administrators would be well advised to adapt some of the previous and following code to create canned NT performance log sets and corresponding Log Parser queries. The following section addresses the other side—an NT performance log that has a variable number of columns, which complicates the analysis with Log Parser significantly. However, with the following code, you should be able to handle most NT performance logs without much trouble. The code is commented, so modifying it to adapt to your enterprise or environment should not be difficult.

While Log Parser does not intrinsically support finding column names and then querying for them, you can write add-on code to pull those names and then query for them. The following C# example pulls the column names from any CSV Perfmon file and then stores those names for querying one at a time for minimum, maximum, and average values for the entire file. This can also be accomplished a little more brutally by using a temp file and then interrogating it via a second query inside a batch file. Both examples are given. Which you choose is more of a matter of preference, as the performance is similar.

```
---CH04LP_perfmon.cs---
using System;
using LQC     = Interop.MSUtil.LogQueryClassClass;
using LCI     = Interop.MSUtil.COMCSVInputContextClassClass;

class LogP
{
      public static void Main(string[] Args)
      {
      // construct objects that we just defined in using above

      try
            {
                  LQC obj2 = new LQC();
                  LCI objI = new LCI();

      // getting the number of columns

      objI.headerRow = true;
      string query1 = @"SELECT top1 * from "+Args[0];
      Interop.MSUtil.ILogRecordset recset= obj2.Execute(query1, objI);
      Interop.MSUtil.ILogRecord record = recset.getRecord();

            while (recset.atEnd() != true)
                  {
            for (int I = 4; I < recset.getColumnCount() -1; I++)
```

```
                                {
        //print the NT counternames from the logfile

                                    Console.WriteLine(recset.getColumnName(I));

        // Create a SQL query for Log Parser to query the file

string query2 = "select ";
query2 += @"AVG(TO_INT(["+recset.getColumnName(I)+"])) as avg_value_,";
query2 += @"MIN(TO_REAL(["+recset.getColumnName(I)+"])) as min_value, ";
query2 += @"MAX(TO_REAL(["+recset.getColumnName(I)+"])) as Max_value from ";
query2 += Args[0];

//print the counter min/max/avg to the console

Interop.MSUtil.ILogRecordset recset2= obj2.Execute(query2, objI);
Interop.MSUtil.ILogRecord record2 = recset2.getRecord();
Console.WriteLine(record2.getValue(0).ToString()+
" "+record2.getValue(1).ToString()+" "+record2.getValue(2).ToString());
                                }
                        recset.moveNext();
                        }
                }
            catch (System.IndexOutOfRangeException)
    {
                    Console.WriteLine();
                    Console.WriteLine("must specify a valid perfmon logfile to parse");
                    Console.WriteLine("usage: LP_Perfmon.exe <CSV logfile>");
                    Console.WriteLine("example: LP_Perfmon.exe foo.csv");
    }
            catch (System.IO.FileNotFoundException)
    {
                    Console.WriteLine();
                    Console.WriteLine("must specify a valid perfmon logfile to parse");
                    Console.WriteLine("usage: LP_Perfmon.exe <CSV logfile>");
                    Console.WriteLine("example: LP_Perfmon.exe foo.csv");
    }
            catch (System.Runtime.InteropServices.COMException)
    {
                    Console.WriteLine("you must have the Log Parser.dll registered to run
this");
                    Console.WriteLine(@"get it from http://logparser.com");
    }
    }
}
---CH04LP_perfmon.cs---
```

Perform the following steps to use the C# sample (you need the .NET framework installed):

1. Make an Interop wrapper for LogParser.dll.

```
tlbimp LogParser.dll /out:Interop.MSUtil.dll
```

2. Compile the Ch04LP_Perfmon.cs file into an executable (.EXE) with the following command:

```
csc /r:Interop.MSUtil.dll /out:Ch04LP_perfmon.exe  Ch04LP_perfmon.cs
```

3. Run the new executable:

```
Ch04LP_Perfmon.exe <performance log filename.csv>
```

4. Each output line has the NT counter name, the Average Value, The Minimum Value and the Maximum Value on the following line:

```
\\serverName\Memory\Page Faults/sec
743 15.498725 14296.662888
```

5. To drill down on a particular counter that you find interesting:

```
    ---Ch04CounterDrill.sql---

SELECT
[(PDH-CSV 4.0) (Pacific Standard Time)(480)] AS time,
[\\serverName\Memory\Page Faults/sec]
FROM FOO_Log.CSV
ORDER BY time DESC
    ---Ch04CounterDrill.sql---
```

If you prefer scripting, here is a Windows Shell equivalent.

```
---Ch04LP_perfmon.cmd---
@echo off

if "%1"=="" goto :usage
if "%1"=="-h" goto :usage
if "%1"=="/h" goto :usage
if "%1"=="-?" goto :usage
if "%1"=="/?" goto :usage

REM setup variables
set countername=
set filename=%1
set %filename%=filename

REM make a temp directory and cleanup old ones
```

```
if exist ~lptemp rd ~lptemp /S /Q
md ~lptemp

REM get Column Names onto separate lines
@logparser.exe file:Ch04Top1.sql -q:on -i:csv -o:csv -headerrow:off -headers:off
@logparser.exe file:Ch04CRLF.sql -q:on -i:textline -headers:off -oDQuotes:OFF -o:csv

REM loop through the perfmon file and get the Average/MIN/MAX
FOR /F "skip=3 delims=," %%f in (.\~lptemp\counterlist2.csv) do (
set countername=
set countername=%%f
set %%countername%%=countername
@logparser.exe file:Ch04AVG.sql -q:on -i:csv
@logparser.exe file: Ch04MAX.sql -q:on -i:csv
@logparser.exe file: Ch04MIN.sql -q:on -i:csv)

REM Clean Up
echo cleaning up temp files
rd ~lptemp /S /Q

goto :eof

:usage
@echo Ch04LP_perfmon.cmd (CSVfilename.cmd)
goto :eof
:eof
@echo on
Include files for the previous example:
---Ch04Top1.sql---
SELECT
        TOP 1 *
FROM    %filename%
TO      .\~lptemp\counterlist1.csv
---Ch04LP_perfmon.cmd---
--- Ch04CRLF.sql---
SELECT
        REPLACE_CHR(Text,',','\u000a')
FROM    .\~lptemp\counterlist1.csv
TO      .\~lptemp\counterlist2.csv
--- Ch04CRLF.sql---
--- Ch04AVG.sql---
SELECT
        'Average',
        '%countername%',
        AVG(TO_INT([%countername%]))
FROM    %filename%
--- Ch04AVG.sql---
```

```
---Ch04MAX.sql---
SELECT
        'Maximum',
        '%countername%',
        MAX(TO_REAL([%countername%]))
FROM    %filename%
---Ch04MAX.sql---
---Ch04MIN.sql---
SELECT
        'Minimum',
        '%countername%',
        MIN(TO_REAL([%countername%]))
FROM    %filename%
---Ch04MAX.sql---
```

TIP

Windows NT performance counters usually display a very long name with spaces and punctuation included as identifiers. To avoid parsing errors, encapsulate these names in brackets [] as shown in the aforementioned code for Log Parser to correctly identify them as valid column names, for example,
`[\\serverName\Memory\Page Faults/sec]`.

Advanced Graphing Windows NT Performance Data with Log Parser

The Windows NT performance monitor is a good tool for gathering data and generating simple views, but deep analysis of performance logs with multiple data points may prove to be too much for the Perfmon interface, as it mainly supports linear graphs and is designed more for real-time monitoring. Here is a script that will use LogMan and Log Parser to pull virtual memory data for all processes on a system and aggregate it into files that are then graphed to show the data visually.

TIP

Log Parser does not support parsing column names as previously mentioned. In order for this example to work, the columns (an the performance counters that they represent) collected per process must be in the same order in each NT performance log file for the columns to line up correctly and show the correct aggregated data. In this case, we only have one data column, so that simplifies the process.

```
---Ch04CreateLog.cmd---
@echo off

if "%1"=="/?" goto :usage
if "%1"=="" goto :usage

REM drop the countergroup if it exists
@echo stopping and deleting any old copies of the logset...
logman stop %1>nul
logman delete %1>nul
REM create a new set
logman create counter %1 -cf %1 -rf 00:00:02 -o c:\perflogs\ -si 00:00:01 -f csv --v
REM start the set for 2 seconds and then stop
goto :eof
:usage
ECHO Ch04CreateLog.cmd {NTCounterlistFile}
ECHO Example: Ch04CreateLog.cmd Ch04taskman
goto :eof

:eof
@echo on
---Ch04CreateLog.cmd---
---Ch04LP_PerProcess.cmd---
@echo off

if "%1"=="" goto :usage
if "%1"=="-h" goto :usage
if "%1"=="/h" goto :usage
if "%1"=="-?" goto :usage
if "%1"=="/?" goto :usage

setlocal ENABLEDELAYEDEXPANSION

REM setup variables

set vALL=
set filename=%1
set %filename%=filename

REM make a temp directory and cleanup old ones
if exist ~lptemp rd ~lptemp /S /Q
md ~lptemp

REM get Column Names onto separate lines
logparser.exe file:Ch04Top1.sql -q:on -i:csv -o:csv -headerrow:off -headers:off
```

```
logparser.exe file:Ch04CRLF.sql -q:on -i:textline -headers:off -oDQuotes:OFF -o:csv
logparser.exe file:Ch04GetProcess.sql -q:on -i:textline  -headers:off -oDQuotes:OFF -o:csv


REM get numbers
REM get the processname
REM and then get the counternames for that process
REM it is best to control the counters with what is gathered -- see logman portion
for /f "delims=," %%w in (.\~lptemp\Processlist.csv) do (logparser -q:on -i:textline
"select Text from .\~lptemp\counterlist2.csv to .\~lptemp\%%w.txt where
SUBSTR(EXTRACT_TOKEN(Text,1,'\Process('),0,INDEX_OF(EXTRACT_TOKEN(Text, 1, '\Process('
),')')')) = '%%w'"
REM aggregate the variables together
for /f "delims=;" %%z in (.\~lptemp\%%w.txt) do set vALL=!vALL!Avg^(TO_INT^(^[%%z^]^)^)^,
set vall=!vall:~0,-1!
REM query for the average value in the perflog
logparser -q:on -i:csv -o:csv "select !vALL! from %filename% to .\~lptemp\%%w.csv"
set vall=)


REM cleaning up list files
Del .\~lptemp\counterlist1.csv
Del .\~lptemp\counterlist2.csv
Del .\~lptemp\processlist.csv


REM graph the files
LogParser file:CH04graph.sql -i:csv -headerrow:off -nSkipLines:1 -Charttype:BarClustered -
view:on -GroupSize:800x600


REM Clean Up
REM read out the files we just did - use this if you want to keep
REM the tempfiles below and comment out the RD command
REM @echo files written:
REM @for /f %%q in (.\~lptemp\processlist.csv) do dir .\~lptemp\%%q.csv /b
ECHO cleaning up the rest of the temp files
rd ~lptemp /S /Q
goto :eof


:usage
@echo Ch04LP_PerProcess.cmd (CSVfilename.cmd)
goto :eof


:eof
@echo on
---Ch04LP_PerProcess.cmd---
---Ch04log_vbytes---
"\Process(*)\Virtual Bytes"
---Ch04log_vbytes---
```

```
---Ch04GetProcess.sql---
SELECT
        DISTINCT SUBSTR(EXTRACT_TOKEN(Text, 1, '\Process('),0,INDEX_OF(EXTRACT_TOKEN(Text,
1, '\Process(' ),')')'))
FROM   .\~lptemp\counterlist2.csv
TO     .\~lptemp\Processlist.csv
---Ch04GetProcess.sql---
---Ch04Graph.sql---
SELECT
        EXTRACT_TOKEN( EXTRACT_TOKEN(Filename, -1, '\\'), 0, '.') AS ProcessName,
        Field1 AS VirtualMemoryUsage
INTO   allvm.gif
FROM   ~lptemp\*.csv
ORDER BY VirtualMemoryUsage DESC
---Ch04Graph.sql---
```

The output of this is shown in Figure 4.2.

Figure 4.2 Output of Ch04LP_PerProcess.cmd

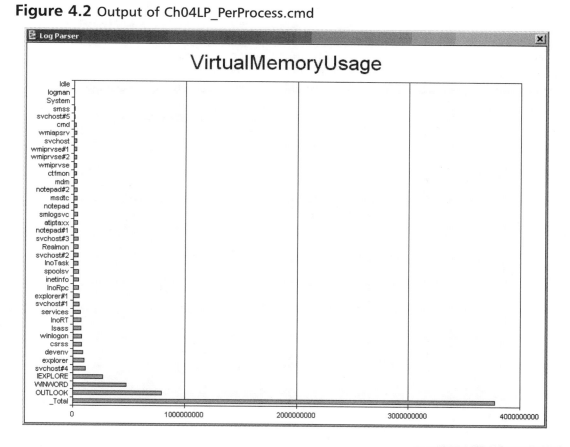

TIP

This goes without saying, but since I know many of you will chain these scripts together to make this a one command process, here is one caveat – the log collection happens silently: make sure you leave enough time for the logs to finish collecting data before you query them or you might get odd results. You can check to see if it is running or not by using LogMan.exe QUERY (logsetName). You can also use tools like SLEEP.exe to add artificial pauses in NT .cmd scripts between programs.

Final Touches

The ability to read such low level formats is a testament to the flexible, generic nature of Log Parser. While many other programs and scripts can be used to examine log files, Log Parser's native support of the Netmon format set it apart in many important ways. Ordinary scripts and parsers simply cannot read these files reliably. Where and while Netmon can read it, it cannot read and display the data in the incredibly flexible ways that Log Parser can. Similarly, many programs can read NT performance logs, but not with the unique extensibility and power of Log Parser. Hopefully these Netmon examples will inspire administrators to look more at the low levels of their network to leverage this existing functionality in a much more flexible and simple way than ever before. As for the NT performance logs, hopefully those giant files that are delivered do not look as intimidating as they once did, but rather appear as an opportunity to settle a problem once and for all.

Chapter 5

Managing Snort Alerts

Scripts and Samples in this Chapter

- **Gathering Snort Logs**
- **Building an Alerts Detail Report**
- **Building an Alerts Overview Report**
- **Managing Snort Rules**

In This Toolbox

Snort is an open source intrusion detection system (IDS) used in a wide variety of network environments. Snort is a lightweight, but extremely powerful tool for detecting malicious traffic on your network. With a flexible and robust rules definition language, Snort is capable of detecting nearly any threat that crosses your network.

However, if you use Snort, you already know that reporting is not its strength. On a busy network you might find that it records tens or hundreds of thousands of suspicious events every day. Fortunately, Log Parser is a perfect match for Snort for managing intrusion detection logs.

Building Snort IDS Reports

An intrusion detection system is only valuable if you review and act on the data it produces. Unfortunately, sometimes an IDS will produce overwhelming amounts of data that make it difficult to process. To aid in our interpretation of the data, we can use Log Parser to take snapshots of our IDS logs and present them in different easy-to-read reports. In this chapter, we will build an example IDS report using nothing more than the power of Log Parser.

Gathering Snort Logs

To process the alert data, we first need a consistent method for gathering the data. Log Parser is an excellent method for managing Snort logs because you can query the file while Snort still has the log open. Many administrators schedule scripts to regularly cycle the Snort logs, but this requires stopping the service to release the file so a script can move it. Using Log Parser, we can use checkpoints to read the most recent data from the file.

Although Snort supports several output formats that Log Parser could use, I have found the CSV format most flexible and consistent. To configure Snort to use the CSV output format, simply add the following line in the snort.conf file:

```
output alert_csv: alert.csv default
```

This configures Snort to create a CSV log file named alert.csv in the configured logs directory using the default output fields. By default the CSV output processor includes these fields:

- timestamp
- sig_generator
- sig_id
- sig_rev
- msg
- proto
- src

- srcport
- dst
- dstport
- ethsrc
- ethdst
- ethlen
- tcpfags

- tcpseq
- tcpack
- tcplen
- tcpwindow
- ttl
- tos
- id

- dgmlen
- iplen
- icmptype
- icmpcode
- icmpid
- icmpseq

Snort CSV logs do not include a header row, so we need a separate file to name each column. In the file download for this chapter, I have included the file AlertHeader.csv to use for this purpose. To read CSV Snort alerts, you would use a command like this:

```
logparser.exe file:alert.sql -i:csv -headerRow:off  -iHeaderFile:AlertHeader.csv -
iTsFormat:mm/dd/yy-hh:mm:ss
```

Note that we specify the CSV input format, but instead of using the header row, we specify a header file using the **iHeaderFile** option. We also specify the timestamp format so Log Parser can interpret that field as an actual time stamp rather than a string.

NOTE

All of the queries in this chapter use the year in the timestamp date, which Snort does not log by default. To configure Snort to log the year, use the –**y** option when starting Snort. If your timestamps do not include the year, the queries in this chapter will return the error, "Semantic Error: argument of function TO_TIME must be a TIMESTAMP."

Building an Alerts Detail Report

In our IDS report we likely want to view summaries of the alert data such as:

- Most common alerts
- Most common source IP (Internet Protocol) addresses
- Most common target IP addresses

Using Log Parser's multiplex feature and template output format we can very easily create interactive HTML (Hypertext Markup Language) reports directly from the Snort logs.

Most Common Alerts

To begin our report, we will create HTML pages for the most common alerts. We will start with an index page showing the most common alert messages. Each line will have a link to a more detailed HTML page listing individual alerts with that message. The query for the index page is simple:

```
---Ch05Alerts-Index.sql---
SELECT DISTINCT
    sig_id,
    msg,
    Count(msg) as Alerts
INTO report\alerts.html
FROM alert.csv
GROUP BY msg, sig_id
ORDER BY Alerts DESC
---Ch05Alerts-Index.sql---
```

The key component here is the so much the query but the output template:

```
---Ch05Alerts-Index.tpl---
<LPHEADER>
    <html>
    <head>
        <meta http-equiv="Content-Type" content="text/html; charset=windows-1252">
        <link rel="stylesheet" type="text/css" href="snort.css">
        <title>Snort Alert Messages</title>
    </head>
    <body>
    <p><h1>Snort Alerts Summary</h1><br/>
    <i>Created %SYSTEM_TIMESTAMP% </i></p>
            <table border="0" width="75%" cellspacing="2">
            <tr>
                <th><b>Signature</b></th>
                <th><b>Message</b></th>
                <th><b>Alerts</b></th>
            </tr>
</LPHEADER>
<LPBODY>
            <tr>
                <td><a href=http://www.snort.org/snort-
db/sid.html?sid=%sig_id%> %sig_id%</a></td>
                <td> %msg%</td>
                <td><a href=alert\%sig_id%.html> %Alerts%</a></td>
            </tr>
</LPBODY>
<LPFOOTER>
        </table>
```

```
    </p>
    </body>
    </html>
</LPFOOTER>
---Ch05Alerts-Index.tpl---
```

You can run the query using the output template using this command:

```
logparser.exe file:Ch05Alerts-Index.sql -i:csv -iHeaderFile:AlertHeader.csv -
iTsFormat:mm/dd/yy-hh:mm:ss -headerRow:off -o:tpl -tpl:Ch05Alerts-Index.tpl
```

Run this command and in a matter of seconds you should have a file named alerts.html that looks like the one shown in Figure 5.1. Note that the report lists the alerts in order, starting with the most common messages. If you click on the signature ID, it will jump to the reference page at www.snort.org. Note that the alert total is also a hyperlink, but we have not created that page yet. We now need to run another query to generate log details for each alert message.

Figure 5.1 Snort Alert Messages Summary

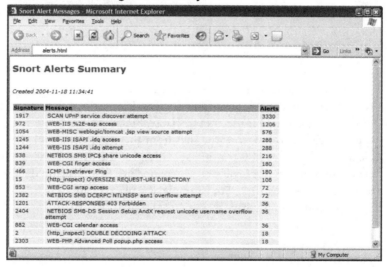

Creating a detail page for every individual message is surprisingly simple:

```
---Ch05Alerts-Detail.sql---
SELECT
    sig_id,
    TO_TIME(timestamp) AS Time,
    msg,
    proto,
    src,
    srcport,
```

```
       dst,
       dstport,
       ethsrc,
       ethdst,
       ethlen,
       tcpflags,
       tcpseq,
       tcpack,
       tcplen,
       tcpwindow,
       ttl,
       tos,
       id,
       dgmlen,
       iplen,
       icmptype,
       icmpcode,
       icmpid,
       icmpseq
INTO report\alert\*.html
FROM alert.csv
---Ch05Alerts-Detail.sql---
```

This query takes advantage of Log Parser's multiplex feature and creates a unique output file for each unique value of **sig_id**, the first field in the query. It uses this value in place of the asterisk (*) in the filename specified on the INTO clause. Since we use the signature ID in the output filename, it is easy for us to link to those files from the main alert.html page.

For the alert detail pages, I wanted use a title at the top of the page showing the particular alert message, as shown in Figure 5.2. However, you cannot use field placeholders in the LPHEADER portion of the template file. For example, if I placed **%msg%** in the LPHEADER, each page would simply have %msg% as the title.

Figure 5.2 Detailed Alert Messages.

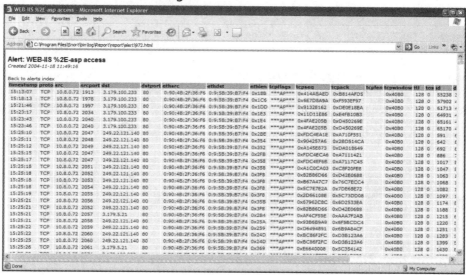

Nevertheless, sometimes a little creativity can make up for Log Parser's limitations. To write the individual titles, I actually run the query twice, once to write the headers and again to write the detail information. For the first pass I use this query and template file:

```
---Ch05Alerts-DetailHeader.sql---
SELECT DISTINCT
      sig_id,
      msg
INTO report\alert\*.html
FROM alert.csv
---Ch05Alerts-DetailHeader.sql---


---Ch05Alerts-DetailHeader.tlp---
<LPBODY>
        <html>
        <head>
        <meta http-equiv="Content-Type" content="text/html; charset=windows-1252">
        <link rel="stylesheet" type="text/css" href="..\snort.css">
        <title>%msg%</title>
        </head>
        <body>
        <p><b><font face="Arial" size="3">Alert: %msg%</font></b><br/>
        <i>Created %SYSTEM_TIMESTAMP% </i></p>
        <a href=..\alerts.html>Back to alerts index</a>
</LPBODY>
```

```
---Ch05Alerts-DetailHeader.tlp---
```

Run the query with this command:

```
logparser.exe file:Ch05Alerts-DetailHeader.sql -i:csv -iHeaderFile:AlertHeader.csv -
iTsFormat:mm/dd/yy-hh:mm:ss -headerRow:off -o:tpl -tpl:Ch05Alerts-DetailHeader.tpl
```

The query first pulls the **sig_id** and **msg** and creates a unique file for each **sig_id** and writes a header using **msg** in the LPBODY. At this point we have a set of files with nothing but a header. Next, we run another set of queries using Ch05Alerts-Detail.sql and this template:

```
---Ch05Alerts-Detail.tpl---
<LPHEADER>
                              <table border="0" width="100%" cellspacing="2">
                              <tr>
                                      <th><b>timestamp</b></th>
                                      <th><b>proto</b></th>
                                      <th><b>src</b></th>
                                      <th><b>srcport</b></th>
                                      <th><b>dst</b></th>
                                      <th><b>dstport</b></th>
                                      <th><b>ethsrc</b></th>
                                      <th><b>ethdst</b></th>
                                      <th><b>ethlen</b></th>
                                      <th><b>tcpflags</b></th>
                                      <th><b>tcpseq</b></th>
                                      <th><b>tcpack</b></th>
                                      <th><b>tcplen</b></th>
                                      <th><b>tcpwindow</b></th>
                                      <th><b>ttl</b></th>
                                      <th><b>tos</b></th>
                                      <th><b>id</b></th>
                                      <th><b>dgmlen</b></th>
                                      <th><b>iplen</b></th>
                                      <th><b>icmptype</b></th>
                                      <th><b>icmpcode</b></th>
                                      <th><b>icmpid</b></th>
                                      <th><b>icmpseq</b></th>
                              </tr>
</LPHEADER>
<LPBODY>
                              <tr>
                                  <td> %time%</td>
                                      <td> %proto%</td>
                                      <td> <a href=..\src\%src%.html>%src%</a></td>
                                      <td> %srcport%</td>
                                      <td> <a href=..\dst\%dst%.html>%dst%</a></td>
```

```
                    <td> %dstport%</td>
                    <td> %ethsrc%</td>
                    <td> %ethdst%</td>
                    <td> %ethlen%</td>
                    <td> %tcpflags%</td>
                    <td> %tcpseq%</td>
                    <td> %tcpack%</td>
                    <td> %tcplen%</td>
                    <td> %tcpwindow%</td>
                    <td> %ttl%</td>
                    <td> %tos%</td>
                    <td> %id%</td>
                    <td> %dgmlen%</td>
                    <td> %iplen%</td>
                    <td> %icmptype%</td>
                    <td> %icmpcode%</td>
                    <td> %icmpid%</td>
                    <td> %icmpseq%</td>
                </tr>
</LPBODY>
<LPFOOTER>

                </table>
            </p>
            </body>
            </html>
</LPFOOTER>
---Ch05Alerts-Detail.tp---
```

This time when we run the query, we use this command:

```
logparser.exe file:Ch05Alerts-Detail.sql -i:csv -iHeaderFile:AlertHeader.csv -
iTsFormat:mm/dd/yy-hh:mm:ss -headerRow:off -o:tpl -tpl:Ch05Alerts-Detail.tpl -fileMode:0
```

Note that I used **–fileMode:0** in the command to instruct Log Parser to append to the files rather than overwrite them. In this pass, Log Parser will take the files already containing titles and append the alert details as shown earlier in Figure 5.2. The two-pass approach will obviously slow down report creation time with very large alert files, but it is still surprisingly effective for most purposes.

 TIP

If you find that the two-pass approach is too slow, another option is to use Log Parser as a COM component in a script and process each output record individually.

Alerts by IP Address

Each IP address in the alerts report shown in Figure 5.2 is a clickable hyperlink that leads to a detail page showing all alerts for that IP address. Using a process similar to that used previously for the alert messages, I created a summary page (Figure 5.3), and detail pages (Figure 5.4) using a two-pass approach. I repeated this process for both source and destination IP addresses to produce a fully interactive HTML IDS report. At this point, you can run the entire report with these Log Parser commands:

```
logparser.exe file:Ch05Alerts-Index.sql -i:csv -iHeaderFile:AlertHeader.csv -
iTsFormat:mm/dd/yy-hh:mm:ss -headerRow:off -o:tpl -tpl:Ch05Alerts-Index.tpl

logparser.exe file:Ch05Alerts-DetailHeader.sql -i:csv -iHeaderFile:AlertHeader.csv -
iTsFormat:mm/dd/yy-hh:mm:ss -headerRow:off -o:tpl -tpl:Ch05Alerts-DetailHeader.tpl

logparser.exe file:Ch05Alerts-Detail.sql -i:csv -iHeaderFile:AlertHeader.csv -
iTsFormat:mm/dd/yy-hh:mm:ss -headerRow:off -o:tpl -tpl:Ch05Alerts-Detail.tpl -fileMode:0

logparser.exe file:Ch05SrcIP-Index.sql -i:csv -iHeaderFile:AlertHeader.csv -
iTsFormat:mm/dd/yy-hh:mm:ss -headerRow:off -o:tpl -tpl:Ch05SrcIP-Index.tpl

logparser.exe file:Ch05SrcIP-DetailHeader.sql -i:csv -iHeaderFile:AlertHeader.csv -
iTsFormat:mm/dd/yy-hh:mm:ss -headerRow:off -o:tpl -tpl:Ch05SrcIP-DetailHeader.tpl

logparser.exe file:Ch05SrcIP-Detail.sql -i:csv -iHeaderFile:AlertHeader.csv -
iTsFormat:mm/dd/yy-hh:mm:ss -headerRow:off -o:tpl -tpl:Ch05SrcIP-Detail.tpl -fileMode:0

logparser.exe file:Ch05DstIP-Index.sql -i:csv -iHeaderFile:AlertHeader.csv -
iTsFormat:mm/dd/yy-hh:mm:ss -headerRow:off -o:tpl -tpl:Ch05DstIP-Index.tpl

logparser.exe file:Ch05DstIP-DetailHeader.sql -i:csv -iHeaderFile:AlertHeader.csv -
iTsFormat:mm/dd/yy-hh:mm:ss -headerRow:off -o:tpl -tpl:Ch05DstIP-DetailHeader.tpl

logparser.exe file:Ch05DstIP-Detail.sql -i:csv -iHeaderFile:AlertHeader.csv -
iTsFormat:mm/dd/yy-hh:mm:ss -headerRow:off -o:tpl -tpl:Ch05DstIP-Detail.tpl -fileMode:0
```

Figure 5.3 Snort Alerts by Destination IP Address

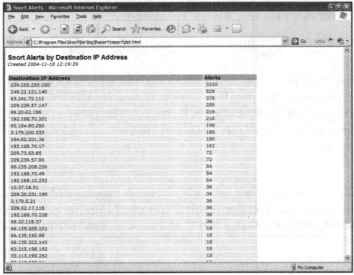

Figure 5.4 IP Address Details

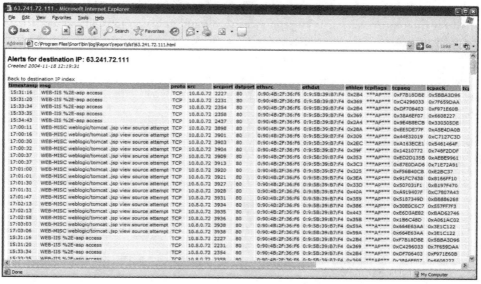

Building an Alerts Overview Report

Now that we have a detailed alerts report, we might want to build a summary index page. This page should include links to the detailed reports and also display graphs and short summaries of the data to get a quick overview of the network. Figure 5.5 shows the final report.

Figure 5.5 Snort Alerts Summary

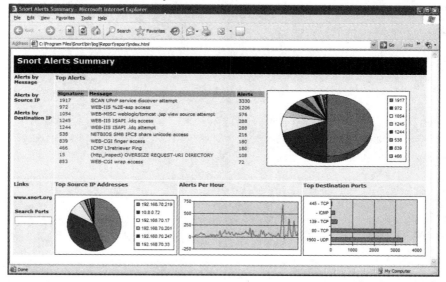

Since the summary report includes only one table of data with multiple graphs, I placed the entire HTML markup in a single template file, Ch05Summary-Index.tpl. This template creates the HTML for the report that includes references to the individual graphs. The query for the top alerts is similar to that used for the alerts index page, but only includes the top 10 records:

```
---Ch05Summary-Index.sql---
SELECT TOP 10
    sig_id,
    msg,
    Count(msg) as Alerts
INTO report\index.html
FROM alert.csv
GROUP BY msg, sig_id
ORDER BY Alerts DESC
---Ch05Summary-Index.sql---
```

The query for the pie graph is similar, but does not include the actual message and this time processes all records:

```
---Ch05Summary-GraphTopAlerts.sql---
SELECT
    sig_id,
    Count(msg) as Alerts
INTO report\AlertsTopAlerts.gif
FROM alert.csv
GROUP BY sig_id
ORDER BY Alerts DESC
---Ch05Summary-GraphTopAlerts.sql---
```

Finally, there are three queries for the remaining graphs:

```
---Ch05Summary-GraphTopSrcIPs.sql---
SELECT
    src,
    Count(msg) as Alerts
INTO report\AlertsTopSrcIPs.gif
FROM alert.csv
GROUP BY src
ORDER BY Alerts DESC
---Ch05Summary-GraphTopSrcIPs.sql---


---Ch05Summary-GraphAlertsPerHour.sql---
SELECt
    Count(*) as Alerts
USING QUANTIZE(timestamp,360) as Hour
INTO report\AlertsByHour.gif
FROM alert.csv
```

```
GROUP BY Hour
---Ch05Summary-GraphAlertsPerHour.sql---


---Ch05Summary-GraphTopDstPorts.sql---
SELECT TOP 5
    STRCAT(STRCAT(TO_STRING(dstport),' - '), proto) AS Destination,
    Count(*) as Alerts
    USING dst as DestinationPort
INTO report\AlertsTopDstPorts.gif
FROM alert.csv
GROUP BY Destination
ORDER BY Alerts DESC
---Ch05Summary-GraphTopDstPorts.sql---
```

Finally, we can generate the entire index page with these commands:

```
logparser.exe file:Ch05Summary-Index.sql -i:csv -iHeaderFile:AlertHeader.csv -
iTsFormat:mm/dd/yy-hh:mm:ss -headerRow:off -o:tpl -tpl:Ch05Summary-Index.tpl
logparser.exe file:Ch05Summary-GraphTopAlerts.sql -i:csv -iHeaderFile:AlertHeader.csv -
iTsFormat:mm/dd/yy-hh:mm:ss -headerRow:off -o:chart -chartType:Pie3D -groupSize:350x190 -
values:OFF -chartTitle:"" -categories:OFF
logparser.exe file:Ch05Summary-GraphTopSrcIPs.sql -i:csv -iHeaderFile:AlertHeader.csv -
iTsFormat:mm/dd/yy-hh:mm:ss -headerRow:off -o:chart -chartType:Pie -groupSize:300x150 -
values:OFF -chartTitle:"" -categories:OFF
logparser.exe file:Ch05Summary-GraphAlertsPerHour.sql -i:csv -iHeaderFile:AlertHeader.csv
-iTsFormat:mm/dd/yy-hh:mm:ss -headerRow:off -o:chart -chartType:smoothline -
groupSize:300x150 -values:OFF -chartTitle:"" -categories:OFF
logparser.exe file:Ch05Summary-GraphTopDstPorts.sql -i:csv -iHeaderFile:AlertHeader.csv -
iTsFormat:mm/dd/yy-hh:mm:ss -headerRow:off -o:chart -chartType:BarStacked -
groupSize:300x150 -values:OFF -chartTitle:""
```

The final result is a fully interactive IDS report using nothing more than Log Parser.

NOTE

You can create the entire report shown here using the CreateReport.cmd batch file
included with the file download for this chapter.

Managing Snort Rules

Log Parser complements Snort with more than just reporting. Log Parser's powerful parsing features make it an ideal tool for managing and updating Snort rule definitions.

Snort's intrusion detection engine is nothing more than a network sniffer. The rule definitions are what give it the ability to identify attack patterns. For Snort to be most effective, you should customize the rules for your particular environment. You should also keep it up to date with the most recent rule definitions.

Snort uses dozens of rule files, each categorized by attack category. You might find it useful to combine these rules into a single file for easier management. Because Log Parser can easily read and parse all files in a directory, rule management is simple.

The following query reads all rule files in a directory and sorts them by the signature ID, removing any duplicate rules you might have:

```
---Ch05RulesBySID.sql---
SELECT DISTINCT
    TO_INT(EXTRACT_VALUE(Params, 'sid')) AS SID,
    Rule
USING
    Field1 AS Rule,
REPLACE_STR(REPLACE_CHR(SUBSTR(Rule,ADD(INDEX_OF(Rule,'('),1),LAST_INDEX_OF(Rule,')')),':'
,'='),'; ','&') AS Params,
INTO all.rules
FROM *.rules
ORDER BY SID
---Ch05RulesBySID.sql---


---Ch05RulesBySID.tpl---
<LPHEADER>
#----------------------------------------------------------
# Snort Rules sorted by SID
#       Generated %SYSTEM_TIMESTAMP%
# by %USERDOMAIN%\%USERNAME%
#----------------------------------------------------------

</LPHEADER>
<LPBODY>%Rule%
</LPBODY>
---Ch05RulesBySID.tpl---
```

Run this query with the following command:

```
logparser file:Ch05Rulesbysid.sql -i:tsv -headerRow:off -lineFilter:-# -o:tpl -
tpl:Ch05RulesBySID.tpl
```

Note in the query that I did not use SUBSTR and INDEX_OF to extract the **sid** value, but rather used the replace functions to make the parameters look like a URL (Uniform Resource Locator) query string. This allows me to use the EXTRCT_VALUE functions to easily grab any value I want from the rule. Note also that I used a template file rather than outputting directly to a file. This is so I can include a comment header but also because I want to sort by SID, but not include the value in the output. You cannot sort by a field specified in the USING clause.

Using this same technique, you might find it useful to create a rules reference page. This query reads all rule definitions and generates the HTML reference page shown in Figure 5.6:

```
---Ch05RulesRef.sql---
SELECT DISTINCT
    TO_INT(EXTRACT_VALUE(Params, 'sid')) AS SID,
        EXTRACT_VALUE(Params, 'classtype') AS Category,
        REPLACE_CHR(EXTRACT_VALUE(Params, 'msg'),'"','') AS Message,
        Rule
USING
        Field1 AS Rule,

REPLACE_STR(REPLACE_CHR(SUBSTR(Rule,ADD(INDEX_OF(Rule,'('),1),LAST_INDEX_OF(Rule,')'))),':'
,'='),'; ','&') AS Params
INTO Rules.htm
FROM *.rules
ORDER BY SID
---Ch05RulesRef.sql---


---Ch05RulesRef.tpl---
<LPHEADER>
        <html>
        <head>
                <meta http-equiv="Content-Type" content="text/html; charset=windows-
1252">
                <title>Snort Rules Reference</title>
                <style>
<!--
H1 {
        font : bold 14pt Verdana, Geneva, Arial, Helvetica, sans-serif;
        color : #4A4322;
        }
TD {
        COLOR: Black; FONT: 11px Verdana, arial, geneva, helvetica, sans-serif;
                        border : 0px solid #EBE7D3;
                        vertical-align : top;
                        background-color : #EBE7D3;
                        }
TH {
        COLOR: Black; FONT: 11px  Verdana, arial, geneva, helvetica, sans-serif;
        background-color : #9F9B64;
        text-align : left;
}
-->
</style>
        </head>
        <body>
        <h1>Snort Rules Reference</h1><br/>
```

www.syngress.com

```
                        <table border="0" width="75%" cellspacing="2">
                        <tr>
                                <th><b>Signature</b></th>
                                <th><b>Message</b></th>
                                <th><b>Category</b></th>
                        </tr>
</LPHEADER>
<LPBODY>

                        <tr>
                                <td><a href=http://www.snort.org/snort-
db/sid.html?sid=%SID%> %SID%</a></td>
                            <td> %Message%</td>
                                <td>%Category%</td>
                        </tr>
</LPBODY>
<LPFOOTER>
                </table>
        </p>
        </body>
        </html>
</LPFOOTER>
---Ch05RulesRef.tpl---
```

Run this query with the following command:

```
logparser file:ch05RulesRef.sql -i:tsv -headerRow:off -lineFilter:-# -o:tpl -
tpl:Ch05RulesRef.tpl
```

Figure 5.6 Snort Rules Reference

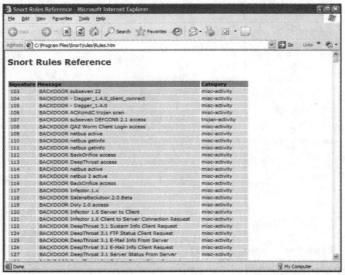

Log Parser has a powerful feature that allows you to parse files directly from a URL. You can use this feature to download new Snort rule definitions. The following command downloads the newest Bleeding Snort rules from www.bleedingsnort.com.

```
logparser "SELECT Field1 INTO bleeding.rules FROM http://www.bleedingsnort.com/bleeding-
all.rules" -i:tsv -headerRow:off -o:tsv -headers:off
```

Of course, once you download the rules, you can merge and sort them as shown previously in this chapter.

Final Touches

As you can see, Log Parser is a powerful addition to Snort, both for reporting and for rules management. In very little time and using nothing more than Log Parser itself, you can create elaborate interactive HTML reports to view and drill down through thousands of IDS alerts. With Log Parser's charting features, you can view the data from different angles to help identify high priority alerts.

Chapter 6

Managing Log Files

Scripts and Samples in this Chapter:

- **Log File Conversion**
- **Log Rotation and Archival**
- **Separating Logs**

In This Toolbox

Log files are the most critical source of data for most of your information technology systems. As such, they need to be properly managed. There are several areas to focus on when managing log files including conversion, rotation, archival, and separation. In this chapter we will be going over each of these primary areas of focus and showing you some techniques you can use to best manage your log files.

Log File Conversion

When managing log files from various systems, it quickly becomes apparent that just about every vendor of software or hardware wants to use their own format for log file data. Some log files are stored in plain text and some in binary format. Some include tab-separated data and others simply drop whatever information comes in next to the next line in the file. In order to work with all of these files, most technical professionals must learn the formats used for the log files of each application or piece of hardware that they work with regularly.

With Log Parser, there is a new way to work with log file data. Rather than dealing with several different formats of log data, Log Parser allows you to convert log file data to another format. This conversion process goes a long way to making log file data accessible to more people because you can convert the log data into a format that they are familiar with. Throughout this section, we will be going over some conversion techniques and show you some techniques you can use after the conversion to perform better analysis.

Standardizing Log Formats

The first step in log file conversion is to decide on a standard format of log file that will work best for you and the other technical people you work with regularly. Log parser supports many different formats including CSV, TSV, XML, DATAGRID, CHART, SYSLOG, NAT, W3C, IIS, SQL, and TPL. Some of these formats such as DATAGRID, CHART, and NAT are intended for immediate display or presenting a graph and are not appropriate for conversion or standardization efforts. Each of the other formats presents some value in standardization.

Choosing the format that is right for you is completely dependant on your needs and the formats that you understand the easiest. For example, if you are well versed in working with the SYSLOG format, then it would be best for you to standardize on that specific format. Each of the available formats store the data in a slightly different way and some are better for specific purposes than others. For example, you could easily open up a CSV file in Excel and work with the data whereas a W3C file wouldn't give you that option.

All of the specific syntax for each Log Parser output file is included in the program itself and in our quick reference guide so we won't be going through every option for every format in this chapter. However, we will go over a quick overview of each format and give some examples of how to perform these conversions in a couple different ways.

First up are the CSV and TSV formats. These are the *comma-separated values* and *tab-separated values* formats, respectively. Each of these formats will output a plain text file that separates the values for each column with either a comma or a tab. The TSV format will also let you use more than just tabs for the separator. You can actually use tabs, spaces, or any specific string in this format by specifying what separator you'd like to use in the Log Parser command line. This allows for a great deal of flexibility in your TSV format.

XML is a very powerful format that Log Parser supports for output. XML allows you a huge amount of flexibility in both the output of your specific data as well as the format that the data is displayed in when you later display the results. Log Parser allows you to use multiple XML structures, specify the schema for the XML, and even use a UNICODE or non-UNICODE codepage. Many applications are moving to XML as a standard for data output and data conversion and Log Parser's support of this format is very well implemented.

The SYSLOG format is incredibly useful for enterprises that are moving towards using Syslog servers for monitoring log and informational data from all pieces of the corporate infrastructure. When using a Syslog server, you have a single point of reference for everything that is happening in your environment and Log Parser supports the use of this type of monitoring. By using the SYSLOG format, Log Parser will send your converted log file data directly to a Syslog server and format it in a method that the server will understand.

The W3C format is the same format that IIS (Internet Information Server) now uses by default for its log files and many applications have been written to read and interpret this log file format. Log Parser allows you to convert log data into the W3C Extended Format File specification and subsequent programs that support this format can then read data that has been converted from other sources. This would allow you to perform standardization of log files and use existing log utilities to read the result.

Log Parser's IIS Log Format supports the older format that Internet Information Server used to use for its logging. This format has been mostly replaced with the W3C format, but some companies still prefer to use the original IIS format so that existing third-party programs supporting this format can remain in use. Consequently, Log Parser supports this format and will allow you to convert your log file data to IIS Log Format if you so choose.

The SQL format allows you to convert your log file data into a SQL table and store it in a relational database. This capability is a huge step forward in the concepts of log file storage and correlation and will be covered extensively in another chapter.

Finally, FileTemplate Output Format, or TPL, allows you to output the format of your converted data based on a specific user-defined template. By specifying a template file for the output, you can generate reports and reformat log file data to fit a specific need. While this isn't typically used for standardization of the actual data, it can be used for standardization of your data output.

All of the formats we've gone over can be used as your own standard format to convert your log files to. Whichever format you choose, Log Parser will allow you to take existing log file data from many sources and convert it over to your standard format to be viewed and analyzed. This capability will help you a great deal in simplifying the task of viewing data from multiple log sources and give you a single formatting style to work with.

To see how this is done, let's go through a quick example. Let's assume that you have some data stored in the W3C format from IIS that you wish to standardize to correspond with some of your other log file data. To standardize the format of your log files, you want to convert the W3C format to XML. This is done through the use of a couple simple commands with Log Parser. To convert the W3C data, we simply use the following command:

```
logparser.exe file:Ch06ConvertW3CtoXML.sql -i:W3C
```

```
--- Ch06ConvertW3CtoXML.sql ---
SELECT
    *
INTO ex041008.xml
FROM ex041008.log
--- Ch06ConvertW3CtoXML.sql ---
```

When you run this command (against valid log files), you will end up with a new XML file that contains all of the data from your original W3C file. The SQL used for this can be further refined to only include records that show errors for example. If we want a list of all errors converted to XML, we could use this code instead:

```
Logparser.exe file:Ch06ConvertW3CErrorstoXML.sql -i:W3C
```

```
--- Ch06ConvertW3CErrorstoXML.sql ---
SELECT
    *
INTO ex041008.xml
FROM ex041008.log
WHERE sc-status >= 400
--- Ch06ConvertW3CErrorstoXML.sql ---
```

After running this conversion, you will have a file named ex041008.xml that contains only the errors from your original W3C log file. If you open this file in Internet Explorer, it should look similar to the screenshot shown in Figure 6.1.

Figure 6.1 W3C File Converted to XML

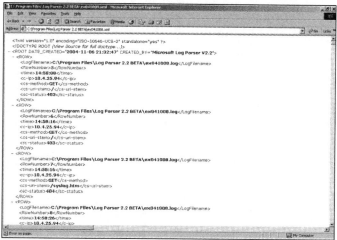

Using XML for Reporting

XML is a very versatile format that can easily be used to generate report data. By using an XSL template when you convert your logs to XML, you can change the result from the standard XML display to something more readable. Figure 6.1 shows an XML file that has had no additional formatting applied to it. While it contains all the data you need and provides an excellent standardized format for your data, it's not easily readable.

In order to apply formatting to your XML file, Log Parser allows you to define an XSL template. This template will be applied by any XSL-enabled XML browser to the resulting XML output and will change the format of the resulting data file. An excellent sample XSL template, included with Log Parser, formats incoming data into a table view. This sample is shown below:

```
--- Ch06Table.xsl ---
<?xml version="1.0"?>
<xsl:stylesheet xmlns:xsl="http://www.w3.org/TR/WD-xsl">

 <xsl:template match="/">
  <xsl:for-each select="ROOT">
   <HTML>
    <HEAD><TITLE><xsl:value-of select="@CREATED_BY"/> Generated Log</TITLE></HEAD>
    <BODY>

     <CENTER><H1><xsl:value-of select="@CREATED_BY"/> Generated Log</H1></CENTER>
     <CENTER><H2>Generated on <xsl:value-of select="@DATE_CREATED"/></H2></CENTER>

     <CENTER>
      <TABLE BORDER="0" BGCOLOR="#E0E0E0" CELLPADDING="5">
```

```
      <xsl:apply-templates select="ROW"/>
    </TABLE>
   </CENTER>


   </BODY>
  </HTML>
 </xsl:for-each>
</xsl:template>


<xsl:template match="ROW">
    <TR BGCOLOR="#F0F0F0">
     <xsl:for-each select="*">
      <TD>
       <xsl:value-of select="."/>
      </TD>
     </xsl:for-each>
    </TR>
 </xsl:template>


</xsl:stylesheet>
--- Ch06Table.xsl ---
```

In order to use this XSL file, we simply add it to the command line we use to run Log Parser. For example, to use this formatting option with the query we used previously to output W3C log file errors, we would use the following command:

```
logparser.exe file:Ch06ConvertW3CErrorstoXML.sql -i:W3C -xslLink:Ch06table.xsl
```

After running this command, you will have generated a new file named ex041008.xml. This file will contain a link referencing the XSL file you specified for formatting the data. When the new XML file is opened in an XSL-enabled browser, the browser will follow the link, load the XSL, and format the XML document as specified. Figure 6.2 shows the difference in formatting when our new file is displayed in Internet Explorer.

Swiss Army Knife

Using XSL Files

Using XSL files is a very powerful way of formatting XML to be very readable and easy to understand. Along with the sample that comes with Log Parser, you can find a large number of samples and information about XSL on the Web. Using these template files with XML will allow to you take any XML file that you create with Log Parser and present it in a more understandable format than the standard XML display. Make sure that you utilize these XSL files to their full potential and format your Log Parser XML files in the manner that best suits your needs.

Figure 6.2 XML File Formatted with XSL

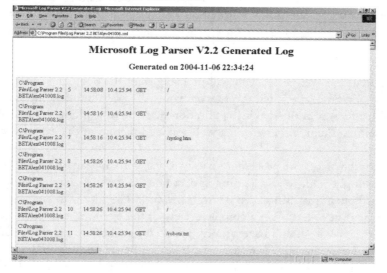

Correlating Log File Data

One of the more difficult tasks any systems administrator faces is the correlation of log file data from multiple sources. This problem is very apparent in the area of security administration when log files from many different systems, devices, and applications must be parsed through to find information that might relate to a specific event. However, even in normal systems administration work, you may have to correlate data from multiple sources in order to track down the root cause for a failure or events that led up to a system crash

Log Parser can help a great deal in this area with both the extensive queries that can be created as well as the conversion capabilities of the utility. Since Log Parser accepts so many possible input types and supports a large number of standard output types, it is the obvious choice of tool for correlating log file data from all of your source systems or applications.

The greatest benefit of correlating log file data using Log Parser is the speed and ease in which this work can be done. Using traditional troubleshooting methodologies, an admin may look at a system log, then a Web server log, then an application server log, then some other log simply to try and find where a failure actually occurred in the chain of interlinked systems. With Log Parser, the data from each of these sources can be combined and queries performed against the data as if it were from a single source. This means that it will take less time and less effort to track down important data.

Identifying Related Data

The first step in setting up a log file correlation process is to determine which log file data is related. For example, if you are working with a multi-tiered application with a Web server tier, an application server tier, and a database tier, you might consider correlating the log data from all systems in the hierarchy as a single source of log data. On the other hand, if you're only dealing with a specific tier, you might want only information from the multiple systems in the tier that you're involved with. Identifying the related data that you need is fairly simple once you've determined where your focus lies.

Let's take an example where you want to gather data from a single web server and a single application server. From the Web server, you will probably want the operating system event logs and the Web server logs. From the application server, you will want the operating system logs and the individual log files from the specific application that you're working with. Collecting these logs and combining them will give you a well-rounded picture of the events within your environment.

On the other hand, what if the problem you're working with appears to be network or security related, you might want to also add in log data from routers or switches as well as any network security equipment that is installed on your network. The idea is to correlate all data from point A to point B in order to get a complete view of the environment you're working in.

From these examples, you should have a pretty good idea on how to identify related data. Always go with the premise that the more data you have, the better results you'll get when trying to use correlated data to solve a problem. Since Log Parser is so versatile in the log file formats it can use, it's very easy to gather data from all the sources in an environment and use their related data.

Converting Related Log Files

Step two in correlating log file data using Log Parser is to convert the log files that you're working with into a standardized format. Typically you will be gathering data from a number of sources and each will be coming to you in a slightly different format. As we've already discussed, Log Parser is very capable of converting from a multitude of formats and storing the result in a single, standardized format for your future use.

In the example listed above, we discussed an environment where you want to gather W3C logs from a Web server's IIS installation as well as operating system event logs. To correlate the data from these two sources, it is easiest to convert them to a format such as XML. For the purposes of this example, we'll do just that and convert these log files into a single XML document.

First, we'll need to design the SQL for Log Parser to use for the conversion. We'll have to do the conversion in two distinct steps, as Log Parser does not currently support converting from multiple formats simultaneously. Therefore our first query will be to gather the data from the W3C log file and convert it into an XML document that uses the same fields that an event log uses. Using the following command and query will accomplish this:

```
logparser.exe file:Ch06ConvertW3CtoCombinedXML.sql -i:W3C -o:XML
```

```
--- Ch06ConvertW3CtoCombinedXML.sql ---
SELECT
    LogFilename AS EventLog,
    RowNumber AS RecordNumber,
    to_timestamp( SYSTEM_DATE(), time) AS TimeGenerated,
    time AS TimeWritten,
    sc-status AS EventID,
    cs-method AS EventType,
    cs-method AS EventTypeName,
    cs-method AS EventCateagory,
    c-ip AS SourceName,
    cs-uri-stem AS Strings,
    c-ip AS ComputerName,
    c-ip AS SID,
    cs-uri-stem AS Message,
    cs-uri-stem AS Data
INTO combined.xml
FROM ex041008.log
--- Ch06ConvertW3CtoCombinedXML.sql ---
```

After running this code, we now have an XML file called combined.xml, which contains the W3C log file data in a new format. In order to properly combine the data from the W3C with the event log data, we must make the format of the XML match. To see a better view of how the fields are mapped in this XML file, refer to Table 6.1.

Table 6.1 W3C to XML Field Mappings

W3C Data Field	XML Data Field
LogFilename	EventLog
RowNumber	RecordNumber
to_timestamp(SYSTEM_DATE(), time)	TimeGenerated
time	TimeWritten

Continued

Table 6.1 W3C to XML Field Mappings

W3C Data Field	XML Data Field
sc-status	EventID
cs-method	EventType
cs-method	EventTypeName
cs-method	EventCategory
c-ip	SourceName
cs-uri-stem	Strings
c-ip	ComputerName
c-ip	SID
cs-uri-stem	Message
cs-uri-stem	Data

Master Craftsman

Conversion Mapping

As you can see in Table 6.1, we've mapped out the columns between the W3C format and the EventLog format as it fit our needs for this example. Whenever you start a conversion process, you should always map out your fields first. If you're converting to a standard format of your own, then you already have a pretty good idea of which fields in the source should convert to which fields in the destination. However if you're converting from one standard format to another, a little guesswork is involved. Regardless, mapping out your fields in a table similar to that shown will make your conversion effort go a lot smoothly and give you accurate documentation on how to repeat the process in the future.

The next step in our task of converting this data is to add the appropriate operating system event logs to the combined.xml file. Log parser can easily add in all three event logs for the same date as the W3C log at once using the following command:

```
logparser.exe file:Ch06ConvertEVTtoCombinedXML.sql -i:EVT -o:XML -filemode:0


--- Ch06ConvertEVTtoCombinedXML.sql ---
SELECT
    *
INTO combined.xml
FROM system,
    security,
```

```
        application
WHERE TO_DATE(timegenerated) = TIMESTAMP('2004-11-06', 'yyyy-MM-dd')
--- Ch06ConvertEVTtoCombinedXML.sql ---
```

Make sure you note the *filemode* parameter for the Log Parser command line. This parameter instructs Log Parser to append the output to an existing XML file rather than overwrite it. After running this code, the combined.xml file now contains the event log data from all three event logs as well as the log data from the W3C log in a standardized format using the same field names.

There is one final step in completing this task. When we added in the event log data, we simply appended the data to the existing XML file. When doing so, Log Parser automatically added in the XML header prior to the new data. This problem wouldn't occur when using a CSV, TSV, or SQL database, but must be fixed when using XML. To do so, simply open up the combined.xml file using a text editor such as notepad and remove the second header. In our example, the header that should be removed looks like this:

```
</ROOT>?<?xml version="1.0" encoding="ISO-10646-UCS-2" standalone="yes" ?>
<!DOCTYPE ROOT[
 <!ATTLIST ROOT DATE_CREATED CDATA #REQUIRED>
 <!ATTLIST ROOT CREATED_BY CDATA #REQUIRED>
 <!ELEMENT EventLog (#PCDATA)>
 <!ELEMENT RecordNumber (#PCDATA)>
 <!ELEMENT TimeGenerated (#PCDATA)>
 <!ELEMENT TimeWritten (#PCDATA)>
 <!ELEMENT EventID (#PCDATA)>
 <!ELEMENT EventType (#PCDATA)>
 <!ELEMENT EventTypeName (#PCDATA)>
 <!ELEMENT EventCategory (#PCDATA)>
 <!ELEMENT SourceName (#PCDATA)>
 <!ELEMENT Strings (#PCDATA)>
 <!ELEMENT ComputerName (#PCDATA)>
 <!ELEMENT SID (#PCDATA)>
 <!ELEMENT Message (#PCDATA)>
 <!ELEMENT Data (#PCDATA)>
 <!ELEMENT ROW (EventLog, RecordNumber, TimeGenerated, TimeWritten, EventID, EventType,
EventTypeName, EventCategory, SourceName, Strings, ComputerName, SID, Message, Data)>
 <!ELEMENT ROOT (ROW*)>
]>
<ROOT DATE_CREATED="2004-11-07 04:18:44" CREATED_BY="Microsoft Log Parser V2.2">
```

Basically, you'll need to remove all the data from the last </ROW> of your first XML segment to the first <ROW> of your second XML segment. This manual data change is required to change the file to a valid XML file and must be done before you can run any queries against the new XML file that you've created. In this manner, we now have converted four log files into a single standardized log file format and can query against the new XML file to correlate the log data.

Analyzing Related Log File Data

In the previous sections we have gone through the process of identifying related data and converting the related data into a standardized format. Now it's time to do something with the data we've gathered. Performing a query against the combined.xml file that we created in the last section is the same as performing a query against any standard XML file. To identify fields for your query, simply use the fields specified in Table 6.1.

As an example, let's say that we want to find all the events that occurred at around 1:00 P.M. from the combined log set. To do this, we could use the following command and query:

```
logparser.exe file:Ch06EventsWithinanHour.sql -i:XML -o:XML -xslLink:ch06table.xsl


--- Ch06EventsWithinanHour.sql ---
SELECT
     *
INTO 1pmEvents.xml
FROM combined.xml
WHERE TO_STRING(timegenerated, 'yyyy-MM-dd HH') = '2004-11-06 15'
ORDER BY timegenerated
--- Ch06EventsWithinanHour.sql ---
```

Using this code will parse through the XML file that we created by combining a W3C log file with three event log files and identify all events that occurred at 3:00 P.M. It will then take this data and output it to another XML file while formatting it according to the format specified in the XSL file we used previously. The end result is an easily read XML file that contains all of the data for the hour that we're interested in. Viewing the resulting XML file in Internet Explorer should give you a result similar to that shown in Figure 6.3.

Figure 6.3 Formatted, Limited, and Combined XML

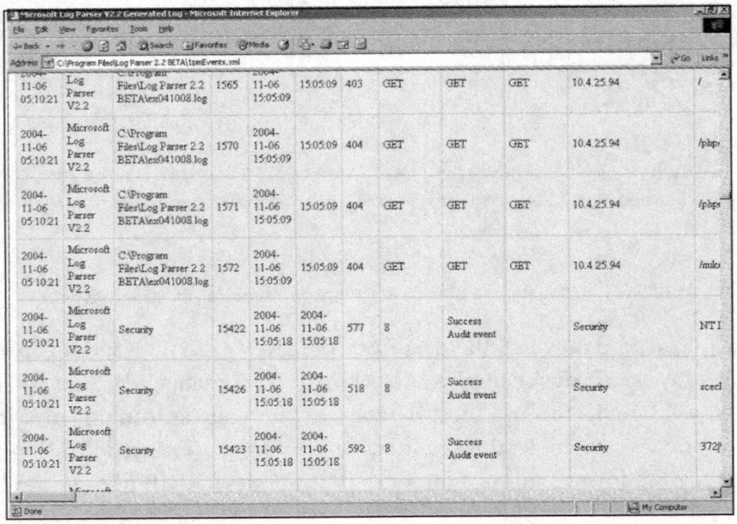

Further queries and analysis can be done on your combined log file to use the correlated data in a way that best fits your needs. As previously mentioned, you can run any query against this combined XML file that you can against a standard event log file as they use the same field names.

You can see by this example that it's relatively simple to combine multiple log files as well as multiple log files from multiple sources into the same final log file. This process will help you a great deal with correlating log file data and using Log Parser to further analyze the resulting data. Keep in mind that while I used an XML file for this example, you can also use almost any format that Log Parser supports for output to combine your data.

Log Rotation and Archival

We all realize that log files are a critical part of tracking system functionality and ensuring that everything within your enterprise is functioning up to spec. There is one overwhelming problem with all the logging that occurs to create these files, however; it never stops. Therefore the log files just keep getting larger and larger to the point that if not properly taken care of, they can fill up system drives.

This becomes more and more apparent in larger enterprises where disk space is critical and hundreds or thousands of systems must be monitored to ensure that the various log files stored on the systems are not growing too large. Some applications provide specific logging features to allow for log rotation and archival, but you as an administrator must decide upon the strategy you wish to use and ensure that it is consistent across multiple systems and multiple applications.

In this section, we're going to cover some basic techniques of log file rotation and log file archiving that will help you accomplish two main goals. The first goal is to keep your systems clean and prevent log files from filling up the drives. Second, you want to ensure that you have an adequate amount of historical log data retained for reporting or tracking of ongoing system problems.

Rotating Log Files

One method of keeping log files from piling up on any given system is to rotate the log files out. This basically involves specifying at what point the log file is considered full or complete and moving to a new log file when that point is reached.

There are two major methods used to determine when a log file is complete. First, you can base your completion criteria on the size of the log file itself. Second, you can base your completion criteria on a specific date or time match, for example, rotate log files hourly or daily.

While log file rotation may initially seem the same as log file archival, there are some differences and we'll discuss those as we go along. Remember, the primary goal of a log file rotation is to stop writing to a log file that is deemed complete and to start writing a new log file. No movement of the log files is necessarily done in a straight log file rotation method.

Rotating Log Files Based on Size

When working with log files, you'll find that every operating system or application looks at logging in a different way. Some actually allow you to modify the way the application does its logging and define a specific rotation strategy, but most require some form of manual intervention in order to accomplish any log file rotations.

For example, Windows 2000 allows you to set a maximum log file size, but does not allow you to specify a way to rotate out the log files themselves. It simply allows you to choose whether or not you wish to overwrite previous entries. This feature is better than many applications, however, because at least you have some options to help you eliminate the possibility of log files filling up the system drives.

To further refine this process, you'll want to implement some form of archival. We'll explain how that is done later in the chapter. In the meantime, let's look at an application that has no default log file rotation mechanism. For the purposes of this example, we'll use the iPass Connect VPN solution. iPass stores its log file as C:\Program Files\iPass\iPassConnect\log\connection.log. It does not rotate the log files and simply appends any new data at the bottom of the existing file. This is pretty standard for most applications.

In order to create your own log rotation process for these log files manually, you simply need to rename the old file to something useful and create a new blank file for storing future data. However, since you want to rotate the log files based on size, you only want to do this for files that are above the size that you specify. There are some methods you can use to automate this process, and we'll cover those a little later in this section.

Rotating Log Files Based on Date

Another method of handling log file rotation is to rotate log files based on the file date or time. Some applications create so much logging data that you'll want to rotate the log files on an hourly basis to keep the log files from growing too large. In order to perform this type of rotation, you'll need to determine, on average, how much data is being placed in your log files during a specific timeframe. When you have this information, you will be able to determine what frequency you'll need to use in rotating out the log files.

Similar to the example above with an iPass Connect log file, any log file can be rotated out based on a date structure and typically this is easier than relying on file size. By implementing a log file rotation schedule based on date, you'll have specific times that your automated log rotation process will need to run in order to rotate the log file out. An example of a program that does this by default is Microsoft IIS. IIS rotates out its logs every night and stores one day's worth of data in each log file. While this process does not automatically archive the data, it does rotate the logs so that they can be more easily archived by using another process.

Automating Log File Rotation

Our discussion of log file rotation so far has given you the basic methods and methodologies of log file rotation. Now you should understand the purpose and benefits of rotating log files and have a pretty clear idea of how this process is accomplished. But how do you actually implement this in a real-world environment in such a way that it is easily managed? The answer is automated log file rotation.

The method you choose to automate your log file rotation will vary depending on the specific applications that you're working with. Every application is different, but you can apply the same reasoning regardless of the way the application works and apply some sort of log rotation. Let's go through a couple examples on how to set this up.

First, let's look at doing an automatic log file rotation of the Windows 2000 application log. Let's assume that you want to set this up to only occur when the log file reaches 500k. The best way to set up something along those lines is to create a visual basic script file or a batch file that checks the size of the application event log and starts Log Parser to grab out the data if the file is larger than 500k. You then use the Microsoft Task Scheduler to schedule this file to execute on a regular basis. An appropriate command line to use with Log Parser would be:

```
logparser.exe file:Ch06RotateApplicationLog.sql -i:EVT -o:XML
--- Ch06RotateApplicationLog.sql ---
SELECT
    *
INTO AppLog.xml
FROM application
--- Ch06RotateApplicationLog.sql ---
```

You would then follow this up with a purge of the application event log using a third-party utility. Using this method of log rotation isn't necessarily the cleanest, but it gets the job done. It's usually very difficult to set up a good log rotation system when the applications that you're working with don't natively support a function such as this.

For another example, let's do something similar with the system event log, but this time base it on date instead of log file size. This is much easier to set up than a file size-based log rotation because you simply schedule the automated run of Log Parser followed by an event log purge utility on the specific dates or times that you want the process to run. There's no need to check for file size, etc. So to use Log Parser in this manner, you might use the following command and query:

```
logparser.exe file:Ch06RotateSystemLog.sql -i:EVT -o:XML
--- Ch06RotateSystemLog.sql ---
SELECT
    *
INTO SysLog.xml
FROM system
--- Ch06RotateSystemLog.sql ---
```

Determining an Archiving Methodology

Throughout this section, we've discussed log file rotation and extracting data from log files for storage and future analysis. But where should all those log files go? You certainly don't want to create and retain gigs upon gigs of log file data on every system in your enterprise. The answer to this is log file archival.

There are several reasons for archiving logs. First is the obvious space savings on individual servers, but there are other reasons that are sometimes even more important. First, in the event of a security breach, you should try to have as much data as possible available to parse through in search of clues to the security problem. Setting up a log file rotation is the first step of this, but you want to move those log files to a secure location regularly so they aren't compromised when the system itself is.

Second, there are sometimes legal or policy requirements that force you to retain logs of important data for several years. Typically the best way to meet this need is to archive the files off of the system where they were generated and store them with other data that has a long-term retention need.

You may also need to archive log files to protect yourself or your company. This sometimes falls under legal requirements, but even if the situation you're in isn't being viewed from a legal perspective, it may be wise to protect yourself.

Whatever the most pressing reason is, there is always some justification that proves log archiving to be necessary. Through the remainder of this section we will be going over some of the reasons why you might want to archive logs and specific methodologies to use based on your reasoning. We'll also go over some industry best practices as they relate to log archival and storage.

Meeting Legal or Policy Requirements

Often there are legal or policy requirements around log retention. In order to comply with several corporate audit standards such as Sarbanes-Oxley, ISO-9000, and VISA CISP you must have a corporate policy in place that covers the subject of critical system log archive retention. Depending on the standards, the retention duration and other requirements vary. However, they all require some specific duration that you must keep log files.

In order to meet these requirements, many companies are quickly implementing corporate policies around log file archiving and retention. Some are using Syslog servers and storing the data on their Syslog server for the specified duration. Others are simply doing a file copy and storing the log files on a centralized file share. Another option is writing log files to one exclusive backup tape system so they are stored long-term on tape.

Regardless of which methodology is chosen, the best base concept behind all of them is centralized storage in one manner or another. Using this type of system moves the responsibility of the log file retention and archival from the individual systems and to a centralized system or set of systems. This allows for easier purging when the storage duration has been exceeded as well as a single place to look for log files regardless of which system or application generated them.

One major benefit of this centralized storage scheme is that you have a single place to look for information from all of your systems. Using Log Parser, you can easily look through multiple logs simultaneously and cut down on the amount of time necessary to query for data. For example, if you wanted to gather all system startup events from a series of logs in the same directory, you might use the following command and query:

```
logparser.exe file:Ch06MultipleFileStartupEvents.sql -i:EVT -o:datagrid
```

```
--- Ch06MultipleFileStartupEvents.sql ---
SELECT
     timegenerated AS EventTime,
     message AS Message
FROM *.evt
WHERE eventid= '6005'
--- Ch06MultipleFileStartupEvents.sql ---
```

Archiving Logs for Non-Repudiation

Another reason many companies require log file archival is for non-repudiation. The purpose of this is for proof that a transaction happened so it cannot be refuted later. One example of this is digitally signing e-mail messages. If you digitally sign a message, the receiver knows that you sent this message and you cannot deny it later.

The same thing applies to system logs. If an event is captured in a system log and later this log is to be used for legal purposes, you need to ensure that the log files are archived and protected. In many situations, you may actually be required to encrypt the files as well, but usually placing them on a secure system on the network or even an out-of-band system will suffice.

WARNING

Whenever you're working with non-repudiation, make sure that you coordinate with your company's Legal department prior to changing any existing processes. There may be a specific reason for storing files in a particular manner based on state or local law. Always make sure that a company attorney is aware of your efforts and helps you to ensure that you have complied appropriately with any legal requirements.

Regardless of where the log files go, you need to have a policy in place to cover this situation in the event that it occurs. By coupling this policy with your standard log file archival and retention policy, you can cut down on the number of documents that have to be maintained and use a single point of reference for your logging requirements.

Log Parser can help you with this effort by automatically sending the data from log files on individual systems over to a storage location on a centralized system in a standard format. For example, in order to copy security event log data to a central server you could use the following command and query:

```
logparser.exe file:Ch06RemoteServerSecurityLog.sql -i:EVT -o:XML
```

```
--- Ch06RemoteServerSecurityLog.sql ---
SELECT
    *
INTO \\server1\log$\server23.xml
FROM security
--- Ch06RemoteServerSecurityLog.sql ---
```

Swiss Army Knife

Using Remote Systems

When you're working on remote systems with Log Parser, remember that with the exception of a Syslog server, you're simply using UNC shares to perform your work. With that in mind, if you want to use a share on a remote system to store all of your log files, simpye create it, assign appropriate permissions, and use Log Parser to send the data over as you're converting it. Rather than coping the files over after they're converted, you can use Log Parser to combine these steps and save yourself some time.

Building a Hierarchical Logging Directory Structure

When you begin to use a centralized server to store your enterprise log files, you'll quickly learn that the system becomes unmanageable without using good naming conventions and file structures. If all of the event logs or application logs from multiple systems are simply dumped into a single directory, you risk overwriting existing files or not being able to identify which system a specific log file originated from. This can cause a great deal of confusion or even make the entire process of log archiving useless.

To prevent this, there are two key steps you must take. First, name your log files in an accurate and easy to understand naming convention. Be consistent on this because as with most services offered in IT, once this is available its use will grow. You want to ensure that you have a solid standard in place from the beginning.

Second, you should use a hierarchical directory structure to store the log files. The way you set this up will differ depending on your specific needs. Some administrators prefer to use the system names as the top level in their hierarchy. Others prefer to base them on what the system is used for and put the name on the next level. Another method I've seen is to use the application name as the top level, followed by system function, followed by name. It's all a matter of preference. Whichever you choose, just be consistent. If you set up the log file storage differently for different systems then you will run into problems locating files and retrieving data later.

Figures 6.4, 6.5, and 6.6 show three examples of how this can be done. Again, don't use multiple methods on a single system. Choose the hierarchy that works best for you and stick with it.

Figure 6.4 Sample Hierarchical Logging Directory Structures – Application-Based

Figure 6.5 Sample Hierarchical Logging Directory Structures – Function-Based

Figure 6.6 Sample Hierarchical Logging Directory Structures – System-Based

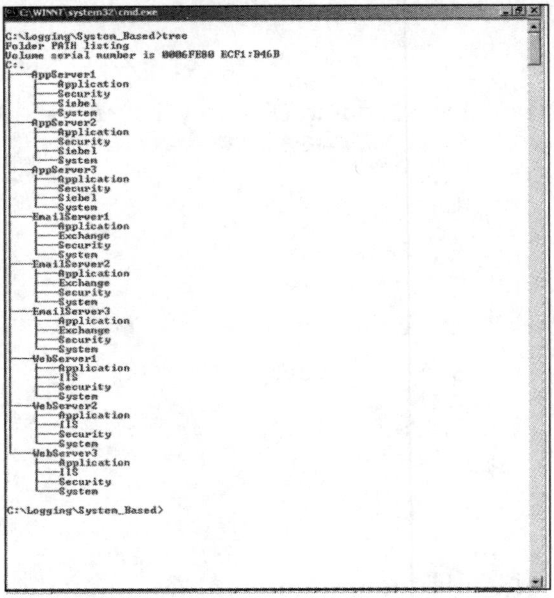

Using a Syslog Server

Many corporations make use of a Syslog server to centralize storage of their log files. Syslog messaging was originally used on UNIX systems for application, network, and operating-system logging. Many network devices can now also be configured to generate Syslog messages. These Syslog messages are then transmitted via UDP to a server configured with a Syslog daemon to accept the messages.

As more and more devices support Syslog messages, many enterprises are moving toward using a Syslog server as their primary archival location of event messages from across the enterprise. Syslog servers can also be set up to do automatic notifications if specific critical events are sent to it. This feature allows for a faster response time from IT personnel to system outages and helps to reduce the overall amount of downtime.

By using a Syslog server, you have a centralized point on your network to receive, alert on, and archive log files. However, many systems don't yet support this method of sending log files and this leads many enterprises to having both a hierarchical logging system and a Syslog server. Log Parser can help alleviate the pain of keeping two logging points on your network by sending log messages to a Syslog server.

Log Parser natively supports the use of a Syslog server as an output type and can use this function to convert and forward your log files to your enterprise's corporate Syslog server regardless of the support of individual applications. To use this feature, you must know the server and port (optional) to which you need to send the Syslog messages. In addition, there are a number of features specific to Syslog servers that Log Parser supports. A quick example follows that shows the conversion and transmission of event logs to a Syslog server:

```
logparser.exe file:Ch06EventlogtoSyslog.sql -i:EVT -o:SYSLOG
--- Ch06EventlogtoSyslog.sql ---
SELECT
    *
INTO @syslogserver:514
FROM system,
    application,
    security
--- Ch06EventlogtoSyslog.sql ---
```

Separating Logs

Throughout this chapter we've been discussing the conversion and centralization of enterprise log files. The processes and methods we've discussed serve several very useful purposes including drive space utilization reduction, centralized log data for reference and correlation, and centralized archival for legal or policy needs. However, there are occasions when you need to use a slightly different method for working with your log files.

Log file separation is the process by which centralized files are broken down into specific categories and referenced based on their category. If you have a centralized system in place using a hierarchical directory structure, you may need to gather files from multiple places in the structure in order to correlate them for a specific purpose. For example, if a specific set of systems and hardware devices were involved in a security breach of the enterprise, you may want to gather a subset of the log files consisting of the log files specific to those systems and devices.

Another reason for log file separation is to separate a single log file into categories. An occasion where you may need to do this is when you have a very large log file containing multiple days of data and you want to break up this log file by date. Doing so can make the log more meaningful or be a first step in preparing the file for inclusion with other log files from the same individual dates so that it fits properly into your hierarchical structure.

In this section we'll be going over some of the strategies and methods of using separated logs. You'll find at times that this seems in direct contradiction to the strategies we discussed in the section on log file correlation, but as we go along you'll see how log file separation and correlation/consolidation can go hand in hand.

Determining Log File Separation Strategies

The first step in putting a log separation process in place is to determine your strategy behind the process. There are many different reasons for setting up log file separation. As I've mentioned, you may be separating log files for ease of use, correlation with other like files, or as a preparation task for centralizing the files in a hierarchical structure. All of these are valid reasons for implementing log file separation and all fall into specific strategies.

The three main strategies of log file separation are separation by date, separation by type, and separation by system. Using one of these strategies will help break your log files down to more manageable chunks for analysis. We'll go through each strategy in detail and discuss how each one is implemented.

Separating by Date

The first log separation strategy we'll discuss is separating by date. This is probably the most common form of log file separation and one of the most frequently implemented. The basic premise behind separating by date is pretty obvious; you want to separate out a log file based on the date that the event occurred and was logged. This is usually used in cases where an application continues writing within a single large log file regardless of date until some criteria is filled, such as an application restart.

When considering this strategy, you need to determine the type of log file you're dealing with and the way the application handles logging. Based on the way the application works, you may need to answer the following questions:

- Does the application start overwriting the log file after it reaches a specific size?

- How does the application store time stamps in the logs? Since date is your primary criteria here, this is critical.

- Are there specific criteria that the application uses to determine that it should rotate to another log file?

- Do the log files from multiple systems have to be recombined after the individual system logs have been separated by date?

Answering these questions based on your specific environment will help you to determine the best way to separate your log files by date. Many administrators find that it is helpful to extract out the previous day's worth of data out of a log file and store that in a hierarchical structure similar to the structures discussed previously. This is one of the major ways that log file separation by date is used.

Separating by Event Type

Another form of log file separation is separation by type. This strategy basically involves separating out log file messages based on the type of message. An example is the separation of error messages from benign messages. This form of separation is primarily used to limit the amount of data that an administrator must go through in order to find important information about the ongoing operation of a system, device, or application.

While Log Parser can easily parse through a log file and output the results of a query for this information on the fly, it's sometimes necessary to actually maintain a constant output of this data on a daily basis. One reason that this is done is to support an automated reporting or statistics gathering tool. When this is the case, it makes more sense to separate out the events of interest and store them in another file.

To use this strategy, you'll probably want to set up an automated process through Windows Task Scheduler or some other means in order to start up Log Parser. The parameters and query that you use for Log Parser would be similar to that used earlier in this chapter to convert the log file data to another format gathering only the data matching your specific criteria. These new files can then be used for any automated or manual evaluation process.

Separating by System

Some administrators are more concerned about the overall operations of individual servers, rather than each specific application running on those servers. In this case, an administrator may want to separate out all log file data for all applications on a system and look though this data independently from the data retrieved from other systems.

In the event that you are doing centralized storage and archival of log data, you may need to extract data out of the central store to serve this need. This form of separation is what is considered separation by system. Typically this strategy is used to either fill the need mentioned above or to help consolidate logs by system for future review. Figure 6.7 shows a breakdown of this process and should make it a little more understandable.

Figure 6.7 Log File Separation by System

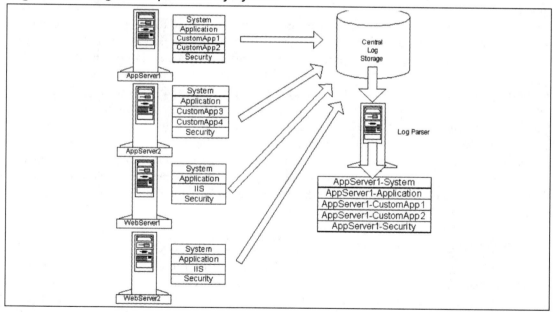

As you can see, all of the application and Web servers in this environment are sending their system, application, and security logs to a centralized store in addition to any log from other software on the system. To illustrate this example, an administrator uses Log Parser to pull all data related to AppServer1 from the centralized store for a full system analysis.

While the administrator could have simply gathered this information directly from the server, using the centralized store allows the administrator to get more historical information than what would be available on the server. In addition, the use of the centralized store makes it easy for the administrator to also run a query that looks at applications across multiple servers, etc depending on their needs.

Using Separated Log Files

Now that we've examined the various log file separation strategies, it's time to learn how to use them. So far we've covered the three main strategies that are used with log file separation and learned how each can benefit you as an administrator depending on your specific needs. Before going forward and implementing any one strategy, make sure that you thoroughly understand your enterprise and choose the strategy that best suits the needs of your organization.

There are three steps to using separated log files. First, you must create them. Throughout this book, we've gone over various ways to use Log Parser to query against log files of various types. In this chapter, we've covered how to convert and centralize log files within an enterprise. Using all of this information together is all you need to know on how to create separated log files. Basically, you are simply extracting the log data that you want from the centrally stored log files using Log Parser queries and storing the newly separated log file in a format of your choosing.

Second, since you have now created separated log files, you have to store them somewhere to make them useful. This doesn't necessarily have to be the same storage location as your central log archive, but you do need some method of keeping the separated log files organized.

Finally, you must make use of the data within the separated log files. This means using Log Parser to query against one or more of your separated log files to find information or display data. Since your separated log files are a subset of your centralized log files, querying against them should be slightly faster and you can be sure that any data you receive is directly related to the subset of data you requested when creating the separated log file.

Now we'll go over a method you can use to store your separated log files. Using this suggestion in combination with everything else you've learned in this chapter and a well thought out log file strategy will allow you to leverage the power of Log Parser and use this tool to help you troubleshoot or understand your enterprise better.

Developing a Separated Log File Hierarchy

In order to utilize the separated log files that you create, you need to ensure that they are stored in a logical manner. This is where a separated log file hierarchy comes into place. Similar to the hierarchical logging directory structure that we discussed earlier in the chapter, a separated log file hierarchy allows you to logically separate out separated log files so that they are easy to find and use.

Fefer to Figures 6.4, 6.5, and 6.6 earlier in this chapter for some sample hierarchical structures. These structures apply to separated logs as well as your centralized log storage location. The primary difference is that you don't necessarily need to store the separated log files at the same location. In this case the log file hierarchy is simply used for organizing the files for your personal temporary use, not to position them for log time archival.

You'll find that if your centralized log storage hierarchy is set up in such a manner that it really fits the needs of your enterprise, you may be able to simply use the same hierarchy for your separated log files as well. While this may seem to mean that you're duplicating data, in reality you're simplifying the use of the data by making a temporary duplicate.

Final Touches

Throughout this chapter, we have covered several of the more administrative aspects of using Log Parser. We went over using Log Parser to convert multiple types of log files into standard formats for easy future reference as well as consolidation. In addition, we went over some methods you can use to store your log files in a logical hierarchical manner so that they are very easy to access and use at a future time. Finally, we went over how to work backwards and separate the consolidated log files in order to run queries faster and limit the data to exactly what you need a little easier.

As we've gone over each section within this chapter, you should have mastered performing conversion efforts using Log Parser. Using this powerful tool, it's very quick and easy to convert data from the plethora of formats that Log Parser supports. In addition, you should have a good understanding of how and why log files should be consolidated as well as when you should separate them back out for ease of use. Mastering these techniques and understanding these procedures will help you to be more effective in your ongoing use of Log Parser.

Chapter 7

Investigating Intrusions

Scripts and Samples in this Chapter:

- **Monitoring Logons**
- **Identifying Suspicious Files**
- **Finding Modification Dates**
- **Reconstructing Intrusions**

In This Toolbox

Investigating intrusions is usually a difficult and tedious task. Faced with megabytes and sometimes gigabytes of log file data, it is easy to overlook some of the most critical evidence. Often it is difficult to determine that a security incident has even occurred.

But Log Parser changes that. Log Parser can combine, sort, and parse through log files to give you a unique perspective of your data. With the right queries, important evidence tends to float into view. Our goal in this chapter is to build a toolbox of queries that we will have ready to use as needed. Here you will learn powerful features and capabilities of Log Parser that will help you track down almost any intrusion.

Locating Intrusions

To locate intruders, you must first detect the intrusion. Fortunately, most attacks leave some kind of trail. The trick is in knowing how to find these intrusions among thousands of normal log entries. The secret is to start with high-level queries then work your way down to more and more specific conditions in your WHERE clause. In this chapter, we will focus on the most common and the most obvious threats.

TIP

If you anticipate prosecuting an intruder with the information you gather, you should take careful steps to preserve the original evidence, and only run these queries on copies of log data. If you expect legal proceedings, you should always consult a forensics expert on how to best preserve evidence for use in court.

Suspicious behavior is usually abnormal behavior. Knowing this, it is usually possible to identify an intrusion just by measuring normal behavior. Suspicious log entries often show up on top 10 lists or cluster around specific pieces of information. For example, you can often identify SQL injection attacks by watching for unusually high hits to one page, especially from a single IP (Internet Protocol) address. However, you must also be creative. For example, sometimes an attacker will not show much activity in any single day, but if you do a top 10 list for six months, the attacker's IP address will show up.

The key is to look at your data in many different ways. By doing this you will find that suspicious data tends to bring itself to your attention.

Monitoring Logons

The most basic element of a security system is user account access. Many security mechanisms rely upon authenticating a user and then authorizing that user to take actions or access resources on a server. If properly configured to audit logon events, a Windows server records account activity in the Security Event Log. Browsing through the Security Event Log, it is difficult to identify anything suspicious, but by using Log Parser to summarize the data, it is very easy to spot malicious activity. Monitoring account logon activity is an essential element of intrusion detection.

Excessive Failed Logons

One common sign of intrusion is excessive failed logins, either for a single user or across your domain. Although login failures are common, abnormally high login failures are a good indication of attack. The query Ch07UserLogins.sql will list the total number of failed and successful logons for each user account, with the highest number of logins listed first. This query looks for all events with an EventCategory of 2, which is any logon/logoff event. It also filters results to only include those events with an EventID less than 541 and where the username is not blank.

Run this query with the following command:

```
logparser.exe file:Ch07UserLogins.sql
```

```
--- Ch07UserLogins.sql---
SELECT
     TO_LOWERCASE(EXTRACT_TOKEN(Strings,0,'|')) AS Account,
     SUM(CASE EventType WHEN 16 THEN 1 ELSE 0 END) AS Failed,
     SUM(CASE EventType WHEN 8 THEN 1 ELSE 0 END) AS Success,
     COUNT(*) AS Total
FROM m1Security.evt
WHERE EventCategory=2
     AND EventID < 541
     AND User<>''
GROUP BY User
ORDER BY Total DESC
--- Ch07UserLogins.sql---
```

The query should return something like this:

Account	Failed	Success	Total
PCW204$	0	218	218
PCW218$	0	114	114
administrator	27	103	130
anonymous logon	0	108	108
awest	12	86	98
network service	0	87	87
local service	0	67	67
cnorth	19	24	43
PCW205$	0	28	28

Review these results for users with abnormally high failed logins, high total number of failed logins, or failed logins for invalid accounts.

Note that failed logins and successful logins are separate records in the event log, but here we want to see the totals for each account on a single line. I accomplished that with these two lines:

```
SUM(CASE EventType WHEN 16 THEN 1 ELSE 0 END) AS Failed,
SUM(CASE EventType WHEN 8 THEN 1 ELSE 0 END) AS Success,
```

These lines use the CASE statement to check for the values of 16 and 8 and if they exist, change the field value to 1. The SUM statement then totals these 1's for each user as specified in the GROUP BY clause.

Terminal Services Logons

Because Terminal Services allows for remote console access to a server, it is an attractive target for hackers. If you have a Terminal Server exposed to the Internet, it is critical that you monitor the logins to this server. If you are investigating an intrusion, it is important that you check logins to all public Terminal Servers. The query Ch07TSLogins.sql lists all failed logins to Windows 2003 Terminal Services along with the originating IP address.

```
--- Ch07TSFailedLogins.sql---
SELECT
    Count(*) AS Failed,
    EXTRACT_TOKEN(Strings,1,'|') AS Domain,
    EXTRACT_TOKEN(Strings,0,'|') AS User,
    EXTRACT_TOKEN(Strings,11,'|') AS Source
USING EXTRACT_TOKEN(Strings,2,'|') AS Type
FROM Security
WHERE EventID=529
    AND Type='10'
GROUP BY Domain, User, Source
ORDER BY Logins DESC
--- Ch07TSFailedLogins.sql---
```

Although failed logins are interesting, perhaps more interesting is checking for successful logins from unrecognized IP addresses. Ch07TSLogins.sql is similar to the previous query, except that this time it lists all successful logins.

```
--- Ch07TSLogins.sql---
SELECT
    Count(*) AS Logins,
    EXTRACT_TOKEN(Strings,1,'|') AS Domain,
    EXTRACT_TOKEN(Strings,0,'|') AS User,
    EXTRACT_TOKEN(Strings,13,'|') AS Source
USING EXTRACT_TOKEN(Strings,3,'|') AS Type
FROM Security
WHERE EventID=528
    AND Type='10'
```

```
GROUP BY Domain, User, Source
ORDER BY Logins DESC
--- Ch07TSLogins.sql---
```

Swiss Army Knife

Terminal Services Logins with Windows 2000

Microsoft introduced the login type 10 with Windows XP and Windows 2003 to indicate a Terminal Services login. This event, therefore, is not available in Windows 2000. Instead, Windows 2000 uses type 2, which is the same as a console login. Furthermore, Windows 2000 does not record the IP address of the remote system.

Windows 2000 does, however, record the IP address when a user disconnects from or reconnects to a session. Windows records session disconnects with event 683 and session reconnects with event 682. Although this information is by no means complete, it nevertheless might prove useful when investigating an intrusion. To list the IP addresses from Terminal Services disconnects and reconnects, use the Ch07Win2kTSConnectsDisconnects.sql query.

```
--- Ch07Win2kTSConnectsDisconnects.sql ---
SELECT
    Count(*) AS Events,
    EXTRACT_TOKEN(Strings,0,'|') AS User,
    EXTRACT_TOKEN(Strings,5,'|') AS Source,
    CASE Event
        WHEN '682' THEN 'Reconnect'
        WHEN '683' THEN 'Disconnect'
    END AS Reason
USING TO_STRING(EventID) AS Event
FROM Security
WHERE EventID=682
    OR EventID=683
GROUP BY User, Source, Reason
ORDER BY Events DESC
--- Ch07Win2kTSConnectsDisconnects.sql ---
```

Monitoring IIS

Having a web presence is a critical business strategy for many companies, sometimes providing the only storefront for their business. However, because they are exposed to the world and their complexity often provides a large attack surface, IIS (Internet Information Server) logs are often the most obvious place to look for signs of an intrusion. Fortunately, web-based attacks usually leave enough evidence to identify the attack and help track down the attacker.

Identifying Suspicious Files

A quick and easy way to identify an attack is to check your web directories for suspicious files. A suspicious file might be an unidentified executable or a recently modified server side script. Although this query might not reveal anything suspicious, if it does turn up something this will significantly reduce your effort to identify an intrusion and is therefore a good place to start.

The query Ch07NewWebFiles.sql identifies the twenty files most recently modified or created in your web directories. Run the query with this command:

```
logparser.exe -i:fs file:Ch07NewWebFiles.sql -rtp:-1
--- Ch07NewWebFiles.sql ---
SELECT TOP 20
    Path,
    COALESCE(REPLACE_IF_NOT_NULL(TO_STRING(LastWrite,'yyyy'),'Modified'),'Created') AS
Action,
        COALESCE(LastWrite,CreationTime) AS TimeStamp


USING

TO_TIMESTAMP(REPLACE_IF_NOT_NULL(TO_STRING(INDEX_OF(TO_STRING(SUB(TO_INT(CreationTime),TO_
INT(LastWriteTime)),'yy'),'-')),TO_STRING(LastWriteTime,'yyyy-MM-dd hh:mm:ss')),'yyyy-MM-
dd hh:mm:ss') As LastWrite


FROM c:\*.* /* put your path here */
ORDER BY TimeStamp DESC
--- Ch07NewWebFiles.sql ---
```

The query should output results such as this:

```
Name                              Action     TimeStamp
------------------------------    --------   ----------------------
c:\inetpub\wwwroot\global.asa     Modified   2004-10-18 20:20:14.0
c:\inetpub\wwwroot\default.asp    Modified   2004-10-18 20:20:13.0
c:\inetpub\wwwroot\database.asp   Created    2004-10-14 13:50:58.853
c:\inetpub\wwwroot\orders.asp     Modified   2004-10-08 10:51:50.0
c:\inetpub\wwwroot\download       Modified   2004-09-24 21:27:07.0
c:\inetpub\wwwroot\about.asp      Modified   2004-09-03 11:37:52.0
```

This query is particularly interesting because it demonstrates both the weaknesses and strengths of Log Parser. Its weakness is that it does not support SQL joins or unions, making it difficult to combine data into a single column. However, its strength is that with a little creativity, it is surprisingly capable of compensating for its weaknesses.

In this case, we wanted to combine the file modification time and file creation time in a single list and sort by the time of the action taken. The value of the Action column will be either *Modified* or *Created* and the TimeStamp column will contain the date of that action. The key to accomplishing this is the LastWrite field, which consists of numerous nested functions. Here is a breakdown of how we built that field:

1. Log Parser subtracts the integer value of LastWriteTime from the integer value of CreationTime and converts the result to a string.

2. If the LastWriteTime is later than the CreationTime, then the result will be a negative timestamp, so we use the INDEX_OF function to look for a minus sign (-). we convert this value to a string so the next function can use it.

3. At this point, the value is either a zero if it found a minus sign, or null if it didn't. we use the REPLACE_IF_NOT_NULL to replace all zeros with the actual LastWriteTime, which we first have to convert to a string for use with the REPLACE_IF_NOT_NULL function.

4. Finally, we take the result and convert it back to a timestamp.

At this point, the LastWrite field contains the LastWriteTime value if that is the latest date, otherwise it will contain a null. we finish the process when defining the TimeStamp field: we use the COALESCE function to take the first non-null value of either the LastWrite or the CreationTime field. In other words, if the LastWrite field contains a null, Log Parser will instead use the value of the CreationTime. The result is the greater of the creation and modified dates in a single column.

The Action field works similar to the TimeStamp field, but in this case we use the REPLACE_IF_NOT_NULL function to convert all non-null dates to the word *Modified*. The COALESCE function then uses either this value, or if it is null, the constant *Created*. The result is a column that indicates which date we are using in that row.

Finding Modification Dates

Unfortunately, some hackers are smart enough to change file dates, which is by no means difficult to do. Fortunately, if you know that someone modified a file on your website and you want to determine when this happened, there is a trick you can use to narrow it down. First, you must understand something about IIS status codes.

When a user requests a file from your website, the server will send the file and record a status code of 200 in the IIS logs. The user's web browser will usually store this file in a local disk cache to speed up subsequent requests. So the second time the user requests the file, the web browser will make a quick check on the server to make sure the file has not changed. If the file has not changed since the last request, the web server will return a 304 status code. The web browser will then return the locally cached file to the user.

Now suppose that a hacker is somehow able to remotely modify files on your website. Chances are the hacker will visit the page before and after modifying the file to verify the change. This might result in a scenario such as this:

1. The hacker visits a page and IIS records a 200 entry in the website logs.

2. The hacker browses the site, looking for a file to target.

3. The hacker returns to one page, and IIS returns a 304 because is has not changed.

4. The hacker modifies the file, planting some malicious code.

5. The hacker returns to the page, and since it has changed, once again logs a 200 status code.

Therefore, by looking for a 200–304–200 combination from a single IP address, you have a good chance of identifying when the file contents changed. You can do this with Ch07IISFileModified.sql using the following command:

```
logparser.exe file:Ch07IISFileModified.sql?Source=ex*.log
```

```
--- Ch07IISFileModified.sql ---
SELECT DISTINCT
    date,
    time,
    c-ip,
    cs-uri-stem,
    sc-status
FROM %Source%
WHERE c-ip in
    (
    SELECT DISTINCT
        c-ip
    FROM %Source%
    WHERE sc-status=304
    )
    AND
    (
        sc-status=200
        OR sc-status=304
    )
ORDER BY date,
    c-ip
--- Ch07IISFileModified.sql ---
```

Reconstructing Intrusions

When you investigate an intrusion, you usually have several goals:

- Identify the hole that let the intruder in.
- Identify the intruder for possible prosecution
- Determine the scope of the intrusion and damage assessment.

We have investigated many small intrusions where the victim is not so much interested in finding and prosecuting the intruder as they are assessing the damage and patching the holes. To accomplish any of this, it is helpful to determine exactly what the intruder did to your system. This section will help you reconstruct the intruder's actions.

Most Recently Used Lists

Many users express concern about privacy and the numerous ways that Windows tracks your actions. Fortunately, we can use this same information to track an intruder.

Many Windows applications track your most recently used files so that you can later access them quickly. Here are some examples of most recently used lists found in Windows:

- Internet Explorer's history of recently visited sites.
- The Recent Documents selection on the Start Menu.
- The My Recent Documents button in the Open File dialog box of Microsoft Office applications.
- The list of recently executed programs in the Run dialog box launched from the Start Menu.

All of this information is extremely valuable to an investigation and because there are so many different recently used lists, it is very difficult for an intruder to effectively clean all traces.

The following query, Ch07ListRegistryMRU.sql, searches the Windows Registry for any entries that either look like recently used lists or that might contain information such as last access times. Because this information can be extensive, it saves the lists to a CSV file named RegistryMRU.csv that you can easily open with Microsoft Excel.

Execute this query with the following command:

```
logparser.exe file:Ch07ListRegistryMRU.sql
--- Ch07ListRegistryMRU.sql ---
SELECT
    Path,
    ValueName,
    Value,
    HEX_TO_ASC(Value) AS Value2
INTO RegistryMRU.csv
FROM \HKCU
WHERE  Path LIKE '%MRU%'
```

```
     OR Path LIKE '%recent%'
     OR Path LIKE '%Used%'
     OR Path LIKE '%Usage%'
     OR Path LIKE '%Time%'
     OR Path LIKE '%Date%'
     OR Path LIKE '%Last%'
     OR Path LIKE '%Updated%'
     OR Path LIKE '%History%'
     OR Path LIKE '%Accessed%'
     OR Path LIKE '%Last%'
     OR ValueName LIKE '%MRU%'
     OR ValueName LIKE '%recent%'
     OR ValueName LIKE '%Used%'
     OR ValueName LIKE '%Usage%'
     OR ValueName LIKE '%Time%'
     OR ValueName LIKE '%Date%'
     OR ValueName LIKE '%Last%'
     OR ValueName LIKE '%Updated%'
     OR ValueName LIKE '%History%'
     OR ValueName LIKE '%Accessed%'
     OR ValueName LIKE '%Last%'
ORDER BY Path, ValueName
--- Ch07ListRegistryMRU.sql ---
```

You might be surprised by the number of records returned with this query, but in an effort to be complete, you will get many unrelated results. If your results are very large, you might want to adjust the query to further constrain the data or run the results through another Log Parser query to further mine this data.

Some applications store recent file lists as shortcuts in a directory. This is the case with Windows Explorer, Internet Explorer, and Microsoft Office. To view these and other lists, execute the query Ch07FileMRU.sql with the following command:

```
logparser.exe file:Ch07FileMRU.sql -i:fs
```

```
--- Ch07FileMRU.sql ---
SELECT
     LastWriteTime,
     CreationTime,
     Path
INTO FileMRU.csv
FROM '%SystemDrive%\documents and settings\*.*'
WHERE Path LIKE '%recent%'
     AND Path NOT LIKE '%.'
ORDER BY LastWriteTime DESC
--- Ch07FileMRU.sql ---
```

Downloading Stolen Data

Usually when someone breaks into a system, he or she has some goal in mind. It might be a malicious attempt to damage the system or to use the system as a launching pad for other attacks. Often the motivation is to steal something such as private databases, sensitive files, software, or intellectual property. Somehow, the intruder has to move this information off the system and IIS is a good way to accomplish this.

It might be a long shot, but it is worth checking the IIS logs for any large file transfers. The query Ch07TopIISDownloadBytes.sql lists all web files, along with the average, maximum, and minimum number of bytes sent to the client. Run the query with the following command:

```
logparser.exe file:Ch07TopIISDownloadBytes.sql
```

```
--- Ch07TopIISDownloadBytes.sql ---
SELECT
    cs-uri-stem,
    Count(*) AS Hits,
    AVG(sc-bytes) AS Avg,
    Max(sc-bytes) AS Max,
    Min(sc-bytes) AS Min,
    Sum(sc-bytes) AS Total
FROM ex*.log
GROUP BY cs-uri-stem
ORDER BY cs-uri-stem
--- Ch07TopIISDownloadBytes.sql ---
```

DNS Name Cache

Many people do not realize that Windows keeps a cache of recently used DNS (Domain Name System) names. You can view this cache with the following command:

```
Ipconfig /displaydns
```

This is interesting because if the attacker resolved any DNS names, those names might still be in the cache, especially on a server that has little client traffic. The query Ch07DNSCache.sql lists all the unique DNS names in the DNS cache. Run this query with the following command:

```
ipconfig /displaydns | logparser.exe file:Ch07DNSCache.sql -i:textline -rtp:-1
```

```
--- Ch07DNSCache.sql ---
SELECT DISTINCT
    SUBSTR(text,ADD(INDEX_OF(text,':'),2)) AS [DNS Name]
FROM stdin
WHERE text like '%record name%'
ORDER BY [DNS Name]
--- Ch07DNSCache.sql ---
```

Your results might look something like this:

```
DNS Name
---------------------------
1.0.0.127.in-addr.arpa.
m2.doubleclick.net
news.microsoft.com
ns1.msft.net
ns3.msft.net
ns5.msft.net
use1.akam.net
```

Using these results, you might be able to identify recent client DNS activity on the machine, possibly giving some indications of the attacker's motivations.

User Activity

Some attacks involve the attacker logging in with a new user account or using domain credentials to access a system. The first time any user logs in to a system interactively, Windows creates a profile for that user under the Documents and Settings directory. By looking at the creation time of those directories, you can know exactly when a user first logged in to a system.

The query Ch07NewUserProfiles.sql parses through these directories and displays them by date, starting with the most recently created directories. Run the query with this command:

```
logparser.exe file:Ch07NewUserProfiles.sql -i:fs -recurse:0 -rtp:-1


--- Ch07NewUserProfiles.sql ---
SELECT
    Name,
    CreationTime
FROM '%SystemDrive%\Documents and Settings\*.*'
WHERE Name <> '.'
  AND Name <> '..'
ORDER BY CreationTime DESC
--- Ch07NewUserProfiles.sql ---
```

Your query output should look something like this:

```
Name                CreationTime
------------------  -----------------------
m1.Burnett          2004-08-03 23:50:36.516
Administrator       2004-08-01 11:12:26.15
TSInternetUser      2004-07-23 19:47:05.951
LocalService        2004-07-23 19:43:05.875
NetworkService      2004-07-23 19:43:05.15
Default User        2004-07-23 09:03:52.46
All Users           2004-07-23 09:03:52.46
```

Note that in the previous query, the date for All Users is usually the Windows installation date and time. This query allows you to see when a user first logged in to a machine and potentially allows you to identify unauthorized users who have logged into a machine. Review this list to identify all users who have recently logged in to the system and pay special attention to user accounts such as TSInternetUser, which should not have a login profile if you do not use Terminal Services in application mode. Sometimes intruders use this and other accounts to gain access and avoid raising suspicion.

Master Craftsman

Reviewing the Event Log for Logins

If you wish to review the Event Log for logins from suspicious accounts, use the query Ch07SuspiciousAccountLogins.sql.

```
--- SuspiciousAccountLogins.sql ---
SELECT
    TimeGenerated,
    CASE Type
        WHEN '2' THEN 'Interactive'
        WHEN '10' THEN 'RemoteInteractive'
      WHEN '11' THEN 'CachedInteractive'
      WHEN '12' THEN 'CachedRemoteInteractive'
    END AS [Login Type],
    EXTRACT_TOKEN(Strings,1,'|') AS Domain,
    EXTRACT_TOKEN(Strings,0,'|') AS User
USING EXTRACT_TOKEN(Strings,3,'|') AS Type
FROM Security
WHERE EventID=528
    AND Type IN ('2'; '10'; '11'; '13')
    AND (
        User LIKE '%ASPNET%'
        OR User LIKE '%guest%'
        OR User LIKE 'helpassistant'
        OR User LIKE 'IUSR_%'
        OR User LIKE 'IWAM_%'
        OR User LIKE 'TSInternetUser'
        )
ORDER BY TimeGenerated DESC
--- Ch07SuspiciousAccountLogins.sql ---
```

Any logins returned from this query are suspicious and you should thoroughly investigate each one.

Managing local Administrator accounts on each machine on your network is a tedious and time-consuming task. You cannot disable these accounts, and managing these passwords is inconvenient. Consequently, many administrators use the same password or predictable passwords for these accounts. This, and the fact that these accounts provide full control over a machine, makes them an attractive target for hackers. The query Ch07LastAdminLogin.sql will report the last login time for all Administrator accounts on your network. Run the query with this command:

```
logparser.exe file:Ch07LastAdminLogin.sql?Domain=mydomain.net
```

```
--- Ch07LastAdminLogin.sql ---
SELECT
    ObjectPath AS Path,
    PropertyValue AS [Last Login]
FROM WINNT://%Domain%/
WHERE ObjectName='Administrator'
    AND PropertyName='LastLogin'
--- Ch07LastAdminLogin.sql ---
```

Due to the nature of Microsoft Active Directory Service Interfaces (ADSI) and the structure of this query, it will likely take several minutes to run, even more on a large network. Nevertheless, this information is extremely valuable in detecting abuse of local Administrator accounts.

Login Count

Sometimes Log Parser is useful in enhancing other tools. For example, Windows XP and 2003 come with a tool named wmic.exe for executing Windows Management Instrumentation (WMI) queries from the command line. Wmic.exe uses an SQL-like query language, but is not as robust as that provided with Log Parser. However, you can get the best of both worlds by piping the results of wmic.exe into Log Parser. The following is a command that accomplishes this:

```
Wmic.exe /locale:ms_409 netlogin GET Name, NumberOfLogons | Logparser.exe "SELECT
TO_INT(TRIM(NumberOfLogons)) AS Logins, Name from StdIn where Logins IS NOT NULL ORDER BY
Logins DESC " -i:tsv -iSeparator:space -nSep:2 -fixedSep:off -nFields:2
```

This query takes the result of the wmic.exe command and pipes it into Log Parser. Log Parser then adds additional checking and sorting before displaying the results. Using the iSeparator, nSep and fixedSep parameters of the TSV input format, we can parse the variable output of wmic.exe into distinct fields. Log Parser reads the header line of the wmic.exe output and lets you refer to these fields by name (NumberOfLogons and Name).

This particular query displays a list of users on the system and shows how many times each user has logged in, starting with the most logins. This is useful in identifying unusual login activity from a particular account.

Services

When you re-create an attack, you do not always know the exact environment that existed at that time. For example, you might want to know which services are running to see if any of those services might have been used to compromise the system. But suppose that someone later turns off a service and there is no way to know if it was running at the time of an attack.

Although there is no way to know for sure what services were running at any point in time, we can determine if a service's startup mode changed since the time of an attack. The query Ch07ServiceStartChanged.sql searches through the services portion of the registry and lists the ten services with the most recently changed start modes.

Run this query with the following command:

```
logparser.exe file:Ch07ServiceStartChanged.sql
```

```
--- Ch07ServiceStartChanged.sql ---
SELECT TOP 10
    KeyName,
    Startup,
    LastWriteTime
USING
    CASE Value
        WHEN '2'
        THEN 'Automatic'
        WHEN '3'
        THEN 'Manual'
        WHEN '4'
        THEN 'Disabled'
    END AS Startup
FROM HKLM\System\CurrentControlSet\Services\
WHERE ValueName='Start'
    AND Value<>'1'
ORDER BY LastWriteTime DESC
--- Ch07ServiceStartChanged.sql ---
```

Although the Registry Editor does not show dates, the registry records the last modified date for all keys. This information is extremely useful in this case because Windows stores the startup mode for each service in the registry. By checking the last write time for this value, we can determine when the startup mode for a service changed. Since this field contains a value from 1 through 4, we use the CASE statement to convert these values into readable text. Note that a value of 1 indicates that the service is a system driver, so we will disregard those in this query.

If a service is set to Disabled, but that value recently changed, we might assume that the service previously was enabled. Again, this isn't solid evidence, but it gives you a better picture of the server environment at the time of an attack.

Installed Programs

The last write time on registry keys is also useful for viewing the installation dates of recently installed applications. It is not uncommon for an intruder to install applications or tools on a target system. The query Ch07RecentSoftware.sql demonstrates how to gather this installation information. Run the query with the following command:

```
logparser.exe file:Ch07RecentSoftware.sql
```

```
--- Ch07RecentSoftware.sql ---
SELECT TOP 10
    Value AS Product,
    LastWriteTime AS [Date Installed]
FROM HKLM\SOFTWARE\Microsoft\Windows\CurrentVersion\Installer\UserData
WHERE ValueName='DisplayName'
ORDER BY LastWriteTime DESC
--- Ch07RecentSoftware.sql ---
```

This query will list the same applications in the Add or Remove Programs Control Panel applet, but only shows the 10 most recent applications, sorted by the order in which they were installed, most recent first. Note that this query will not show programs that were installed then later uninstalled. However, some applications will leave files on the system even after uninstalling the application. In addition to the previous query, the query Ch07RecentProgramFiles.sql might also turn up programs installed by an intruder. Run the query with the following command:

```
logparser.exe file:Ch07RecentProgramFiles.sql -i:fs -recurse:0
```

```
--- Ch07RecentProgramFiles.sql ---
SELECT
    TOP 10 Name,
    CreationTime
FROM 'C:\program files\*.*'
ORDER BY CreationTime DESC
--- Ch07RecentProgramFiles.sql ---
```

Related to installed programs is adding or removing Windows components. If you add or remove any Windows component, the Optional Components Manager goes through every component and generates an installation log, even if you did not change that particular component. Therefore, by running the query Ch07OptionalComponents.sql, we can determine precisely when a component was added or removed.

Run the query with this command:

```
logparser.exe file:Ch07OptionalComponents.sql -i:fs -recurse:0
```

```
--- Ch07OptionalComponents.sql ---
SELECT
    Name,
```

```
      LastWriteTime
FROM c:\windows\*.*
WHERE name like '%oc%.log%'
--- Ch07OptionalComponents.sql ---
```

This query will produce results something like this:

```
Name              LastWriteTime
-----------       -----------------------
medctroc.Log      2004-10-13 22:50:09.328
msgsocm.log       2004-10-13 22:50:09.203
netfxocm.log      2004-10-13 22:50:09.343
ocgen.log         2004-10-13 22:50:09.328
ocmsn.log         2004-10-13 22:50:09.984
tabletoc.log      2004-10-13 22:50:10.0
tsoc.log          2004-10-13 22:50:10.78
```

Notice how all dates and times are approximately the same, indicating that Windows updated all component logs, even if the component remained unmodified. This information further contributes to re-creating the environment at the time of the attack and recreating the intrusion.

Final Touches

Investigating an intrusion is a long and complex process, but by parsing through data and viewing this information from different angles, you gradually build a picture of what occurred. The key here is to summarize, sort, and slice your data enough times until key evidence emerges. As you gather information, use it to further refine your queries, but be careful to not let it blind you to other evidence that may be out there. Investigating intrusions is tedious work, but tools like Log Parser have put the odds of finding the intruder in our favor.

Chapter 8

Security Auditing

Scripts and Samples in this Chapter:

- **Assessing IIS Configurations**
- **Monitoring IIS Contents**

In This Toolbox

In Chapter 2, we covered analyzing different log files to obtain information about a server's performance, usage, security, and health status. However, it is important to note that this information is derived from captured log files; in other words – its history, as it represents the requests or server actions that have already occurred.

Security auditing, on the other hand, checks and scans through related settings and configurations to help determine where things might go wrong if the system is not configured properly. With this in mind, auditing is a critical element when it comes to security processes and protecting the servers. Security auditing of an IIS server covers the IIS configurations as well as IIS contents that reside on file system. This chapter showcases many useful queries that you can employ during the auditing process.

Auditing IIS

Auditing IIS mainly focuses on the IIS configurations that reside in the Metabase file. Prior to IIS 6.0, the Metabase was stored in a single binary (.bin) file. With IIS 6.0, the Extensible Markup Language (XML) file was introduced to replace these binary files. The Metabase.xml file holds the configuration settings and MBSchema.xml contains the schema for the XML configuration file.

> **TIP**
>
> Auditing an IIS configuration requires a general understanding of IIS metabase knowledge, as well as the metabase property keys. To learn more about this, please refer to: www.microsoft.com/resources/documentation/IIS/6/all/techref/en-us/iisRG_MET_1.mspx.

Metabase.xml is a plain-text XML file that can be opened via Notepad or another text editor. However, it is not advisable to edit Metabase.xml directly in this manner; instead, it is recommended that you configure IIS via IIS Microsoft Management Console (MMC), or via Active Directory Service Interfaces (ADSI).

Assessing IIS Configurations

To audit and verify IIS configurations, Log parser uses Active Directory Service (ADS) as the input format and IIS as the service provider. ADS is a new input format supported by Microsoft Log parser 2.2. Accessing IIS configuration settings is an important routine to ensure that IIS is configured properly and associated security risks are minimized.

TIP

To learn more about the ADS input format, refer to the Appendix section in this book, or enter **logparser.exe -i -h:ADS** at the command prompt to see information on supported command switches and available property fields.

Although IIS 6.0 is secure by design, there might be configuration settings that have been reconfigured or customized to suit certain applications running on the server. It is also possible, when the system is managed by many different system administrators, that one might overlook some configurations that may lead to certain security risks.

The focus of the configuration assessment includes IIS services properties, content location, logging format and configuration, authentication methods, application pool identity, and many more. Before we move on to the sample queries, it is important to know about available field properties that can be queried via ADS format. Table 8.1 includes the supported fields and their descriptions.

Table 8.1 Active Directory Service Query Fields

Property	Field	Description
Object Path	ObjectPath	The ADS hierarchical path of the object.
Object Name	ObjectName	The name of the ADS object.
Object Class	ObjectClass	Object classes, for example, IIsWebServer and IIsFtpServer.
Property Name	PropertyName	The property field name.
Property Value	PropertyValue	The value held by the property.
Property Type	PropertyType	The type of the field property, for example, string or integer.

Installed IIS Services

Before determining which services to audit, it is important to know which services have been installed and which related sites have been created. The Ch08IISservices.sql query scans through the Metabase via the IIS provider to obtain the list of services running and their respective sites. The results generated include site service ID associated with the services and the name of the site and services it belongs to.

```
---Ch08IISservices.sql---
SELECT
    ObjectName AS SiteID,
    PropertyValue AS SiteName,
    CASE ObjectClass
        WHEN 'IIsWebServer' THEN 'HTTP'
        WHEN 'IIsFtpServer' THEN 'FTP'
```

```
        WHEN 'IIsSmtpServer' THEN 'SMTP'
        WHEN 'IIsNntpServer' THEN 'NNTP'
        ELSE 'Unknown Service'
    END AS Service
FROM IIS://LOCALHOST/
WHERE
    (ObjectClass LIKE '%Server')
    AND
    (ObjectPath NOT LIKE '%/W3SVC/Info/%')
    AND
    (ObjectPath NOT LIKE '%/MSFTPSVC/Info/%')
    AND
    (PropertyName = 'ServerComment')
ORDER BY Service, SiteID
---Ch08IISservices.sql---
```

The output will show you how many sites were created and associated with which types of service. If any of the services are not needed, you should uninstall the specific service component using **Add or Remove Programs** in Control Panel.

In the previous query, **IIS://LOCALHOST/** is specified in the *FROM* clause. The query first declares the *ObjectName* column alias as *SiteID*, then declares *PropertyValue* as the *SiteName*, and uses a *CASE* clause to categorize the component as *Services*.

The *WHERE* clause is the key in this query, and it is determines whether a particular service is installed, as each services' site existing in the *ObjectClass* property with a format for IIs*XXX*Server, where *XXX* represents the service name. For example, *IIsFtpServer* indicates that the site belongs to IIS FTP (File Transfer Protocol) services. Next, you can filter out rows with *ObjectPath* containing the string **/W3VC/Info/** and **/MSFTPSVC/Info/**. These are default IIS service templates for creating new sites. Normal site creation will be in W3SVC/*XXX*/ format, where the *XXX* represents the site ID. And finally, the query checks for *ServerComment* in *PropertName*. This property holds the value of the server site description, for example, "Default Web Site."

TIP

Unlike W3C extended format log files, the IIS Metabase structure is not well defined and not flexible to parse; this is because data structures are stored in a property field and value in rows. For example, look at the following excerpt from a generic *SELECT* statement:

```
ObjectName      ObjectClass          PropertyName
IIsWebServer    KeyType              IIsWebServer
IIsWebServer    ServerState          2
IIsWebServer    ServerComment  www.mysite.com
```

However, with a little effort and a better understanding of the row structure, you should be able to formulate useful queries. One way to learn more about the structure output is to do a simple query using **SELECT FROM**

IIS://LOCALHOST/ and redirect the output to a text file, then spend some time exploring the generated text file. It also helps to run Metabase Explorer to explore the Metabase hierarchy and structure of the IIS configuration file. Metabase Explorer is included in the IIS 6 resource kit tools. For more information about the resource kits, please refer to: www.microsoft.com/windowsserver2003/iis/downloads/default.mspx.

To run the query, first go to Command Prompt, navigate to the directory where you installed the query samples, and enter the following:

```
logparser .exe file:Ch08IISservices.sql
-stats:OFF -o:NAT –i:ADS -rtp:-1
```

The command syntax tells Log parser to read the example query and output it in *NATIVE* format. **–i:ADS** specifies the input format as Active Directory Service object. Note that this input switch can be ignored, as Log parser is smart enough to figure out the input format using the *FROM* clause. The following shows a sample result of the query:

```
SiteID SiteName                                  Services
------ ----------------------------------- --------
1      Default FTP Site                          FTP
2      My FTP Site                               FTP
1      mywebsite                                 HTTP
2      Microsoft SharePoint Administration  HTTP
8560   Administration                            HTTP
1      Default NNTP Virtual Server               NNTP
1      Default SMTP Virtual Server               SMTP
```

Swiss Army Knife

Retrieving IP and Port Bindings

After determining which services are currently running on the IIS server, it is also important to audit the IP (Internet Protocol) address and port bindings of each service. By modifying the sample query to the following, you can get a list of all IIS service site IP addresses and port binding details:

```
---Ch08SvrPorts.sql---
SELECT Services, SiteID, IPAddr, Port
    USING STRLEN(EXTRACT_TOKEN(PropertyValue,0,':')) AS IPValue,
    CASE ObjectClass
```

Continued

```
              WHEN 'IIsWebServer' THEN 'HTTP'
              WHEN 'IIsFtpServer' THEN 'FTP'
              WHEN 'IIsSmtpServer' THEN 'SMTP'
              WHEN 'IIsNntpServer' THEN 'NNTP'
              ELSE 'Unknown Service'
        END AS Services,
        ObjectName AS SiteID,
        CASE IPValue
              WHEN 0 THEN 'All Unassigned'
                    ELSE EXTRACT_TOKEN(PropertyValue,0,':')
        END AS IPAddr,
        EXTRACT_TOKEN(PropertyValue,1,':') AS Port
FROM IIS://LOCALHOST
WHERE
        (PropertyName = 'ServerBindings')
        AND
        (ObjectClass LIKE '%Server')
        AND
        (ObjectPath NOT LIKE '%/W3SVC/Info/%')
        AND
        (ObjectPath NOT LIKE '%/MSFTPSVC/Info/%')
---Ch08SvrPorts.sql---
```

The results can help you to troubleshoot any connectivity issues. For example, if services are not binding to the default port, this query will tell you which port it binds to. The result could also be a requirement list for a firewall administrator to configure related policies if such services are accessed from another network or the Internet.

A *USING* clause is used to declare the *IPValue*, which contains the string length of the IP address. This variable is used to determine whether the service IP binding is to a specific IP address or all IP addresses registered in the machine. *ServerBindings* is the property name that holds IP and port binding details.

Auditing Content Paths

By default, during IIS installation, many service folders and file contents are created on the system volume partition. For example, the FTP default root path is typically located at C:\Inetpub\ftproot>. It is recommended that you relocate IIS content files to another partition or hard drive in order to restrict access to sensitive system information located on the system drive if there is a security breach.

Moving web content to a new disk volume will also protect you from directory traversal attacks; an attack that involves an attacker accessing a file outside the web folder structure. Though IIS 6.0 is not currently vulnerable to traversal attacks, by moving contents to a standalone disk volume, you can minimize the potential exposure to future attacks.

The Ch08SysVolContents.sql query analyzes the Metabase to gather sites or virtual directory configurations that are mapped to a system partition. The output covers the related sites and virtual directories mapping along with the actual content path.

```
---Ch08SysVolContents.sql---
SELECT
    EXTRACT_TOKEN(ObjectPath,1,'LOCALHOST/') AS [Sites or virtual directories],
    TO_LOWERCASE(PropertyValue) AS MappedPath
FROM IIS://LOCALHOST
WHERE
    (PropertyName = 'Path')
    AND
    (PropertyValue LIKE '%SystemDrive%%')
ORDER BY [Sites or virtual directories]
---Ch08SysVolContents.sql---
```

This query is simple and straight-forward; it searches for the *PATH* property value, which contains the content path of virtual directories and service sites. The filter checking in the *WHERE* clause specifies the property name as *Path* and *PropertyValue* should contain the string **%SystemDrive%**, which is a system environment variable and the typical the value is **C:**.

To run the query, first go to Command Prompt, navigate to the directory where you installed the query samples, and enter the following:

```
logparser .exe file:Ch08SysVolContents.sql
-o:NAT -rtp:-1 > SysVolContents.txt
```

This instructs Log parser to read the query and generate the output in *NATIVE* format and redirect the output to a text file named *SysVolContents.txt*. The following shows the sample result of the query:

```
Sites or virtual directories        MappedPath
--------------------------- ----------------------------------------------------------
--
MSFTPSVC/1/ROOT                     c:\inetpub\ftproot
MSFTPSVC/2/ROOT                     c:\inetpub\ftproot
NNTPSVC/1/ROOT                      c:\inetpub\nntpfile\root
NNTPSVC/1/ROOT/_slavegroup          c:\inetpub\nntpfile\root\_slavegroup
NNTPSVC/1/ROOT/control              c:\inetpub\nntpfile\root\control
W3SVC/1/ROOT                        c:\inetpub\wwwroot
W3SVC/1/ROOT/CertControl            c:\windows\system32\certsrv\certcontrol
W3SVC/1/ROOT/CertEnroll             c:\windows\system32\certsrv\certenroll
W3SVC/1/ROOT/CertSrv                c:\windows\system32\certsrv
W3SVC/1/ROOT/Printers               c:\windows\web\printers
W3SVC/1/ROOT/_vti_bin               c:\program files\common files\microsoft shared\web
                                        server extensions\50\isapi
W3SVC/2/Root                        c:\program files\common files\microsoft shared\web
                                        server extensions\50\isapi\_vti_adm
W3SVC/8560/Root                     c:\windows\system32\serverappliance\web
W3SVC/8560/Root/tsweb               c:\windows\system32\serverappliance\web\admin\tsweb\
```

```
Statistics:
-----------
Elements processed: 6467
Elements output:    14
Execution time:     6.99 seconds
```

With the output, you will have a better idea about which sites and virtual directories are mapping content paths on your system volume. It is suggested that you move this content to a new disk volume and secure it with strong NT File System (NTFS) permissions.

Auditing Authentication Methods

There are many authentication methods supported in IIS 6.0. These methods determine the authentication mechanism required for content access, either through anonymous access or via basic, integrated Windows and other methods. The reason for auditing authentication modes is to allow you understand which authentication modes are enabled for a particular site or virtual directory. For example, if a certain virtual directory contains sensitive data, you might want to disable anonymous access and further secure it with NTFS permission.

TIP

To learn more about IIS authentication methods, please refer to the IIS help documentation or access it online at:
www.microsoft.com/resources/documentation/iis/6/all/proddocs/en-us/sec_auth_aboutauth.mspx.

IIS includes many built-in authentication methods, including the latest Microsoft Passport authentication. These built-in authentication modes are easy to configure and allow simple control of access without any additional coding. The Ch08IISAuths.sql query analyzes Metabase to gather each site's or virtual directory's configured authentication methods. The output covers the related sites and virtual directories and its related authentication mode.

```
---Ch08IISAuths.sql---
SELECT
    EXTRACT_TOKEN(ObjectPath,1,'LOCALHOST/') AS [Sites or virtual directories],
    CASE TO_INT(PropertyValue)
        WHEN 1 THEN 'Anonymous Auth'
        WHEN 2 THEN 'Basic Auth'
        WHEN 3 THEN 'Anonymous|Basic'
        WHEN 4 THEN 'Integrated Windows Auth'
        WHEN 5 THEN 'Anonymous|Integrated'
        WHEN 6 THEN 'Basic|Integrated'
        WHEN 7 THEN 'Anonymous|Basic|Integrated'
        WHEN 16 THEN 'Digest Auth'
```

```
        WHEN 17 THEN 'Anonymous|Digest'
        WHEN 18 THEN 'Basic|Digest'
        WHEN 19 THEN 'Anonymous|Basic|Digest'
        WHEN 20 THEN 'Integrated|Digest'
        WHEN 21 THEN 'Anonymous|Integrated|Digest'
        WHEN 22 THEN 'Basic|Integrated|Digest'
        WHEN 23 THEN 'Anonymous|Basic|Integrated|Digest'
        WHEN 64 THEN 'Passport Auth'
        WHEN 65 THEN 'Anonymous|Passport'
        ELSE 'Unknown methods'
    END AS Authentication
FROM IIS://LOCALHOST
WHERE
    (PropertyName = 'AuthFlags')
    AND
    (ObjectClass NOT LIKE '%Service')
    AND
    (ObjectClass NOT LIKE '%WebServer')
    AND
    (ObjectPath NOT LIKE '%/W3SVC/Info/%')
    AND
    (ObjectPath NOT LIKE '%/MSFTPSVC/Info/%')
---Ch08IISAuths.sql---
```

> ### NOTE
>
> The query parses IIS services authentication methods except the FTP service because the FTP service does not contain the property *AuthFlags*, and it only supports anonymous and basic authentication.
>
> It is important to note that when enabling Microsoft Passport authentication, the only other method you can select is anonymous access. Passport authentication cannot coexist with other methods.

When analyzing this sample query, you must interpret the property value from a numeric value to a meaningful description. For example, according to Metabase documentation, the value **1** is defined as anonymous authentication only. The other key point is to filter out unneeded rows, hence there are many *NOT LIKE* statements. To see which record rows are being filtered out, you can simply remove the condition checking and run the query to see the output.

To run the query, first go to Command Prompt, navigate to the directory where you installed the query samples, and enter the following:

```
logparser .exe file:Ch08IISAuths.sql
-o:NAT -rtp:-1
```

This instructs Log parser read the query generate the output in *NATIVE* format with no Row to Print restriction. The following shows the sample result of the query:

```
Sites or virtual directories Authentication
---------------------------- -------------------------------
NNTPSVC/1                     Anonymous Auth
SmtpSvc/1                     Anonymous|Basic|Integrated
W3SVC/1/ROOT                  Anonymous|Basic
W3SVC/1/ROOT/_private         Anonymous|Basic
W3SVC/1/ROOT/_vti_bin         Anonymous|Basic
W3SVC/1/ROOT/_vti_cnf         Anonymous|Basic
W3SVC/1/ROOT/_vti_log         Anonymous|Basic
W3SVC/1/ROOT/_vti_pvt         Anonymous|Basic
W3SVC/1/ROOT/_vti_script      Anonymous|Basic
W3SVC/1/ROOT/_vti_txt         Anonymous|Basic
W3SVC/1/ROOT/aspnet_client    Anonymous|Basic
W3SVC/1/ROOT/CertControl      Integrated Windows Auth
W3SVC/1/ROOT/CertEnroll       Integrated Windows Auth
W3SVC/1/ROOT/CertSrv          Integrated Windows Auth
W3SVC/1/ROOT/Printers         Anonymous|Passport
W3SVC/1/ROOT/test1            Anonymous|Basic|Integrated
W3SVC/1/ROOT/wmpub            Integrated Windows Auth
W3SVC/2/Root                  Anonymous|Integrated
W3SVC/2/Root/aspnet_client    Anonymous|Integrated
W3SVC/8560/Root               Anonymous|Basic|Integrated|Digest
W3SVC/8560/Root/tsweb         Anonymous|Basic|Integrated|Digest
```

Master Craftsman

More Authentication Analysis

So how do you obtain FTP authentication information? The answer is easy – by using a similar query with different *WHERE* clause checking. For example, try:

```
---Ch08FtpAuths.sql---
SELECT
    EXTRACT_TOKEN(ObjectPath,1,'LOCALHOST/') AS [Sites or virtual directories],
    CASE TO_INT(PropertyValue)
            WHEN 1 THEN 'Anonymous|Basic'
            ELSE 'Basic only'
    END AS Authentication
FROM IIS://LOCALHOST
```

Continued

```
WHERE
     (PropertyName = 'AllowAnonymous')
     AND
     (ObjectClass = 'IIsFtpServer')
     AND
     (ObjectPath NOT LIKE '%/MSFTPSVC/Info/%')
---Ch08FtpAuths.sql---
```

As discussed previously, FTP configuration does not contain the *AuthFlags* property; hence to obtain authentication methods configured for FTP, the *AllowAnonymous* key is used.

Basic authentication is the most common, widely adopted industry standard for user authentication; this is because it is supported by many browsers such as Internet Explorer, Netscape, Mozilla, and others. However, basic authentication uses Base64 encoding to encode user credentials. In other words, it is in plain-text format. Because it is not encrypted, it can be easily decoded. To prevent the data from being intercepted, it is always recommended that you deploy a Secure Sockets Layer (SSL) connection to secure the communication channel when using basic authentication. The following query scans for websites with basic authentication enabled but without SSL protection.

```
---Ch08BasicNoSSL.sql---
SELECT
     EXTRACT_TOKEN(ObjectPath,1,'LOCALHOST/') AS [Basic Auth enabled without SSL]
FROM IIS://LOCALHOST/W3SVC
WHERE
     (PropertyName='AccessSSL')
     AND
     (PropertyValue='0')
HAVING ObjectPath
IN
(SELECT
     ObjectPath
FROM IIS://LOCALHOST/W3SVC
WHERE
     (PropertyName = 'AuthBasic')
     AND
     (PropertyValue = '1')
     AND
     (ObjectPath NOT LIKE '%/W3SVC/Info/%'))
---Ch08BasicNoSSL.sql---
```

Based on the results, it is recommended that you deploy SSL cert for the respective website. It is important to note that secure basic authentication via SSL is only applicable to W3SVC; it is not available for FTPSVC because the IIS 6.0 FTP component does not support SSL. It is recommended to secure FTP connections via other means such as using a Virtual Private Network (VPN) or IP Security (IPSec).

Next, in basic authentication, there are additional settings to determine the types of logon. The *LogonMethod* key holds this information. IIS 6.0 introduces a new logon

Continued

type, NETWORK_CLEARTEXT. This is the default logon type with a value of **3** in the property. With this logon type, basic authentication is no longer required to logon locally, hence it is important to audit and verify if there another logon type had been configured.

```
---Ch08LogonMethods.sql---
SELECT
    EXTRACT_TOKEN(ObjectPath,1,'LOCALHOST/') AS [Sites or virtual directories],
    CASE TO_INT(PropertyValue)
      WHEN 0 THEN 'Interactive Logon'
      WHEN 1 THEN 'Batch Logon'
      WHEN 2 THEN 'Network Logon'
      ELSE STRCAT('Unknown Method:',PropertyValue)
    END AS [Logon Method]
FROM IIS://LOCALHOST/
WHERE
    (PropertyName = 'LogonMethod')
    AND
    (PropertyValue <> '3')
---Ch08LogonMethods.sql---
```

This query analyzes the Metabase configuration and generates a list of sites or directories that are using different logon types other than the default NETWORK_CLEARTEXT type.

Auditing Site Access Properties

Now that you understand the authentication methods used in each site, it is time to look at the site access properties. These access properties refer to types of access are allowed for web content. These access types are divided into two main categories, including site permissions and execute permissions:

- **Site Permissions**:
  - **Read** (enabled by default) allows users to view directory and file content.
  - **Write** allows users to modify directory or file content.
  - **Script source access** allows users to access source files, including source code for scripts.

- **Execute Permissions:**
  - **None** disallows running of any programs or scripts.
  - **Scripts only** enables scripting engine application mapping.
  - **Scripts and Executables** enables any scripting engines and Windows binaries to run in this directory.

Most of these permissions apply to web components. The only access properties applicable to FTP service are read and write, which matches the AccessRead and AccessWrite property keys in the Metabase.

The Ch08WriteAccess.sql query analyzes the Metabase to locate write-enabled virtual directories along with other configured access permissions. The result includes the site path and the configured properties.

```
---Ch08WriteAccess.sql---
SELECT
    EXTRACT_TOKEN(ObjectPath,1,'LOCALHOST/') AS [Sites or virtual directories],
    CASE TO_INT(PropertyValue)
      WHEN 2 THEN 'Write Only'
      WHEN 3 THEN 'Read|Write'
      WHEN 18 THEN 'Write|Script Source Access'
      WHEN 19 THEN 'Read|Write|Script Source Access'
      WHEN 514 THEN 'Write|Scripts Only'
      WHEN 515 THEN 'Read|Write|Scripts Only'
      WHEN 518 THEN 'Write|Scripts and Executables'
      WHEN 530 THEN 'Write|Script Source Access|Scripts Only'
      WHEN 531 THEN 'Read|Write|Script Source Access|Scripts Only'
      WHEN 534 THEN 'Write|Script Source Access|Scripts and Executables'
      WHEN 535 THEN 'Read|Write|Script Source Access|Scripts and Executables'
      ELSE STRCAT('Unknown properties :',PropertyValue)
    END AS [Access Mode]
FROM IIS://LOCALHOST
WHERE
    (PropertyName = 'AccessFlags')
    AND
    ((ObjectPath LIKE '%MSFTPSVC%')
    OR
    (ObjectPath LIKE '%W3SVC%'))
HAVING ObjectPath
IN
(SELECT
    ObjectPath
FROM IIS://LOCALHOST
WHERE
    (PropertyName = 'AccessWrite')
    AND
    (PropertyValue='1'))
---Ch08WriteAccess.sql---
```

This is another example of a *SELECT* within a *SELECT*, where the inner *SELECT* statement looks for sites or virtual directories with write access enabled (in which the value for the *AccessWrite* key is **1**). The main *SELECT* statement further processes the result and determines other configured permissions; this is done by obtaining the value of *AccessFlags* in the Metabase.

This is a very useful query, as enabling special permissions such as *Write, Script source access, Scripts and Executables* are considered high risk because they might lead to potential security issues if they are not properly locked down with authentication and strong NTFS permissions. It is recommended that these settings not be enabled on production machines unless it is absolutely necessary.

WARNING

The risks of enabling special permissions:

Write enables users to create or modify existing file contents. Potential security threats to the server exist, as attackers might upload malicious scripts and attack the server. For example, an online accounting system running with write permissions might enable attackers to modify sensitive accounting data.

Script source access allows user to directly access script source code via IIS. Enabling this access grants users the ability to download and view script source files remotely, revealing internal application structure, business logic, database schema, and configuration detail. For example, hackers can use this access to retrieve Active Server Pages (ASP) application configuration files (global.asa), which normally holds the database connection details of the application. Hackers then use the login details to gain unauthorized access to the database server.

Scripts and Executables allows users to invoke scripting engines and execute Windows binaries files. Binary application executable files may include Common Gateway Interface (CGI), such as a Perl interpreter running as an executable file (.exe). Although, by default, IIS does not serve all unknown CGI or ISAPI extensions, it is not recommended that you grant this permission unless it is needed.

To run the query, first go to Command Prompt, navigate to the directory where you installed the query samples, and enter the following:

```
logparser .exe file:Ch08WriteAccess.sql
-o:NAT -rtp:-1 > WriteAccess.txt
```

This instructs Log parser to read the query and generate output in *NATIVE* format and redirect the output to a text file named WriteAccess.txt. The following shows the sample result of the query:

```
Sites or virtual directories Access Mode
---------------------------- --------------------------------
MSFTPSVC/1/ROOT/             Read|Write
MSFTPSVC/2/ROOT/MyVirDir     Write Only
W3SVC/1/ROOT/images          Read|Write|Scripts Only
W3SVC/1/ROOT/MyDir           Read|Write|Scripts and Executables
W3SVC/1/ROOT/upload          Read|Write|Scripts Only
```

Swiss Army Knife

Auditing Other Site Properties

Directory browsing is a special website or directory access property that exhibits a folder and file listing of the mapped path. Enabling directory browsing could lead to information disclosure of file and folder structures. Unless necessary, it is not recommended that you allow directory browsing. When directory browsing is enabled and default documents are not set, IIS will return a directory listing of the requested path.

The following query analyzes existing website structure and lists paths with directory browsing enabled together with default document configuration.

```
---Ch08DirBrowsing.sql---
SELECT
    EXTRACT_TOKEN(ObjectPath,1,'LOCALHOST/') AS [Directory Browsing Enabled Path],
    CASE TO_INT(PropertyValue)
        WHEN 0 THEN 'Not Configured'
        WHEN 1 THEN 'Configured'
        ELSE STRCAT('Unknown status:',PropertyValue)
    END AS DefaultDoc
FROM IIS://LOCALHOST/W3SVC
WHERE (PropertyName = 'EnableDefaultDoc')
HAVING ObjectPath
IN
(SELECT
    ObjectPath
FROM IIS://LOCALHOST/W3SVC
WHERE
    (PropertyName = 'EnableDirBrowsing')
    AND
    (PropertyValue = '1'))
---Ch08DirBrowsing.sql---
```

The Metabase keys focused on here will be *EnableDirBrowsing* and *EnableDefaultDoc*, both of which represent directory listing and default document configuration. It is recommended that you configure at least one default document for websites and directories.

As discussed in Chapter 2, site activities logging is important in understanding server performance, usage, and health status. Hence, it is important that each service component be configured with proper logging. The following query generates information about sites that do not have logging enabled (represented by a *LogType* of **0**.

```
---Ch08NoLogs.sql---
SELECT
```

Continued

```
      EXTRACT_TOKEN(ObjectPath,1,'LOCALHOST/') AS [Path with logging disabled]
FROM IIS://LOCALHOST/
WHERE
    (PropertyName = 'LogType')
    AND
    (PropertyValue = '0')
    AND
    (ObjectClass LIKE '%Server')
---Ch08NoLogs.sql---
```

Auditing Application Pools

Application pool identity, more commonly known as *Process Identity* in the Microsoft Windows operating system, denotes the account identity that a process runs under. By default, work processes run under the *Network Service* identity. This account is predefined and has fewer privileges than *LocalSystem*, which is the default process identity for in-process IIS 5.0 applications.

When configuring the application pool identity, you can either choose from predefined built-in accounts or the configurable accounts. Configurable accounts refer to any Windows registered user account. It is recommended that you choose from predefined accounts unless you are sure what you are configuring. The predefined accounts are:

- **LocalSystem** application pool with full access to the entire system.

- **Network Service** low-level access rights to the system and network resources while equipped to run normal worker processes.

- **LocalService** least privileges account, suitable for application pools and does not require access to network resources.

TIP

For more information about predefined application pool identities and procedures to customize the identity, please refer to: www.microsoft.com/resources/documentation/iis/6/all/proddocs/en-us/ca_wpim.mspx.

The Ch08AppPoolId.sql query scans configured application pools and determines the process identity used. The output includes the application pool name and the configured identity type.

```
---Ch08AppPoolId.sql---
SELECT
    ObjectName AS [Application Pool],
    CASE TO_INT(PropertyValue)
        WHEN 0 THEN 'Local System'
```

```
      WHEN 1 THEN 'Local Service'
      WHEN 2 THEN 'Network Service (default)'
      WHEN 3 THEN 'Customize User'
      ELSE STRCAT('Unknown Identity:',PropertyValue)
    END AS [Application Identity]
FROM IIS://LOCALHOST/W3SVC
WHERE (PropertyName = 'AppPoolIdentityType')
HAVING ObjectPath
IN
(SELECT
    DISTINCT ObjectPath
FROM IIS://LOCALHOST/W3SVC
WHERE (ObjectClass = 'IIsApplicationPool'))
---Ch08AppPoolId.sql---
```

From the generated result, you can easily identify which application identity was configured for each pool. If an application does not require the identity access privileges, it is recommended that you reconfigure the process identity to a lower privileges account.

The query starts by gathering the application pool running in the server. The *DISTINCT* clause is used to filter out duplicated rows that exist in the *IisApplicationPool,* which belongs to *ObjectClass.* The main *SELECT* statement searches the value in *AppPoolIdentityType* and determines the logon type by comparing the value using a *CASE* clause.

To run the query, first go to Command Prompt, navigate to the directory where you installed the query samples, and enter the following:

```
logparser .exe file:Ch08AppPoolId.sql
-o:NAT -rtp:-1
```

This instructs Log parser to read the query and generate output in the *NATIVE* format. The following shows the sample result of the query:

```
Application Pool      Application Identity
------------------    ------------------------
DefaultAppPool        Network Service (default)
MSSharePointAppPool   Local System
MyAppPool             Customize User
```

Auditing ASP Configurations

There are many ASP configurations that might leak information disclosure and pose certain security implications. These configurations include ASP parent path, query error message, secure session ID, error to event log, request entity, and more. These configurations must be audited to help lower the security risks associated with them. The following briefly discusses each setting's usage and default value:

- **Event Log** (*AspErrorsToNTLog*) default value is false. This property determines whether to capture additional error details in the Windows Event viewer when the ASP application is experiencing errors. It is recommended that you enable this in your Metabase key to gather maximum information when errors occur.

- **Request Entity** (*AspMaxRequestEntityAllowed*) default value is 200k. This property specifies the maximum bytes allowed in the body of an ASP request. Setting this limit prevents huge ASP entity posting. It is advised that you only increase the entity size on an as-needed basis.

- **Parent Path** (*AspEnableParentPaths*) default value is false. This property specifies whether the ASP application allows access to relative paths using the (../) notation to access the parent directory. This poses a security risk if a web application is located on the system drive and requests are being made to access related system files. It is not recommended that you enable this feature; instead, the application should use the absolute path when referencing other content.

- **Query Error Message** (*AspScriptErrorSentToBrowser*) default value is true. This property controls whether IIS should return ASP error messages including filename, line number, and the error description to the client browser. This information can be helpful in troubleshooting, but also poses a security risk, as it exposes the query name, path information, and more. It is recommended that this setting be turned off in the production stage.

- **Secure Session ID** (*AspKeepSessionIDSecure*) default value is false. This property ensures the session ID details are sent in secure mode if assigned over a SSL channel. ASP sessions use the session ID to maintain each client connection detail. The session ID and connection detail can be spoofed by an attacker if intercepted, so it is recommended that you enable this property to minimize the security risk.

The following sample queries cover the auditing of these settings and list the corresponding websites and virtual directory path details. The first, the Ch08AspEventLog.sql query, gathers ASP content sites and directories that did not send query errors to the Windows Event Log.

```
---Ch08AspEventLog.sql---
SELECT
    PropertyValue AS [Websites without AspErrorsToNTLog enabled]
FROM IIS://LOCALHOST/W3SVC
WHERE (PropertyName = 'ServerComment')
HAVING ObjectPath
IN
(SELECT
    ObjectPath
FROM IIS://LOCALHOST/W3SVC
WHERE
    (PropertyName = 'AspErrorsToNTLog')
```

```
    AND
    (PropertyValue = '0')
    AND
    (ObjectClass =  'IIsWebServer')
    AND
    (ObjectPath NOT LIKE '%/W3SVC/Info/%'))
---Ch08AspEventLog.sql---
```

The Ch08AspMaxRequestEntity.sql query looks for websites or directories that have **AspMaxRequestEntityAllowed** size configured higher than the default value.

```
---Ch08AspMaxRequestEntity.sql---
SELECT
    EXTRACT_TOKEN(ObjectPath,1,'LOCALHOST/') AS [Sites or virtual directories],
    STRCAT(TO_STRING(DIV(TO_INT(PropertyValue),1024)),'k') AS AspMaxRequestEntity
FROM IIS://LOCALHOST/W3SVC
WHERE
    (PropertyName = 'AspMaxRequestEntityAllowed')
    AND
    (ObjectClass NOT LIKE '%WebServer')
HAVING (TO_INT(PropertyValue) > 204800)
---Ch08AspMaxRequestEntity.sql---
```

The Ch08AspparentPath.sql query lists sites that have the parent path enabled.

```
---Ch08AspParentPath.sql---
SELECT
    EXTRACT_TOKEN(ObjectPath,1,'LOCALHOST/') AS [Sites or virtual directories with ASP
Parent Path enabled]
FROM IIS://LOCALHOST/W3SVC
WHERE
    (PropertyName = 'AspEnableParentPaths')
    AND
    (PropertyValue = '1')
    AND
    (ObjectPath NOT LIKE '%/W3SVC/Info/%')
---Ch08AspParentPath.sql---
```

The Ch08AspScriptError.sql query gathers a list of websites and directories that are not supposed to send detail ASP script error to client browsers.

```
---Ch08AspScriptError.sql---
SELECT
    EXTRACT_TOKEN(ObjectPath,1,'LOCALHOST/') AS [Sites or virtual directories with ASP
Script Error sent to client]
FROM IIS://LOCALHOST/W3SVC
WHERE
    (PropertyName = 'AspScriptErrorSentToBrowser')
```

```
    AND
    (PropertyValue = '1')
    AND
    (ObjectClass NOT LIKE '%Service')
    AND
    (ObjectClass NOT LIKE '%WebServer')
    AND
    (ObjectPath NOT LIKE '%/W3SVC/Info/%')
---Ch08AspScriptError.sql---
```

The Ch08AspSecureSessionID.sql query analyzes the Metabase to determine whether secure session ID has been configured for an ASP session-enabled website.

```
---Ch08AspSecureSessionID.sql---
SELECT
    EXTRACT_TOKEN(ObjectPath,1,'LOCALHOST/') AS [Asp Website],
    CASE TO_INT(PropertyValue)
        WHEN 0 THEN 'Not configured'
        WHEN 1 THEN 'Secure SessionID configured'
        ELSE STRCAT('Unknown status:',PropertyValue)
    END AS [Secure SessionID]
FROM IIS://LOCALHOST/W3SVC
WHERE (PropertyName = 'AspKeepSessionIDSecure')
HAVING ObjectPath
IN
(SELECT
     ObjectPath
FROM IIS://LOCALHOST/W3SVC
WHERE
    (PropertyName = 'AspAllowSessionState')
    AND
    (PropertyValue = '1')
    AND
    (ObjectClass = 'IIsWebServer')
    AND
    (ObjectPath NOT LIKE '%/W3SVC/Info/%'))
---Ch08AspSecureSessionID.sql---
```

To make this auditing more effective, take the following batch file, audit these configurations, and redirect all results to one file:

```
::Ch08AspAudit.cmd
::Auditing ASP Configuration Batch File
::Chapter 8 - Auditing IIS

@ECHO OFF
SETLOCAL
```

```
SET Result="AspAudit.txt"
ECHO Scanning ASP Configuration...
ECHO Start... > %Result%

ECHO AspErrorsToNTLog >> %Result%
@logparser .exe file:Ch08AspEventLog.sql -stats:OFF -rtp:-1 >> %Result%
ECHO. >> %Result%

ECHO AspMaxRequestEntityAllowed >> %Result%
@logparser .exe file:Ch08AspMaxRequestEntity.sql -stats:OFF -rtp:-1 >> %Result%
ECHO. >> %Result%

ECHO AspEnableParentPaths >> %Result%
@logparser .exe file:Ch08AspParentPath.sql -stats:OFF -rtp:-1 >> %Result%
ECHO. >> %Result%

ECHO AspScriptErrorSentToBrowser >> %Result%
@logparser .exe file:Ch08AspScriptError.sql -stats:OFF -rtp:-1 >> %Result%
ECHO. >> %Result%

ECHO AspKeepSessionIDSecure >> %Result%
@logparser .exe file:Ch08AspSecureSessionID.sql -stats:OFF -rtp:-1 >> %Result%
ECHO. >> %Result%

ECHO ...End >>   %Result%
ECHO Completed. Result:
MORE < %Result%
```

This batch file runs individual ASP audit query and outputs to a text file named AspAudit.txt. To run the query, first go to Command Prompt, navigate to the directory where you installed the query samples, and enter the following:

```
logparser.exe file:>Ch08AspAudit.cmd
```

The batch file also displays the results at the end of processing, and you can also use any text editor to open the result file. Based on the results, it is recommended that you configure the required Metabase property key to further lock down related websites and directories.

Auditing the File System

File system refers to the methods and data structure that an operating system allocates to keep track of files and folders stored on a disk media. Windows Server 2003 supports different file systems including File Allocation Table (FAT) 16, FAT32 and NTFS. The FAT file systems are not recommended, as they do not provide file-level security. It is always recommended that you use NTFS for Windows Server operation systems, as it provides full security access control via Access Control Lists (ACLs) and supports long filenames and large storage media.

The concept of auditing the file system presented here leans more toward IIS-related files and folder monitoring as opposed to general ideas of auditing, which may include access auditing on selected files, file ownership information, folder and file ACL verifications, and more.

TIP

To learn more about NTFS structure and technologies supported, please refer to: www.microsoft.com/resources/documentation/WindowsServ/2003/all/techref/en-us/W2K3TR_ntfs_intro.asp.

Monitoring IIS Contents

IIS contents are static (images, text) or dynamic (ASP, CGI) files served by IIS. To audit these file contents, Log parser uses File System (FS) as the input format. Auditing IIS contents not only provides details on content types used by different services, but also serves as a security channel to check if there are additional unknown or illegal files that have been copied to the content paths. These illegal contents might be dangerous or occupy huge disk spaces. For example, dangerous contents might include virus-infected files or worm queries. Huge disk space usage might be due to attackers uploading pirated software, movie files, and others that tag the server as a distribution server.

TIP

To learn more about FS input format, you can refer to the Appendix section at the end of this book or enter **logparser.exe -i -h:FS** at the command prompt to see the help information on supported command switches and available property fields.

The audit process primary focuses on World Wide Web (WWW) and FTP contents, as both services are involved in accepting client requests and sending the requested content directly. The audit covers scanning of file types, file size, creation date, file attributes, and others. Before we move on to the sample queries, it is important to know about available field properties that can be queried via FS format. Table 8.2 lists the supported field properties and their descriptions:

Table 8.2 File System Query Fields

Property	Field	Description
File Path	path	The content path of the file.
File Name	name	The name of the file.
File Size	size	The file size in bytes.
File Attributes	attributes	The associated file attributes.

Continued

Table 8.2 File System Query Fields

Property	Field	Description
Creation Date	creationtime	The creation date and time of the file.
Last Access Time	lastaccesstime	The date and time of last access.
Last Write Time	lastwritetime	The date and time of last write.
File Version	fileversion	The version number of the file.
Product Version	productversion	The file product version number.
Internal Name	internalname	The file name referred to internally.
Product Name	productname	The product name that the file belongs to.
Company Name	companyname	The company that owns the file.
Copyright detail	legalcopyright	The copyright information of the product.
Trademarks	legaltrademarks	The trademarks details.
Private Build No.	privatebuild	The internal build number of the file.
Special Build No.	specialbuild	The special build reference number.
Comments	comments	The comment information of the file.
File Description	filedescription	The description of the file.
Original File Name	originalfilename	The original name of the file.

While there are many query fields supported in FS format, the contents audit primarily focuses on the following property fields:

- path
- name
- size
- attributes
- creationtime
- lastaccesstime
- lastwritetime
- comments

Auditing Content Types

Content or file types are determined by the file extensions. For example *.gif* and *.jpg* are image file types. As well as getting details on the type of contents used, auditing content types can help discover illegal file types that are located in the content path. It serves as a monitoring channel if prohibited contents exist in the content path.

The Ch08ContentTypes.sql script scans through an input content path and analyzes the types of content used. It uses **–i:FS** to inform Log parser for file system input format.

```
---Ch08ContentTypes.sql---
SELECT
    [File Type], Total
    USING TO_LOWERCASE(EXTRACT_EXTENSION(name)) AS Type,
    CASE STRLEN(Type)
        WHEN 0 THEN 'No extension'
        ELSE Type
    END AS [File Type],
    COUNT() AS Total
INTO %chartname%
FROM %source%
WHERE (attributes NOT LIKE 'D%')
GROUP BY [File Type]
ORDER BY Total DESC
---Ch08ContentTypes.sql---
```

This query generates output as a chart diagram image. It expects two input parameters; the first one, **%chartname%**, is the output image name of the chart image, and **%source%** refers the file path that Log parser will analyze.

The *USING* clause defines the variable *Type,* where it converts the string value to lowercase format from the file extension. The purpose of the *CASE* clause is to determine if there are files without extensions. If such files exist, it will assign *No extension* as the file extension. The *WHERE* clause condition instructs Log parser to ignore folder names that have the value **D** in the attributes field.

TIP

The following example uses **d:\web\.** as the example content path. You will need to change . to your web content path. Also, the same concept applies to FTP contents. You can also specify the **%source%** as **d:\web\.,d:\ftp\.** to instruct Log parser to analyze the content types of both paths. Use a comma to separate each content path.

To run the query, first go to Command Prompt, navigate to the directory where you installed the query samples, and enter the following:

```
logparser .exe
file:Ch08ContentTypes.sql?chartname="webcontenttypes.gif"
+source="d:\web\." -i:fs -o:chart -chartType:PieExploded3d
-chartTitle:"Website Content Types" -values:on -view
-groupSize:800x600
```

This command instructs Log parser to read from the Ch08ContentTypes.sql query file. It specifies the output image file parameter as **webcontenttypes.gif**, and **d:\web\.** as the content path. The chart type used in the example is *PieExploded3d*, and specifies *Website Content Types* as the chart title. The *-value:on* switch outputs the total number of each file type in the diagram, and finally, *-view* instructs Log parser to view the image file at the end of the process and *-groupSize* sets the image resolution size. See Figure 8.1 for a sample chart diagram.

NOTE

The example shown in this section only uses one chart type (PieExploded3d). To learn more about different chart types, refer to the Appendix section, or access the help document using the following command:

logparser.exe -h -o:chart | more

This will show you the available chart type details as well as the parameters you can specify when using the *-o:chart* method. However, it is important to note that the chart diagram output requires Microsoft Office XP or later to be installed. This is because the chart diagram output uses the Office application library when generating the output.

Figure 8.1 Sample Chart Diagram – Website Content Types

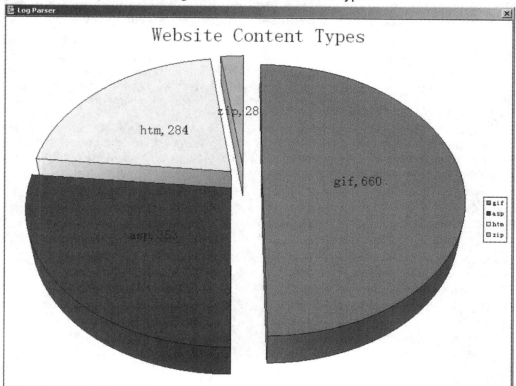

Master Craftsman

Advanced Content Types Auditing

From the sample output diagram, what if you noticed the presence of illegal file types? How do you find their paths? Refer to the following:

```
---Ch08FindContentTypes.sql---
SELECT
    EXTRACT_PATH(path) AS ContentPath,
    name AS ContentName
FROM %source%
WHERE (TO_LOWERCASE(EXTRACT_EXTENSION(name)) = '%filetype%')
ORDER BY ContentPath
---Ch08FindContentTypes.sql---
```

This query parses the content path and looks for the content type specified in the **%file%** parameter. To run the query, enter the following at the command prompt:

```
logparser .exe file:Ch08FindContentTypes.sql?source="d:\web\.*"+filetype="mov"
```

This query is also particularly useful to find include files, which have the file extension .inc. This file type should be mapped to the ASP engine because a direct request for an .inc file can display the file content in a client browser, as IIS serves it as plain text. Although IIS 6.0 prevents this request due to its new security implementation, previous versions of IIS do not prevent this.

Next, Ch08IllegalContents.sql scans for content path and looks for suspicious file names. This normally happens when the FTP server is *tagged*, whereby attackers have taken control in order to upload *warez*-related contents. *Warez* contents are normally associated with pirated software, pornographic content, illegal music, or movies.

```
---Ch08IllegalContents.sql---
SELECT
    EXTRACT_PATH(path) AS ContentPath,
    name AS ContentName
FROM %source%
WHERE
    (name LIKE '%tagged%')
    OR (name LIKE '%xxx%')
    OR (name LIKE '%warez%')
    OR (name LIKE '%.nfo%')
    OR (name LIKE '%porn%')
    OR (name LIKE '%pr0n%')
    OR (name LIKE '%owned%')
```

Continued

```
    OR (name LIKE '%0wn3d%')
    OR (name LIKE '%0wnz%')
    OR (name LIKE '%crackz%')
    OR (name LIKE '%0-day%')
    OR (name = 'iso')
ORDER BY ContentPath
---Ch08IllegalContents.sql---
```

This query looks for warez-like contents and generates a listing that includes the file path and content name.

There are times when a system administrator might accidentally place a sensitive file in the IIS content path. These types of content may include FTP log files, configuration files, system information data files, and more. The Ch08SensitiveContents.sql query scans the content path and looks for sensitive data contents.

```
---Ch08SensitiveContents.sql---
SELECT
    EXTRACT_PATH(path) AS ContentPath,
    name AS ContentName
FROM %source%
WHERE
    (name = 'ws_ftp.log')
    OR (name LIKE '%.log')
    OR (name LIKE '%.mdb')
    OR (name LIKE '%.dbf')
    OR (name LIKE '%.sql')
    OR (name = 'stats')
    OR (name = 'log')
    OR (name = 'logs')
    OR (name LIKE '%usage%')
    OR (name LIKE '%admin%')
    OR (name LIKE '%orders%')
    OR (name LIKE '%private%')
ORDER BY ContentPath
---Ch08SensitiveContents.sql---
```

These files may contain sensitive data that, if leaked, will post a security risk. For example, the FTP log file may reveal information of uploaded contents name, its path, FTP client IP address, and more.

To scan for possible signs of worms, trojans, or malformed queries, the Ch08BadContents.sql query looks for possible content that might related to torjans and malformed queries.

```
---Ch08BadContents.sql---
SELECT
    EXTRACT_PATH(path) AS ContentPath,
    name AS ContentName
FROM %source%
```

Continued

```
WHERE
    (name = 'cmd.exe')
    OR (name like 'cmd%.asp')
    OR (name = 'shell.asp')
    OR (name = 'perl.exe')
    OR (name = 'nc.exe')
    OR (name = 'tini.exe')
    OR (name = 'root.exe')
    OR (name = 'upload.asp')
    OR (name = 'upload.inc')
    OR (name = 'osql.exe')
    OR (name = 'pslist.exe')
    OR (name = 'tasklist.exe')
    OR (name = 'tlist.exe')
    OR (name = 'tftp.exe')
    OR (name = 'telnet.exe')
    OR (name LIKE 'showcode%')
    OR (name LIKE 'viewcode%')
    OR (originalfilename ='cmd.exe')
ORDER BY ContentPath
---Ch08BadContents.sql---
```

Auditing Contents Access

To know more about requested content characteristics, we need to looks at their properties. These properties can help identify the popularity of the content, when it was created, when it was last accessed, and more.

The Ch08ContentCreationDate.sql script scans through an input content path and outputs the content names that have been created within the specified time period. This is particularly useful in identifying new contents that are created on the IIS server. This audit check allows you acknowledge that these contents are valid.

```
---Ch08ContentCreationDate.sql---
SELECT
    ContentPath, FileName, [Creation Date Time]
    USING creationtime AS [Creation Date Time],
    TO_DATE([Creation Date Time]) AS Cdate,
    TO_DATE(TO_LOCALTIME(SUB(SYSTEM_TIMESTAMP(), TIMESTAMP('%day%', 'd')))) AS Days,
    EXTRACT_PATH(TO_LOWERCASE(path)) AS ContentPath,
    TO_LOWERCASE(name) AS FileName
FROM %source%
WHERE
    (attributes NOT LIKE 'D%')
    AND
    (Cdate >= Days)
```

```
ORDER BY [Creation Date Time] DESC
---Ch08ContentCreationDate.sql---
```

This query parses through the content directories and looks for content that has been created within the specified number of days. It uses two parameters, the **%source%** as the input of the content path, and **%day%** as the time period in days. The *SYSTEM_TIMESTAMP()* function is used to obtain the current date and time. This value is then converted to the local time zone using the *TO_LOCALTIME* function. After that, the query takes this value and subtracts the input parameter.

To run the query, first go to Command Prompt, navigate to the directory where you installed the query samples, and enter the following:

```
logparser .exe file:Ch08ContentCreationDate.sql?source="d:\web\."+day="15"
-i:FS -preserveLastAccTime
```

The syntax instructs Log parser to read the **d:\web\.** content path and looks for files that have been created in the past two weeks (15 days). Since it does not specify the output format, the default *NATIVE* mode is used. The *+day* parameter specifies the number of days. **1** indicates today. To specify the past two weeks, the value will be **15**. For example, *+day="15"*. Note that the maximum days that you can specify is 31, which is equivalent to one month.

> **NOTE**
>
> The *-preservelastAccTime* switch tells Log parser to preserve the files' last access time. This property indicates when the content was last accessed. Using this switch to ensures that Log parser will not change the access time when it scans through the content path.

The following shows the sample result of the query:

```
ContentPath        FileName         Creation Date Time
-----------        --------------   ------------------
d:\web\asp         latest.html      2004-09-05 15:33:43.715
d:\web\clienttemp  input.asp        2004-09-04 02:12:30.012
d:\web\clienttemp  updatepro.asp    2004-08-31 22:19:51.220
....
```

Swiss Army Knife

Advanced Contents Access Auditing

The example query will allow you to scan for the latest content update time. By using the *lastwritetime* property, you will be able to obtain when the content was last updated. Notice that *creationtime* refers to the date and time it was created, whereas *lastwritetime* specifies when the content was updated.

```
---Ch08ContentLastWriteDate.sql---
SELECT
    ContentPath, FileName, [Last Write Date]
    USING lastwritetime AS [Last Write Date],
    TO_DATE([Last Write Date]) AS Ldate,
    TO_DATE(TO_LOCALTIME(SUB(SYSTEM_TIMESTAMP(), TIMESTAMP('%day%', 'd')))) AS Days
    EXTRACT_PATH(TO_LOWERCASE(path)) AS ContentPath,
    TO_LOWERCASE(name) AS FileName
FROM %source%
WHERE
    (attributes NOT LIKE 'D%')
    AND
    (Ldate >= Days)
ORDER BY [Last Write Date] DESC
---Ch08ContentLastWriteDate.sql---
```

Notice that the this code is similar to the example query, but instead of looking for creation date, the query now looks for modification date. This query is useful in determining if the content was updated, and if the update was not made known to you, you might want to audit the content to see if it contains any illegal or malformed coding that might harm the server.

Now, how do you determine which files are not very popular or are no longer valid? The same concept applies here, but this time you will focus on *lastaccesstime*. This property specifies when the content was last requested. If the content has not been accessed for a long time, you might want to check if the content is still valid and useful. The Ch08OldContents.sql query lists the top 10 oldest contents located in the content path. The output includes the folder path, the content name, and the time period that it was last accessed.

```
---Ch08OldContents.sql---

SELECT

    Top 10

    ContentPath, FileName, AccessDate, [Days (Old)]
```

Continued

```
        USING lastaccesstime AS Ltime,

        TO_DATE(Ltime) AS AccessDate,

        SUB(TO_LOCALTIME(SYSTEM_TIMESTAMP()), AccessDate) AS ODate,

        TO_INT(ODate) AS Seconds,

        DIV(Seconds,86400) As [Days (Old)],

        EXTRACT_PATH(TO_LOWERCASE(path)) AS ContentPath,

        TO_LOWERCASE(name) AS FileName

    FROM %source%

    WHERE (attributes NOT LIKE 'D%')

    ORDER BY AccessDate

    ---Ch08OldContents.sql---
```

This query is not as complicated as it may look. The *USING* clause declares many variables referenced throughout the query. The main logic is to obtain the current date, and subtract the last access time to determine the number of days for which the content was not accessed. The *TO_INT* function helps convert the date value to number of seconds which then *DIV* divided by 86400 to obtain the number of days.

Auditing Contents Properties

In this section, we will look at other file properties that might be interesting to audit and can help you gather useful information. For example, if the content name and original name do not match, the content might have been renamed to hide from normal inspection; such content might be a threat and have to be analyzed.

The Ch08OriginalFileName.sql script scans through an input content path and list contents that do not match the original file name. The property field used in this query is *originalfilename*.

```
---Ch08OriginalFileName.sql---
SELECT
    EXTRACT_PATH(TO_LOWERCASE(path)) AS ContentPath,
    TO_LOWERCASE(name) AS FileName,
    TO_LOWERCASE(originalfilename) AS OriginalFileName
FROM %source%
WHERE
    (originalfilename IS NOT NULL)
    AND
    (TO_LOWERCASE(name) <> TO_LOWERCASE(originalfilename))
ORDER BY ContentPath
---Ch08OriginalFileName.sql---
```

The output columns include the content directory path, the current filename, and the orginal filename. It is important to note that this query targets binary files, which compile with original filenames included. Normal application query and static files do not have this property.

To run the query, first go to Command Prompt, navigate to the directory where you installed the query samples, and enter the following:

```
logparser .exe file:Ch08OriginalFileName.sql?source="d:\web\." -i:FS
```

The command instructs Log parser to scan the content path and look for contents in which the current name does not match the original filename. The following shows the sample result of the query:

```
ContentPath            FileName       OriginalFileName
--------------------   ------------   ----------------------
d:\web\casino\         loginchk.dll   upload.exe
d:\web\upload\temp     test.exe       cmd.exe
...
```

Swiss Army Knife

Exploring Other Content Properties

In Chapter 2, we were able to identify the top requested contents that use most of the bandwidth. In the following example, Ch08Top10FileSize.sql identifies the top 10 contents according to file size.

```
---Ch08Top10FileSize.sql---
SELECT
    TOP 10
    EXTRACT_PATH(TO_LOWERCASE(path)) AS ContentPath,
    TO_LOWERCASE(name) AS FileName,
    DIV(size,1024) AS FileSize(K)
FROM %source%
ORDER BY FileSize(K) DESC
---Ch08Top10FileSize.sql---
```

This query outputs the largest file size located in the content path. This is useful when you need to find out any big content files in FTP content path. The query output includes the content path, content name, and the file size in kilobytes.

A file with an attribute **H** indicates that it is hidden from normal directory listings. Typically, hidden files are system-related and should not be displayed within IIS content

Continued

paths. The Ch08HiddenFiles.sql query scans for any hidden content inside the content path.

```
---Ch08HiddenFiles.sql---
SELECT
    EXTRACT_PATH(TO_LOWERCASE(path)) AS ContentPath,
    TO_LOWERCASE(name) AS FileName,
    size AS FileSize,
    creationtime AS CreationDate
FROM %source%
WHERE
    (attributes LIKE '%H%')
    AND
    (attributes NOT LIKE 'D%')
ORDER BY CreationDate DESC
---Ch08HiddenFiles.sql---
```

This query looks for hidden contents in the specified path. It lists out the creation date of the file, the size of the file, and its path details. These contents could be hidden by attackers to bypass normal checking and might become threat to the server if not properly audited.

Final Touches

To formulate useful queries, first determine what information is needed, then investigate the available properties to construct the output. Start with a simple query to obtain required data, and then apply filtering, checking, and listing orders to produce the required information. The core elements in this chapter are getting to know more about the available key properties and understand important IIS configurations and content properties that should be audited. Auditing is a critical process in security assessement and really must be implemented in order to have a secure and healthy server.

Chapter 9

Enhancing
Log Parser

Scripts and Samples in this Chapter:

- Parsing Windows Cluster Service Logs
- Parsing Excel Spreadsheets
- Examining Windows Service Configuration
- Parsing Internet Explorer Favorites
- Querying Arbitrary WMI Classes
- Simplifying Query Creation
- Data-Driven Formatting
- Managing Identity Flow to Remote Input Sources
- Maintaining a Responsive User Interface
- Combining Query Output with External Data
- Using Script Parameters to Configure Log Parser Commands
- Publishing LogQuery Output by E-mail
- Using Query Results to Construct an .REG File
- Storing LogQuery Output in a new Access Database

In This Toolbox

Log Parser Version 2.2 includes extensive functionality that allows administrators to extract and examine data from a wide range of input sources, but its use as a stand-alone tool is sometimes limited. In this chapter, we'll demonstrate ways you can extend the Log Parser's capabilities to handle additional input formats, and methods by which you can make Log Parser's default capabilities more accessible to non-administrators. In addition, we'll examine ways to incorporate Log Parser as a core component within scripts that provide powerful business solutions.

Building Input Processors

One of the key extensibility features introduced in Log Parser 2.2 is the new COM input format, which enables developers to write COM plug-ins or *input processors* that allow Log Parser to extract input from new input formats. Written as COM objects, these input processors can be used through both the Log Parser command-line application and the scriptable Log Parser COM components.

Log Parser input processors expose *records* to the Log Parser engine. Each of these records consists of one or more fields defined by the input processor itself. It is the responsibility of the input processor author to determine how data will be extracted from an input source and mapped into the fields to create a record.

All custom input processors follow the same general methodology to extract data from an input source and expose it to the Log Parser engine as a series of records. First, the input processor opens the specified input source so that the contents can be read. Next, using the field definitions contained within the input processor itself, the input processor reads data from the input source and associates the data with the fields to create records. In many ways, the process is analogous to mapping data from an input source to the columns and rows of an SQL table whose structure is defined by the input processor. This process is independent of the query that has been passed to the Log Parser query engine; the input processor always fully populates its table with rows, and the query engine uses the query to manipulate and return records from this table.

There are two methods by which a COM object can be written to function as a Log Parser input processor:

- The object can implement the *ILogParserInputContext* interface, whose declaration can be found in the COM\ILogParserInputContext.hxx file that is installed below the Log Parser 2.2 application directory.

- The object can implement the *IDispatch* interface, and support the same methods exposed by the ILogParserInputContext interface.

The Log Parser 2.2 documentation lists the methods exposed by the ILogParserInputContext interface, explains the order in which they are called, and details the field types that can be returned to the Log Parser query engine.

In addition to the methods required by the ILogParserInputContext interface, input processors can expose properties or *parameters* that can be used to significantly alter the behavior of the input processor—anything from changing the fields exposed to changing the methodology by which the processor gathers the data. In this section, we'll examine several input processors that implement the ILogParserInputContext interface and demonstrate possible usage scenarios for plug-in parameters.

Parsing Windows Cluster Service Logs

Windows Cluster Service logs contain a wealth of information that is invaluable in troubleshooting issues with cluster stability and/or performance. Unfortunately, the compact ASCII format and the vast amount of information the logs contain make them difficult to interpret.

Although cluster log entries seem impenetrable when viewed through a text editor such as Notepad, they are actually fairly easy to parse into separate fields. There are two types of cluster log entries: component event log entries and resource DLL log entries. In addition to several mandatory fields that are common to all entries, each type contains one or more type-specific fields. Full details on the anatomy of cluster log entries can be found in the Windows 2000 Server Distributed Systems Guide, located at www.microsoft.com/resources/documentation/windows/2000/server/reskit/en-us/distsys/part3/dsgch20.mspx.

The following lists the source code for the LP_ToolKit.ClusterLog input processor, written in C# by implementing the ILogParserInputContext interface tool:

```
---Ch09ClusterLogs.cs---
// Windows Cluster Service Log Input format sample
namespace LP_Toolkit
{
    using System;
    using System.Collections;
    using System.Runtime.InteropServices;
    using System.Text.RegularExpressions;
    using System.IO;

    public interface ILogParserInputContext
    {
        void OpenInput(string from);
        int GetFieldCount();
        string GetFieldName(int index);
        int GetFieldType(int index);
        bool ReadRecord();
        object GetValue(int index);
        void CloseInput(bool abort);
    }

    // ClusterLog input processor for LogParser
```

```
[Guid("7a495293-727c-4fec-baff-1ec5cc24b862")]
public class ClusterLog : ILogParserInputContext
{
    // For a Cluster log, the following 'fields' are available:
    // ProcessPID, ThreadPID, EventTime, Component
    // ResourceName, ResourceType, Description

    FileStream fstr;
    StreamReader sr;
    ArrayList logFields;
    string currentLogEntry;

    Regex ProcPidRegex = new Regex(@"^(?<ProcessPID>\w+)\.");
    Regex ThreadPidRegex = new Regex(@"\.(?<ThreadPID>\w+)");
    Regex DateRegex = new Regex(@"::(?<EventTime>\S+)\s");
    Regex CompRegex = new Regex(@"^(\S+)\s\[(?<Component>\S+)\]");
    Regex ResTypeRegex =
        new Regex(@"\s(?<ResourceType>[^<:]+)[<:]");
    Regex ResNameRegex = new Regex(@"<(?<ResourceName>.+)>:");
    Regex DesComRegex = new Regex(@"(\])s?(?<Description>.+)$");
    Regex DesResRegex =
        new Regex(@"(::)(.)+:\s?(?<Description>.+$)");)
    Match m;

    #region LogField Class
    private class LogField
    {
        string fieldName;
        FieldType fieldType;

        public LogField(string FieldName, FieldType FieldType)
        {
            fieldName = FieldName;
            fieldType = FieldType;
        }

        public string FieldName
        {
            get { return fieldName; }
            set { fieldName = value; }
        }

        public FieldType FieldType
        {
            get { return fieldType; }
```

```
            set { fieldType = value; }
        }
    }
    #endregion

    // ClusterLog constructor
    public ClusterLog()
    {
        logFields = new ArrayList();

        logFields.Add(new LogField("ProcessPID", FieldType.String));
        logFields.Add(new LogField("ThreadPID", FieldType.String));
        logFields.Add(new LogField("EventTime",
            FieldType.Timestamp));
        logFields.Add(new LogField("Component", FieldType.String));
        logFields.Add(new LogField("ResourceType",
            FieldType.String));
        logFields.Add(new LogField("ResourceName",
            FieldType.String));
        logFields.Add(new LogField("Description",
            FieldType.String));
    }

    //  Open a log file or resource
    //  "from" is the entity to open, specified in the FROM clause
    public void OpenInput(string from)
    {
        if( from != "" )
        {
            // Load the cluster log file
            fstr = new FileStream(from, FileMode.Open,
                FileAccess.Read, FileShare.ReadWrite);
            sr = new StreamReader(fstr);

        }
    }

    public object GetValue(int index)
    {
        LogField lf = (LogField)logFields[index];
        // currentLogEntry = (string) logEntries.Current;

        switch (lf.FieldName)
        {
            case "ProcessPID":
```

```
            m = ProcPidRegex.Match(currentLogEntry);
            return m.Groups["ProcessPID"].Value;
        case "ThreadPID":
            m = ThreadPidRegex.Match(currentLogEntry);
            return m.Groups["ThreadPID"].Value;
        case "EventTime":
            m = DateRegex.Match(currentLogEntry);
            return DateTime.Parse(
                m.Groups["EventTime"].Value).ToLocalTime();
        case "Component":
            m = CompRegex.Match(currentLogEntry);
            if ( m.Success )
                return m.Groups["Component"].Value;
            else
                return null;
```

**Script truncated, please refer to the book's accompanying website,
www.syngress.com/solutions for the entire code.
---Ch09ClusterLogs.cs---

Perform the following steps to use this input format:

1. Compile the Ch09ClusterLog.cs file with the following command (substitute the .NET Framework system assemblies path with the path on your computer):

```
csc.exe /r:C:\winnt\Microsoft.NET\Framework\v1.0.3705\System.dll
    /target:library /out:ClusterLog.dll Ch09ClusterLog.cs AssemblyInfo.cs
```

2. Install the ClusterLog.dll assembly into the GAC using the following command:

```
Gacutil.exe /i ClusterLog.dll
```

3. Register the ClusterLog.dll assembly with the following command:

```
Regasm.exe ClusterLog.dll
```

4. To see the fields returned by this input format, execute the following Log Parser command:

```
logparser.exe -h -i:COM -iprogid:LP_Toolkit.ClusterLog
```

5. Execute the following Log Parser query to retrieve the 50 most recent records from a Windows Cluster service log (subsitute the path to a Windows Cluster Service log file)

```
logparser.exe "SELECT EventTime, Component, Description FROM
C:\WINNT\Cluster\cluster.log" -i:COM
-iProgId:LP_Toolkit.ClusterLog
```

6. Execute the following Log Parser query to obtain the distribution of cluster log events by component type (subsitute the path to a Windows Cluster Service log file):

```
logparser.exe "SELECT Component, Count(*) as 'Number of Events' FROM
C:\WINNT\Cluster\cluster.log GROUP BY Component" -i:COM
-iProgId:LP_Toolkit.ClusterLog
```

7. Execute the following Log Parser query to retrieve all Windows Cluster service events within the last 12 hours triggered by physical disk resources (subsitute the path to a Windows Cluster Service log file):

```
logparser.exe "SELECT * FROM C:\WINNT\Cluster\cluster.log WHERE ResourceType =
'Physical Disk'and EventTime >= TO_LOCALTIME(SUB(SYSTEM_TIMESTAMP(),
TIMESTAMP('12', 'h')))" -i:COM -iProgId:LP_Toolkit.ClusterLog
```

Parsing Excel Spreadsheets

Excel spreadsheets are commonly used as the target of cut and paste operations by administrators who want to easily sort and/or format tabular data, such as output from batch file that executes tasks within a loop. Unfortunately, this usage pattern results in *data islands* that prevent these administrators from easily combining the spreadsheet data with output from previous operations.

The following code lists the source code for the LP_ToolKit.Excel input processor, a Windows Script Component (WSC) that uses VBScript and opendatabase connectivity (ODBC) to allow the Log Parser to extract data from an Excel workbook, which is specified in the query WHERE clause. This input processor exposes a read-only *Worksheet* property, which can be provided at the command line to target a specific worksheet within a given workbook. If not provided, the Worksheet property defaults to a value of *Sheet1*.

```
---Ch09ExcelInput.wsc---
logParser.exe Types
Public Const ftInteger = 0
Public Const ftReal = 1
Public Const ftString = 2
Public Const ftTimeStamp = 3

Dim oConn
Dim oRS
Dim m_Worksheet

Set oRS = CreateObject("ADODB.Recordset")

Function OpenInput(strWorkbook)
    ' Make sure the .xls file has been specified
    If IsNull(strWorkbook) or Len(strWorkbook) = 0 Then
      Exit Function
```

```
        End If

    If IsNull(m_Worksheet) or Len(m_Worksheet) = 0 Then
        m_Worksheet = "[Sheet1$]"
    End If

    ' Retrieve the spreadsheet contents into an
    ' ADO Recordset
    Set oConn = CreateObject("ADODB.Connection")
    oConn.Open "Provider=Microsoft.Jet.OLEDB.4.0;" & _
               "Data Source=" & strWorkbook & ";" & _
          "Extended Properties=""Excel 8.0;"""

    Set oRS = CreateObject("ADODB.Recordset")
    oRS.Open "SELECT * FROM " & m_Worksheet, oConn
    If Not oRS.EOF And oRS.BOF Then
        oRS.MoveFirst
    End if
End Function

Function GetFieldType(nFieldIndex)
    If oRS.State=0 Then
        GetFieldType = ftString
    Else
        Select Case oRS.Fields.Item(nFieldIndex).Type
            Case 5
                ' numeric (adDouble)
                GetFieldType = ftReal
            Case 6
                ' currency (adCurrency)
                GetFieldType = ftInteger
            Case 11
                ' boolean (adBoolean)
                GetFieldType = ftInteger
            Case 7
                ' date (adDate)
                GetFieldType = ftTimestamp
            Case Else
                'text (an ADO ad...Char type, such as 202, adVarChar,
                '    200, adVarWChar or similar)
                GetFieldType = ftString
        End Select
    End if
End Function
```

```
Function ReadRecord()
    If Not oRS.State = 0 then
        If oRS.EOF or oRS.BOF Then
            ReadRecord = False
        Else
            oRS.MoveNext
            ReadRecord = True
        End If
    End if
End Function


Function GetValue(nFieldIndex)
    If Not oRS.State = 0 then
        If Not oRS.EOF then
            GetValue = oRS.Fields.Item(nFieldIndex).Value
        End If
    End If
End Function


Function put_Worksheet(strWorksheet)
    ' If the user specifies a specific worksheet, ensure
    '   that the query will reference it;  otherwise,
    '   assume the Excel default worksheet name "Sheet1"
    If IsNull(strWorksheet) or Len(strWorksheet) = 0 Then
        m_Worksheet = "[Sheet1$]"
    Else
        m_Worksheet = "[" & strWorksheet & "$]"
    End If
End Function
```

```
**Script truncated, please refer to the book's accompanying website,
www.syngress.com/solutions for the entire code.
---Ch09ExcelInput.wsc---
```

Perform the following steps to use this input format:

1. Register the LP_Toolkit.Excel scriptlet with the following command:

   ```
   regsvr32 Ch09ExcelInput.wsc
   ```

2. Execute the following Log Parser query to retrieve information from the Sheet1 worksheet within the C:\sample.xls workbook:

   ```
   logparser.exe "SELECT * FROM C:\sample.xls" -i:COM
       -iprogid:LP_Toolkit.ExcelInput
   ```

3. To extract data from another worksheet, specify the worksheet name using the iComParams parameter as follows:

```
logparser.exe "SELECT * FROM C:\sample.xls" -i:COM
    -iprogid:LP_Toolkit.ExcelInput -iCOMParams:Worksheet=Sheet2
```

Swiss Army Knife

Accessing data from OBDC-compliant data sources

The LP_Toolkit.Excel input processor uses ActiveX Data Objects (ADO) and a hard-coded reference to the Microsoft Jet OLE DB 4.0 Provider to access the data stored within the Excel spreadsheets. By modifying the processor to accept provider and connection string details through command-line parameters, this tool could be extended to access data from virtually any ODBC-compliant data source.

Examining Windows Service Configuration

The management of Windows services is a crucial part of any system administrator's job. While there are numerous ways in which administrators can view information about the configuration of these services—Services.msc, net start, sc.exe, Regedit.exe—none of them provide the built-in capacity to query, filter, group, and sort the configuration data as if it were stored in an SQL table. The following lists the source code for the LP_ToolKit.Win32Services input processor, a Visual Basic 6.0 COM component that uses Windows Management Instrumentation (WMI) to extract information about services installed on a specified computer.

This processor combines several Win32_Service class properties retrieved through a WMI Query Language (WQL) *SELECT* statement with service dependency information obtained through the WQL *ASSOCIATORS OF* statement.

```
---Ch09Win32Services.cls---
'Module-level variables
Dim m_objWin32ServiceArray() As Service   'Array of processed results
Dim m_lIndex As Long       'Current record
Dim strDependencies As String
Dim m_bFirstDependency As Boolean
Dim m_DepMode As String


Public Sub OpenInput(strComputerName)


    Dim objWMIService As SWbemServices
    Dim objWin32Service, objDependentService As SWbemObject
```

```
Dim objWin32Services, objDependencies As SWbemObjectSet

' Default computer name is local machine
If (IsNull(strComputerName) Or Len(strComputerName) = 0) Then
    strComputerName = "."
End If


' Query for all the Windows services on the specified machine
Set objWMIService = GetObject("winmgmts:" _
    & "{impersonationLevel=impersonate}!\\" & strComputerName _
    & "\root\cimv2")
Set objWin32Services = objWMIService.ExecQuery( _
    "Select * from Win32_Service", , 0)


' Store in array

' If we're not adding a separate row for every dependency,
' set the array size to equal the number of services retrieved

If m_DepMode = "list" Or m_DepMode = "off" Then
    ' Using a fixed size array, with one element per service
    ReDim Preserve m_objWin32ServiceArray(objWin32Services.Count)
End If


m_lIndex = 0
For Each objWin32Service In objWin32Services
    Dim m_Service As Service

    m_Service.mName = objWin32Service.Name
    m_Service.mDescription = _
        IIf(IsNull(objWin32Service.Description), "", _
        objWin32Service.Description)
    m_Service.mDisplayName = objWin32Service.DisplayName
    m_Service.mPathName = objWin32Service.PathName
    m_Service.mProcessID = objWin32Service.ProcessID
    m_Service.mServiceType = objWin32Service.ServiceType
    m_Service.mStarted = objWin32Service.Started
    m_Service.mStartMode = objWin32Service.StartMode
    m_Service.mStartName = objWin32Service.StartName
    m_Service.mState = objWin32Service.State
    m_Service.mStatus = objWin32Service.Status

    Select Case m_DepMode
      Case "off"
        ' Add a single entry to the array of services
```

```
        ' Using a fixed size array, so assign the service
        ' to the current array position

        m_objWin32ServiceArray(m_lIndex) = m_Service
        m_lIndex = m_lIndex + 1

    Case "list"
        ' Create a comma-separated list of dependencies,
        ' and assign it to the mDependsOn member

        ' retrieve dependencies
        Set objDependencies = objWMIService.ExecQuery( _
            "Associators of {Win32_Service.Name='" & _
            objWin32Service.Name & "'} _Where AssocClass=" _
            & "Win32_DependentService Role=Dependent", , 0)

        If objDependencies.Count > 0 Then
            m_bFirstDependency = True
            For Each objDependentService In objDependencies
                If m_bFirstDependency = True Then
                    strDependencies = objDependentService.Name
                    m_bFirstDependency = False
                Else
                    strDependencies = strDependencies & ", " _
                    & objDependentService.Name
                End If
            Next
            m_Service.mDependsOn = strDependencies
        End If

        ' Add a single entry to the array of services
        ' Using a fixed size array, so assign the service
        ' to the current array position

        m_objWin32ServiceArray(m_lIndex) = m_Service
        m_lIndex = m_lIndex + 1
    Case "normalize"
        ' retrieve dependencies
        Set objDependencies = objWMIService.ExecQuery( _
            "Associators of {Win32_Service.Name='" & _
            objWin32Service.Name & "'} _Where AssocClass=" _
            & "Win32_DependentService Role=Dependent", , 0)

        If objDependencies.Count > 0 Then
            ' This service has depencies
            For Each objDependentService In objDependencies
```

```
                   ' Create one array entry for each dependency
                   ' Have to increment the array length to
                   ' accomodate each new entry

                   m_Service.mDependsOn = _
                     objDependentService.Name
                   ReDim Preserve m_objWin32ServiceArray( _
                     UBound(m_objWin32ServiceArray) + 1)
                   m_objWin32ServiceArray(UBound( _
                     m_objWin32ServiceArray)) = m_Service
                 Next
               Else
                 ' No dependencies, so we add a single entry to
                 ' the array of services
                 ReDim Preserve m_objWin32ServiceArray( _
                     UBound(m_objWin32ServiceArray) + 1)
                 m_objWin32ServiceArray(UBound( _
                     m_objWin32ServiceArray)) = m_Service
               End If
            End Select
        Next

    ' move the state pointer to the first array entry
    m_lIndex = LBound(m_objWin32ServiceArray)

    Set objDependentService = Nothing
    Set objDependencies = Nothing
    Set objWin32Services = Nothing
    Set objWin32Service = Nothing
End Sub

Public Function ReadRecord() As Boolean
    If m_lIndex >= UBound(m_objWin32ServiceArray) Then
        ReadRecord = False
    Else
        m_lIndex = m_lIndex + 1
        ReadRecord = True
    End If
End Function

Function GetFieldCount()
    GetFieldCount = IIf(m_DepMode = "off", 11, 12)
End Function

Private Sub Class_Initialize()
```

```
        m_DepMode = "list"
        ReDim m_objWin32ServiceArray(0)
End Sub

Public Property Let Dependencies(ByVal strDependencies As String)
        If Not (IsNull(strDependencies) Or Len(strDependencies) = 0) Then
            Select Case LCase(strDependencies)
                Case "off"
                    m_DepMode = "off"
                Case "normalize"
                    m_DepMode = "normalize"
                Case Else
                    m_DepMode = "list"
            End Select
        Else
            m_DepMode = "list"
        End If
End Property

Public Function GetValue(ByVal nFieldIndex As Integer) _
  As Variant
    Select Case nFieldIndex
      Case 0
        ' Description
        GetValue = _
          m_objWin32ServiceArray(m_lIndex).mDescription
      Case 1
        ' DisplayName
        GetValue = m_objWin32ServiceArray(m_lIndex).mDisplayName
      Case 2
        ' Name
        GetValue = m_objWin32ServiceArray(m_lIndex).mName
      Case 3
        ' Path To Executable
        GetValue = m_objWin32ServiceArray(m_lIndex).mPathName
      Case 4
        ' ProcessId
        GetValue = m_objWin32ServiceArray(m_lIndex).mProcessID
      Case 5
        ' ServiceType
        GetValue = m_objWin32ServiceArray(m_lIndex).mServiceType
      Case 6
        ' Started
        If m_objWin32ServiceArray(m_lIndex).mStarted Then
          GetValue = "Yes"
```

```
      Else
         GetValue = "No"
      End If
```

```
**Script truncated, please refer to the book's accompanying website,
www.syngress.com/solutions for the entire code.
---Ch09Win32Services.cls---
```

Perform the following steps to use this LP_Toolkit.Win32Service format:

1. Open the LP_Toolkit.vbp project with Microsoft Visual Basic 6.0 and build LP_Toolkit.dll

2. Register the LP_Toolkit.dll component with the following command:

   ```
   regsvr32 lp_toolkit.dll
   ```

NOTE

The LP_Toolkit.vbp project includes the source code for three tools (Win32Service, Favorites, and WMIQuery). You only need to build and compile LP_Toolkit.dll once in order to use all three tools.

3. To see the fields returned by this input format, execute the following Log Parser command:

   ```
   logparser.exe -h -i:COM -iprogid:LP_Toolkit.Win32Services
   ```

4. Execute the following command to list each service on the local machine that is dependent on the TCPIP service:

   ```
   logparser.exe "SELECT DisplayName FROM . WHERE DependsOn= 'Tcpip'"
   -i:COM -iProgID:LP_Toolkit.Win32Services
   -iCOMParams:Dependencies=normalize
   ```

5. Execute the following command to list the display name of each stopped service on a server named **Server1**:

   ```
   logparser.exe "SELECT DisplayName FROM Server1 WHERE Started='No'"
   -i:COM -iProgID:LP_Toolkit.Win32Services
   -iCOMParams:Dependencies=off
   ```

6. Execute the following command to list the the services on which a service named **MyService** on the local computer depends, with all information written in a single row of output:

```
logparser.exe "SELECT DependsOn FROM . WHERE Name='MyService'"
-i:COM -iProgID:LP_Toolkit.Win32Services
```

Because this technique generates multiple results per Win32_Service instance, the input processor provides the user with a *Dependencies* parameter to determine how the dependency information should be maintained internally. Table 9.1 lists the supported dependency values and the impact each has on how the dependency information is maintained internally:

Table 9.1 Dependency Parameter Values for the Win32Services Input Processor

Parameter Value	Internal Storage Representation
Off	Dependency information is not gathered, and the **DependsOn** field is removed from the output. This parameter value produces a significant performance increase, but sacrifices dependency information.
List (default)	Each service instance is represented as a single entry (row). Dependency entries for each service are stored within the **DependsOn** field as a comma-separated list. This parameter value results in fewer total rows, but sacrifices internal normalization between each service and the services it depends on.
Normalize	Service instances are represented as one or more rows. For each service, a separate row is created for each dependency entry, with the corresponding **DependsOn** field containing a single entry (or NULL). This parameter value results in a higher total number of rows, but allows queries to search and group by individual service dependencies.

Parsing Internet Explorer Favorites

Windows maintains Internet Explorer Favorites as individual ASCII text files, indicated by a .url extension. These .url files are Internet shortcuts stored within the Favorites special folder, which has its location determined by the setting stored in the HKEY_CURRENT_USER\Software\Microsoft\Windows\CurrentVersion\Explorer\User Shell Folders\Favorites registry key.

While the .url files are structured internally as simple initialization files (similar to .INI files), the Windows shell uses special handling of these shortcuts; if you right-click an Internet shortcut and try to edit it with Notepad, then you'll get its actual target, plus a few other options. The action of resolving an Internet shortcut in order to find the target URL is managed by a OS-level COM component that is part of the shell.

The following lists the source code for the LP_ToolKit.Favorites input processor, a Visual Basic 6.0 COM component that extracts selected information about each IE Favorite. The component uses the *FileSystemObject* provided by the Windows Scripting Runtime to locate and gather details about the actual .url file, and uses the *GetPrivateProfileString* Win32API method to parse the file contents.

```
---Ch09Favorites.cls---
Option Explicit

Private Type FavoriteRecord
    Title As String
     URL As String
     CreatedDate As Variant
     LastModDate As Variant
     Folder As String
 End Type


'Module-level variables
Dim m_Favorites() As FavoriteRecord   'Array of query results
Dim m_Files() As Files
Dim m_FullPaths As Boolean
Dim m_lIndex As Long                 'Current record

Public Sub OpenInput(ByVal FromEntity As String)
    ' Don't care about "FromEntity", since we'll only work with
    ' the current user

    Dim fso As FileSystemObject
    Dim mFolder, mSubFolder As Folder

    Set fso = CreateObject("Scripting.FileSystemObject")
    Set mFolder = fso.GetFolder(Environ("USERPROFILE") _
     & "\Favorites")

    ' gather info from .url files in Favorites folder
    GatherFavoriteInfo mFolder

    ' gather info from .url files in Favorites subfolders
    For Each mSubFolder In mFolder.SubFolders
        GatherFavoriteInfo mSubFolder
    Next

    Set mFolder = Nothing
    Set fso = Nothing

    ' move state tracker to first record
    m_lIndex = LBound(m_Favorites)

End Sub


Private Sub GatherFavoriteInfo(ByVal mFolder As Folder)
```

```
    Dim x As Long
    Dim sValue, sRetBuf As String
    Dim iLenBuf As Integer
    Dim strTitle As String

    sRetBuf$ = String$(256, 0)    '256 null characters
    iLenBuf% = Len(sRetBuf$)

    Dim myFavorite As FavoriteRecord

    Dim mFile As File
    For Each mFile In mFolder.Files
        x = GetPrivateProfileString("InternetShortcut", "URL", "", _
            sRetBuf$, iLenBuf%, mFile.Path)

        sValue = Left$(sRetBuf$, x)

        If LCase(Right$(mFile.Name, 3)) = "url" Then
        ' Valid shortcut
        strTitle = Left(mFile.Name, Len(mFile.Name) - 4)

            ReDim Preserve m_Favorites(UBound(m_Favorites) + 1)
            m_Favorites(UBound(m_Favorites)).Title = strTitle
            m_Favorites(UBound(m_Favorites)).url = sValue
            m_Favorites(UBound(m_Favorites)).CreatedDate = _
                mFile.DateCreated
            m_Favorites(UBound(m_Favorites)).LastModDate = _
                mFile.DateLastModified
            If m_FullPaths Then
                m_Favorites(UBound(m_Favorites)).Folder = _
                    mFile.ParentFolder.Path
            Else
                m_Favorites(UBound(m_Favorites)).Folder = _
                    mFile.ParentFolder.Name
            End If
        End If
    Next
    Set mFile = Nothing
End Sub
```

```
**Script truncated, please refer to the book's accompanying website,
www.syngress.com/solutions for the entire code.
---Ch09Favorites.cls---
```

Perform the following steps to use this LP_Toolkit.Favorites format:

1. Open the LP_Toolkit.vbp project with Microsoft Visual Basic 6.0 and build LP_Toolkit.dll.

2. Register the LP_Toolkit.dll component with the following command:

   ```
   regsvr32 lp_toolkit.dll
   ```

3. To see the fields returned by this input format, execute the following Log Parser command:

   ```
   logparser.exe -h -i:COM -iprogid:LP_Toolkit.Favorites
   ```

4. Execute the following command to list the display name, address, and containing folder name of each IE Favorite that is configured to use HTTPS (HyperText Transfer Protocol Secure):

   ```
   C:\Program Files\Log Parser 2.2 BETA5>logparser "SELECT Title, URL, Folder FROM
   . WHERE URL Like 'https%' " -i:COM -iProgID:LP_Toolkit.Favorites -
   iCOMParams:FullPaths=off
   ```

The LP_ToolKit.Favorites input processor exposes a read-only *FullPaths* property, which can be provided at the command line to determine whether the *Folder* field will store the full path of the containing folder or only the name of the containing folder. Table 9.2 lists the accepted values for the FullPaths property:

Table 9.2 FullPaths Parameter Values for the IE Favorites Input Processor

Parameter Value	Effect on Folder Field Values
Off (default)	Values will contain the name of the folder in which the corresponding .url file resides.
On	Values will contain the absolute path of the folder in which the corresponding .url file resides.

Querying Arbitrary WMI Classes

WMI makes managing Windows-based computers much more convenient than it has been in the past, by providing a consistent way to access comprehensive system management information. For virtually any manageable resource—computer hardware, computer software, services, user accounts, and more—there is a corresponding WMI class that succinctly lists the properties of the resource and the actions that WMI can perform to manage that resource.

WMI is a natural fit for use with Log Parser, since WMI supports SQL-like queries that return collection-based results. These collections are easily translated into a format that Log Parser can use internally, thereby exposing the results to the rich processing and output formatting options that Log Parser provides.

The following lists the source code for the LP_ToolKit.WMIQuery input processor, a Visual Basic 6.0 COM component that executes WQL queries against arbitrary WMI classes, which are specified in the Log Parser command *WHERE* clause. Administrators can use this tool to quickly access management information, leveraging Log Parser's rich output options to assist in interpreting the results.

```
---Ch09WMIQuery.cls---
Option Explicit

Private Type WMIProperty
    Name As String
    Type As Integer
End Type

'Module-level variables
Dim m_wpFields() As WMIProperty     'Array of field properites
Dim m_oItems() As SWbemObject      'Array of query results
Dim m_sFromEntity As String            'FROM clause
Dim m_lIndex As Long                      'Current record

'local variable(s) to hold property value(s)
Private mvarComputerName As String

Public Property Let ComputerName(ByVal vData As String)
    mvarComputerName = vData
End Property

Public Property Get ComputerName() As String
    ComputerName = mvarComputerName
End Property

Public Sub OpenInput(ByVal FromEntity As String)
    Dim sComputer As String
    Dim oWMIService As SWbemServices
    Dim oClass As SWbemObject
    Dim oProperty As SWbemProperty
    Dim x As Integer
    Dim cItems As SWbemObjectSet
    Dim oItem As SWbemObject
    Dim lCount As Long

    m_sFromEntity = FromEntity
    sComputer = mvarComputerName
    Set oWMIService = GetObject("winmgmts:\\" & sComputer & "\root\cimv2")
    Set oClass = oWMIService.Get(m_sFromEntity)
```

```
    'Enumerate fields
    ReDim m_wpFields(oClass.Properties_.Count)
    For Each oProperty In oClass.Properties_
        m_wpFields(x).Name = oProperty.Name
        m_wpFields(x).Type = oProperty.CIMType
        x = x + 1
    Next


    'Retrieve query results and save in array
    Set cItems = oWMIService.ExecQuery( _
        "Select * from " & m_sFromEntity, , 0)
    ReDim m_oItems(cItems.Count)
    For Each oItem In cItems
        Set m_oItems(lCount) = oItem
        lCount = lCount + 1
    Next
End Sub


Public Function GetFieldCount() As Long
    GetFieldCount = UBound(m_wpFields) - 1
End Function


Public Function GetFieldName(ByVal Index As Integer) As String
    GetFieldName = m_wpFields(Index).Name
End Function


Public Function GetFieldType(ByVal Index As Integer) As Integer
    GetFieldType = ConvertType(m_wpFields(Index).Type)
End Function


Public Function ReadRecord() As Boolean
    If m_lIndex >= UBound(m_oItems) Then
        ReadRecord = False
    Else
        m_lIndex = m_lIndex + 1
        ReadRecord = True
    End If
End Function


Public Function GetValue(ByVal Index As Integer) As Variant
    Dim i As Integer
    Dim vValue As Variant
    Dim iType As Integer
    iType = m_wpFields(Index).Type
```

```
        vValue = m_oItems(m_lIndex - 1).Properties_( _
            m_wpFields(Index).Name).Value
    If IsArray(vValue) Then
        GetValue = ConvertValue(vValue(0), iType)
        For i = LBound(vValue) + 1 To UBound(vValue)
            GetValue = GetValue & "|" _
                & ConvertValue(vValue(i), iType)
        Next i
    Else
        GetValue = ConvertValue(vValue, iType)
    End If
End Function


Private Function ConvertValue(ByVal Value As Variant, DataType As Integer) As Variant
    Dim swTimeStamp As SWbemDateTime

    If Len(Value) Then
        Select Case DataType
            Case wbemCimtypeObject, wbemCimtypeReference
                ConvertValue = "<object>"
            Case wbemCimtypeDatetime
                Set swTimeStamp = New SWbemDateTime
                swTimeStamp = Value
                ConvertValue = swTimeStamp.GetVarDate
            Case Else
                ConvertValue = Value
        End Select
    End If
End Function


Private Sub Class_Initialize()
    mvarComputerName = "."
End Sub
```

**Script truncated, please refer to the book's accompanying website,
www.syngress.com/solutions for the entire code.
---Ch09WMIQuery.cls---

Perform the following steps to use this LP_Toolkit.WMIQuery tool:

1. Open the LP_Toolkit.vbp project with Microsoft Visual Basic 6.0 and build
   LP_Toolkit.dll.

2. Register the LP_Toolkit.dll component with the following command:

   ```
   regsvr32 lp_toolkit.dll
   ```

3. Execute the following command to retrieve the current height and width (in pixels) of the display settings on the local computer:

```
logparser.exe "SELECT PelsHeight, PelsWidth FROM Win32_DisplayConfiguration"
-i:COM -iProgID:LP_Toolkit.WMIQuery
```

4. Execute the following command to create a pie chart (shown in Figure 9.1) depicting the percentage of allocated memory used by each running process:

```
logparser.exe "SELECT Name, MUL(PROPSUM(ThreadCount), 100.0) AS Percent INTO
Processes.GIF FROM Win32_Process GROUP BY Name ORDER BY Percent DESC" -i:COM -
iProgID:LP_Toolkit.WMIQuery
-chartType:PieExploded -View -ChartTitle:"Percent Memory Used"
-categories:off
```

Figure 9.1 Processes.gif Output from LP_Toolkit.WMIQuery Input Format

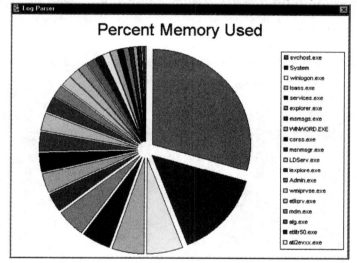

Using a Front End

Log Parser is accessible through two independent architectures:

- The LogParser.exe command-line tool
- A set of COM objects contained in LogParser.dll

While systems administrators can usually work comfortably with both of these formats, the information that Log Parser extracts and outputs is often invaluable to managers and business analysts who are more comfortable working through graphical user interfaces (GUIs). In this section, we'll examine several ways that a graphical front end can make Log Parser more accessible to non-administrators. In addition, we'll see how we can use a GUI to selectively highlight key query output.

Simplifying Query Creation

Whether it's used from the command line or through its COM objects, all Log Parser processing is driven by a query. Unfortunately, not everyone understands query syntax or knows the names of specific fields they'd like to query. A user interface provides a great chance to shield end users from query complexities while letting users specify the information they'd like to review.

In this section, we'll examine the LP_QueryBuilder tool, an HTML (HyperText Markup Language) Application (HTA) that dynamically crafts Log Parser queries based on input from several user interface controls.

NOTE

You must have Microsoft Internet Explorer 5.0 or later installed in order to use an HTA.

LP_QueryBuilder, shown in Figure 9.2, uses an event-driven programming model in which static HTML elements combine with VBScript event handlers.

Figure 9.2 LP_QueryBuilder User Interface

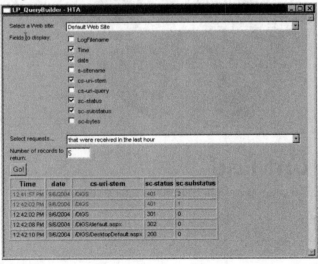

The following code is a partial listing of the LP_QueryBuilder source code, containing all static HTML elements and the *<HTA:APPLICATION>* element. In the sections that follow, we'll look at how several LP_QueryBuilder event handlers are used to simplify user interaction with Log Parser.

```
---Ch09LP_QueryBuilder.hta---
<html>
<head>
<title>LP_QueryBuilder - HTA</title>
<HTA:APPLICATION
      ID="objLogParser2HTA"
      APPLICATIONNAME="LP_QueryBuilder - HTA"
      SCROLL="yes"
      SINGLEINSTANCE="yes"
      WINDOWSTATE="maximize">
<body>
<table width="100%">
<tr valign="top">
    <td width="150">Select a Web site:</td>
    <td width="80%"><select size="1" name="lstWebSites"
style="display:none"></select></td>
</tr>
<tr valign="top">
    <td>Fields to display: </td>
    <td><span id="spanLogFields"></span></td>
</tr>
<tr valign="top">
    <td>Select requests... </td>
    <td><select size="1" name="lstWhere">
    <option value="lastHour">that were received in the last hour
    <option value="Today">that were received today
    <option value="Yesterday">that were received yesterday
    <option value="Anonymous">by anonymous users
    <option value="AuthFailure">with authorization errors
    <option value="30KB">for pages larger than 30 KB
    </select></td>
</tr>
<tr valign="top">
    <td>Number of records to return: </td>
    <td><input type="text" id="txtCount" name="txtCount" size="4"></td>
</tr>
<tr valign="top"">
    <td colspan="2">
    <input id=gobutton  name="go_button" onClick="GetData"type="button" value="Go!">
    </td>
</tr>
</table>
<span id="OutputArea"></span>
```

```
</body>
</html>


**Script truncated, please refer to the book's accompanying website,
www.syngress.com/solutions for the entire code.
---Ch09LP_QueryBuilder.hta---
```

Building the FROM Clause from Discovered Input Sources

A great way to help users specify the input source they'd like to review is to provide the users with a list of available sources from which to choose. For example, suppose your manager wanted to examine usage patterns for an intranet website, but didn't know the exact name that IIS (Internet Information Server) used internally to refer to the site. By using Log Parser to query the IIS configuration, you could create a drop-down list of available sites and your boss could select the site he'd like to examine.

The following VBScript code shows the LP_QueryBuilder.hta *DisplayWebSites* procedure, which (since it's called from the *Window_Onload* procedure) executes when a user starts or refreshes the HTA. This procedure uses the Log Parser ADS input format to enumerate the IIS websites on the local computer, adding a corresponding entry for each into the lstWebSites drop-down list. The entry selected by the user is later used within the *FROM* clause of a Log Parser query to specify which site's log files to use as input.

```
---Ch09LP_QueryBuilder.hta---
Sub DisplayWebSites
    Dim ILogQuery, Iw3c, strCol, myRS, myRecord
    Set ILogQuery = CreateObject("MSUtil.LogQuery")
    Set ADS = CreateObject("MSUtil.LogQuery.ADSInputFormat")

    Dim strQuery
    strQuery = _
        "SELECT ObjectPath, PropertyValue FROM IIS://Localhost/W3SVC" _
        & " WHERE ObjectClass='IIsWebServer' And" _
        & " PropertyName='ServerComment' " _
        & "And NOT ObjectPath LIKE '%W3SVC/Info%'"

    Set myRS = ILogQuery.Execute(strQuery, ADS)
    Dim iCounter
    iCounter=0
    While Not myRS.atEnd
        Set myRecord = myRS.getRecord()
        Set objOption = Document.createElement("OPTION")
        objOption.Text = myRecord.getValue("PropertyValue")
        objOption.Value = myRecord.getValue("PropertyValue")
```

```
        lstWebSites.Add(objOption)
        iCounter = iCounter + 1
        myRS.moveNext
    Wend


    myRS.close


    If iCounter > 0 Then
        lstWebSites.Options(0).Selected=True
        lstWebSites.style.display=""
    End if
End Sub
```

```
**Script truncated, please refer to the book's accompanying website,
www.syngress.com/solutions for the entire code.
---Ch09LP_QueryBuilder.hta---
```

Helping the User Create the SELECT Clause

Another mandatory clause in any query is the *SELECT* clause, which specifies the fields that the user is interested in. A great way to allow users to specify one or more fields is to provide checkboxes that correspond to the fields from which the user can choose.

The following VBScript code shows the LP_QueryBuilder *DisplayLogFields* procedure, which (like the DisplayWebSites procedure) executes when a user starts the HTA. The key element of this procedure is a loop that iterates through a list of fields supported by the specified input format. In addition to generating HTML checkboxes for the available fields, this loop dynamically creates text for the *GetSelectedFields* procedure, which will be used to determine which log fields the user has specified by looking at the *Checked* value of the corresponding controls. After this procedure text is created, it is assigned to the named *FieldScript SCRIPT* element, which serves as a placeholder for the dynamically constructed procedure.

```
---Ch09LP_QueryBuilder.hta---
Sub DisplayFieldCheckboxes
    Dim IISLogFields, iCurrentField
    IISLogFields = Array("LogFilename", "LogRow", "time", "date", _
      "s-sitename", "cs-uri-stem", "cs-uri-query," , _
      "sc-status", "sc-substatus", "sc-bytes")
    iCurrentField = 0

    Dim dynamicControls
    '  dymamicControls will be used to contain a string of HTML
    '  markup that will be dynamically constructed and added to
    '  the page

    strSub = "Sub GetSelectedFields" & VbCrLf
```

```
    For iCurrentField = 0 to UBound(IISLogFields)
        fieldname = IISLogFields(iCurrentField)
        dynamicControls = dynamicControls _
         & "<input type=checkbox name=chk"& fieldname _
         "value=" & fieldname & " checked> " & fieldname & "<br>"

        iCurrentField = iCurrentField + 1
        strSub = strSub _
         & "    If chk" & fieldname & ".Checked Then"' & VbCrLf _
         & "        If Len(columns) > 0 Then"  & VbCrLf _
         & "            columns = columns & " & Chr(34) & ", " _
         & Chr(34) & VbCrLf _
         & "        End If" & VbCrLf _
         & "    columns = columns & " & Chr(34) & fieldname _
         & Chr(34) & VbCrLf _
         & "    End If" & VbCrLf
    Next
    strSub = strSub & "End Sub"

    '  Render the dynamically contructed controls within the
    '   spanLogFields placeholder
    spanLogFields.innerHTML = dynamicControls & "<br>"

    '  The GetSelectedFields procedure will be used to determine
    '  which logfields the user has specified, by looking at the
    '  "Checked" value of the corresponding controls.

    '  The text of this procedure was dynamically constructed
    '  above when we created the controls we need to examine,
    '  and was stored in the strSub variable. Now, we'll put the
    '  procedure text into a <SCRIPT> block that serves as
    '  placeholder

    FieldScript.Text = strSub
End Sub

</SCRIPT>
<SCRIPT Language="VBScript" id="FieldScript">
    Sub GetSelectedFields
        MsgBox "Hello World"    ' This gets replaced dynamically
    End Sub
</SCRIPT>

**Script truncated, please refer to the book's accompanying website,
www.syngress.com/solutions for the entire code.
---Ch09LP_QueryBuilder.hta---
```

Because the Log Parser COM interfaces don't provide a way to programmatically discover the available fields for input formats that Log Parser natively supports, such as the IISW3C format used within this example, this example uses static list of field names. However, Log Parser COM plug-ins that implement the ILogParserInputContext—such as the LP_Toolkit.Favorites tool discussed earlier in this chapter—expose three public methods that enable you to auto-discover their supported fields. The *GetFieldCount*, *GetFieldName*, and *GetFieldType* methods can be combined to allow you to list each field and its properties. This autodiscovery is extremely powerful, allowing you to reuse code that discovers fields and generates corresponding controls and procedure code on the fly.

Providing WHERE Clause Options

The *WHERE* clause is an optional query clause that reduces output to only those records that meet a specific selection criteria, such as "requests for Web pages with the .aspx file extension". A user interface can help users specify their selection criteria in many different ways, such as allowing a user to:

- Specify a field, comparison operator, and reference value (for example, **date = '08-30-2004'**).

- Specify an aggregate function (such as **count(*) > 5**) that filters records based on groups of data.

- Choose from a list of pre-built selection criteria (such as **requests for static content that experienced authentication failures yesterday**) that shield the user from the underlying fields of the corresponding input processor.

As compared to the SELECT clause, which is built from a constrained list of fields, or the FROM clause, which is built by specifying a specific input source, the WHERE clause can be extremely complex. When using a GUI to generate the WHERE clause, this complexity is both a blessing and a curse. Because you can use virtually any combination of UI (user interface) controls to provide your users with options, you have to choose between functionality and flexibility. For instance, if you provide a textbox that allows users to specify a WHERE clause using free text, you give your users a great deal of query flexibility, but you provide virtually no query-creation assistance. Alternatively, if your only user interface control is a checkbox that determines whether a complex filter should be applied, you greatly alleviate your users' need to understand the underlying field structure, but at the expense of severely restricting the ways in which they can filter the records. The best approach for meeting your users' needs is to ensure that they are consulted during the design of the user interface.

The following code sample demonstrates the filtering options made available within the LP_QueryBuilder tool. The user interface provides a drop-down list (**lstWhere**) from which users can select one of several pre-built filters. The user's selection is used to directly specify the WHERE clause of the executed query. While the implementations vary among the filter options provided, users aren't provided the ability to specify any filtering options besides those explicitly listed.

```
---Ch09LP_QueryBuilder.hta---
Select Case lstWhere.Value
    Case "lastHour"
        strWHERE = "time > " &
        strWHERE = "TO_TIMESTAMP(date,time) >"
            & " SUB(SYSTEM_TIMESTAMP(), " _
            & "TIMESTAMP('1', 'h')) "
    Case "Today"
        strWHERE = "date=SYSTEM_DATE()"
    Case "Yesterday"
        strWHERE = "date=TO_DATE(SUB(" &
            "SYSTEM_TIMESTAMP(), TIMESTAMP('2', 'd')))"
    Case "Anonymous"
        strWHERE = "cs-username is NULL"
    Case "AuthFailure"
        strWHERE = "sc-status in (401,402,403)"
    Case "30KB"
        strWHERE = "sc-bytes > 30720"
 End Select


Script truncated, please refer to the book's accompanying website,
www.syngress.com/solutions for the entire code.
---Ch09LP_QueryBuilder.hta---
```

Data-Driven Formatting

Developers frequently choose to display data that consists of records and fields—such as output from a Log Parser query—in a tabular format, since this format closely mirrors the structure of the data and can be created easily. Unfortunately, because this display option renders each record in an identical format, it can be ill-suited for situations that require the user to locate records that have particular significance. An excellent way to provide users with the visual clues they need while retaining the simplicity of the tabular display is to perform data-driven formatting.

The following LP_QueryBuilder code excerpt demonstrates a common technique for highlighting specific data elements within a query resultset. The application invokes a Log Parser *Execute* command, using the previously constructed query string and IISW3C input format. This command returns an *ILogRecordset*, which is assigned to the *myRS* variable. This ILogRecordset is used to dynamically construct an HTML table that will display the query results.

```
---Ch09LP_QueryBuilder.hta---
Set myRS = ILogQuery.Execute(strQuery, IW3C)


While Not myRS.atEnd
    i=i+1
```

```
Set myRecord = myRS.getRecord()
Select Case myRecord.getValue("sc-status")
    Case 401, 402, 403
        '   authorization error
        strHTML = strHTML  & "<tr style='color:red;'>"
    Case 500
        '   server error
        strHTML = strHTML  & "<tr bgColor='#FF0000'>"
    Case Else
        strHTML = strHTML  & "<tr bgColor='#FFFFFF'>"
    End Select

    For j = 0 To strCol - 1
        myVal=myRecord.getValue(Cint(j))
        If LCase(myRS.getColumnName(Cint(j)))="time" Then
            myVal=Right(myVal, Len(myVal)-InStr(myval, " "))
        End If
        strHTML = strHTML  & ("<td> " & myVal & "</td>")
    Next
    strHTML = strHTML  & ("</tr>")
    myRS.moveNext()
Wend
strHTML = strHTML  & ("</table>")

OutputArea.InnerHTML=strHTML

**Script truncated, please refer to the book's accompanying website,
www.syngress.com/solutions for the entire code.
---Ch09LP_QueryBuilder.hta---
```

The application creates an HTML table header row by iterating through the columns in the ILogRecordset, creating an HTML table cell that displays the name of each corresponding ILogRecordset column. Once the header row has been created, the application uses a *While…Wend* loop to iterate through the query records, so that a corresponding HTML table row can be created for each.

Before rendering the contents of a given record, the application examines the value of the record's *sc-status* field. If the value indicates an authorization error, the corresponding HTML row is modified to display red text. If the value indicates a server error, the row is rendered with a red background. If neither of these conditions is found, the row is rendered with the default display style. Finally, after each row has been examined, the HTML table is written to the screen.

Managing Identity Flow to Remote Input Sources

Any time you use an application to access remote resources, the action must be performed using a security context or *identity* that has rights and/or permissions to perform access the specific remote resource. For simple client applications (desktop applications such as HTAs or Win32 applications), the remote resource is usually accessed using the identity of the user who launched the application. For distributed applications, however, the case may be different.

Distributed applications—such as web-based applications—are comprised of multiple tiers, each of which performs authentication and authorization. For instance, an ASP website that uses Log Parser to retrieve Event Log entries from a remote computer is actually made up of three tiers:

- A client tier (the browser)

- A server tier (the IIS server that hosts the ASP site)

- A data tier (the remote computer on which the data – in this case, the Event Log entries—resides)

In this scenario, the application service provider (ASP) requests will impersonate the identity of the user browsing the page, or, if the site allows anonymous access, will impersonate the configured anonymous account. When the pages attempt to access the remote resource (the Event Log on the remote computer), delegation is required. Specifically, the impersonated caller's token must have network credentials. If it doesn't, all remote resource access is performed as the using user (AUTHORITY\ANONYMOUS LOGON).

There are a number of factors including the authentication method used by IIS that determine whether or not a security context can be delegated in an IIS application. A security context can always be delegated if IIS uses *basic* authentication, but can never be delegated if the site uses *digest* authentication. For Integrated Windows authentication, the answer depends on whether the authentication results in NT Lan Manager (NTLM, which does not support delegation) or Kerberos (which does support delegation in a suitably configured environment).

To avoid the complexities of delegation, which can be extremely difficult to troubleshoot in an ASP or ASP.NET application, you can implement a trusted subsystem model to allow Log Parser to access remote resources by using a fixed identity. This approach greatly simplifies the process of troubleshooting failed access to remote input sources, as the remote access permissions of individual users is irrelevant; only the fixed identity needs permissions to the resources.

To ensure that your Log Parser application sends a known identity to a remote system, you can perform your Log Parser calls from within a COM+ server application, which can be assigned a fixed identity under which its component(s) will run. If you're concerned that this approach may provide users with the ability to access remote resources for which they're not authorized, you can use COM+ roles to manage authorization locally.

Master Craftsman

Wrapping Log Parser in a COM+ Application

Using Log Parser from within a COM+ application is not trivial. If you're developing the COM+ application using managed code (such as VB.NET, C#, or managed C++), you must first generate a strongly named Log Parser type library and create a reference to the type library from your Visual Studio .NET project. You can use the following procedure to generate and reference the strongly named Log Parser type library.

1. Open a Visual Studio command prompt and navigate to the Log Parser installation directory.

2. Run the following command to create a strong key pair with which to sign the assembly (DLL) you'll be generating: **sn -k LogParserComponent.snk**

3. Run the following command to export the strongly-named Log Parser type library: **tlbimp.exe LogParser.dll /out:InteropLogParser.dll /keyfile:LogParserComponent.snk /namespace:MSUtil**

4. From the Visual Studio .NET Solution Explorer, select your project and click **Add Reference**.

5. In the Add Reference dialog box, click the **Browse...** button, navigate to your Log Parser installation directory, and select the InteropLogParser.dll you just created.

The following code lists the source for the LogParserComponent class, a COM+ application written in VB.NET that exposes a subset of Log Parser's functionality. This component exposes a single method, which accepts a string query and a string *InputType* and returns an ADO.NET DataTable. Internally, the tool uses the specified InputType string to instantiate an appropriate Log Parser input type COM object, and uses the LogQuery Execute method to create an ILogRecordSet, and dynamically constructs the DataTable.

```
---Ch09LogParserComponent.vb---
Imports MSUtil
Imports System.EnterpriseServices
Imports System.Reflection

Public Class LogParserComponent
    Inherits ServicedComponent

    Dim myRS As ILogRecordset
    Dim myRecord As ILogRecord
```

```
Dim i, iColCount As Integer
Dim myDT As New DataTable
Dim myDataRow As DataRow

Public Function Execute(ByVal szQuery As String, _
    ByVal InputType As String) As DataTable

    Dim myparser As New LogQueryClassClass
    Dim myInput As Object

    Select Case InputType
        Case "IISW3C"
            myInput = New COMIISW3CInputContextClassClass
        Case "NCSA"
            myInput = New COMIISNCSAInputContextClassClass
        Case "IIS"
            myInput = New COMIISIISInputContextClassClass
        Case "W3C"
            myInput = New COMW3CInputContextClassClass
        Case "BIN"
            myInput = New COMIISBINInputContextClassClass
        Case "FS"
            Dim fsInput As New COMFileSystemInputContextClassClass
            fsInput.preserveLastAccTime = True
            fsInput.recurse = 0
            myInput = fsInput
        Case "XML"
            myInput = New COMXMLInputContextClassClass
    End Select

    myRS = myparser.Execute(szQuery, myInput)

    Dim i, iCol As Int16
    For iCol = 0 To myRS.getColumnCount - 1
        Dim myCol As New DataColumn
        myCol.ColumnName = myRS.getColumnName(iCol)
        Select Case myRS.getColumnType(iCol)
            Case myRS.INTEGER_TYPE
                myCol.DataType = GetType(System.Int32)
            Case myRS.REAL_TYPE
                myCol.DataType = GetType(System.Double)
            Case myRS.STRING_TYPE
                myCol.DataType = GetType(String)
            Case myRS.TIMESTAMP_TYPE
                myCol.DataType = GetType(DateTime)
```

```
        End Select
        myDT.Columns.Add(myCol)

    Next

    While Not myRS.atEnd
        myRecord = myRS.getRecord
        myDataRow = myDT.NewRow
        For i = 0 To myRS.getColumnCount - 1
            myDataRow(i) = myRecord.getValue(i)
        Next
        myDT.Rows.Add(myDataRow)

        myRS.moveNext()
    End While

    myRS.close()

    Return myDT
End Function

End Class
```

```
**Script truncated, please refer to the book's accompanying website,
www.syngress.com/solutions for the entire code.
---Ch09LogParserComponent.vb---
```

Use the following steps to use this tool:

1. Use Visual Studio .NET 2003 to compile the LogParserComPlusApp.vbproj project. This compilation will build the LogParserComPlusApp.dll assembly.

2. Open the Visual Studio .NET command prompt and type the following command to register the assembly with COM+ and create the LogParserComPlus COM+ application:

   ```
   regsvcs <full path to LogParserComPlusApp.dll>
   ```

3. Using the Component Services Microsoft Management Console (MMC), right-click the LogParserComPlus application and select **Properties**.

4. On the **Activation** tab, set the **Activation Type** to **Server Application**.

5. On the **Identity** tab, select the **This user** option to specify the username and password for the identity under which the application will run.

> **NOTE**
>
> When specifying the account credentials for your COM+ application, you should ensure that you follow the principle of least privilege to mitigate the threat associated with a process compromise. Rather than specifying a high privileged account (such as a member of the Domain Admins group), you should create a low privileged account specifically for the application. This account should be granted the minimum rights and privileges necessary to accecss the remote resources that will be used as input for your Log Parser applications.

Maintaining a Responsive User Interface

A Log Parser query can be a long-running process, especially when executed against large or remote input sources. Users are usually content to wait for such things, as long as they believe that progress is being made. When developing a UI that launches a potentially long-running query, you need to provide the user with a visual indication that the application is working properly. The techniques available for providing this feedback are generally dependent on both the technology chosen to implement the UI, and your level of expertise with the technology.

If you've chosen to develop your UI using a technology that doesn't easily support multiple threads of execution—such as a Visual Basic 6.0 form or a HTA—it's very difficult to ensure that the UI stays responsive while a long-running query executes. Since the application only has one thread of execution, you're unable to update the UI to indicate progress while the query is extracting and manipulating data from the input source. In this scenario, since you can't actually make the UI more responsive, you can give your users more confidence in the application's progress by giving the *appearance* of a more responsive user interface.

The following code illustrates the technique used within the LP_QueryBuilder tool to give the appearance of continued reponsiveness during a remote query. Immediately before invoking the remote query, the application launches a dialog box that states, "Please Wait – Executing Query…" Once the results are returned and have been prepared for display, the results are rendered and the dialog box is hidden.

```
---Ch09LP_QueryBuilder.hta---
Call ShowWaitDialog("Executing Query...")

Set myRS = ILogQuery.Execute(strQuery, IW3C)

Call HideWaitDialog()

Sub ShowWaitDialog(Message)
    Set objDialogWindow = window.Open("about:blank",_
      "ProgressWindow","height=15,width=250,left=300,top=300," _
      & "status=no,titlebar=no,toolbar=no,menubar=no," _
      & "location=no,scrollbars=no")
```

```
   objDialogWindow.Focus()
   objDialogWindow.document.writeln "<html><body>" _
      & Message & "</body></html>"
   objDialogWindow.document.title = "Please wait."
End Sub

Sub HideWaitDialog
   objDialogWindow.Close
   self.Focus()
End Sub
```
**Script truncated, please refer to the book's accompanying website,
www.syngress.com/solutions for the entire code.
---Ch09LP_QueryBuilder.hta---

When developing a Log Parser UI using a technology with strong multi-threading support (such as a C# Windows application), you should consider spawning a new thread to execute long-running Log Parser queries. By using a dedicated thread to perform your query processing, you ensure that the UI thread will continue to receive user input.

WARNING

Use caution when programming with multiple threads. Be sure you're familiar with both the hazards and thread-safe techniques that are appropriate for the technology you're using for your UI. Keep in mind one of the fundamental rules of Windows programming: "Though shalt not operate on a window from other than its creating thread." In other words, make sure you never allow background threads to directly invoke UI methods or properties.

The LP_Rich_Client application, shown in Figure 9.3, is a C# Windows Forms application that demonstrates this multithreaded concept. When the user clicks the **Execute Query!** button, the UI thread invokes Log Parser processing on a background thread through the use of a delegate. Once the Log Parser processing has completed, the background thread uses another delegate to inform the UI thread that the display grid has an updated data source to display.

Figure 9.3 The LP Rich Client User Interface

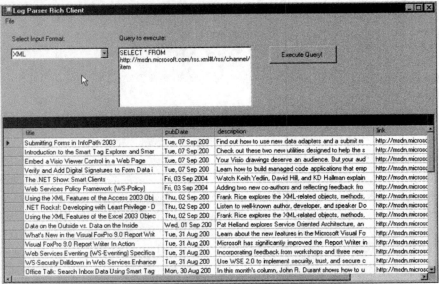

The following C# code shows the implementation of the application's logic.

```
---Ch09frmMainRichClient.cs---
using MSUtil;
using System;
using System.Drawing;
using System.Collections;
using System.ComponentModel;
using System.Windows.Forms;
using System.Threading;
using System.Data;

namespace LP_RichClient
{
    public class Form1 : Form
    {

        private void Form1_Load(object sender, System.EventArgs e)
        {
            arrInputFormats = new ArrayList();
            arrInputFormats.Add("IISW3C");
            arrInputFormats.Add("NCSA");
            arrInputFormats.Add("IIS");
            arrInputFormats.Add("W3C");
            arrInputFormats.Add("BIN");
```

```
      arrInputFormats.Add("HTTPERR");
      arrInputFormats.Add("URLSCAN");
      arrInputFormats.Add("CSV");
      arrInputFormats.Add("EVT");
      arrInputFormats.Add("REG");
      arrInputFormats.Add("ADS");
      arrInputFormats.Add("FS");
      arrInputFormats.Add("XML");
      cboInputFormat.DataSource=arrInputFormats;
}

private void btnExecute_Click(object sender, System.EventArgs e)
{
      ExecQueryDelegate execQ = new ExecQueryDelegate(ExecQuery);
      execQ.BeginInvoke(null, null);
}

delegate void UpdateDataGridDelegate(DataTable dt);

private void UpdateDataGrid(DataTable dt)
{
      UpdateDataGridDelegate updateGrid =
          new UpdateDataGridDelegate(UpdateDataGrid);

      BeginInvoke(updateGrid, new object[] { dt });
}

delegate void ExecQueryDelegate();

private void ExecQuery()
{
      LogQueryClassClass myparser = new LogQueryClassClass();
      ILogRecordset myRS = null;
      ILogRecord myRecord = null;
      object myInput = null;

      switch (cboInputFormat.SelectedValue.ToString())
      {
          case "IISW3C":
              myInput = new COMIISW3CInputContextClassClass();
              break;
          case "NCSA":
              myInput = new COMIISNCSAInputContextClassClass();
              break;
          case "IIS":
```

```
        myInput = new COMIISIIISInputContextClassClass();
        break;
    case "W3C":
        myInput = new COMW3CInputContextClassClass();
        break;
    case "FS":
        COMFileSystemInputContextClassClass fsInput =
            new COMFileSystemInputContextClassClass();
        fsInput.preserveLastAccTime = true;
        fsInput.recurse = 0;
        myInput=fsInput;
        break;
    case "XML":
        COMXMLInputContextClass xmlInput =
            new COMXMLInputContextClassClass();
        myInput=xmlInput;
        break;
}

try
{
    myRS=myparser.Execute(txtQuery.Text, myInput);

    if (myRS.atEnd())
    {
        return;
    }

    DataTable myDT = new DataTable();
    DataRow myDR;

    int i, iCol;
    for (iCol=0; iCol < myRS.getColumnCount(); iCol++)
    {
        DataColumn myCol = new DataColumn();
        myCol.ColumnName=myRS.getColumnName(iCol);
        switch (myRS.getColumnType(iCol))
        {
            case 1:
                myCol.DataType = Type.GetType("System.Int32");
                break;
            case 2:
                myCol.DataType = Type.GetType("System.Double");
                break;
            case 3:
```

```
                    myCol.DataType = Type.GetType("System.String");
                break;
            case 4:
                myCol.DataType = Type.GetType("System.DateTime");
                break;
        }
        myDT.Columns.Add(myCol);
    }
    while(!myRS.atEnd())
    {
        myRecord = (ILogRecord) myRS.getRecord();

        myDR = myDT.NewRow();
        for (i = 0; i < myRS.getColumnCount();i++)
        {
            object col=i;
            myDR[i] =  myRecord.getValue(ref col);
        }
        myDT.Rows.Add(myDR);

        myRS.moveNext();
    }
    UpdateDataGrid(myDT);
    myRS.close();
}
catch (Exception e)
{
    MessageBox.Show(e.StackTrace, e.Message);
```

**Script truncated, please refer to the book's accompanying website, www.syngress.com/solutions for the entire code.
---Ch09frmMainRichClient.cs---

Swiss Army Knife

Caching Query Results to Improve Performance

If your Log Parser application repeatedly executes a query that is expensive in terms of time and/or resource consumption (for example, in order to allow users to page through query results), you can improve the application's performance by caching the Log Query output. By caching the results, you remove the cost of generating the results for subsequent user requests, which can substantially improve the responsiveness of your UI and overall user experience.

The COM+ application discussed earlier returns results as an ADO.NET DataTable rather than as an MSUtil.ILogRecordSet because the DataTable includes native support for both caching and data binding.

Developing Log Parser Scripts

The most common way for system administrators to extend Log Parser is by developing scripts built around Log Parser functionality. A script is a file that describes the steps required to complete a specific task. After you create the script, you can run the script and it will perform all of the steps needed to perform the task, saving you a great deal of time and energy and minimizing the chances that the task will be executed incorrectly.

Of the two methods of invoking Log Parser functionality—the command-line LogParser.exe executable binary or the Log Parser scriptable COM components—most administrators will agree that the scriptable COM components offer numerous advantages and flexibility for use in custom scripts. For example, with the Log Parser scriptable COM components, your script can execute a query without providing an output format, retrieve the resultant output records, and perform custom processing on the output records. By doing so, your scripts are able to generate custom output formats, or use Log Parser query output to directly drive business process. The scripts in this section each take advantage of these benefits.

Combining Query Output with External Data

An inherent limitation in Log Parser 2.2 is the inability to perform an SQL join within the Log Parser query, which hampers your ability to incorporate external data in your script output. However, you can leverage built-in Log Parser output formats to enable your script to manipulate the query output outside of the Log Parser processing. Let's look at an example that illustrates a common scenario.

Thousands of public and private ASP.NET websites—including the popular www.asp.net website—have been built using the template provided by the IBuySpy Portal Solution Kit example site (which has been extended significantly through the open source DotNetNuke application—www.dotnetnuke.com). This site architecture uses a base web page (typically

default.aspx or **DesktopDefault.aspx**) that dynamically loads content modules based on the value passed in the *TabID* query string parameter. Each TabID value corresponds to a site tab, or predefined collection of content modules. These tab definitions—including the tab display name and list of roles authorized to view the tab's content—is maintained in a SQL Server database table. As users navigate through site links, they pass different TabID query string values, loading the default page with the corresponding content.

This site architecture, although widely adopted for its ease of use, poses a challenge to administrators trying to view site usage patterns. As an overwhelming majority of page hits are for the default page, the corresponding IIS logs cannot provide the administrators with a clear picture of the site usage patterns. In order to correlate page hits with the content that was requested, administrators must extract the TabID value from the cs-uri-query log field and retrieve the corresponding Tab name from the site configuration database.

The following Jscript script code uses the following methodology to perform analysis similar to the scenario described earlier:

- A LogParser query is executed to retrieve raw site usage metrics from the site's IISW3C log files.

- The query output is inserted into a table in the site configuration database.

- An ADO command is executed to combine the newly inserted data with the tab definitions through an SQL JOIN.

- The ADO command output is written to the console.

```
---Ch09ExternalData.js---
/*
//Parse arguments first
var szInputLogFilename=null;
var szConnString=null;
var szTable=null;
var szArgs = WScript.Arguments.Named;
var bClearTable=true;

szInputLogFilename = szArgs.Item("Log");
szConnString = szArgs.Item("ConnString");
szTable = szArgs.Item("Table");

if (szArgs.Exists("ClearTable"))
{
    if (szArgs.Item("ClearTable").toLowerCase()=="off")
    {
        bClearTable=false;
    }
}
```

```
//Create the main Log Parser Query object
var myQuery=new ActiveXObject("MSUtil.LogQuery");
var myInput=new ActiveXObject("MSUtil.LogQuery.IISW3CInputFormat");
var myOutput=new ActiveXObject("MSUtil.LogQuery.SQLOutputFormat");

myOutput.oConnString=szConnString;
myOutput.createTable=true;
myOutput.clearTable=bClearTable;

//Create the text of the query
var szQuery =
    "SELECT EXTRACT_Token(cs-uri-stem,1,'/') as Application, " +
    "EXTRACT_VALUE(cs-uri-query,'tabid','&') as TabID, " +
    "count(*) as Hits " +
    "INTO " + szTable + " " +
    "FROM " + szInputLogFilename + " WHERE TabId IS NOT NULL " +
    "GROUP BY Application, TabID " +
    "ORDER BY Application, Hits DESC";

// //Execute the query and populate the SQL table
WScript.Echo("Trying LogQuery.ExecuteBatch()...");
try {
    myQuery.ExecuteBatch(szQuery,myInput,myOutput);
}
    catch(e){
        WScript.Echo(e);
    }


// Now that SQL has the new table and the existing "Tabs" table
// that contains the Tab name, use ADO to perform a JOIN so we
// can output a readable report

var vConn=new ActiveXObject("ADODB.Connection");
vConn.Open(szConnString);
var vRS=new ActiveXObject("ADODB.Recordset");
vRS.Open("SELECT Application, TabName, S.Hits, TabName "
    + " FROM " + szTable + " S "
    + " INNER JOIN Tabs ON S.TabID=Tabs.TabID "
    + " ORDER BY S.Hits DESC", vConn);

if (vRS.EOF == true)
{
    WScript.Echo("No results returned from the SQL join");
    WScript.Quit();
}
```

```
vRS.MoveFirst();
var szAppColumn="Application";
var szTabColumn="TabId";
var szHits="Hits";
//
// create tabular output
var szColSpaces = "                    ";
var sz30Spaces = "                              ";

WScript.Echo("");
WScript.Echo(szAppColumn + szColSpaces.substr(0, 20-szAppColumn.length)
    + szTabColumn + sz30Spaces.substr(0, 30-szTabColumn.length) +
    szHits + szColSpaces.substr(0, 20-szHits.length));
WScript.Echo("--------------------" +
          "------------------------------" +
          "--------------------");
while (vRS.EOF != true)
{
    WScript.Echo(
        vRS(0) + szColSpaces.substr(0, 20 - vRS(0).Value.length) +
        vRS(1) + sz30Spaces.substr(0, 30 - vRS(1).Value.length) +
        vRS(2) + szColSpaces.substr(0, 20 - vRS(2).Value.length));

    vRS.MoveNext();
}
```

**Script truncated, please refer to the book's accompanying website,
www.syngress.com/solutions for the entire code.
---Ch09ExternalData.js---

The following console output illustrates example script output:

```
C:\> Ch09ExternalData.js /Log:"<1>" /Table:Sitehits /ConnString:"driver=SQL
Server;Server=myserver;database=portal"

Microsoft (R) Windows Script Host Version 5.6
Copyright (C) Microsoft Corporation 1996-2001. All rights reserved.

Trying LogQuery.ExecuteBatch()...
Application           TabId                         Hits
----------------------------------------------------------------
Portal                Audit Runs                    1863
Portal                Packages                      322
Portal                Home                          130
Portal                Data By Package               114
Portal                Data by Server                67
Portal                Data for Multiple Servers     41
Portal                Admin                         30
```

Using Script Parameters to Configure Log Parser Commands

Scripts provide an excellent way to invoke Log Parser queries without having to explicitly specify every command option each time you want to execute the query. That said, there is clearly a penalty for hardcoding command options into the script source code. If you want to change any command options, you must open and edit the script source. This is usually undesirable, as it requires the user to understand the syntax required within the script and introduces the possibility that a syntax or logic error will be introduced into a script that had been working properly.

The best way to provide flexibility in your scripts is to enable them to accept command-line parameters. The scripts in this chapter provide excellent examples of how you can use parameters to modify the behavior of your scripts. The script shown earlier (which combines Log Parser query output with SQL data) uses command-line parameters to configure three aspects of the Log Parser command:

1.   The *Log* parameter specifies the input source for the query.

2.   The *ConnString* parameter specifies the connection string used to establish the connection to the output destination database.

3.   The *Table* parameter specifies the name of the SQL table into which the query output is inserted.

Similarly, you can use script parameters to configure virtually any aspect of a Log Parser command. The basic procedure is as follows:

1.   Retrieve the parameters passed to the script.

2.   Verify that the user has specified values for any parameter your script requires. Optionally, you can specify default values for any parameters not provided.

3.   Use the parameters to configure the aspects on the Log Parser command that you wish to adjust.

TIP

Scripts written in VBScript or Jscript run within the Windows Script Host (WSH), which supports both named and unnamed parameters. Although you can use unnamed parameters to simplify the syntax by which users invoke a one-parameter script, you should use named parameters any time your script supports multiple parameters. Doing so ensures that your script won't exhibit unexpected behavior if the user specifies parameter values in an order your script does not expect.

Swiss Army Knife

Retrieving Script Parameters from an External Data Source

Your scripts are not limited to retrieving parameters only from the command line. You can retrieve script parameters from virtually any data source, such as a text file, SQL database, Registry key, or Active Directory Container. The method you choose to implement is dependent only on the needs of your users and the viability of the external source for your scenario.

Publishing LogQuery Output by E-mail

Enabling a script to send automated e-mail messages provides an excellent way to distribute information to a particular administrator or group of administrators regardless of their physical location. Administrators can even receive the information even if they are off-site. Because most administrators read their e-mail more often than they read event logs or consult intranet websites, the ability to programmatically distribute information is extremely valuable.

The following script uses the Collaboration Data Objects (CDO) technology to send Log Parser query output by e-mail. To use the script properly, you must modify the address (and possibly the port) of the SMTP (Simple Mail Transfer Protocol) server through which the e-mail will be sent.

```
---Ch09Email.vbs---
' Get required command-line parameter

Set oParams=WScript.Arguments.Named

Dim strMailTo
strMailTo = oParams.Item("MailTo")

Dim objLogParser
Set objLogParser = CreateObject("MSUtil.LogQuery")

Dim objEvtInput
Set objEvtInput = CreateObject("MSUtil.LogQuery.EventLogInputFormat")

strQuery = "Select TimeGenerated, EventID, EventTypeName, " _
    & "SourceName, Message FROM APPLICATION " _
    & "WHERE TimeGenerated >= " _
    & "TO_LOCALTIME(Sub(SYSTEM_TIMESTAMP(),TIMESTAMP('2', 'h'))) " _
    & "ORDER BY TimeGenerated DESC"
```

```
WScript.Echo "Running query..."
Dim objRS
Set objRS = objLogParser.Execute(strQuery,objEvtInput)

If objRS.atEnd Then
    WScript.Echo "Email will not be sent as query returned no records"
    objRS.close
    WScript.Quit
End If

Dim htmlBody
' Create table header row
htmlBody = htmlBody & "<tr>"
For i=0 To objRS.getColumnCount-1
    htmlBody = htmlBody & "<th>" & objRS.getColumnName(i) _
      & "</th>"
Next
htmlBody = htmlBody & "</tr>"

' Create record rows
Dim myRecord
Do While Not objRS.atEnd
    Set myRecord = objRS.getRecord()
    htmlBody = htmlBody & "<tr>"
    For j=0 To objRS.getColumnCount-1
        htmlBody = htmlBody & "<td>" & myRecord.GetValue(j) & "</td>"
    Next
    htmlBody = htmlBody & "</tr>"
    objRS.moveNext
Loop
htmlBody = htmlBody & "</table>"

objRS.close

Dim objEmail
Set objEmail=CreateObject("CDO.Message")
objEmail.From="LogParser@example.com"
objEmail.To=strMailTo
objEmail.Subject="Log Parser Query Output"
objEmail.htmlBody=htmlBody
objEmail.AutoGenerateTextBody=True
objEmail.Configuration.Fields( _
    "http://schemas.microsoft.com/cdo/configuration/sendusing") = 2
objEmail.Configuration.Fields( _
    "http://schemas.microsoft.com/cdo/configuration/smtpserver") = _
    "MySmtpServer"
```

```
objEmail.Configuration.Fields( _
    "http://schemas.microsoft.com/cdo/configuration/smtpserverport") = 25
objEmail.Configuration.Fields.Update
objEmail.Send
WScript.Echo "Message Sent Successfully!"
---Ch09Email.vbs---
```

Swiss Army Knife

Publishing Script Output by E-mail

It's highly likely that you'll want your e-mails to contain more information than just the Log Parser query output. Instead of using the LogQuery.Execute method to create the e-mail body, you can specify script-specific content for the e-mail body, and use the LogQuery.ExecuteBatch method to create an output file that you attach to the e-mail message using the CDO.Message *AddAttachment* method. This is a great technique for publishing the results of scheduled Log Parser queries.

Using Query Results to Construct an .REG File

Registration entry (.reg) files contain information regarding the specific keys, data types, and values below a given registry path, and are extremely useful for archiving registry settings, distributing registry changes, or adding new keys and values. These files are rarely created from scratch; typically, they are created by exporting registry keys and values through Regedit.exe, and then modifying the .reg file as needed with new values.

Log Parser provides a built-in registry input format that allows users to query local or remote registry keys and values. This script uses the output of a registry query performed with the Log Parser COM objects to generate an export a .reg file that archives the settings of a specified key.

WARNING

Before you modify the registry, make sure to back it up and make sure you understand how to restore the registry if a problem occurs. You should always use extreme caution when modifying registry information, as improper changes can cause problems that may require you to reinstall your operating system. When you run a .reg file, the contents are merged into the local registry; therefore, you must distribute and use .reg files with caution.

```
---Ch09ExportToRegFile.js---
//Parse arguments first
```

```
var szRegKey=null;
var szSaveAs=null;
var szArgs = WScript.Arguments.Named;
var bClearTable=true;

szRegKey = szArgs.Item("Key");
szSaveAs = szArgs.Item("SaveAs");

//Create the main Log Parser Query object
var myQuery=new ActiveXObject("MSUtil.LogQuery");
var myInput=new ActiveXObject("MSUtil.LogQuery.RegistryInputFormat");
myInput.binaryFormat="HEX"

//Create the text of the query
var szQuery = "SELECT Path, ValueName, ValueType, " +
      "CASE ValueType " +
         "WHEN 'REG_DWORD' " +
         " THEN SUBSTR(TO_STRING(TO_HEX(To_Int(Value))), 2) " +
         "WHEN 'REG_BINARY' THEN TO_STRING(Value) " +
         "ELSE Value " +
      "END AS Value " +
            "FROM " + szRegKey + " ";
//Execute the query and populate the SQL table
WScript.Echo("Trying LogQuery.Execute()...");
var vRS;
vRS=myQuery.Execute(szQuery,myInput);

var fso=new ActiveXObject("Scripting.FileSystemObject");
var regFile=fso.CreateTextFile(szSaveAs,true,true);

regFile.WriteLine("Windows Registry Editor Version 5.00");

var szPrevKey=null;

var szCurrentKey=null;
var szQuote="\"";
var szPath=null;
//Walk thru the recordset
for(; !vRS.atEnd(); vRS.moveNext())
{
    //Retrieve the values
    var record=vRS.getRecord();
    szCurrentKey=record.GetValue("Path");
    if (szCurrentKey!=szPrevKey)
    {
        // new key, so write the key path to the file
```

```
        regFile.WriteLine();

        //   Expand hive names
        var szSlashIndex=szCurrentKey.indexOf("\\");
        WScript.Echo();
        var szHive = szCurrentKey.substr(0, szSlashIndex);
        switch (szHive)
        {
            case "HKLM":
                // HKLM --> HKEY_LOCAL_MACHINE
                regFile.WriteLine("[HKEY_LOCAL_MACHINE" +
                szCurrentKey.substr(szSlashIndex) + "]");
                break;
            case "HKCR":
                //    HKCR --> HKEY_CLASSES_ROOT
                regFile.WriteLine("[HKEY_CLASSES_ROOT" +
                szCurrentKey.substr(szSlashIndex) + "]");
                break;
            case "HKCU":
                //    HKCU --> HKEY_CURRENT_USER
                regFile.WriteLine("[HKEY_CURRENT_USER" +
                szCurrentKey.substr(szSlashIndex) + "]");
                break;
            case "HKU":
                //    HKU  --> HKEY_USERS
                regFile.WriteLine("[HKEY_USERS" +
                szCurrentKey.substr(szSlashIndex) + "]");
                break;
            case "HKCC":
                //    HKCC --> HKEY_CURRENT_CONFIG
                regFile.WriteLine("[HKEY_CURRENT_CONFIG" +
                szCurrentKey.substr(szSlashIndex) + "]");
                break;
        }
}

var szValueName = record.getValue("ValueName");

// Write out ValueName
if (szValueName=="(Default)")
{
    regFile.Write("@=");
}
else
{
regFile.Write(szQuote + szValueName + szQuote
```

```
       + "=");
}


// Convert Value to required .REG format
var szValueType=record.getValue("ValueType");
var szValue=record.getValue("Value");
switch (szValueType)
{
    case 'REG_SZ':
        regFile.Write(szQuote);

        // escape special \, ", and '
        for (i=0; i<szValue.length; i++)
        {
            switch (szValue.charAt(i))
            {
                case ("\\"):
                case ("\""):
                case ("\'"):
                    regFile.Write("\\");
                default:
            }
            regFile.Write(szValue.charAt(i));
        }
        regFile.Write(szQuote);
        break;
    case 'REG_DWORD':
        regFile.Write("dword:" + szValue);
        break;
    case 'REG_MULTI_SZ':
        regFile.Write("hex(7):");
        for (i=0; i<szValue.length; i++)
        {
            if (szValue.charAt(i)=="|")
            {
            regFile.Write("00,00");
            }
            else
            {
                regFile.Write(szValue.charCodeAt(i).toString(16));
                regFile.Write(",00");
            }
            if (i<szValue.length)
            {
                regFile.Write(",");
            }
```

```
        }
        if (szValue.length>0)
        {
            regFile.Write("00,00,00,00");
        }
        else
        {
            regFile.Write("00,00");
        }
        break;
```

**Script truncated, please refer to the book's accompanying website, www.syngress.com/solutions for the entire code.
---Ch09ExportToRegFile.js---

Master Craftsman

Dynamically Constructing "Corrective Action" Scripts

A common usage scenario for Log Parser queries is the search for configuration settings that are incorrect or unexpected. Rather than simply creating reports that display the results, why not use the results to generate scripts that will rectify the situation? By doing so, you have the ability to apply the changes at a later date, or to delegate the remediation to another administrator, even if the administrator is unfamiliar with the procedure that would be required if the script wasn't provided.

The technique for generating these corrective action scripts is similar to the procedure used in the .reg script and in the LP_QueryBuilder HTA application. You simply begin with a skeleton script—broken into a series of strings—insert values that you extract from your query results, and save the generated text to the target location.

Storing LogQuery Output in a new Access Database

We began this chapter by examining how Log Parser can be extended by creating custom input formats. Let's close the chapter by demonstrating a script to allow you to save Log Parser query results in a custom output format.

The following VBScript code can be used to save Log Parser output into a new Access database. The script uses the Microsoft Jet OLE DB Provider and Microsoft ADO Ext. 2.7 for DDL and Security (ADOX) to create the MDB file, and uses Log Parser's SQL output format to save the results to a new table within the file.

```
---Ch09CreateMDB.vbs---
Const ForReading = 1
Dim fileParam
Dim strMDB
Dim strTable
Dim oParams

' Get required command-line parameters
Set oParams=WScript.Arguments.Named

fileParam = oParams.Item("File")
strMDB = oParams.Item("MDB")

Dim strfile
Dim strParams
Dim params

Dim iParamIndex
iParamIndex=InStr(fileParam,"?")

If iParamIndex > 0 Then
    ' query parameters have been passed

    ' extract the file name
    strfile=Left(fileParam,iParamIndex - 1)

    ' extract the list of query parameters
    strParams=Right(fileParam,len(fileParam) - iParamIndex)
Else
    strfile=fileParam
    strParams=""
End If

' Open the query file
Dim fso
Set fso=CreateObject("Scripting.FileSystemObject")

If Not fso.FileExists(strfile) Then
    WScript.Echo "Error opening " & strfile & ""
    WScript.Echo "File not found"
    WScript.Quit 2
 End If

Dim myFile
Set myFile=fso.OpenTextFile(strfile,ForReading)
Dim szQuery
```

```
szQuery=myFile.ReadAll

' if the user specified query parameters, apply them now
If Len(strParams) > 0 Then
    params=Split(strParams, "+")
    For i=LBound(params) To UBound(params)
        Dim strKey
        Dim strValue

        ' Convert the parameter set to a name-value pair
        strKey=Left(params(i),InStr(params(i),"=") - 1)
        strValue=Right(params(i),len(params(i)) - InStr(params(i),"="))

        szQuery = Replace(szQuery,"%" & strKey & "%", _
            CStr(strValue), 1, -1, 1)
    Next
End if


Dim cat
Set cat = CreateObject("ADOX.Catalog.2.80")
cat.Create "Provider=Microsoft.Jet.OLEDB.4.0;" & _
        "Data Source=" & strMDB & ";"

WScript.Echo "Database Created Successfully"
Set cat = Nothing


Dim myParser
Set myParser=CreateObject("MSUtil.LogQuery")
Dim myInputContext
Set myInputContext=CreateObject("MSUtil.LogQuery.EventLogInputFormat")
Dim myOutputContext
Set myOutputContext=CreateObject("MSUtil.LogQuery.SQLOutputFormat")
myOutputContext.createTable=True
myOutputContext.oConnString= _
    "Driver={Microsoft Access Driver (*.mdb)};Dbq=" & strMDB _
    & ";Uid=admin;Pwd="

myParser.ExecuteBatch szQuery, myInputContext, myOutputContext

' Check to see if any errors occurred
If myParser.lastError <> 0 Then
    WScript.Echo "Errors occurred!"

    For Each strMessage In myParser.errorMessages
        WScript.Echo "Error Message: " + strMessage
```

```
    Next
Else
    WScript.Echo "Query executed with no errors"
End If

WScript.Echo "Data successfully saved to database!"
WScript.Quit
---Ch09CreateMDB.vbs---
```

Final Touches

The tools in this chapter provide just a glimpse of the possibilities for extending Log functionality. Whether you use these tools "as is" or modify them to suit your specific needs, it's clear that the Log Parser COM architecture provides you with flexibility to create great tools to simplify your network administration.

Chapter 10

Formatting, Reporting, and Charting

Scripts and Samples in this Chapter:

- **Creating Data on the Fly**
- **Storing Data to a File**
- **Leveraging the Multiplex Feature**
- **Creating Chart Output**

In This Toolbox

Thus far in this guide, we've been focused primarily on constructing queries to extract information from any number of sources: IIS (Internet Information Server) log files, file system information, even router and IDS (intrusion detection system) logs. However, all of this doesn't mean much if we aren't able to format this data into meaningful and useful output. In our final chapter, we'll take a look at how Log Parser will allow you to create reports and charts that will help you understand and analyze the results of your well-crafted queries.

Formatting Output

As you're about to see, Log Parser offers you almost as much flexibility in deciding how your data should be displayed as it does is designing your queries in the first place. Log Parser 2.2 offers you ten potential output choices, ranging from an on-screen display for a one-off or ad hoc query, to a pie chart or graph created for you automatically, to the ability to log your results to an SQL or Syslog server. And each of these choices can be further customized to meet the specific needs of your task.

Creating Data on the Fly

The simplest way to view the output of a Log Parser query is to simply echo it to your monitor screen (that's **stdout** to you C programmers or **system.out.println** to Java devotees). You have two options for displaying your query results on-screen: the text-based Native format, and the built-in Datagrid Windows GUI. We'll discuss each of these in turn before moving on to ways to store your query results in a more permanent form.

Native

To use *Native format*, simply execute your query without any corresponding **TO** statement, and the query results will print on your monitor screen. You'll find that this is mostly useful for on-the-fly queries; you'll use it during the troubleshooting process or to quickly verify something from a specific log file. You should use caution with this option, though, since a long or complex query can wrap within your console window and quickly become unreadable. In Figure 10.1, you can see how even a simple file system query (**logparser.exe "SELECT PATH, NAME, SIZE FROM 'C:\LogParser\.*** –i:FS**) can overrun the default size of the Windows command prompt. In a case like this, you can include a *TO* clause that will pipe the output to a text file for better readability by appending a simple **> filename.txt** to the end of the command.

Figure 10.1 Long Filenames Printed to the Console Can Quickly become Unreadable

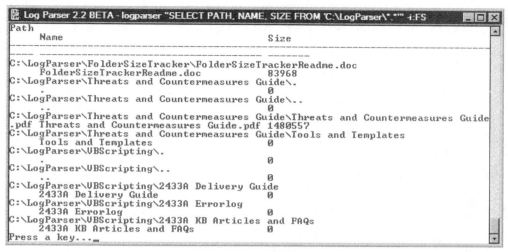

Even this seemingly simple output format can be customized quite a bit to fit your needs. By specifying the **-o:NAT** switch, you have a number of options available to you, listed in Table 10.1.

Table 10.1 Command Line Switches for Native-Format Output

Option	Definition
-rtp <rowsnumber>	Rows to print together [-1=all] [default value=10]
-headers ON|OFF	Print headers [default value=ON]
-spaceCol ON|OFF	Space columns [default value=ON]
-rAlign ON|OFF	Align columns to the right [default value=OFF]
-colSep <string>	Column separator [default value=' ']
-direct ON|OFF	Enable direct mode (no buffering, no spacing) [default value=OFF]
-oCodepage <codepage_ID>	File codepage (special values: 0=system codepage, -1=UNICODE) [default value=0]
-fileMode 0|1|2	Action to perform when the file already exists: 0=append, 1=overwrite, 2=ignore [default value=1]

For example, the query in the following code will create output 20 lines at a time, aligned to the right.

```
---Ch10CreatingNativeOutput.sql---
SELECT
    NAME,
    SIZE
```

```
FROM C:\LogParser\.
---Ch10CreatingNativeOutput.sql---

logparser.exe file: Ch10CreatingNativeOutput.sql -i:FS -o:NAT -rtp:20 -rAlign:ON

                                  Name    Size
---------------------------------- -------
                                     .       0
                                    ..       0
                                   COM       0
                              EULA.doc   34816
                          LogParser.dll 1131248
                          LogParser.doc  389632
                          LogParser.exe 1077488
                               Samples       0
         Threats and Countermeasures Guide   0
                          Whatsnew.htm   11269
         Windows Server 2003 Security Guide   0
                                     .       0
                                    ..       0
              ILogParserInputContext.hxx    1293
                           Readme.htm    7721
                                     .       0
                                    ..       0
                                   COM       0
                               Queries       0
                               Scripts       0
Press a key...
```

And even this Native mode output can be stored to a file for later viewing. The following code demonstrates a query that stores Native output to a text file; the **fileMode** switch indicates that the file will be appended if it already exists. You can see the resultant text file in Figure 10.2.

```
---Ch10SendingNativeOutputToATextFile.sql---
SELECT
    NAME,
    SIZE
FROM C:\LogParser\. TO C:\LogParser\output.txt
---Ch10SendingNativeOutputToATextFile.sql---

logparser.exe file: Ch10SendingNativeOutputToATextFile.sql -i:FS -o:NAT -fileMode 1

Statistics:
-----------
Elements processed: 205
Elements output:    205
Execution time:     0.57 seconds
```

```
C:\LogParser>C:>
```

Figure 10.2 Creating Native Mode Output Saved to Text File

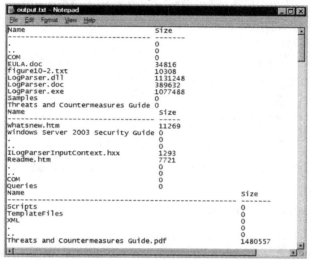

Datagrid

Another useful output format for one-off queries is the Datagrid, which displays results on-screen like Native Mode output. Instead of a command window, though, Datagrid output is presented within a Windows dialog box. Within this dialog box, you have the option of scrolling through the results of the query, customizing the font size for better readability, and copying content to the Windows Clipboard. As you can see in Figure 10.3, a query that was nearly impossible to read from the command window in Native format is far more legible and manageable when presented in Datagrid format. Because this output format is designed to be so simple, there aren't many command line switches available to customize it. The two that are available for Datagrid output are:

- **-rtp <*rowsnumber*>** is used to specify how many rows will print at a time. The default value is 10 rows at a time, and a **-1** here will print all rows at once.

- **-autoScroll ON|OFF** will control whether the Datagrid window automatically scrolls when new a new query is run. The default value is **ON**.

Figure 10.3 Datagrids Provide an Easy-to-Read Output for Ad Hoc Queries

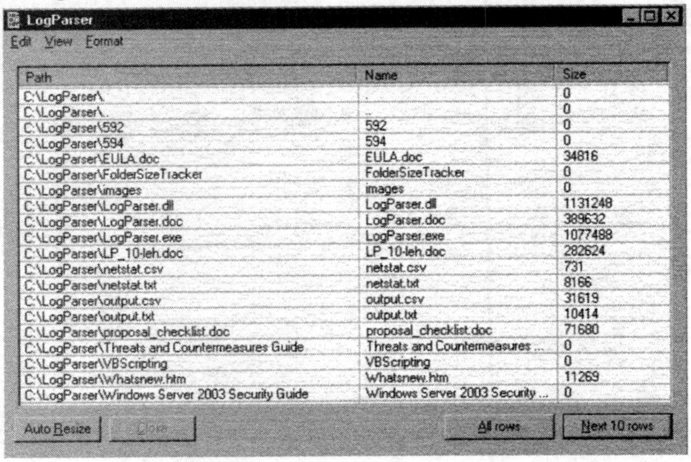

Path	Name	Size
C:\LogParser\.	.	0
C:\LogParser\..	..	0
C:\LogParser\592	592	0
C:\LogParser\594	594	0
C:\LogParser\EULA.doc	EULA.doc	34816
C:\LogParser\FolderSizeTracker	FolderSizeTracker	0
C:\LogParser\images	images	0
C:\LogParser\LogParser.dll	LogParser.dll	1131248
C:\LogParser\LogParser.doc	LogParser.doc	389632
C:\LogParser\LogParser.exe	LogParser.exe	1077488
C:\LogParser\LP_10-leh.doc	LP_10-leh.doc	282624
C:\LogParser\netstat.csv	netstat.csv	731
C:\LogParser\netstat.txt	netstat.txt	8166
C:\LogParser\output.csv	output.csv	31619
C:\LogParser\output.txt	output.txt	10414
C:\LogParser\proposal_checklist.doc	proposal_checklist.doc	71680
C:\LogParser\Threats and Countermeasures Guide	Threats and Countermeasures ...	0
C:\LogParser\VBScripting	VBScripting	0
C:\LogParser\Whatsnew.htm	Whatsnew.htm	11269
C:\LogParser\Windows Server 2003 Security Guide	Windows Server 2003 Security ...	0

Storing Data to a File

Even beyond the ad hoc data output that we've already covered, Log Parser also allows you to create output in various file formats for archiving and further analysis. You can store output in flat text files like the W3C (World Wide Web Consortium) or IIS file formats, or into an SQL database table for more extensive analysis capabilities. Your options become quite flexible when you create XML output, and you can create your own output format using template files that you can generate and format as you see fit.

W3C & IIS

You'll use the **-o:W3C** output switch to create output in the W3C Extended Log File format, which allows you to store detailed and extensive information, including client IP (Internet Protocol) addresses and the amount of data sent and received from your web or proxy server. You can create W3C-formatted output in order to perform further analysis using another utility, or if you have pre-existing log files that you want to convert to the more extensible W3C format (we'll talk about log file conversion a little later in the chapter). Table 10.2 lists the parameters that are available to you when you create W3C output files.

Table 10.2 Command Line Switches for W3C-Formatted Output

Option	Definition
-rtp <rowsnumber>	Row to print at a time, -1=all [default value=10]
-oCodepage <codepage_ID>	File codepage (special values: 0=system codepage, -1=UNICODE) [default value=0]
-oDQuotes ON|OFF	Double-quote strings [default value=OFF]

Continued

Table 10.2 Command Line Switches for W3C-Formatted Output

Option	Definition
-oDirTime <STRING>	Content of the "#Date" directive header [default value=Actual date and time]
-encodeDelim ON|OFF	Automatically substitute space characters with '+' within string values [default value=OFF]
-fileMode 0|1|2	Action to perform when the file already exists: 0=append, 1=overwrite, 2=ignore[default value=1]

NOTE

The W3C format is used in a number of Microsoft products and applications, Windows Media Services, Microsoft Internet Security & Acceleration Server (ISA Server), Microsoft Exchange Server, Personal Firewall, FTP server, or SMTP server.

Likewise, if you have a business need to convert or store your log files in the IIS format, you can use the **-o:IIS** switch to create Log Parser output in the IIS log format. Table 10.3 lists the additional switches available when creating IIS-formatted Log Parser output.

Table 10.3 Command Line Switches for IIS-Formatted Output

Option	Definition
-rtp <rowsnumber>	Row to print at a time, -1=all [default value=10]
-oCodepage <codepage_ID>	File codepage (special values: 0=system codepage, -1=UNICODE) [default value=0]
-fileMode 0|1|2	Action to perform when the file already exists: 0=append, 1=overwrite, 2=ignore[default value=1]

For example, the following query demonstrates how to create W3C-formatted output, while the query Ch10CreatingIISOutput.sql takes the same query and formats the output in IIS format.

```
---Ch10CreatingW3COutput.sql---
SELECT
    cs-username AS Source,
    cs-uri-query AS FileRequested
FROM ex011115.log
---Ch10SendingNativeOutputToATextFile.sql---

logparser.exe file: Ch10CreatingW3COutput.sql -o:w3c
```

```
#Software: Microsoft Log Parser
#Version: 1.0
#Date: 2004-09-18 15:06:42
#Fields: Source File
ex1.example.com /dir1/html/subhtml/sub/jobs/33_153a.htm
ex1.example.com /home/dir1/html/subhtml/sub/jobs/33_17a.htm
ex1.example.com /home/dir1/html/subhtml/sub/jobs/33_43.htm
ex1.example.com /dir1/html/subhtml/sub/jobs/33_17a.htm
ex2.example.com /default.htm
ex2.example.com /home/images/finance_bg1.jpg
ex2.example.com /home/images/B_Title.gif
ex2.example.com /home/index.html
ex2.example.com /home/contents.htm
ex2.example.com /home/financebase.htm
ex1.example.com /dir1/html/subhtml/sub/jobs/33_43.htm
ex2.example.com /home/images/financecapblue.gif
ex2.example.com /home/images/finass.gif
ex2.example.com /home/images/formpub.gif
ex2.example.com /home/images/home.gif
ex2.example.com /home/images/invoicestu.gif
ex2.example.com /home/images/loancredit.gif
```

Here is the same query as before, using the IIS output format.

```
---Ch10CreatingIISOutput.sql---
SELECT
    c-ip AS UserIP,
    cs-uri-stem AS Target
INTO output.iis
FROM ex011115.log
---Ch10CreatingIISOutput.sql---


logparser.exe file: Ch10CreatingIISOutput.sql -o:iis


ex1.example.com, /dir1/html/subhtml/sub/jobs/33_153a.htm,
ex1.example.com, /home/dir1/html/subhtml/sub/jobs/33_17a.htm,
ex1.example.com, /home/dir1/html/subhtml/sub/jobs/33_43.htm,
ex1.example.com, /dir1/html/subhtml/sub/jobs/33_17a.htm,
ex2.example.com, /default.htm,
ex2.example.com, /home/images/finance_bg1.jpg,
ex2.example.com, /home/images/B_Title.gif,
ex2.example.com, /home/index.html,
ex2.example.com, /home/contents.htm,
ex2.example.com, /home/financebase.htm,
ex1.example.com, /dir1/html/subhtml/sub/jobs/33_43.htm,
ex2.example.com, /home/images/financecapblue.gif,
```

```
ex2.example.com,  /home/images/finass.gif,
ex2.example.com,  /home/images/formpub.gif,
ex2.example.com,  /home/images/home.gif,
ex2.example.com,  /home/images/invoicestu.gif,
ex2.example.com,  /home/images/loancredit.gif,
```

Swiss Army Knife

When What You Have Isn't Quite What You Need

Probably the main benefit of the W3C output format is the ability to transform your existing data into something that can be fed into other analysis tools. Because the W3C format was standardized in 1995 and is platform- and operating system-independent, many Microsoft and third-party analysis tools can accept log files that are formatted this way. In fact, Log Parser includes a built-in conversion utility between IIS and W3C formats, for those situations where you've been storing your log files in the IIS native format and then discover that you need to start using the W3C format. For example, you could use this utility to convert another log file format into the W3C format that analysis tools like AWStats (http://awstats.sourceforge.net) or Urchin (//www.urchin.com) will be able to analyze.

Log Parser 2.2 includes a built-in query that will convert a file from the IIS log format to W3C Extended log format, as illustrated in the following code. This query renames the IIS fields according to the W3C naming standard and converts the timestamp from local time (used by IIS logs) to the UTC time format required by W3C.

```
SELECT
    TO_DATE(TO_UTCTIME(TO_TIMESTAMP(Date, Time))) AS date,
    TO_TIME(TO_UTCTIME( TO_TIMESTAMP(Date, Time))) AS time,
    ServiceInstance AS s-sitename,
    HostName AS s-computername,
    ServerIP AS s-ip,
    RequestType AS cs-method,
    REPLACE_CHR(Target, ' \u0009\u000a\u000d', '+') AS cs-uri-stem,
    Parameters AS cs-uri-query,
    UserName AS cs-username,
    UserIP AS c-ip,
    StatusCode AS sc-status,
    Win32StatusCode AS sc-win32-status,
    BytesSent AS sc-bytes,
    BytesReceived AS cs-bytes,
    TimeTaken AS time-taken
```

Continued

You can see the difference between the two file formats in the following lists. For IIS File Field Names:

- LogFilename
- LogRow
- Date
- Time
- c-ip
- cs-username
- s-sitename
- s-computername
- s-ip
- s-port
- cs-method
- cs-uri-stem
- cs-uri-query
- sc-status
- sc-substatus
- sc-win32-status
- sc-bytes
- cs-bytes
- time-taken
- cs-version
- cs-host
- cs(User-Agent)
- cs(Cookie)
- cs(Referer)
- s-event
- s-process-type
- s-user-time
- s-kernel-time
- s-page-faults
- s-total-procs
- s-active-procs
- s-stopped-procs

For W3C log file field names:

- LogFilename
- LogRow
- Date

Continued

- Time
- c-ip
- cs-username
- s-sitename
- s-computername
- s-ip
- s-port
- cs-method
- cs-uri-stem
- cs-uri-query
- sc-status
- sc-substatus
- sc-win32-status
- sc-bytes
- cs-bytes
- time-taken
- cs-version
- cs-host
- cs(User-Agent)
- cs(Cookie)
- cs(Referer)
- s-event
- s-process-type
- s-user-time
- s-kernel-time
- s-page-faults
- s-total-procs
- s-active-procs
- s-stopped-procs

Formatting CSV and TSV output

Two more standards for data storage that have been around even longer than the W3C format are the CSV (comma-separated values) and TSV (tab-separated values) files. These two file formats create possibly the ultimate in interoperability and flexibility in storing data, since information stored in these formats can be easily imported into line-of-business applications like Excel and Access, and even into mainframes for storage or processing.

As the name implies, the CSV file format will produce an output file that contains one record per line with each field separated by a comma. To produce a CSV file from your Log Parser query, simply include an **INTO** *<filename>* phrase within your SQL query, as illustrated in the code listing the Ch10CreatingCSVOutput.sql. You can see the output of the query in Figure 10.4.

```
---Ch10CreatingCSVOutput.sql---
SELECT
    c-ip AS IP,
    cs-uri-stem AS File
INTO c:\logparser\output.csv
FROM c:\logparser\ex011115.log
---Ch10CreatingCSVOutput.sql---


Logparser.exe file: Ch10CreatingCSVOutput.sql -i:W3C -o:csv –fileMode 1
```

Figure 10.4 Viewing the CSV File in Notepad

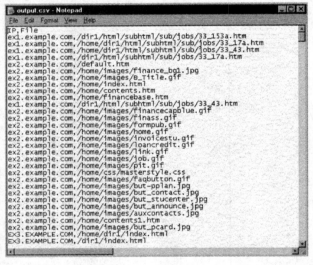

Table 10.4 details the additional command line switches available for CSV-formatted output, including whether or not to include a header row containing the field names, how to format timestamp fields, and whether to append to or overwrite an existing file if one is present.

> **NOTE**
>
> The **-headers AUTO** option will insert field names onto the first line of a CVS file, except when the **-fileMode** option is set to *append* to an existing file.

Table 10.4 Command Line Switches for CSV-Formatted Output

Option	Definition
-headers ON|OFF|AUTO	Write field names on first line; when AUTO, don't write headers when appending to an existing file [default value=AUTO]
-oDQuotes ON|OFF|AUTO	Enclose fields within double quotes; when AUTO, quote fields only if contain separators [default value=AUTO]
-tabs ON|OFF	Write a tab character between values [default value=OFF]
-oTsFormat *<timestamp-format>*	Format in which TIMESTAMP fields are rendered [default value=yyyy-MM-dd hh:mm:ss]
-oCodepage *<codepage_ID>*	File codepage (special values: 0=system codepage, -1=UNICODE) [default value=0]
-fileMode 0|1|2	Action to perform when the file already exists: 0=append, 1=overwrite, 2=ignore[default value=1]

TSV

The TSV format is fundamentally similar to CSV, except that the delimiting character is a Tab instead of a comma. Table 10.5 lists the command line parameters available.

Table 10.5 Command Line Switches for TSV-Formatted Output

Option	Definition
-headers ON|OFF|AUTO	Write field names on first line; when AUTO, don't write headers when appending to an existing file [default value=AUTO]
-oSeparator *<separator>*	Separator between fields; '<string>', 'spaces' (any space character), 'space', or 'tab' [default value='tab']
-oTsFormat *<timestamp-format>*	Format in which TIMESTAMP fields are rendered [default value=yyyy-MM-dd hh:mm:ss]
-oCodepage *<codepage_ID>*	File codepage (special values: 0=system codepage, -1=UNICODE) [default value=0]
-fileMode 0|1|2	Action to perform when the file already exists: 0=append, 1=overwrite, 2=ignore [default value=1]

SQL

For long-term log archiving and the ability to perform detailed data analysis, Log Parser's ability to output query information directly into an SQL database is perhaps its most useful feature. You can either import the results of your queries into an existing SQL table, or Log Parser can create a table for you based on the structure of your query. The command line switches in Table 10.6 provide you with great flexibility in customizing the behavior of your queries as they interact with SQL.

For example, the query in the following code, listing Ch10CreateSQLTable.sql, will return the 20 most-requested URLs for each day. This will be recorded in the SQL database called *StatisticsArchive* on server *SQL-1*. Since no username or password is specified, Log Parser will run the query and connect to the SQL server using the credentials of the currently logged-in user.

```
---Ch10CreateSQLTable.sql---
SELECT
    TOP 20 date AS Date,
    cs-uri-stem,
    COUNT() AS Total,
    MAX(time-taken) AS MaxTime,
    AVG(time-taken) AS AvgTime,
    AVG(sc-bytes) AS AvgBytesSent
FROM ex.log
---Ch10CreateSQLTable.sql---

logparser.exe file: Ch10CreateSQLTable.sql -o:SQL -server:SQL1 -database:StatisticsArchive
```

You can also use Log Parser to query SQL itself, like the following query, which will log any SQL errors to a new *SQLEvents* table in the *Logs* database. In this case, the **–cleartable:on** switch will empty the table each time the query is run.

```
---Ch10AnalyzeSQLErrors.sql---
SELECT
    'SQLServer1' AS Server,
    TO_TIMESTAMP(substr(Text,0,19), 'yyyy-MM-dd hh:mm:ss') AS TimeGenerated,
    substr(Text,23,9) AS Source,
    substr(Text,33) AS Message
FROM c:\Program Files\Microsoft SQL Server\MSSQL\LOG TO Sql_Events
WHERE
    (
        NOT TimeGenerated IS NULL
    )
    AND
INDEX_OF(TO_STRING(SUB(TO_LOCALTIME(SYSTEM_TIMESTAMP()),TimeGenerated),'MM/dd/yyyy'),'11/3
0/') = 0
---Ch10AnalyzeSQLErrors.sql---

logparser file: Ch10AnalyzeSQLErrors.sql -i:textline -o:SQL -database:Logs -cleartable:on
```

When working with SQL output, keep in mind that you're not restricted to using Microsoft SQL Server as your output source, either. Log Parser can send output to any ODBC–compatible database by using the **–dsn** option to specify the Data Source Name. This should allow you to export your Log Parser data to Microsoft SQL, Oracle and other database formats that you require.

Table 10.6 Command Line Switches for SQL-Formatted Output

Option	Definition
-server *<server name>*	Database server [default value=<empty>]
-database *<database name>*	Database name [default value=<empty>]
-driver *<driver>*	ODBC Driver [default value=SQL Server]
-dsn *<dsn name>*	Name of the DSN to use [default value=<empty>]
-username *<SQL username>*	Database username; if not specified, will use the current user's credentials through Windows Integrated Authentication [default value=use current user's credentials]
-password *<SQL password>*	Database user password [default value=<empty>]
-oConnString *<connection string>*	Connection string (overrides 'server', 'database', 'driver', 'dsn', 'username', and 'password' parameters) [default value=<empty>]
-createTable ON|OFF	Create a new table if the specified table doesn't exist [default value=OFF]
-clearTable ON|OFF	Clear existing table before inserting rows [default value=OFF]
-fixColNames ON|OFF	Automatically remove invalid characters from column names when creating table [default value=ON]
-maxStrFieldLen *<max_field_len>*	Declared maximum number of characters in string fields when creating table [default value=255]
-transactionRowCount -1|0| *<rows_number>*	Number of rows enclosed in a SQL transaction (0=auto commit for each row, -1=all rows in a single transaction) [default value=0]
-ignoreMinWarns ON|OFF	Ignore minor warnings [default value=ON]
-ignoreIdCols ON|OFF	Ignore Identity columns [default value=OFF]

Formatting XML Data

The Extensible Markup Language, or XML, was designed as a way to store and describe data in a highly flexible manner. It serves a number of purposes, especially exchanging data between dissimilar systems, and allowing you to segregate an application's data from the medium used to display it, like HTML (Hypertext Markup Language). Instead of having a specific set of pre–defined tags, XML requires you to define your own tags in order to classify your data. For example, you can create a set of tags that will describe a cooking recipe, like the one shown in the following code. In this example, **recipe** is considered a *root element*, while **title** and **ingredient** are considered *child elements*.

```
<recipe>
        <title>Chicken Kiev</title>
        <ingredient>
                <name>Chicken breast</name>
                <quantity>4</quantity>
        </ingredient>
        <ingredient>
                <name>Butter</name>
                <quantity>2 sticks</quantity>
        </ingredient>
...
</recipe>
```

Since you will be defining your own XML tags, you also need a way to define what those elements are so that you can *validate* your XML (it's like making up your own schoolyard game – you need to define the rules of the game so that other people know how to play). You do this using either a Document Type Definition (DTD) or an XML schema. A DTD defines the document structure with a list of legal elements, while an XML schema does the following:

- defines elements that can appear in a document
- defines attributes that can appear in a document
- defines which elements are child elements
- defines the order of child elements
- defines the number of child elements
- defines whether an element is empty or can include text
- defines data types for elements and attributes
- defines default and fixed values for elements and attributes

In order to create XML output from your Log Parser queries, you'll use **INTO** *filename*.**xml** within your SQL query. Table 10.7 defines the command line switches available when creating XML output.

NOTE

-**xslLink** refers to an Extensible Style Language document, which is an XML-based style sheet similar to CSS.

Table 10.7 Command Line Switches for XML-Formatted Output

Option	Definition
-structure 1|2|3|4	Type of XML structure [default value=1]
-rootName *<rootname>*	Name of the ROOT element [default value=ROOT]
-rowName *<rowname>*	Name of the ROW element [default value=ROW]
-fieldName *<fieldname>*	Name of the FIELD element [default value=FIELD]
-xslLink *<xsl_document_path>*	Path of an XSL document to be referenced in the output [default value=NONE]
-schemaType 0|1	Type of schema to be written inline (0=none, 1=DTD) [default value=1]
-compact ON|OFF	Suppress spaces and carriage returns in output [default value=OFF]
-noEmptyField ON|OFF	Suppress empty tags for NULL field values [default value=OFF]
-standAlone ON|OFF	When OFF, does not write any <XML> header nor <ROOT> tags (generates an invalid XML document) [default value=ON]
-fileMode 0|1|2	Action to perform when the file already exists: 0=append, 1=overwrite, 2=ignore [default value=1]
-oCodepage *<codepage_ID>*	File codepage (special values: 0=system codepage, -1=UNICODE) [defaultvalue=-1]

Ch10CreateXMLOutput.sql illustrates how an IIS log is formatted when transformed into an XML document.

```
---Ch10CreateXMLOutput.sql---
 SELECT

INTO output.xml
FROM ex011115.log
---Ch10CreateXMLOutput.sql---

logparser.exe fie: Ch10CreateXMLOutput.sql -i:W3C -o:XML

<?xml version="1.0" encoding="ISO-10646-UCS-2" standalone="yes" ?>
<!DOCTYPE ROOT[
 <!ATTLIST ROOT DATE_CREATED CDATA #REQUIRED>
 <!ATTLIST ROOT CREATED_BY CDATA #REQUIRED>
 <!ELEMENT LogFilename (#PCDATA)>
 <!ELEMENT RowNumber (#PCDATA)>
 <!ELEMENT date (#PCDATA)>
 <!ELEMENT time (#PCDATA)>
 <!ELEMENT c-ip (#PCDATA)>
 <!ELEMENT cs-username (#PCDATA)>
```

```
<!ELEMENT s-ip (#PCDATA)>
<!ELEMENT s-port (#PCDATA)>
<!ELEMENT cs-method (#PCDATA)>
<!ELEMENT cs-uri-stem (#PCDATA)>
<!ELEMENT cs-uri-query (#PCDATA)>
<!ELEMENT sc-status (#PCDATA)>
<!ELEMENT cs_User-Agent_ (#PCDATA)>
<!ELEMENT ROW (LogFilename, RowNumber, date, time, c-ip, cs-username, s-ip, s-port, cs-
method, cs-uri-stem, cs-uri-query, sc-status, cs_User-Agent_)>
<!ELEMENT ROOT (ROW)>
]>
<ROOT DATE_CREATED="2004-09-19 18:23:12" CREATED_BY="Microsoft Log Parser V2.2">
 <ROW>
  <LogFilename>
  C:\LogParser\ex011115.log
  </LogFilename>
  <RowNumber>
  5
  </RowNumber>
  <date>
  2001-11-15
  </date>
  <time>
  00:02:33
  </time>
  <c-ip>
  ex1.example.com
  </c-ip>
  <cs-username>
  </cs-username>
  <s-ip>
  webserver
  </s-ip>
  <s-port>
  80
  </s-port>
  <cs-method>
  GET
  </cs-method>
  <cs-uri-stem>
  /dir1/html/subhtml/sub/jobs/33_153a.htm
  </cs-uri-stem>
  <cs-uri-query>
  </cs-uri-query>
  <sc-status>
```

```
    404
    </sc-status>
    <cs_User-Agent_>
    example1/3.14+(user1@example.com;+http://example1.com/example1/)
    </cs_User-Agent_>
  </ROW>
```

Using Templates

If you need to create even more customized output for your queries, you can use the Log Parser template format. This format will remind you more than a little of doing a mail merge in Microsoft Word or another word processor, where you use placeholder syntax to indicate where the query information should be placed. The remainder of the file contains freeform plain text. Table 10.8 illustrates the command parameters available for template output.

Table 10.8 Formatting Options for Template Output

Option	Definition
-tpl <template file path>	Path of the template file [default value=<none set>]
-tplHeader <header file path>	Path of the header file [default value=<none set>]
-tplFooter <footer file path>	Path of the footer file [default value=<none set>]
-noEmptyFile ON|OFF	When no row is generated, do not write a file [default value=ON]
-fileMode 0|1|2	Action to perform when the file already exists: 0=append, 1=overwrite, 2=ignore [default value=1]
-oCodepage <codepage_ID>	File codepage (special values: 0=system codepage, -1=UNICODE) [default value=0]

Implementing templates is a two-step process: first you need to create the Log Parser query as usual, but you must also create the template file that will dictate how the output will be formatted. So the Log Parser syntax for creating template file output will look like the following:

```
---Ch10CreateTemplateOutput.sql---
SELECT


FROM ex011115.log TO tpl.txt
---Ch10CreateTemplateOutput.sql---
logparser.exe file: CreateTemplateOutput.sql -i:W3C -o:TPL -tpl:mytemplate.txt
```

Template files can have two types of formatting: raw and structured. The raw template format looks remarkably similar to the master document in a mail merge, where the field names are offset by percent signs (%). In this case, you can create a template file similar to the following, where the text corresponds to one row of query output:

```
RL %cs-uri-stem% was requested by IP:%c-ip% at %time%.
The request took %time-taken% milliseconds to process.
<CR>
```

> **NOTE**
>
> The **<CR>** listed in the format file is for illustration purposes only—you would simply leave a blank line when creating an actual template.

The combination of the query and the template file produces the following output:

```
The following URL /dir1/html/subhtml/sub/jobs/33_153a.htm was requested by
IP:ex1.example.com at 00:02:33.
The request took 45 milliseconds to process.

The following URL /home/dir1/html/subhtml/sub/jobs/33_17a.htm was requested by
IP:ex1.example.com at 00:04:36.
The request took 73 milliseconds to process.

The following URL /home/dir1/html/subhtml/sub/jobs/33_43.htm was requested by
IP:ex1.example.com at 00:06:20.
The request took 102 milliseconds to process.

The following URL /dir1/html/subhtml/sub/jobs/33_17a.htm was requested by
IP:ex1.example.com at 00:08:08.
The request took 86 milliseconds to process.

The following URL /default.htm was requested by IP:ex2.example.com at 00:09:48.
The request took 251 milliseconds to process.

The following URL /home/images/finance_bg1.jpg was requested by IP:ex2.example.com at
00:09:59.
The request took 35 milliseconds to process.

The following URL /home/images/B_Title.gif was requested by IP:ex2.example.com at
00:09:59.
The request took 72 milliseconds to process.

The following URL /home/index.html was requested by IP:ex2.example.com at 00:10:23.
The request took 102 milliseconds to process.

The following URL /home/contents.htm was requested by IP:ex2.example.com at 00:10:33.
The request took 17 milliseconds to process.
```

WARNING

Don't confuse the *template* file, which defines how your output is formatted, with the *output* file that actually contains the results of your query.

Using Structured format allows you to create a header and footer for your output file, to create a more polished look for your query results. A structured template file begins with the raw formatting, then adds <LPHEADER></LPHEADER>, <LPBODY></LPBODY> and <LPFOOTER></LPFOOTER> tags, as follows:

```
<LPHEADER>This query contains %FIELDS_NUM% records.</LPHEADER>
<LPBODY> The following URL %cs-uri-stem% was requested by IP:%c-ip% at %time%.
The request took %time-taken% milliseconds to process.
<CR>
</LPBODY>
<LPFOOTER>Thank you for reading.
</LPFOOTER>
```

While the Log Parser query is identical to the one used to create raw format, the output appears slightly different, as follows:

```
This query contains 13 records.

 The following URL /dir1/html/subhtml/sub/jobs/33_153a.htm was requested by
IP:ex1.example.com at 00:02:33.
The request took 51 milliseconds to process.

 The following URL /home/dir1/html/subhtml/sub/jobs/33_17a.htm was requested by
IP:ex1.example.com at 00:04:36.
The request took 79 milliseconds to process.
…

 The following URL /home/netpay/index.html was requested by IP:ex28.example.com at
02:42:25.
The request took 126 milliseconds to process.

 The following URL /home/images/plogotype.gif was requested by IP:ex28.example.com at
02:42:26.
The request took 64 milliseconds to process.

 The following URL /home/ was requested by IP:EX29.EXAMPLE.COM at 02:42:46.
The request took 27 milliseconds to process.

Thank you for reading.
```

In addition to the command line options available with template format, you can use the wildcards listed in Table 10.9 to customize the header, body, and Footer of a Structured template file:

Table 10.9 Wildcard Values for Template Output

Tag	Example	Substitution	Can Be Used In:
%FIELDS_NUM%	This query contains %FIELDS_NUM% fields.	Number of fields in the SELECT clause.	Header, Body, Footer
%FIELD_<N>%	First field value: %FIELD_1%	Value of the specified field.	Body
%<field name>%	First field value: %cs-bytes%	Value of the specified field.	Body
%FIELDNAME_<N>%	%FIELDNAME_1% value: %FIELD_1%	Name of the specified field	Header, Body, Footer

Sending Data to a Syslog Server

For monitoring an enterprise network, many administrators create a central Syslog Server to collect and store monitoring information for the devices on their network. This provides great flexibility since you can collect information from any device that can communicate with the server, including Log Parser output. In order to send your data to a syslog server, you need to know the name of the server, as well as any necessary authentication information or UDP (User Datagram Protocol) port numbers. For example, the following query would send the results of a web server log to a Syslog server named MONITOR1.EXAMPLE.COM:

```
---Ch10SendingOutputToASyslogServer.sql---
SELECT

FROM ex011115.log TO MONITOR1.EXAMPLE.COM
---Ch10SendingOutputToASyslogServer.sql---

logparser.exe file: Ch10SendingOutputToASyslongServer.sql -i:W3c -o:syslog
```

Table 10.10 lists the command line options for creating syslog output.

Table 10.10 Formatting Options for Syslog Output

Option	Definition
-conf <config_file>	Syslog configuration file [default value=none]
-severity <int> | <name> | $<field>	Message severity level; use $<field> to retrieve this value from a field [default value=info]

Continued

Table 10.10 Formatting Options for Syslog Output

Option	Definition
-facility *<int>* | *<name>* | $*<field>*	Message facility; use $*<field>* to retrieve this value from a field [default value=user]
-oTsFormat *<timestamp_format>*	Format of the TIMESTAMP field [default value=MMM dp hh:mm:ss]
-hostName *<hostname>* | $*<field>*	Value of the HOSTNAME field; use $*<field>* to retrieve this value from a field [default value='localhost']
-processName *<processname>* | $*<field>*	Value of the TAG field; use $*<field>* to retrieve this value from a field [default value='LogParser:']
-separator *<separator_string>*	Separator character(s) between fields; '*<characters>*', 'space', or 'tab' [default value='space']
-maxPacketSize *<max_packet_size>*	Maximum packet size in bytes [default value=1024]
-protocol UDP|TCP	Protocol used for transmission [default value=UDP]
-sourcePort *<source_port>*	Port to use; '' = any [default value=]
-ignoreDspchErrs ON|OFF	Ignore dispatch errors (will be reported as warnings at completion) [default value=OFF]
-discardOversized ON|OFF	Discard oversized packets [default value=OFF]
-oCodepage *<codepage_ID>*	Output codepage (special values: 0=system codepage, -1=UNICODE) [default value=0]

Leveraging the Multiplex Feature

So far in this chapter we've looked at ways to create a single output file using a Log Parser query. In real-world scenarios, however, you'll probably need to process multiple files simultaneously. In this case you'll want to use the Multiplex feature available with Log Parser. This feature allows you to create multiple output files based on the first field name in your query by using the wildcard in your **TO** statement. The following Log Parser output formats support the Multiplex feature:

- W3C
- IIS
- CSV

For example, you may have an extranet site for vendors to access your private sales information, and now you want to create a separate CSV output file for each client that is accessing it. To activate the Multiplex feature in this case, you would create your Log Parser query as follows:

```
---Ch10MultiplexQuery.sql---
SELECT
    c-ip,
```

```
    date,
    time,
    cs-uri-stem
FROM ex011115.log TO c:\multi\.CSV
---Ch10MultiplexQuery.sql---

logparser.exe file: Ch10MultipleQuery.sql -i:W3C -o:CSV
```

In this instance, Log Parser will take the first field name specified in the query (in this case, **c-ip**) and create a separate file called ***%c-ip%*.CSV** in the c:\multi directory, like the listing shown here:

```
09/26/2004   03:22 PM    <DIR>              .
09/26/2004   03:22 PM    <DIR>              ..
09/26/2004   03:20 PM               90 10.0.0.153.CSV
09/26/2004   03:20 PM              241 192.168.1.122.CSV
09/26/2004   03:20 PM            1,470 192.168.1.153.CSV
09/26/2004   03:20 PM            1,664 192.168.1.154.CSV
09/26/2004   03:20 PM              133 192.168.1.169-.CSV
09/26/2004   03:20 PM            7,834 ex1.example.com.CSV
09/26/2004   03:20 PM            1,945 ex10.example.com.CSV
09/26/2004   03:20 PM               74 ex100.example.com.CSV
09/26/2004   03:20 PM            1,771 ex11.example.com.CSV
09/26/2004   03:20 PM              265 ex12.example.com-.CSV
09/26/2004   03:20 PM              246 EX13.EXAMPLE.COM.CSV
09/26/2004   03:20 PM              631 ex14.example.com.CSV
09/26/2004   03:20 PM              476 ex15.example.com.CSV
09/26/2004   03:20 PM              318 ex16.example.com.CSV
...
            40 File(s)         34,838 bytes
             2 Dir(s)  62,213,148,672 bytes free
```

NOTE

While Log Parser has created multiple CSV files for this query, the contents of each file remain essentially the same. Multiplex does not change how a given output is formatted; rather, it controls how many output files are created.

You aren't even limited to a single wildcard when using the Multiplex feature. Log Parser will simply match the first field name of the query with the first wildcard listed in the **TO** statement, the second field name with the second wildcard, and so on. This can allow you to create a detailed directory structure to store multiple log files. We can modify our first query to query multiple log files, creating a separate folder for every day and log files within each folder to correspond to each client.

```
---Ch10UsingMultipleWildcards.sql---
 SELECT
     date,
     c-ip,
     time,
     cs-uri-stem
FROM ex.log TO c:\multi\\.CSV
---Ch10UsingMultipleWildcards.sql---
```

```
logparser.exe file: Ch10UsingMultipleWildcards.sql -i:W3C -o:CSV
```

This query will create the directory structure shown here:

```
Directory of C:\LogParser\multi

09/26/2004   03:41 PM    <DIR>            .
09/26/2004   03:41 PM    <DIR>            ..
09/26/2004   03:41 PM    <DIR>            d2001-11-15
09/26/2004   03:41 PM    <DIR>            d2001-11-16
09/26/2004   03:41 PM    <DIR>            d2001-11-18
09/26/2004   03:41 PM                   0 dir.txt
                 1 File(s)              0 bytes


 Directory of C:\LogParser\multi\d2001-11-15

09/26/2004   03:41 PM    <DIR>            .
09/26/2004   03:41 PM    <DIR>            ..
09/26/2004   03:41 PM              63 c10.0.0.153.csv
09/26/2004   03:41 PM             181 c192.168.1.122.csv
09/26/2004   03:41 PM           1,135 c192.168.1.153.csv
09/26/2004   03:41 PM           1,285 c192.168.1.154.csv
09/26/2004   03:41 PM              73 c192.168.1.169-.csv
09/26/2004   03:41 PM           6,476 cex1.example.com.csv
09/26/2004   03:41 PM           1,522 cex10.example.com.csv
09/26/2004   03:41 PM              58 cex100.example.com.csv
09/26/2004   03:41 PM           1,359 cex11.example.com.csv
...
09/26/2004   03:41 PM              51 cex4.example.com-.csv
09/26/2004   03:41 PM           1,505 cex4.example.comuser2.csv
09/26/2004   03:41 PM             381 cEX5.EXAMPLE.COM-.csv
09/26/2004   03:41 PM              29 cex6.example.com-.csv
09/26/2004   03:41 PM              89 cEx7.example.com-.csv
09/26/2004   03:41 PM             778 cEx7.example.comuser3.csv
09/26/2004   03:41 PM           1,424 cex8.example.com.csv
09/26/2004   03:41 PM             337 cEX9.EXAMPLE.COM-.csv
09/26/2004   03:41 PM              58 cj3411.inktomi.com.csv
```

```
                39 File(s)              26,701 bytes


Directory of C:\LogParser\multi\d2001-11-16

09/26/2004  03:41 PM    <DIR>                  .
09/26/2004  03:41 PM    <DIR>                  ..
09/26/2004  03:41 PM                   63 c10.0.0.153.csv
09/26/2004  03:41 PM                  181 c192.168.1.122.csv
09/26/2004  03:41 PM                1,135 c192.168.1.153.csv
09/26/2004  03:41 PM                1,285 c192.168.1.154.csv
09/26/2004  03:41 PM                   73 c192.168.1.169-.csv
09/26/2004  03:41 PM                6,476 cex1.example.com.csv
09/26/2004  03:41 PM                1,522 cex10.example.com.csv
09/26/2004  03:41 PM                   58 cex100.example.com.csv
...
09/26/2004  03:41 PM                  381 cEX5.EXAMPLE.COM-.csv
09/26/2004  03:41 PM                   29 cex6.example.com-.csv
09/26/2004  03:41 PM                   89 cEx7.example.com-.csv
09/26/2004  03:41 PM                  778 cEx7.example.comuser3.csv
09/26/2004  03:41 PM                1,424 cex8.example.com.csv
09/26/2004  03:41 PM                  337 cEX9.EXAMPLE.COM-.csv
                39 File(s)           26,701 bytes


Directory of C:\LogParser\multi\d2001-11-18

09/26/2004  03:41 PM    <DIR>                  .
09/26/2004  03:41 PM    <DIR>                  ..
09/26/2004  03:41 PM                   63 c10.0.0.153.csv
09/26/2004  03:41 PM                  181 c192.168.1.122.csv
09/26/2004  03:41 PM                1,135 c192.168.1.153.csv
09/26/2004  03:41 PM                1,285 c192.168.1.154.csv
09/26/2004  03:41 PM                   73 c192.168.1.169-.csv
...
09/26/2004  03:41 PM                  113 cHIL-233-213.RESNET.UP.EDU.csv
                39 File(s)           26,701 bytes


        Total Files Listed:
                118 File(s)          80,103 bytes
                 11 Dir(s)  62,211,571,712 bytes free
```

> **WARNING**
>
> You may have noticed that Log Parser won't include the field being used for multi-plexing in the query results themselves. So if you're sorting by date, but also want the date included within the query results, you'll need to list it twice within the SQL query. So the previous query would look something like **SELECT date, date, c-ip**.

Another useful query that takes advantage of Multiplexing will allow you to create MD5 hashes for all files within a particular directory. This is useful in verifying the integrity of a file, such as in cases where you are making something available for public download and want to be able to assure your customers that the file they've downloaded hasn't been tampered with in any way. By providing the MD5 hash of the file, customers can compare it with one generated for the file that they downloaded: if the MD5 values match, then the file is genuine. You can use Log Parser to automate this process as follows:

```
---Ch10GenerateMD5Hash.sql---
SELECT
    Name,
    HASHMD5_FILE(Path)
INTO .md5
FROM '.\*.*'
WHERE Attributes NOT LIKE '%D%'
---Ch10GenerateMD5Hash.sql---
```

```
logparser file: Ch10GenerateMD5Hash.sql -i:fs -o:csv -recurse:0 -headers:off
```

Using Charts

One of the most exciting new features of Log Parser version 2.2 is its ability to automatically generate graphical charts based on your query data. You can generate dozens of chart types, including bar charts, pie charts, line charts, and more. This is a specialized feature that requires Office XP or later to be loaded on the machine you're running your queries from. In this section, we'll look at the types of chart output that you can create using Log Parser, as well as how to customize the output.

Creating Chart Output

Like any chart that you used in school or created in Excel, you're going to have different types of data represented by the different graphical elements of the chart. In the case of *bar* or *line* charts, the most appropriate queries would be those that display aggregate information, like, "Show me the hit counts of the top 20 clients who visited this website." So you would have a *series* of elements on one axis of the chart, in this case the individual clients. This would be followed by an *aggregate* total displayed on the other axis of the chart.

NOTE

> In a two-dimensional graph, the horizontal axis is referred to as the **x-axis**, while the vertical axis is the **y-axis**.

To put this into the context of Log Parser syntax, your query should use a **GROUP BY** clause to create the series of elements that the graph will be displaying, and some type of **COUNT(*)** or other aggregate clause to create the totals for each element in the series. For example, the Log Parser equivalent to the plain English example we just listed would be as follows:

```
---Ch10CreateALineChart.sql---
SELECT
    TOP 20 c-ip AS Client,
    COUNT(*) AS Hits
INTO Chart.gif
FROM ex011115.log
GROUP BY c-ip
ORDER BY Hits DESC
---Ch10CreateALineChart.sql---

logParser file: Ch10CreateALineChart.sql -chartType:Line
```

This would place the client information on the x-axis of the chart, and the number of hits from each client on the y-axis, as shown in Figure 10.5

Figure 10.5 Creating a Line Chart

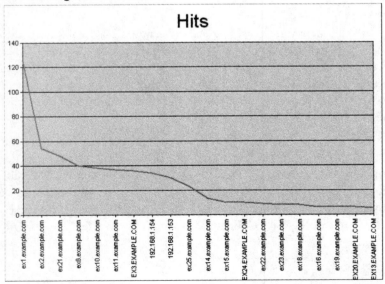

However, you may notice that the Line format for this information may not be the best way to express this information visually. Typically, when you (or a member of management) looks at a line chart, it's more useful for displaying *trends* of information, for example, "Here's how many hits we had on Monday, and here's how that compares to Tuesday, Wednesday and the rest of the week." Luckily, you can create *sixty-four* different types of chart output using the **–o:chart** output flag in Log Parser. By simply changing the **–chartType** parameter in the previous query from **Line** to **BarStacked3D**, we create a much more appropriate graphic, as shown in Figure 10.6.

Figure 10.6 Creating a Bar Chart

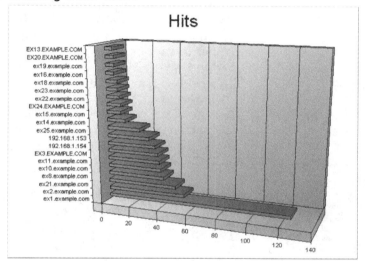

Before we start looking at examples of the many different chart types you can create, Table 10.11 shows the additional command line parameters that you can use to customize your charts. In the next section, we'll look at examples of the different combinations available.

Table 10.11 Command Line Parameters for Chart Output

Option	Definition
-chartType <*chart_type*>	Detailed in the following section – choose from over 60 graphical formats
-categories ON|OFF|AUTO	Display categories along the X-Axis; if AUTO, will display categories if the fields in the first column are STRING values [default value=AUTO]
-maxCategoryLabels <*max_ categories*>	Maximum number of category labels displayed along the X-Axis; 0=auto, -1=unlimited [default value=0]

Continued

Table 10.11 Command Line Parameters for Chart Output

Option	Definition
-legend ON|OFF|AUTO	Print legend for each series; if AUTO, will print legend if there are 2 or more series [default value=AUTO]
-values ON|OFF|AUTO	Print value labels; if AUTO, will decide based on the chart type [default value=AUTO]
-groupSize <WIDTH>x<HEIGHT>	Size of the whole group [default value=640x480]
-fileType GIF|JPG|AUTO	Output file format; when AUTO, uses the specified file extension [default value=AUTO]
-config <config_scripts>	Comma-separated list of configuration script file-names (JScript or VBScript) for futher customization [default value=NONE]
-chartTitle <string>	Title of this chart; if 'Auto' and 1 series only, will use the series' field name [default value=Auto]
-oTsFormat <timestamp-format>	Format in which TIMESTAMP fields are rendered [default value=yyyy-MM-dd hh:mm:ss]
-view ON|OFF	Show the image when done [default value=OFF]

Swiss Army Knife

Even More Fun With Charts

In addition to the Log Parser command line options, you can use configuration scripts to exert granular control over the appearance of your charting output. You'll do this by working with two objects within the Microsoft Office Web Components Object Model: Chart and ChartSpace. Both of these are documented on the MSDN Developer's area of the Microsoft website, and will allow you to customize almost every aspect of your charts. For example, the following script will modify the title, the font size used in the title, as well as the color scheme used by a chart.

```
//Caption
chartSpace.HasChartSpaceTitle=true;
chartSpace.ChartSpaceTitle.Caption="Generated by Log Parser 2.2";
chartSpace.ChartSpaceTitle.Font.Size=6;
chartSpace.ChartSpaceTitle.Position=chartSpace.Constants.chTitlePositionBottom;

//Background color
chart.PlotArea.Interior.Color = chartSpace.Constants.chColorNone;
```

To use this feature, you'll save a script like this one as a VBS or JSCRIPT file, then execute your Log Parser query with the **-config scriptname.vbs** parameter shown in Table 10.11.

Examples of Charting Output

To further customize the bar chart that we created in the previous section, we can use the command line parameters to include a legend for the chart, as well as customizing the title. We'll also illustrate another slightly different chart type so that you can get a feel for the many different styles available. Figure 10.7 shows the chart created by the following Log Parser query:

```
---Ch10CustomizingChartFeatures.sql---
SELECT
    TOP 20 c-ip AS Client,
    COUNT() AS Hits
INTO Chart.gif
FROM ex011115.log
GROUP BY c-ip
ORDER BY Hits ASC
---Ch10CustomizingChartFeatures.sql---


logparser.exe file: Ch10CustomizingChartFeatures.sql -chartType:ColumnClustered3D -legend
ON -chartTitle "Top 20 Resource Requests (DNS)"
```

Figure 10.7 Using Command Line Parameters to Customize Your Chart

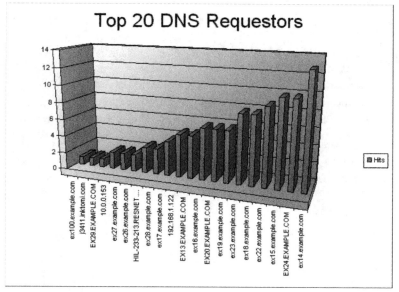

In some instances, showing labels for each element in the series can create unnecessary clutter and make the chart difficult to read, especially in the case of a pie chart. In Figure 10.8, we've created a pie chart for our query and used **–categories OFF** to keep the client DNS (domain name system) names from interfering with the graphic. You'll notice that the legend still allows you to quickly determine which color corresponds to which client DNS name.

Figure 10.8 Creating a Pie Chart

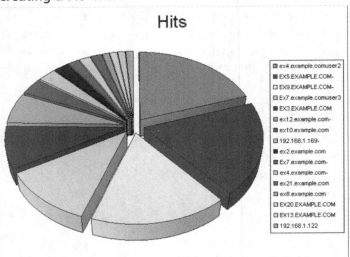

A Poor (Wo)Man's Network Monitor

In a perfect world, we'd all like to be able to shell out for the expensive network monitoring software that will give us a quick graphical view of the status of our critical servers and workstations. In reality, though, this may not be financially feasible for all organizations. But with a bit of creativity, you can rig up a solution with Log Parser that can give you a visual representation of ping times for your mission-critical machines. We've seen the Log Parser syntax for this query elsewhere in the book, but here it is again for review:

```
---Ch10ChartingPingTimes.sql---
SELECT
    TO_INT(REPLACE_STR(EXTRACT_VALUE(Text,'time',' '),'ms','')) AS Response
INTO Ping.gif
FROM stdin
WHERE Text LIKE '%Reply%'
GROUP BY Response
---Ch10ChartingPingTimes.sql---
```

Continued

```
ping -n 10 www.yahoo.com | logparser.exe file: Ch10ChartingPingTimes.sql -i
textline -legend off -chartTitle "Ping Times"
```

The trick now is to take this query and integrate it with other existing Microsoft tools to automate the process. You'll start creating a script that uses the Exec() method to run a command line executable within a VBScript, like this:

```
On Error Resume Next

strPingTarget = "<hostname>" 'IP address or hostname
Set objShell = CreateObject("WScript.Shell")
Set objExec = objShell.Exec (ping -n 10 www.yahoo.com | logparser.exe file:
Ch10ChartingPingTimes.sql -i textline -legend off -chartTitle " & strPingTarget)
```

Use the Scheduled Tasks GUI or the command line scheduler of your choice to re-create this file on a regular basis – as frequently or infrequently as your system resources dictate. You can create multiple scripts to monitor different machines or simply call the Exec() method multiple times.

Once you have your charts created, you can use the **FileSystemObject.MoveFile** command (either from the same or a separate VB script) to copy the chart to an ~/images directory on an Intranet server, running IIS or your web server of choice. At this point it becomes simple to create a basic HTML file that references the GIF files you've created.

To increase the automation of this solution, you can include a **<META HTTP-EQUIV="REFRESH" Content="20;URL=Page.htm">** tag to automatically refresh the HTML page so that it's always updated with the latest information. A very basic HTML page would look something like this, though you can modify and format it to your heart's content:

```
<html>

<head>
<title>Host Availability</title>
</head>

<META HTTP-EQUIV="REFRESH" Content="20;URL=Page.htm">

<body>

<p><img border="0" src="/images/Ping.gif" width="640" height="480"></p>

</body>

</html>
```

While this solution is not as foolproof or feature-rich as the commercial products it's attempting to emulate, it might serve well if your organization is on a tight budget and in need of a creative solution.

Final Touches

In this chapter, we covered the many different types of output that you can create using Log Parser queries. This gives you the flexibility to simply display the output of a quick query directly to your screen, or to save the data to any number of file formats for archiving and further analysis. Log Parser can also help you create reports and charts that you can use in a report for your company's management team or an outside vendor, using both free-form templates and automatically generated pie, line, and bar charts. You can use these files individually for simple reporting or troubleshooting, or, in conjunction with other scripting technologies, you can extend Log Parser's capabilities to create a fully functional reporting or monitoring solution for your network.

Chapter 11

Handling Complex Data

Scripts and Samples in this Chapter:

In This Toolbox

Complex data, as discussed here, is data that is interwoven. It is not cleanly presented as a single field, but buried within a single field with no clean delimiters, or spread across many fields or even files. To obtain the information it holds, the weavings must be undone and inspected. The intent of this chapter is to explain how Log Parser can unravel and inspect the complex data for you, making it more comprehensible.

Embedded Data

Some good examples of embedded data include the event logs from a Windows system. These next queries will use some of the entries for Microsoft's Exchange Server from their Small Business Server 2003. The specific entries sought are those related to the maintenance tasks for permanent removal of deleted items. If you are not familiar with administering a Microsoft Windows Exchange Server, here is a bit of background information that will help the example make more sense. An Exchange Server is often configured for its mail users to store their messages on the server rather than a local hard drive and, if enabled, also provides a second chance to undelete messages even after they have been emptied from your Outlook Deleted Items folder. This Exchange Server is set up to give its users two days to recover deleted mail messages after which the deleted messages are purged from the server as part of the Exchange Server's regular maintenance. To keep track of how many messages and how much space in the message store are being used and cleared we need to look in the event log of the Exchange Server.

The Message field contains the data that on a per-event basis are easy to read and understand. The text of the message is presented as one or more paragraphs of prose containing text and numbers. The numeric data is labeled and there are often links to further information available through the Microsoft website. All of this makes it very easy to read a single event log entry, but it also makes it more difficult to produce a report covering many event log entries. To produce a report about this portion of the Exchange Server maintenance, the pertinent data must be extracted from the Message field while still maintaining the context that it was presented in. Here is an example of the Message field as displayed in the Event Viewer:

```
Cleanup of items past retention date for Item Recovery is complete for database "First
Storage Group\Mailbox Store (BIFS2)".
 Start: 1762 items; 12260 Kbytes
End: 1636 items; 10314 Kbytes


For more information, click http://www.microsoft.com/contentredirect.asp.


For more information, see Help and Support Center at
http://go.microsoft.com/fwlink/events.asp.
```

The message is very easy to read and presents good labels and links for more information. It's wonderful unless you are trying to create a report to indicate how the maintenance processing has been working for the past few months. The important information is embedded with labels that never or seldom change. A good place to start unraveling this data is to determine which parts of the Message field will never be required and exclude them from further consideration. This makes the remainder of the job less complex for the human to understand and reduces the working set of Log Parser.

Having to deal with embedded data can occur with any type of log file, so rather than present a completed solution for just this scenario, there will be several examples provided that show a progression from the original log file to the final extracted data.

Excluding Extraneous Data

The Event Logs have lots of information, but it isn't necessary to use all of it all of the time. Much of the extraneous data is removed by limiting the selected fields to only the data desired. If it turns out the report is too sparse then add the desired fields back in. There are fifteen fields in the Event Logs; seventeen if the select statement is written with the * symbol. This report doesn't need all of those, so most of them will be ignored. In this example, only one field from the event log is selected in its original form, the *TimeGenerated* field. The other field in the SELECT clause is built by slicing and dicing the *Message* field from the event log within the using clause so that it doesn't clutter the result.

```
---Ch11Exclude.sql---
SELECT
  TimeGenerated,
  STRCAT(cat1, cat2) AS Solution
USING
  INDEX_OF(Message, ' For more information, ') AS Exclude,
  SUBSTR(Message, 0, Exclude) AS myMessage,
  SUBSTR(myMessage, INDEX_OF(myMessage, 'Start: ')) AS CutHere,
  SUBSTR(CutHere, 0, INDEX_OF(CutHere, 'End: ')) AS part1,
  SUBSTR(CutHere, INDEX_OF(CutHere, 'End: ')) AS part2,
  TO_INT(EXTRACT_TOKEN(part1, 1, ' ')) AS StartItems,
  TO_INT(EXTRACT_TOKEN(part1, 3, ' ')) AS StartBytes,
  TO_INT(EXTRACT_TOKEN(part2, 1, ' ')) AS EndItems,
  TO_INT(EXTRACT_TOKEN(part2, 3, ' ')) AS EndBytes,
  STRCAT(
    TO_STRING(SUB(StartItems, EndItems)),
    ' items were deleted clearing '
    ) AS cat1,
  STRCAT(TO_STRING(SUB(StartBytes, EndBytes)), 'Kb') AS cat2
FROM
  APPLICATION
WHERE
  EventID = 1207
---Ch11Exclude.sql---
```

This query and all of the other queries presented in this chapter can be found in the samples directory at www.syngress.com/solutions. Look for the Chapter 11 samples. There are several different ways this query can be executed; however, I often use the *datagrid* output format when developing queries, as the output does not wrap in the command window and I find that easier to read. The command line is shown here:

```
logparser.exe -i:evt -o:datagrid -rtp:50 -autoscroll:off file:ch11Exclude.sql
```

Looking at the original Event Log and the Log Parser output shows that the data for these entries is the same, but Log Parser has condensed the log to just the data for the cleanup process, making it much faster to review.

```
2004-10-12 02:00:12 2 items were deleted clearing 932Kb
2004-10-12 02:00:17 123 items were deleted clearing 921Kb
2004-10-13 02:15:06 3 items were deleted clearing 936Kb
2004-10-13 02:15:14 126 items were deleted clearing 1946Kb
2004-10-14 02:15:06 2 items were deleted clearing 932Kb
2004-10-14 02:15:10 96 items were deleted clearing 625Kb
```

Since I was working with one Exchange Server, I put my own labels back in and created a report showing both maintenance operations for each day. If this was being done with multiple Exchange Servers in a data center it would be important to keep the name of the database (see the original message) with its corresponding data and my own labels would likely get in the way with many servers. This query again employs the USING clause to create some fields and then the SELECT clause to add them to the output.

```
---Ch11Exclude2.sql---
SELECT
  TimeGenerated,
  myServer,
  ItemsDeleted,
  BytesCleared
USING
  INDEX_OF(Message, ' For more information, ') AS Exclude,
  SUBSTR(Message, 0, Exclude) AS myMessage,
  SUBSTR(myMessage, ADD(INDEX_OF(myMessage, '"'),1),
    SUB(SUB(LAST_INDEX_OF(myMessage, '"'),
    INDEX_OF(myMessage, '"')),1)) as myServer,
  SUBSTR(myMessage, INDEX_OF(myMessage, 'Start: ')) AS CutHere,
  SUBSTR(CutHere, 0, INDEX_OF(CutHere, 'End: ')) AS part1,
  SUBSTR(CutHere, INDEX_OF(CutHere, 'End: ')) AS part2,
  TO_INT(EXTRACT_TOKEN(part1, 1, ' ')) AS StartItems,
  TO_INT(EXTRACT_TOKEN(part1, 3, ' ')) AS StartBytes,
  TO_INT(EXTRACT_TOKEN(part2, 1, ' ')) AS EndItems,
  TO_INT(EXTRACT_TOKEN(part2, 3, ' ')) AS EndBytes,
  TO_STRING(SUB(StartItems, EndItems)) AS ItemsDeleted,
```

```
    TO_STRING(SUB(StartBytes, EndBytes)) AS BytesCleared
FROM
    APPLICATION
WHERE
    EventID = 1207
---Ch11Exclude2.sql---
```

Swiss Army Knife

Extending Reports Over Time

The event logs of multiple servers can be included in the same query by including more than one machine name in the FROM clause, for example:

```
FROM
    APPLICATION
```

This will read the application event log from the current system but the following will read the application event logs from all three specified servers:

```
FROM
    \\EXCH_HQ\APPLICATION, \\EXCH_WEST\APPLICATION, \\EXCH_NORTH\APPLICATION
```

Log Parser will read these files in the order they are listed, which also means the output will be ordered by server in the same way. If more control over the output is desired, look at using the ORDER BY or GROUP BY clauses in your query.

Privacy Concerns

It wasn't that long ago that the idea of entering your name, e-mail address, and a few pieces of demographic info on a website as part of registering for some service was no big deal. Seventeen million pieces of spam and six new e-mail addresses later, personally identifiable information has become very important and it's everyone business to protect it. There may be iron-clad procedures for dealing with the personal information in the customer registration or marketing databases, but what about dealing with the log files of the servers used to collect that data? It is the same information in a less organized format.

In order to make use of those logs for troubleshooting or other business purposes, the logs may need to have any potentially sensitive data removed to help prevent potential distribution of personal data. This query provides one possible solution for removing personal data from the referrer and parameters fields of an IISMSID-formatted log where it is embedded. The personal information cleaned out in this query is specifically e-mail addresses, but the query can be extended to other types of information.

One of the challenges to overcome with this type of task is with a large distributed website there will likely be many applications from many developers and there will be more than one

way to identify the target information. The COALESCE , REPLACE_IF_NOT_NULL, and
REPLACE_STR functions are a very powerful means to cleanse the logs.

```
---Ch11StripEmail.sql---
SELECT
  -- This first field serves as a file name for the into clause
  -- multiplexing the output to a new file every hour
  TO_STRING(
    QUANTIZE(to_timestamp(date,time), 3600), 'yyyyMMdd-hh') AS stamp,
  time, -- this one maintains the original timestamp for the record
  UserIP,
  SUBSTR(HostName, 7) AS HostName,
  USERAGENT,
  -- This series of functions truncates the referrer
  -- field at the "?" symbol just before the parameters are presented
  -- except when certain desired parameters are present
  REPLACE_IF_NULL
    (
    REPLACE_IF_NOT_NULL
      (
      TO_STRING(RefParm),
      COALESCE(
        CASE TO_LOWERCASE(SUBSTR(Referrer, SUB(RefParm, 8), 8))
          WHEN '/imagedrive.asp' THEN STRCAT(PreRefParm, PostRefParm)
        END,
        CASE TO_LOWERCASE(SUBSTR(Referrer, SUB(RefParm, 14), 14))
          WHEN 'cshift/clrs.asp' THEN STRCAT(PreRefParm, PostRefParm)
        END
        )
      ),
    SUBSTR(Referrer, 0, RefParm)
    ) AS Referrer,

  guid,
  PassportID,
  PartnerID,
  -- This series of functions handle removing the email address
  -- from the parameters field.  For the source logs the email
  -- was taged with 7 different labels and appears in both URL
  -- encoded and un encoded forms. The trick here is to always
  -- wind up with one field regardless of what data was
  -- encountered. The COALESCE function handles that.
  COALESCE
    (
    REPLACE_IF_NOT_NULL(
      URLEnCodedAt,  REPLACE_IF_NOT_NULL(ExtractIDA,  ReplaceOnIDA)),
```

```
REPLACE_IF_NOT_NULL(
    UnURLEnCodedAt, REPLACE_IF_NOT_NULL(ExtractIDA,  ReplaceOnIDA)),
REPLACE_IF_NOT_NULL(
    URLEnCodedAt,  REPLACE_IF_NOT_NULL(ExtractIDQ,  ReplaceOnIDQ)),
REPLACE_IF_NOT_NULL(
    UnURLEnCodedAt, REPLACE_IF_NOT_NULL(ExtractIDQ,  ReplaceOnIDQ)),
REPLACE_IF_NOT_NULL(
    URLEnCodedAt,  REPLACE_IF_NOT_NULL(ExtractIAD,  ReplaceOnIEM)),
REPLACE_IF_NOT_NULL(
    UnURLEnCodedAt, REPLACE_IF_NOT_NULL(ExtractIAD,  ReplaceOnIEM)),
REPLACE_IF_NOT_NULL(
    URLEnCodedAt,  REPLACE_IF_NOT_NULL(ExtractTO,  ReplaceOnTo)),
REPLACE_IF_NOT_NULL(
    UnURLEnCodedAt, REPLACE_IF_NOT_NULL(ExtractTO,   ReplaceOnTo)),
REPLACE_IF_NOT_NULL(
    URLEnCodedAt,  REPLACE_IF_NOT_NULL(ReplaceQQ,   ReplaceOnQQ)),
REPLACE_IF_NOT_NULL(
    UnURLEnCodedAt, REPLACE_IF_NOT_NULL(ReplaceQQ,   ReplaceOnQQ)),
REPLACE_IF_NOT_NULL(
    URLEnCodedAt,  REPLACE_IF_NOT_NULL(ReplaceUIDA,  ReplaceOnUIDA)),
REPLACE_IF_NOT_NULL(
    UnURLEnCodedAt, REPLACE_IF_NOT_NULL(ReplaceUIDA,  ReplaceOnUIDA)),
REPLACE_IF_NOT_NULL(
    URLEnCodedAt,  REPLACE_IF_NOT_NULL(ReplacePQ,   ReplaceOnPQ)),
REPLACE_IF_NOT_NULL(
    UnURLEnCodedAt, REPLACE_IF_NOT_NULL(ReplacePQ,    ReplaceOnPQ)),
Parameters
) AS Parameters
USING
-- much of the field mamipulatin happens here in order to keep
-- the selection statement from being overly hard to read
SUBSTR(Referrer, 0, RefParm) AS PreRefParm,
SUBSTR(Referrer, RefParm, ADD(RefParm, 21)) AS PostRefParm
INDEX_OF(Referrer, '?') AS RefParm,
TO_STRING(index_of(Parameters, '%40')) AS URLEnCodedAt,
TO_STRING(index_of(Parameters, '@')) AS UnURLEnCodedAt,
EXTRACT_VALUE(Parameters, 'id', '&') AS ExtractIDA,
EXTRACT_VALUE(Parameters, 'id', '?') AS ExtractIDQ,
EXTRACT_VALUE(Parameters, 'iad', '&') AS ExtractIAD,
EXTRACT_VALUE(Parameters, 'to', '&') AS ExtractTO,
REPLACE_STR(
  Parameters,
  EXTRACT_VALUE(Parameters, 'iad'),
  'email@servers.foo') AS ReplaceOnIEM,
REPLACE_STR(
```

```
    Parameters,
    EXTRACT_VALUE(Parameters, 'to'),
    'email@servers.foo') AS ReplaceOnTo,
  REPLACE_STR(
    Parameters,
    EXTRACT_VALUE(Parameters, 'id', '&'),
    'email@servers.foo') AS ReplaceOnIDA,
  REPLACE_STR(
    Parameters,
    EXTRACT_VALUE(Parameters, 'id', '?'),
    'email@servers.foo') AS ReplaceOnIDQ,
  REPLACE_STR(
    Parameters,
    EXTRACT_VALUE(Parameters, 'q', '?'),
    'email@servers.foo') AS ReplaceOnQQ,
  REPLACE_STR(
    Parameters,
    EXTRACT_VALUE(Parameters, 'userid', '&'),
    'email@servers.foo') AS ReplaceOnUIDA,
  REPLACE_STR(
    Parameters,
    EXTRACT_VALUE(Parameters, 'p', '?'),
    'email@servers.foo') AS ReplaceOnPQ
-- Hardcoded directory and multiplexed file names for less
-- admin intervention
INTO
  \\logserver\logs\cleaned\*.csv
-- Assumes a separate log rotation process exsits rather
-- than pulling the data directly from the server
FROM
  \\yourservername\logs\*.log
-- Pick up only the rows with the IC values present
WHERE
  TO_INT(EXTRACT_VALUE(Parameters, 'IC'))
IN(66845,66846,66847,66848,53265,53266,53264,11345,11347,11349)
---Ch11StripEmail.sql---
```

This query does not use the standard field names for an IISMSID format log file, so it may not function for you without some modifications to the field names.

Time-Based Queries

The significance of the data is sometimes only in relation to the time period it relates to. When looking at large logs, the sheer amount of data can obscure the important information. Here are a few ways to get past the volume without having to write one.

Intervals and Sampling

Querying for data across intervals of time can be somewhat messy to implement. Uniquely specifying each interval in the WHERE clause would take many statements to implement and be a huge effort to modify. There is an easier and more direct way to accomplish this by using two Log Parser functions together.

The QUANTIZE function is the first one. With it we are able to round down all of the timestamp values within a specified range and once this rounding has occurred all of the records that round down to the same value can be referenced by that value. The sample code we are working up to is from the Security Event log. We will use QUANTIZE on the *Timegenerated* field with a rounding value of 300 seconds (5 minutes). There is no need to output the results of the QUANTIZE function, so the USING clause allows the time value to be manipulated without cluttering the returned fields. This also allows us to reuse the result of that function in another place. Here is a handful of records with the fields *Timegenerated* and *myTime* selected and output. Every record within a 300-second time frame appears as the same time, as shown in Table 11.1.

Table 11.1 Timegenerated Field

Timegenerated	QUANTIZE(Timegenerated, '300')	myTime
2004-09-21 11:15:46	2004-09-21 11:15:00	211962568500
2004-09-21 11:16:23	2004-09-21 11:15:00	211962568500
2004-09-21 11:17:52	2004-09-21 11:15:00	211962568500
2004-09-21 11:19:43	2004-09-21 11:15:00	211962568500
2004-09-21 11:21:15	2004-09-21 11:20:00	211962568800
2004-09-21 11:22:38	2004-09-21 11:20:00	211962568800
2004-09-21 11:24:27	2004-09-21 11:20:00	211962568800
2004-09-21 11:25:06	2004-09-21 11:25:00	211962569100

The query is returning all of the records, so look again at the USING clause and see that the timestamp value is converted to an integer. Next, look at the third column of Table 11.1 and notice that all of the values are evenly divisible by 300. The result of the QUANTIZE function will always end with a multiple equal to the value passed to QUANTIZE. This is important because this degree of consistency provides a basis for a very efficient WHERE clause.

The MOD function returns the leftover parts or remainder of a division equation. The dividend of the MOD function must be an even multiple of the value used in the QUANTIZE function. In this way the WHERE clause will only keep records where the QUANTIZE value and the dividend are both factors of myTime. 900 is divisible 3 times by 300, so the MOD function in the WHERE clause keeps every third 300 second interval. The casual translation of this query is, "Produce 5 minutes of records from the Security log every fifteen minutes".

```
---Ch11Intervals.sql---
SELECT DISTINCT
   timegenerated
USING
   -- duration of sample
   TO_INT(QUANTIZE(timegenerated, 300)) as myTime
FROM
   security
WHERE
   -- frequency of sample
   MOD(myTime, 900) = 0
---Ch11Intervals.sql---
```

Master Craftsman

Time for Log Parser

Having worked with programming languages that provide a time function, but no way to modify its format, we fully endorse Log Parser. It provides an extremely flexible means of specifying and manipulating time formats, as shown in Table 11.2.

Table 11.2 Flexibility in Specifying and Manipulating Time

Function	Parameters
SYSTEM_DATE	()
SYSTEM_TIME	()
SYSTEM_TIMESTAMP	()
SYSTEM_UTCOFFSET	()
TO_DATE	(timestamp <TIMESTAMP>)
TO_LOCALTIME	(timestamp <TIMESTAMP>)
TO_STRING	(argument <INTEGER | REAL>) | (timestamp <TIMESTAMP>, format <STRING>)
TO_TIME	(timestamp <TIMESTAMP>)
TO_TIMESTAMP	(dateTime1 <TIMESTAMP>, dateTime2 <TIMESTAMP>) | (string <STRING>, format <STRING>) (seconds <INTEGER | REAL>)
TO_UTCTIME	(timestamp <TIMESTAMP>)

Continued

This nested function allowed me to extract the date from the Filename field in dealing with log files that did not store the date in the file, but rather embedded it into the filename:

```
\\servername\sharename\directory\20040718.log
TO_DATE(
  TO_TIMESTAMP(
    EXTRACT_PREFIX(EXTRACT_SUFFIX(Filename, 0, '\\'), 0, '.'),
    'yyyyMMdd')
  ) as CollectionDate
```

Note that string manipulation functions were used to extract the date and that it was converted to a timestamp. The extracted data was eight characters and had no formatting to indicate that was not just some number in the 20 millions. The TO_TIMESTAMP function will accept a string value as the time value and a second string to define how that value is interpreted. See Table 11.3.

Table 11.3 Time Versus Log Parser Returns

Date and Format	Log Parser Returns
'January 1, 2005', 'MMMM d, yyyy'	2005-01-01
'20050314', 'yyyyMMdd'	2005-03-14
'050314', 'yyMMdd'	2005-03-14
'050314', 'hhmmss'	05:03:14
'050314', 'MMmmyy'	2014-05-01 00:03:00

Going one step further with TO_TIMESTAMP is the tidbit that if you specify a value and a format that can't work together, such as ('57', 'dd'), Log Parser will return a NULL because 57 is not a valid day of the month. While this is not a complete data validation solution, it is nice to know it is there.

Ranges

The security event log will usually have many entries and, often, interest in that log is time–sensitive, so it makes a good example. Log Parser has a specific statement to make querying with ranges of data very simple. The BETWEEN statement allows the WHERE clause:

```
expressionA BETWEEN expressionB AND expressionC
```

Expression can be a field, alias, function, or constant. Writing this with relational operators has the same results in the output, but would require more typing and increase the chance of errors.

```
---Ch11TimeRange.sql---
SELECT
  TimeGenerated
FROM
  security
```

```
WHERE
    TO_TIME(timegenerated)
        BETWEEN TIMESTAMP('01/01 00:00:00', 'MM/dd hh:mm:ss')
        AND TIMESTAMP('01/01 01:00:00', 'MM/dd hh:mm:ss')
    OR
    TO_TIME(timegenerated)
        BETWEEN TIMESTAMP('01/01 03:07:00', 'MM/dd hh:mm:ss')
          AND TIMESTAMP('01/01 03:08:00', 'MM/dd hh:mm:ss')
```

The equivalent query using relational operators requires more parentheses to keep the grouping together and a little more typing.

```
SELECT
    TimeGenerated
FROM
    security
WHERE
    (TO_TIME(timegenerated) >=
        TIMESTAMP('01/01 00:00:00', 'MM/dd hh:mm:ss')
        AND
        TO_TIME(timegenerated) <=
        TIMESTAMP('01/01 01:00:00', 'MM/dd hh:mm:ss'))
    OR
    (TO_TIME(timegenerated) >=
        TIMESTAMP('01/01 03:07:00', 'MM/dd hh:mm:ss')
        AND
        TO_TIME(timegenerated) <=
        TIMESTAMP('01/01 03:08:00', 'MM/dd hh:mm:ss'))
---Ch11TimeRange.sql---
```

Both queries select all of the records for the first hour of each day and also select all of the records between the seventh and eighth minute of the third hour of each day. These times are not significant, just an example of how the BETWEEN statement provides and easier way to specify a time range.

Correcting For Log Roll Drift

When dealing with very busy Web servers, there can be a number of transactions that start before the logs roll, and due to latency or other issues, do not make it into the logs until after the roll. We call this *log roll drift*. Depending on how busy we are talking about, there could be a few transactions or a few thousand transactions that are now in the wrong log file. The privacy protection query also corrected for log roll drift so that example will be used again with more emphasis on this issue.

```
SELECT
    -- This first field serves as a file name for the INTO clause
    -- multiplexing the output to a new file every hour
    TO_STRING(QUANTIZE(TO_TIMESTAMP(date,time), 3600), 'yyyyMMdd-hh') AS Stamp,
```

```
    Time -- this one maintains the original timestamp for the record
    --and many more fields we don't need for this example
INTO
    \\server\share\directory\*.log
FROM
    -- All of the logs
```

In my last time working with a server farm, the logs rolled every hour so each of the twenty-four daily logs contained drift. If you are working with logs that are rolled daily, the QUANTIZE function has to use 86,400 seconds as a parameter in order to span a whole day. The 3,600 seconds shown here will span a full hour. The field being used for the multiplex must also be a string data type or there will be other problems with creating the file names at the INTO clause. The FROM clause has to cover a period greater than the period in the QUANTIZE function, otherwise the drifted log data won't be pulled back in. The asterisk in the filename instructs Log Parser to use the first field of the select cause as the filename. Every time this field changes, a new file is created and Log Parser writes the following data to it. Use file mode options to overwrite or append to this file as needed.

Obviating the Time-Based Query: iCheckpoint

Once Log Parser introduced the iCheckpoint capability, the need to do all of that manipulation with TIMESTAMPS was greatly diminished for certain instances. When the iCheckpoint option is specified, Log Parser keeps track of how much of the input file was read on the most recent query against that file and then continues on from there with the next query.

To use iCheckpoint the input format must support this option. Formats that support it are IISW3C, NCSA, IIS, IISMSID, HTTPERR, URLSCAN, CSV, EVT, TEXTLINE, TEXTWORD, and TSV. The iCheckpoint feature is used by adding iCheckpoint to the command line and specifying a filename for Log Parser to store the query ending position in. The filename can be just a filename or a fully qualified path either with a drive letter or a UNC (Uniform Naming Convention) path. If the file does not already exist, it will be created. If the file is read-only or cannot be accessed for some creative reason, an error will be generated and the query will abort. This batch file provides a very basic example of how iCheckpoint works. Make a batch file from these two lines of code and save it to a directory that already contains some files and that you have write access to, then execute it.

```
dir > dir.txt
logparser -i:TEXTLINE -rtp:-1 -iCheckpoint:cp.txt "select * from dir.txt"
```

When this executes, it will create a file of all the files in the directory then Log Parser will read that file using the TEXTLINE input format. The Log Parser output will be to the console and will print the summary data from the query when it is done processing. As Log Parser executes, it creates the iCheckpoint file and stores it in the current directory with the name cp.txt. Execute the batch file again and this time the DIR command places both Dir.txt and Cp.txt into the file Dir.txt. Log Parser parses the file with the data in iCheckpoint file and determines that this input file has been read before and there are only two new records to be parsed. The two records displayed are for the files created by the batch file and Log Parser. Execute the file a third time and the summary data indicates that there are no new records in Dir.txt, which is correct again.

Without iCheckpoint the same functionality would require a much more complex set of queries and still have to be wrapped up in a batch file or script to work with the variability of the input files. Before you get carried away with gratitude there are a few more things to consider about iCheckpoint.

Log Parser never stores time stamp information about a file. All of the actions are based on filenames and file sizes so when this option is being used with a dynamic log file rotation some care must be taken to understand what is happening during the queries. To help with that here is the step-by-step procedure carried out when this option is used.

On the first query with iCheckpoint, Log Parser records all of the files that are accessed as inputs (the FROM clause) during the query and the iCheckpoint file is created with a pointer for each input file. On subsequent queries the following behavior could happen for each file in the FROM clause:

- A file is encountered in the FROM clause (FROM *.log) that is not already in the iCheckpoint file; Log Parser processes the file and a new pointer is stored.

- A file is encountered in the FROM clause that is already in the iCheckpoint file; Log Parser uses the iCheckpoint data and continues parsing from where it left off before. This does make an assumption about the encountered file and that assumption is that the file is the same size or larger than when previously parsed.

- If the current file is smaller than the file referenced in the iCheckpoint file, Log Parser will move the pointer to 0, assuming that the file could not have decreased in size unless it was replaced.

- If the current file is larger than the file referenced in the iCheckpoint file, but this is due to the original file being completely replaced by the larger current file, Log Parser will behave just as it did in the second point in this list and will continue parsing with the pointer set in an earlier query. This effectively destroys the validity of your final data since bunches of it would have just been skipped.

As already mentioned, an iCheckpoint file contains a record of every file that is part of the FROM clause. If a subsequent query does not utilize all of those previously recorded files, Log Parser will remove the unreferenced files from the iCheckpoint file. This is great if the log files being parsed all have unique names and are rotated out of the directory regularly, but is not so great if the log file rotation renames files using days of the week or months of the year. Log Parser would be starting over or continuing on with each file based on the contents of the file formerly having that name. There are some definite items to watch out for with this option, but when the environment can be controlled, it is a great aid.

Unsupported Input Formats

Unsupported input formats can come from many sources. Some of the more common would be reports from mainframe computers that are designed to be printed and so have headers and footers for every page and may have data spread across multiple rows. The other place to find inconsistent output is from command line programs that are designed to output to the console. One such program is NETSTAT.exe, a tool used to display active TCP connections and ports.

Command Line Output

This combination of batch file and Log Parser query produces output from NETSTAT and then parses it into a neat set of rows and columns. This line can be typed at a command prompt or placed into a batch file:

```
netstat -a -o -n | logparser -i:csv -nSkipLines:4 -headerrow:off -o:datagrid
file:netstat.sql
```

The output from NETSTAT consists of five columns of data separated by spaces so the output to the console looks nice. The columns will vary in size so the number of spaces between fields will also vary. Not all fields are always present and those that are interpreted by Logparser appear as one large field. There are four lines at the top of the output including the row of column headings. They are also padded with spaces, so are of no real use to Log Parser and are skipped. Here is an abbreviated example of the NETSTAT output to be parsed.

```
Active Connections

  Proto   Local Address          Foreign Address        State         PID
  TCP     0.0.0.0:135            0.0.0.0:0              LISTENING     772
  TCP     0.0.0.0:5000           0.0.0.0:0              LISTENING     1008
  TCP     192.168.2.41:139       0.0.0.0:0              LISTENING     4
  TCP     192.168.2.41:1674      65.86.180.130:21       TIME_WAIT     0
  TCP     192.168.2.41:16713     0.0.0.0:0              LISTENING     1680
  UDP     0.0.0.0:445            *:*                                  4
  UDP     127.0.0.1:1535         *:*                                  1524
  UDP     127.0.0.1:1634         *:*                                  3832
  UDP     127.0.0.1:1900         *:*                                  1008
```

This is piped directly to Log Parser so there is no input file, but in order for the **–nSkipLines** parameter to be available, the CSV input format is used and the lack of headers is also specified with **–headerrow:off**.

Once Log Parser starts to receive the data via STDIN this query begins the process of cleaning things up.

```
---Ch11NetStat.sql---
SELECT
  TRIM(EXTRACT_TOKEN(myData, 0, ' ')) AS Proto,
  EXTRACT_TOKEN(TRIM(SUBSTR(myData, STRLEN(Proto))), 0, ' ') AS LocAddr,
```

```
EXTRACT_TOKEN(TRIM(SUBSTR(myData, ADD(INDEX_OF(myData, LocAddr),
  STRLEN(LocAddr)))), 0, ' ') AS ForgnAddr,
EXTRACT_TOKEN(TRIM(SUBSTR(myData, ADD(INDEX_OF(myData,
  ForgnAddr), STRLEN(ForgnAddr)))), 0, ' ') AS State,
TO_INT(EXTRACT_TOKEN(TRIM(SUBSTR(myData,
  ADD(index_of(myData, State),  STRLEN(State)))), 0, ' ')) as PID
USING
  REPLACE_STR(Field1, '*:* ', '*:* NULL') AS myData
FROM
  STDIN
---Ch11NetStat.sql---
```

A number of string manipulation fields are used together here to clean things up. Since each field that had to be separated presented its own unique parsing challenge, it was not feasible to employ the USING clause to improve the readability of the SELECT clause. Where the USING clause was helpful was in making the data more regular so the EXTRACT_TOKEN function could be used predictably. One way to ease the building of these complex expressions is to write the expression as individual select statements and then, after seeing that they are returning the correct values, combining them into the larger expressions. For example,

```
EXTRACT_TOKEN(TRIM(SUBSTR(myData,
  ADD(INDEX_OF(myData, LocAddr),
  STRLEN(LocAddr)))), 0, ' ') AS ForgnAddr,
```

could be started as

```
INDEX_OF(myData, LocAddr) AS stepone
STRLEN(LocAddr) As steptwo
```

After seeing this return the correct values add the next layer to the expression

```
ADD(INDEX_OF(myData, LocAddr), STRLEN(LocAddr)) AS stepthree
TRIM(SUBSTR(myData,
  ADD(INDEX_OF(myData, LocAddr),
  STRLEN(LocAddr)))) AS stepfour
```

At this point, the last step is to wrap the expression in with the EXTRACT_TOKEN function, which finally produces the value aliased by ForgnAddr.

Skipping Rows

With Log Parser 2.2, skipping rows in a file is very straightforward and much easier than piping the output from Sed, which was one way of doing this with version 2.1. As long as your input format is a CSV or TSV file, there is a command line option called *–nSkiplines* where you simply specify the number of lines to be skipped at the beginning of the file. The lines don't have to be blank or contain any special characters, so this can be a very clean way of removing a header or banner information from command line tool output.

When there are rows that have to be skipped within the body of the input file, there is another option, **-lineFilter**, that allows for a comma-separated list of string values to be specified for either including or excluding every line that begins with those strings. Using the DIR.txt file created in the iCheckpoint example in conjunction with this command line will illustrate.

```
logparser -i:tsv -linefilter:-0 -o:datagrid "select * from dir.txt"
```

In my DIR.txt, the files are listed in the default *dir* output with dates in the MM/DD/YYYY format on the far left. The **-linefilter** option specifies that all lines beginning with **0** are to be skipped so the output no longer shows any files with dates between January through September. Making a small modification on that option to be **–linefilter:+0** will display only the files that were previously excluded.

If your data is so cantankerous as to embed the marker for rows that had to be skipped within the row, there is still another option. This example again uses the DIR.txt file and spits out every row that is not blank and does not list a directory.

```
---Ch11LineSkipper.sql---
SELECT
  myText
USING
  INDEX_OF(Text, '<DIR>') AS GetDir,
  CASE GetDir
    WHEN NULL THEN Text
    ELSE NULL
  END AS myText
FROM
  dir.txt
WHERE
  myText IS NOT NULL
---Ch11LineSkipper.sql---
```

This query executes using the TEXTLINE input format so the entire row of data is one field called **Text**. The USING clause uses the INDEX_OF function to determine the position of the string <DIR> within the field **Text** and returns either an integer for the starting position of the search string, or a null if it cannot be found, and then stores that value as GetDir. Based on GetDir being NULL or having an integer value, the CASE statement either keeps the original data in the **Text** field or blanks the entire row and keeps that result in the alias **myText**. The row skipping ability is completed with the WHERE clause checking all values of **myText** and passing only those that contain data.

Another way to solve this same problem is to use the multiplexing output feature of Log Parser. Employ the USING clause to perform all of the data manipulation to determine if the current record is a desirable record or an undesirable record, much as was done in this last query. Establish the first field of the SELECT clause as the flag for which file the output will go into and use the alias defined in the USING clause as the field expression of the first field. Here is a shorthand example of that for a log containing wanted and unwanted data.

```
SELECT
  KeeperFlag,
  LogData1,
  LogData2,
  LogData3,
USING
  SUBSTR(LogData3, INDEX_OF(LogData3, 'foo'), 5) as KeeperFlag
INTO
  \\server\share\directory\*.txt
FROM
  \\otherserver\othershare\otherdirectory\*.log
```

This query will function as a concentrator and produce a collection of output files grouped by the various values derived into KeeperFlag. This is somewhat similar to using the GROUP BY clause, but provides much greater separation between the groups.

Rows with No Delimiters

Dealing with rows of data that do not have any delimiters is not nearly as awful as it sounds. There will almost always be something in the data that can be used as a key or marker even if it is only the data that is being sought. Log Parser has two input formats for dealing with this, TEXTLINE and TEXTWORD. TEXTLINE will treat all data from the beginning of the file up to the first end-of-record marker as a single record and then the next record will start directly after that and continue until the next end-of-record market and will continue on in that manner to the end of the file. TEXTWORD will treat all of the data from the beginning of the file to the first *space* character as a single record and then the next record will start directly after that space and continue until the next space and will continue on in that manner to the end of the file. If the data being worked with has any cohesion within a row, TEXTLINE will probably be the best choice to have Log Parser maintain that cohesion without extra attention from you.

The **Text** field is unsurprisingly of the string data type. Many of the functions that Log Parser provides can come into play when dealing with this type of data even if they are not string functions. Correctly identifying the desired data could come from using TO_INT and a piece of selected text. If the result is not null, then comparing the result to a known value could be the key to finding your little piece of embedded data. Should you be called to do this often, then very shortly you will likely be writing queries as complex as or more so than the one used to clean up a log for privacy issues.

Passing Data to Log Parser

Many wonderful and amazing queries can be written with Log Parser to drill down to the most specific piece of information, and many of those same queries could be used to find different specific pieces of information, but that would mean either editing the query for each new use or planning ahead and doing something like writing seven different version of the same query for each day of the week or hundreds of different versions for each server in the data center.

Fortunately, that is no longer required with Log Parser 2.2 because parameters can now be passed to the query at run time and be used to modify virtually every part of the query.

Building Dynamic Queries

This query exists only as a batch file until the moment it runs. It was used in a test environment as a batch file and a separate configuration file until the day they became separated and the test failed to execute. Now the batch file creates its own configuration file and then based on the contents of the configuration file, writes out the SQL file anew each time the batch file executes, and finally calls Log Parser to do the real work. Being a single file is less maintainable than separate files for code and configuration, but the portability issue was addressed and being a batch file, it is quick to update.

The objective of the query is to read an XML file and determine if some key information is present. The XML files exist on multiple servers and the key information to be verified could change. Rather than have four queries that are identical except for the server name and have to edit all of them every week to keep up with the code changes, this batch file encapsulates all aspects of the query and presents only one interface to update. Everything is flexible regarding the data being looked for and only has to be maintained in this batch file.

Executing Ch11ServerConfig.cmd

The batch file and query are unique to the test lab they were executed in, so this will likely not run for you without changing server and field name parameters.

```
--- Ch11ServerConfig.cmd---
@echo off
echo.
echo Displays smoke test info.
echo.
rem Create the ini to be used with the FOR command
echo \\actionweb01 > Ch11ServerConfig.ini
echo \\actionweb02 >> Ch11ServerConfig.ini
echo \\stageweb01 >> Ch11ServerConfig.ini
echo \\stageweb02 >> Ch11ServerConfig.ini
--- Ch11ServerConfig.cmd---
```

This echo statement defines which servers are used in the following query:

```
rem Create the sql file to be used with the FOR command
echo SELECT DISTINCT STRCAT('\\','%%server%%'), /ActionConfig/General/TestActionName,
/ActionConfig/Website/Common/AServer, /ActionConfig/ReportingService/DoReporting >
Ch11ServerConfig.sql
echo FROM %%server%%\config\actionconfig.xml >> Ch11ServerConfig.sql
echo WHERE /ActionConfig/Website/Common/AServer IS NOT NULL OR
/ActionConfig/General/ServerName IS NOT NULL OR /ActionConfig/ReportingService/DoReporting
IS NOT NULL >> Ch11ServerConfig.sql
for /F %%i in (Ch11ServerConfig.ini) do logparser -q:on -i:XML -fmode:Branch -fNames:XPath
file: Ch11ServerConfig.sql?server=%%i
```

```
rem clean up
del Ch11ServerConfig.ini > nul
del Ch11ServerConfig.sql > nul
---Ch11ServerConfig.cmd---
```

Emulating Joins

For those not versed in SQL, a join is a means of relating information between more than one table or database. An example of such a practice is a vehicle licensing bureau that must track vehicle owners and their vehicles. They could store all of the owners' personal information with each vehicle, but that would take more time to enter and it increases the chance for errors in data entry. It is more efficient to store the vehicle owner information in one table and all of the vehicle information in a separate one. Vehicles and owners are then related through a piece of shared information or a key such as a driver's license number. By establishing a shared key, the owner information is not duplicated and there is no limit on the number of vehicles that can be related to that owner.

Now that the praises have been sung for relating tables with joins, I will share the bad news: Log Parser does not support joins. They can, however, be successfully emulated and while the method may not be the most elegant, it is functional.

Joins Using Parameter Passing

There are a number of pieces to this example so the actual samples are small and manipulation is done with batch files. You can create a production implementation of this method with batch files, or if even more capabilities were needed, this could be implemented with the Windows Script Host or using the Log Parser COM Object.

The first file introduced here is the log file containing the desired data. It consists of 50 lines of tab-separated values. The first ten are shown here. There are three values to each record; the first is the record number used to reassemble the results, the second is the key that will be joined on and the third is the data to be returned for every record where the key matches in the joined table.

```
---Ch11JoinLog.tsv---
ID      Key      MoreData
1       ABCD     0.509424299
2       DEFG     0.982378588
3       HIJK     0.98108731
4       ABCD     0.297232105
5       DEFG     0.314233204
6       HIJK     0.062696125
7       ABCD     0.45349356
8       DEFG     0.750047108
9       HIJK     0.120907901
---Ch11JoinLog.tsv---
```

The second file presented is the Log Parser query. It selects the three fields from our log file and also defines an alias with the using statement. The EXTRACT_PREFIX function uses a parameter as its first argument. This parameter is replaced during execution with the value provided on the command line of a batch file described in the following example. The results of the query are written to a file called Ch11MidStep.txt, which is the subject of further processing to make this emulation work.

```
---Ch11Join.sql---
SELECT
  ID,
  Key,
  MoreData
USING
  EXTRACT_PREFIX('%idxValue%', 0, '^') AS Index
INTO
  midstep.txt
FROM
  joinlog.tsv
WHERE
  Key = Index
---Ch11Join.sql---
```

The Log Parser query is wrapped with a batch file in order to pass multiple keys into the query. Since only one key can be passed through at a time, Log Parser is called as many times as there are key values in the key file. This action is seen in the second line of the following batch file: the **FOR** command of the Windows Command Shell is used to iterate through each line of the file, Ch11JoinIDX.txt, and parse that line into constituent parts. The contents of that file are shown here with the first piece of text being the key and the second being some amusingly incorrect descriptions.

```
---Ch11Join.cmd---
if exist Ch11MidStep.tsv del /q Ch11MidStep.tsv
for /F "delims=^" %%i in (Ch11JoinIDX.tsv) do
  logparser.exe -i:tsv -o:tsv -headers:off -stats:off -filemode:0
  file:Ch11Join.sql?idxValue=%%i
logparser.exe -i:tsv -iheaderfile:Ch11JoinHeader.txt -o:datagrid -headerRow:off "select
ID, Data from Ch11MidStep.tsv order by ID"
---Ch11Join.cmd---
```

The fifth and sixth lines of the batch file execute Log Parser yet again using this file as an input source. The **–iheaderfile** parameter is used to specify the field names for this last step where the data is re-sorted based on the initial record number, and then displayed using the datagrid.

Log Parser executes as many times as there are rows in joinidx.tsv. Each time, the results are written to the file midstep.tsv using **filemode:0** which appends new data to the existing file. To ensure that a clean starting point is provided for each process run for the target file, Ch11MidStep.tsv, is deleted at the beginnng of the batch file.

TIP

For more information on the Windows Command Shell see the "Command shell overview" and "Command-line reference A-Z" topics in Windows XP Help and Support.

```
---Ch11JoinIDX.tsv---
ABCD^"First Four"
DEFG^"Second Four"
---Ch11JoinIDX.tsv---
```

The first four letters are the key we want and are passed to Log Parser via the **idxValue** parameter where they are used in the WHERE clause for determining which records are selected from the file joinlog.tsv. For the data in our example log file, the Ch11MidStep.tsv file (since Ch11MidStep.tsv is created as part of the query execution it is not provided with the sample files) contains this data after processing the complete FOR statement:

```
---Ch11MidStep.tsv---
1       ABCD       0.509424
4       ABCD       0.297232
7       ABCD       0.453494
2       DEFG       0.982379
5       DEFG       0.314233
8       DEFG       0.750047
---Ch11MidStep.tsv---
```

This output contains only the rows with key values that match the keys in the Ch11JoinIDS.tsvfile, so Log Parser has emulated a join between two files. They appear grouped in the order in which the keys were read and the header row has been suppressed in the output, otherwise it would be appearing once for each row of data and spoil our results.

Joins Embedded in the WHERE Clause

There is another option for emulating a join between two files and that is to embed a SELECT statement within a WHERE clause. This method can be much faster to set up than the parameter passing method previously described, but it is more rigid in its requirements for the format of the input files.

When embedding a selection statement in the WHERE clause, the format of the primary input file must be an exact match to the format of the embedded file. There is a small amount of leeway in this if a CSV or TSV format is used, as Log Parser does not have a definition of which fields are to be present. When using a predefined format such as W3C, that leeway is non-existent.

There are some wonderful uses for this capability, though. Ones that would be much more difficult to put into practice using the parameter passing methods because the values that are joined can be continually changing. Consider the scenario where a report comes in about a group of users that are receiving errors when visiting a certain website you administer. This is not much to go on, but you are going to look at the logs.

```
SELECT
    *
FROM
    \\servername\W3SVC1\ex040215.log
WHERE
    cs-status <> 200
```

For the sake of this example, nothing useful is found and the trouble ticket is closed. Next day comes around, the same report comes in again reporting more errors, and now you're curious so the sleuthing steps into high gear.

```
---Ch11EmbeddedJoin.sql---
SELECT
    *
FROM
    \\servername\W3SVC1\ex040216.log
WHERE
    cs-username IN(SELECT cs-username FROM \\servername\W3SVC1\ex040215.log) AND
    sc-status NOT IN(SELECT sc-status FROM \\servername\W3SVC1\ex040215.log)
---Ch11EmbeddedJoin.sql---
```

This query returns all of the records from February 16, where there is a match between the cs-username fields and no match on the sc-status fields from the log files on February 15. More to the point, it is returning a list of users who were active on both days and encountered different errors on those days. The system administrator writing the query doesn't know who the users are or what the errors were, but now possesses a list of them. This list may be too broad to pinpoint the problem so the query could be run for multiple days by placing a filename wildcard in the FROM clause or by adding another field in the where clause such as the server name.

Swiss Army Knife

SQL Unions

Selecting related information from two tables in SQL is done with the **union** command, similar to the **join** command. However, all selected columns have to be of the same data type when using the **union** command. Since Log Parser doesn't have a **union** function either, that limitation does not exist, but the functionality can be duplicated by running your query multiple times.

```
SELECT
   myDesiredField
INTO
   Temporary.txt
FROM
   \\server\share\logfilename1.log
```

And then executing another query for the same field name on the second log

```
SELECT
   myDesiredField
INTO
   Temporary.txt
FROM
   \\server\share\logfilename2.log
```

For this to work, the file mode of the output file must be 0 (**-filemode:0**), which causes Log Parser to append output to an existing file. The file Temporary.txt becomes the input file for the last query.

```
SELECT DISTICT
   myDesiredField
FROM
   Temporary.txt
INTO
   Final.txt
```

By specifying the DISTINCT keyword, Log Parser will not duplicate any values in the **myDesiredField** field and produce the file, Final.txt, which contains a union of that field from both files.

Final Touches

Log Parser provides a very rich set of functions and operators that have made some of the tasks in my career much easier to complete, and in some cases even made certain tasks possible. For the readers who are just beginning to use Log Parser, I hope that this chapter has opened up some new possibilities for using this tool in some of the more interesting tasks that come the way of professionals. For the few times, if ever, you encounter something that Log Parser can't accomplish, it may be very possible to complete it by breaking the task into smaller pieces and letting Log Parser do part of the job each time like the emulated join does. If that still doesn't work, check with the Log Parser user community at www.logparser.com, and maybe they will have an idea for you.

Appendix A

SQL Grammar Reference

Topics in this Appendix:

- Complete Syntax
- Field-Expressions
- Query Syntax
- SELECT Clause
- USING Clause
- INTO Clause
- FROM Clause
- WHERE Clause
- GROUP BY Clause
- HAVING Clause
- ORDER BY Clause

In This Toolbox

Log Parser works on queries written using a dialect of the Structured Query Language (SQL). Even though the Log Parser SQL dialect draws much from the standard ANSI SQL language, there are some differences whose understanding will help users make the most out of the Log Parser tool.

Complete Syntax

```
<query> -> <select_clause> [ <using_clause>] [ <into_clause> ]
           <from_clause> [ <where_clause> ] [ <group_by_clause> ]
           [ <having_clause> ] [ <order_by_clause> ]


<select_clause> -> SELECT [ TOP <integer> ] [ DISTINCT | ALL ]
                      <selection_list>


<selection_list> -> <selection_list_el> [ , <selection_list> ]


<selection_list_el>     -> <field_expr> [ AS <alias> ] |
                            *


<using_clause>          -> USING <selection_list>


<into_clause>           -> INTO <into_entity>


<from_clause>           -> FROM <from_entity>


<where_clause>          -> WHERE <expression>


<expression>           -> <term1> [ OR <expression> ]


<term1>                -> <term2> [ AND <term1> ]


<term2>   -> <field_expr> <rel_op> <field_expr>                   |
             <field_expr> [ NOT ] LIKE <like_value>               |
             <field_expr> [ NOT ] BETWEEN <field_expr> AND
                 <field_expr>                                     |
             <field_expr> <unary_op>                              |
             <field_expr> <incl_op> <content>                     |
             <field_expr> <rel_op> [ALL|ANY] <content>            |
             ( <field_expr_list> ) <incl_op> <content>            |
             ( <field_expr_list> ) <rel_op> [ALL|ANY] <content>   |
             NOT <term2>                                          |
             ( <expression> )
```

```
<content>    -> ( <value_list> ) |
                ( <query> )

<group_by_clause>       -> GROUP BY <field_expr_list> [ WITH ROLLUP ]

<having_clause>         -> HAVING <expression>

<order_by_clause>       -> ORDER BY <field_expr_list> [ ASC | DESC ] |
                           ORDER BY * [ ASC | DESC ]

<field_expr_list>       -> <field_expr> [ , <field_expr_list> ]

<field_expr>            -> <sqlfunction_expr>       |
                           <function_expr>          |
                           <value>                  |
                           <alias>                  |
                           <field>

<sqlfunction_expr> -> <sqlfunction> ( [ DISTINCT | ALL ] <field_expr> )    |
                      <prop_sqlfunction> ( <field_expr> ) [ <on_fields> ] |
                      COUNT ( [ DISTINCT | ALL ] * )                       |
                      COUNT ( [ DISTINCT | ALL ] <field_expr_list> )       |
                      PROPCOUNT ( * ) [ <on_fields> ]                      |
                      PROPCOUNT ( <field_expr_list> ) [ <on_fields> ]

<function_expr>         -> <function> ( <field_expr_list> ) |
                           <case_statement>

<value_list>            -> <value_list_row> [ ; <value_list> ]

<value_list_row>        -> <value> [ , <value_list_row> ]

<sqlfunction>           -> SUM | AVG | MAX | MIN | GROUPING
```

```
<prop_sqlfunction>      -> PROPSUM

<on_fields>             -> ON ( <field_expr_list> )


<function>  -> ADD | BIT_AND | BIT_NOT | BIT_OR | BIT_SHL        |
               BIT_SHR | BIT_XOR | COALESCE | COMPUTER_NAME | DIV |
               EXP | EXP10 | EXTRACT_EXTENSION | EXTRACT_FILENAME |
               EXTRACT_PATH | EXTRACT_PREFIX | EXTRACT_SUFFIX     |
               EXTRACT_TOKEN | EXTRACT_VALUE | FLOOR              |
               HASHMD5_FILE | HASHSEQ | HEX_TO_ASC | HEX_TO_HEX16 |
               HEX_TO_HEX32 | HEX_TO_HEX8 | HEX_TO_INT            |
               HEX_TO_PRINT | IN_ROW_NUMBER | INDEX_OF            |
               INT_TO_IPV4 | IPV4_TO_INT | LAST_INDEX_OF | LOG    |
               LOG10 | LTRIM | MOD | MUL | OUT_ROW_NUMBER         |
               QNTFLOOR_TO_DIGIT | QNTROUND_TO_DIGIT | QUANTIZE   |
               REPLACE_CHR | REPLACE_IF_NOT_NULL | REPLACE_STR    |
               RESOLVE_SID | REVERSEDNS | ROT13 | ROUND | RTRIM   |
               SEQUENCE | SQR | SQRROOT | STRCAT | STRCNT | STRLEN|
               STRREPEAT | STRREV | SUB | SUBSTR | SYSTEM_DATE    |
               SYSTEM_TIME | SYSTEM_TIMESTAMP | SYSTEM_UTCOFFSET  |
               TO_DATE | TO_HEX | TO_INT | TO_LOCALTIME           |
               TO_LOWERCASE | TO_REAL | TO_STRING | TO_TIME       |
               TO_TIMESTAMP | TO_UPPERCASE | TO_UTCTIME | TRIM    |
               URLESCAPE | URLUNESCAPE | WIN32_ERROR_DESCRIPTION


<case_statement>       -> CASE <field_expression> <when_statement_list>

                            [ <else_statement> ] END


<when_statement_list> -> <when_statement> [ , <when_statement_list> ]
```

```
<when_statement>          -> WHEN <field_expression> THEN <field_expression>


<else_statement>          -> ELSE <field_expression>


<value>                    -> <string_value>  |
                              <real>          |
                              <integer>       |
                              <timestamp>     |
                              NULL



<rel_op>                  -> <  |  >  |  <>  |  =  |  <=  |  >=

<incl_op>                 -> IN  |  NOT IN

<unary_op>                -> IS NULL  |  IS NOT NULL

<timestamp>               -> TIMESTAMP ( <string_value> , <timestamp_format> )

<timestamp_format>        -> ' *( <timestamp_separator> ) *( <timestamp_element>
                              *( <timestamp_separator> ) )'

<timestamp_element>       -> 1*4 y            |
                             1*4 M            |
                             MX | MP          |
                             1*4 d            |
                             dx | dp          |
                             1*2 h            |
                             hx | hp          |
                             1*2 m            |
                             mx | mp          |
                             1*2 s            |
                             sx | sp          |
                             1*2 l            |
                             lx | lp          |
                             1*2 n            |
                             nx | np          |
                             tt
```

```
<timestamp_separator> -> <any_char_except_timestamp_element> |
                         '?'

<field>                 -> '[' <field_name> ']'   |
                         <field_name>

<like_value>            -> ' *( <any_char> | % | _ ) '

<string_value>          -> ' *( <any_char> ) '

<comment>               -> '/*' <text> '*/'     |
                         '//' <text> CRLF
```

Field-Expressions

Field-expressions are the basic elements of any Log Parser SQL query; they define the values on which the various query clauses operate.

A field-expression is one of five possible elements:

- The name of a field.
- The alias of a field-expression.
- A function, taking zero or more field-expressions as arguments.
- An aggregate function, taking zero or more field-expressions as arguments.
- A constant.

Field Names

Field names are names of input record fields. The field-expression in the SELECT clause of the following query is one of the field names in the input records of the IISW3C input format:

```
SELECT cs-uri-stem
FROM extend1.log
```

Aliases

Aliases are alternative names that can be assigned to field-expressions for better readability. The field-expression in the WHERE clause of the following query is the alias of a field-expression in the SELECT clause:

```
SELECT cs-uri-stem AS Url
FROM extend1.log
WHERE Url LIKE '%.asp'
```

Functions

Functions are powerful elements of the Log Parser SQL language; virtually all queries written with the Log Parser SQL language make use of at least one function. Functions take zero or more field-expressions as arguments, process their values, and return a new value. The Log Parser SQL language supports more than 80 functions, ranging from string manipulation functions (for example, SUBSTR, STRCAT) to arithmetical functions (for example, ADD, EXP). The field-expression in the SELECT clause of the following query is a function, which takes two other field-expressions (in this case, field names) as arguments:

```
SELECT ADD(sc-bytes, cs-bytes)
FROM extend1.log
```

For each input record, this function calculates and returns the sum of the values of the two fields. For information on the functions supported by the Log Parser SQL language, refer to Appendix B.

Aggregate Functions

Aggregate functions are *special* functions in the SQL language. Similar to functions, aggregate functions take zero or more field-expressions as arguments, process their values, and return a new value. However, while functions operate on a single input record at a time, aggregate functions operate on *groups* of input records, returning a single value as the result of a calculation on all the input records belonging to a group. When a query does not use the GROUP BY clause, aggregate functions operate on the single group that includes all the input records. For this reason, queries whose SELECT clause contains aggregate functions return a single output record, whose values are the results of the aggregate functions calculated on all the input records. However, when a query uses the GROUP BY clause to define how input records should be grouped together, aggregate functions operate on each individual group. In this case, the query returns an output record for each group, containing the results of the aggregate functions calculated on the input records belonging to the group.

The Log Parser SQL language supports the following aggregate functions:

- COUNT
- SUM
- AVG
- MIN
- MAX
- PROPCOUNT

- PROPSUM
- GROUPING

COUNT Aggregate Function

The COUNT aggregate function calculates the number of items in a group.

This function has two distinct forms. The first form is:

```
COUNT( [ DISTINCT | ALL ] * )
```

When used with the * wildcard, the COUNT aggregate function returns the total number of input records belonging to a group. Using the DISTINCT keyword causes this function to calculate the number of *unique* input records only; using the ALL keyword (or not specifying a keyword) causes this function to calculate the number of *all* the input records, regardless of duplicates.

The second form of the COUNT aggregate function is:

```
COUNT( [ DISTINCT | ALL ] field-expression [ , field-expression … ] )
```

When used with a list of field-expressions as arguments, the COUNT aggregate function returns the total number of input records in which at least one of the specified field-expressions is non-NULL. The DISTINCT and ALL keywords have the same meaning as in the first form. In the Log Parser SQL language, the DISTINCT keyword is not allowed in aggregate functions when queries have a GROUP BY clause.

SUM and AVG Aggregate Functions

The SUM and AVG aggregate functions calculate the sum and the average of their arguments, respectively.

The syntax of these functions is:

```
SUM( [ DISTINCT | ALL ] field-expression )
AVG( [ DISTINCT | ALL ] field-expression )
```

Using the DISTINCT keyword causes these functions to calculate the sum or the average of the *unique* values of the specified field-expression; using the ALL keyword (or not specifying a keyword) causes these functions to calculate the sum or the average of *all* the values of the specified field-expression, regardless of duplicates. In the Log Parser SQL language, the DISTINCT keyword is not allowed in aggregate functions when queries have a GROUP BY clause.

MIN and MAX Aggregate Functions

The MIN and MAX aggregate functions calculate the minimum and the maximum values of their arguments, respectively.

The syntax of these functions is:

```
MIN( [ DISTINCT | ALL ] field-expression )

MAX( [ DISTINCT | ALL ] field-expression )
```

The DISTINCT keyword is supported only for compatibility with SQL standards, and it is meaningless with the MAX and MIN aggregate functions. In the Log Parser SQL language, the DISTINCT keyword is not allowed in aggregate functions when queries have a GROUP BY clause.

PROPCOUNT Aggregate Function

The PROPCOUNT aggregate function calculates the ratio of the number of records in the current group to the total number of records in the query or to the total number of records in a *larger* group containing the current group, thus yielding a *percentage* value.

The syntax of this function is:

```
PROPCOUNT( * ) [ ON field-expression [ , field-expression … ] ]
PROPCOUNT( field-expression [ , field-expression … ] ) [ ON field-expression [ , field-
expression … ] ]
```

The arguments of the PROPCOUNT aggregate function have the same meaning as the arguments of the COUNT aggregate function.

When the ON keyword is not specified, the PROPCOUNT aggregate function operates by calculating a COUNT aggregate function twice. In the first calculation, the COUNT aggregate function is calculated on the group identified by the GROUP BY clause of the query, as is the case with the simple COUNT function. In the second calculation, however, the same COUNT aggregate function is calculated on *all* the input records. The final value returned by the PROP-COUNT function is the ratio of the two values.

For example, consider the following query:

```
SELECT SourceName,
       EventID,
       PROPCOUNT(*)
FROM   System
GROUP BY SourceName,
         EventID
```

The value returned by the PROPCOUNT aggregate function in this example is the ratio of the values of the COUNT aggregate functions calculated by the following two queries:

```
SELECT SourceName,
       EventID,
       COUNT(*)
FROM   System
GROUP BY SourceName,
         EventID


SELECT COUNT(*)
FROM   System
```

When the ON keyword is specified, the second COUNT aggregate function is calculated on the group identified by the field-expressions following the ON keyword, rather than on all the input records. In this case, the list of field-expressions used with the ON keyword acts exactly like a separate GROUP BY clause, and identifies a group larger than the GROUP BY group.

For example, consider the following query:

```
SELECT SourceName,
       EventID,
       PROPCOUNT(*) ON SourceName
FROM   System
GROUP BY SourceName,
         EventID
```

The value returned by the PROPCOUNT aggregate function in this example is the ratio of the values of the COUNT aggregate functions calculated by the following two queries:

```
SELECT SourceName,
       EventID,
       COUNT(*)
FROM   System
GROUP BY SourceName,
         EventID

SELECT COUNT(*)
FROM   System
GROUP BY SourceName
```

Since the ON group must be a group larger than the GROUP BY group, its list of field-expressions must be a subset of the GROUP BY field-expressions, starting with the leftmost field-expression and appearing in the same order. In other words, if a query employs the following GROUP BY clause:

```
GROUP BY Field1, Field2, Field3
```

Then there are only two possible ON groups:

```
ON Field1
ON Field1, Field2
```

PROPSUM Aggregate Function

The PROPSUM aggregate function behaves exactly like the PROPCOUNT aggregate function, with the only difference being that PROPSUM returns the ratio of two SUM aggregate functions, rather than the ratio of two COUNT aggregate functions.

The syntax of this function is:

```
PROPSUM( field-expression ) [ ON field-expression [ , field-expression … ] ]
```

The argument of the PROPSUM aggregate function has the same meaning as the argument of the SUM aggregate function, and the ON keyword behaves like the ON keyword in the PROPCOUNT aggregate function.

GROUPING Aggregate Function

The GROUPING aggregate function is used in conjunction with the ROLLUP operator of the GROUP BY clause. Using the ROLLUP operator causes the query to produce additional output rows representing summary aggregate function calculations on the groups being processed, and these rows contain NULL values for the groups being summarized. The GROUPING aggregate function is used to indicate whether or not a NULL value in a row is a legitimate NULL value of the field-expression or if it is a NULL value generated by the ROLLUP operator.

The syntax of this function is:

```
GROUPING( field-expression )
```

The function returns 1 when the value of its argument field-expression is generated as NULL by the ROLLUP operator, and 0 when the value of its argument field-expression is not NULL, or it is NULL and it has not been generated by the ROLLUP operator.

Query Syntax

A Log Parser SQL query is defined as follows:

```
select_clause
[ using_clause ]
[ into_clause ]
from_clause
[ where_clause ]
[ group_by_clause ]
[ having_clause ]
[ order_by_clause ]
```

SELECT Clause

The SELECT clause specifies the field-expressions that will appear in the query *output records*. This syntax of the SELECT clause is:

```
SELECT [ TOP integer ] [ DISTINCT | ALL ] *
SELECT [ TOP integer ] [ DISTINCT | ALL ] selection_list
```

The TOP keyword specifies that the query should return only the first *n* output records.

The DISTINCT keyword specifies that duplicate output records should be discarded, while the ALL keyword (the default) specifies that all the output records will be returned, even duplicate ones.

When used with the * wildcard, the SELECT clause returns all the input record fields. For example, the output records of the following query contain all the fields of the EVT input format:

```
SELECT *
FROM SYSTEM
```

When used with a *selection_list*, the SELECT clause returns only the field-expressions specified in the *selection_list*. A *selection_list* is defined as follows:

```
field-expression [ AS alias ] [ , field-expression [ AS alias ] … ]
```

For example, the output records of the following query contain the specified two field-expressions only:

```
SELECT TO_UPPERCASE(SourceName),
       TimeGenerated
FROM SYSTEM
```

The field-expressions in the *selection_list* can be *aliased* with the AS keyword followed by a user-defined name. When this happens, the field-expression can be referenced anywhere else in the query by making use of its alias.

For example, the field-expression in the WHERE clause of the following query is the alias of a field-expression in the SELECT clause:

```
SELECT TO_LOWERCASE(cs-uri-stem) AS Url
FROM extend1.log
WHERE Url LIKE '%.asp'
```

If a query includes a GROUP BY clause, then the SELECT clause can only specify aggregate functions or field-expressions appearing in the GROUP BY clause.

Together with the FROM clause, the SELECT clause is one of the two mandatory clauses in Log Parser queries.

USING Clause

The USING clause defines a list of aliased field-expressions that can be referenced anywhere else in the query. The USING clause is a non-standard SQL language element, and its use is targeted at improving the readability of queries.

This syntax of the USING clause is:

```
USING field-expression AS alias [ , field-expression AS alias … ]
```

For example, the SELECT and WHERE clauses of the following query reference a field-expression defined in the USING clause:

```
SELECT cs-uri-stem, ClientAddress
USING REVERSEDNS(c-ip) AS ClientAddress
FROM extend1.log
WHERE ClientAddress <> 'CLIENT01'
```

INTO Clause

The INTO clause specifies the output target to which the currently selected output format should send the output records.

The syntax of the INTO clause is:

```
INTO into_entity
```

The *into_entity* element specifies the output target, and its syntax is dependent on the output format selected. For a description of the *into_entity* values supported by each output format, refer to Appendix D.

FROM Clause

The FROM clause specifies the input data source(s) to be processed by the currently selected input format.

The syntax of the FROM clause is:

```
FROM from_entity
```

The *from_entity* element specifies the input data source, and its syntax is dependent on the input format selected. For a description of the *from_entity* values supported by each input format, refer to Appendix C.

Together with the SELECT clause, the FROM clause is one of the two mandatory clauses in Log Parser queries.

WHERE Clause

The WHERE clause specifies one or more filtering conditions on the values of an input record. If the conditions are not satisfied, the input record is discarded.

The syntax of the WHERE clause is:

```
WHERE expression
```

An expression is a combination of "expression terms" joined together using the AND, OR, and NOT logical operators. An "expression term" can have one of eight different forms.

The first form is a simple relational comparison between two field-expressions:

```
field-expression > | < | = | <> | >= | <= field-expression
```

An example of this form would be:

```
WHERE cs-uri-stem = '/default.asp'
```

The second form is a relational comparison between a single field-expression and a list of constant values:

```
field-expression > | < | = | <> | >= | <= [ ALL | ANY ] ( value_rows )
```

The *value_rows* element is a list of *value_row* elements, separated by the semicolon character. In this form, each *value_row* element must be a single constant. The keyword ANY (the default) specifies that the expression term is satisfied when the comparison operator is true for at least *one* of the values in the right term list; the keyword ALL, on the other hand, specifies that the expression term is satisfied when the comparison operator is true for *all* of the values in the right term list.

```
An example of this form would be:
WHERE cs-bytes = ANY ( 100; 200; 500 )
```

The third form is a comparison between a *list* of field-expressions and a list of *lists* of constant values:

```
( field-expression , field-expression … ) > | < | = | <> | >= | <= [ ALL | ANY ] (
value_rows )
```

In this form, each *value_row* element must be a *list* of constants equaling in number the number of field-expressions on the left side, separated by the comma character. This form works similarly to the previous form, with the distinction that the operands of the comparison operator are multi-valued items, rather than single items.

An example of this form would be:

```
WHERE (cs-uri-stem, cs-bytes) = ANY
        ( '/default.asp', 100;
          '/index.htm', 200;
          '/index.htm', 500
        )
```

The fourth form is a case-insensitive string matching comparison:

```
field-expression [ NOT ] LIKE like_mask
```

The *like_mask* element is a string search pattern that can include any number of two special wildcard characters: the underscore character ('_'), meaning "any character", and the percent character ('%'), meaning "any substring".

An example of this form is:

```
WHERE cs-uri-stem LIKE '%.aspx'
```

The fifth form is a test for inclusion of a value in an interval:

```
field-expression [ NOT ] BETWEEN field-expression AND field-expression
```

The BETWEEN operator is satisfied when the value of the left field-expression is included in the interval whose boundaries are specified by the values of the right field-expressions.

An example of this form is:

```
WHERE TimeGenerated BETWEEN
      TIMESTAMP('2004-05-28 12:00:00', 'yyyy-MM-dd hh:mm:ss')
      AND
      TIMESTAMP('2004-06-06 23:59:59', 'yyyy-MM-dd hh:mm:ss')
```

The sixth form is a test for NULL values:

```
field-expression IS [ NOT ] NULL
```

The IS NULL operator is satisfied when the value of the left field-expression is NULL. An example of this form is:

```
WHERE cs-uri-query IS NULL
```

The seventh form is a test for inclusion of a value in a list of constants:

```
field-expression [ NOT ] IN ( value_rows )
```

The IN operator is satisfied when the value of the left field-expression appears in the list of constants on the right side of the operator.

An example of this form is:

```
WHERE c-ip IN ('192.168.1.100'; '192.168.1.101')
```

The eighth form is a test for inclusion of a multi-valued value in a list of multi-valued constants:

```
( field-expression , field-expression … ) [ NOT ] IN ( value_rows )
```

This form is similar to the previous form, with the only difference being that the values being compared are multi-valued items, rather than single values.

An example of this form is:

```
WHERE (cs-uri-stem, c-ip) IN
      ('/default.htm', '192.168.1.100';
       '/default.asp', '192.168.1.101'
      )
```

Since the conditions in a WHERE clause are applied to the values of an input record, these conditions cannot reference aggregate functions; the HAVING clause can be used to impose filtering conditions on the values of aggregate functions.

GROUP BY Clause

The GROUP BY clause specifies a list of field-expressions whose values are to be used as the grouping criteria when aggregating data. Input records that yield identical values for the GROUP BY field-expressions are considered to belong to the same group.

The syntax of the GROUP BY clause is:

```
GROUP BY field-expression [ , field-expression … ] [ WITH ROLLUP ]
```

When a query includes a GROUP BY clause, its SELECT clause can only specify aggregate functions or field-expressions that appear in the GROUP BY clause.

An example of a query using the GROUP BY clause is:

```
SELECT    cs-uri-stem,
          COUNT(*) AS Hits
FROM      <1>
GROUP BY cs-uri-stem
```

The ROLLUP operator generates additional output records that are constructed by applying group aggregations to all the hierarchical levels specified by the GROUP BY clause. For more information on the ROLLUP operator, consult the Log Parser documentation.

HAVING Clause

The HAVING clause specifies one or more filtering conditions on the values of the records generated by the group aggregation process specified with the GROUP BY clause and with the use of aggregate functions. The HAVING clause works in the same way as the WHERE clause, with the difference being that the conditions in the HAVING clause can reference aggregate functions, while the conditions in the WHERE clause cannot.

The syntax of the HAVING clause is:

```
HAVING expression
```

Expressions in the HAVING clause follow the same rules as the expressions in the WHERE clause.

An example of a query using the HAVING clause is:

```
SELECT    cs-uri-stem,
          COUNT(*) AS Hits
FROM      <1>
GROUP BY cs-uri-stem
HAVING    Hits > 10
```

ORDER BY Clause

The ORDER BY clause specifies sorting criteria on output record values.

The syntax of the ORDER BY clause is:

```
ORDER BY field-expression [ , field-expression … ] [ ASC | DESC ]
```

When an ORDER BY clause is used, the query output records are sorted according to the values of the specified field-expressions, in either ascending order (the default), or in descending order, depending on the use of the ASC or DESC keywords.

Different from the standard SQL language, the Log Parser SQL language requires that the field-expressions in the ORDER BY clause appear in the SELECT clause as well.

Appendix B

Function Reference

In This Toolbox

Functions are powerful elements of the Log Parser SQL language; virtually all queries written with the Log Parser SQL language make use of at least one function. Functions take zero or more field-expressions as arguments, process their values, and return a new value. The Log Parser SQL language supports more than 80 functions, ranging from string manipulation functions (for example, SUBSTR, STRCAT) to arithmetical functions (for example, ADD, EXP).

Functions

The ADD function returns the sum of the two argument values.
```
ADD( addend1 <any type>, addend2 <any type> )
```
When the arguments are of the STRING type, the value returned is the concatenation of the strings.

```
BIT_AND( arg1 <INTEGER>, arg2 <INTEGER> )
BIT_NOT( arg <INTEGER> )
BIT_OR( arg1 <INTEGER>, arg2 <INTEGER> )
BIT_SHL( arg1 <INTEGER>, arg2 <INTEGER> )
BIT_SHR( arg1 <INTEGER>, arg2 <INTEGER> )
BIT_XOR( arg1 <INTEGER>, arg2 <INTEGER> )
```
The BIT... functions calculate the specified bitwise operators on the argument values.

```
CASE <field_expression>
  WHEN <field_expression> THEN <field_expression>
     [ ... ]
     [ ELSE <field_expression> ]
  END
```
The CASE function compares the value of the specified field-expression with the values of the field-expressions in the WHEN statements, returning the value of the field-expression specified in a THEN statement when a match is found. If no match is found, the value of the ELSE statement field-expression is returned, or NULL if no ELSE statement is provided.

```
COALESCE( arg1 <any type>, arg2 <any type> [, ....] )
```
The COALESCE function returns the first non-NULL value found among the specified arguments.
The following example returns **First Value**:
```
COALESCE( NULL, NULL, 'First value', 'Second value')
```

```
COMPUTER_NAME()
```
The COMPUTER_NAME function returns the name of the local computer.

```
DIV( dividend <INTEGER | REAL>, divisor <INTEGER | REAL> )
```
The DIV function returns the quotient of the two argument values.

```
    EXP( argument <INTEGER | REAL> )
EXP10( argument <INTEGER | REAL> )
```

The EXP and EXP10 functions return the natural exponential and the base-10 exponential of their arguments.

```
    EXTRACT_EXTENSION( filepath <STRING> )
    EXTRACT_FILENAME( filepath <STRING> )
EXTRACT_PATH( filepath <STRING> )
```

These functions return the extension, filename, or path portions of a STRING value representing the full path of a file.

```
EXTRACT_PREFIX( argument <STRING>, index <INTEGER>, separator <STRING> )
```

The EXTRACT_PREFIX function returns the prefix of the specified argument string up to the nth appearance of the specified separator. Negative values of the *index* argument are relative to the end of the string.

```
EXTRACT_SUFFIX( argument <STRING>, index <INTEGER>, separator <STRING> )
```

The EXTRACT_SUFFIX function returns the suffix of the specified argument following the nth appearance – in a right-to-left order - of the specified separator. Negative values of the *index* argument are relative to the beginning of the string.

```
EXTRACT_TOKEN( argument <STRING>, index <INTEGER> [ , separator <STRING> ] )
```

The EXTRACT_TOKEN function returns the portion of the specified argument string enclosed within the nth appearance of the specified separator and the next. Negative values of the *index* argument are relative to the end of the string.

```
EXTRACT_VALUE( argument <STRING>, key <STRING> [ , separator <STRING> ] )
```

The EXTRACT_VALUE function parses *key=value* pairs in the argument string, returning the value of the pair whose key matches the specified argument. The *separator* argument specifies the separator used between the pairs, and its default value is *&*.

```
FLOOR( argument <REAL> )
```

The FLOOR function returns the largest integer less than or equal to the specified value. The following example returns **5**:

```
FLOOR( 5.9 )
```

```
HASHMD5_FILE( filePath <STRING> )
```

The HASHMD5_FILE function returns a string containing the MD5 hash of the content of the specified file.

```
HASHSEQ( value <STRING> )
```

The HASHSEQ function returns a sequential integer for each distinct value of the specified argument.

HEX_TO_ASC(hexString <STRING>)
The HEX_TO_ASC function converts a hexadecimal representation of the characters in a string to the string itself, considering only characters belonging to the 0x20-0x7f ASCII character range. Characters outside of this range are returned as period characters.

> **HEX_TO_HEX16(hexString <STRING> [, bigEndian <INTEGER>])**
> **HEX_TO_HEX32(hexString <STRING> [, bigEndian <INTEGER>])**

HEX_TO_HEX8(hexString <STRING>)
These functions convert a hexadecimal representation of an integer to another hexadecimal representation where the individual bytes are grouped together according to the number of bits specified. When the *bigEndian* argument is different than 0, the conversion assumes that the hexadecimal representation of the integer is in the big-endian form.

HEX_TO_INT(hexString <STRING>)
The HEX_TO_INT function converts a hexadecimal representation of an integer to the integer itself.

HEX_TO_PRINT(hexString <STRING>)
The HEX_TO_PRINT function converts a hexadecimal representation of the characters in a string to the string itself, considering only characters that are printable. Non-printable characters are returned as period characters.

IN_ROW_NUMBER()
The IN_ROW_NUMBER returns the sequential index of the input record currently being processed.

INDEX_OF(string <STRING>, searchStr <STRING>)
The INDEX_OF function returns the 0-based index of the first appearance of the specified search string in the first argument.

INT_TO_IPV4(ipV4Address <INTEGER>)
The INT_TO_IPV4 function converts a 32-bit integer containing the network value of an IPV4 address to the string representation of the address.

IPV4_TO_INT(ipV4Address <STRING>)
The IPV4_TO_INT function parses the string representation of an IPV4 address and returns a 32-bit integer containing the network value of the address.

LAST_INDEX_OF(string <STRING>, searchStr <STRING>)

The LAST_INDEX_OF function returns the 0-based index of the last appearance of the specified search string in the first argument.

```
LOG( argument <INTEGER | REAL> )
LOG10( argument <INTEGER | REAL> )
```

The LOG and LOG10 functions return the natural logarithm and the base-10 logarithm of their arguments.

```
LTRIM( string <STRING> )
```

The LTRIM function returns a left-trimmed version of the argument string.

```
MOD( dividend <INTEGER | REAL>, divisor <INTEGER | REAL> )
```

The MOD function returns the remainder of the quotient of its argument.

```
MUL( multiplicand <INTEGER | REAL>, multiplier <INTEGER | REAL> )
```

The MUL function returns the multiplication of its arguments.

```
OUT_ROW_NUMBER()
```

The OUT_ROW_NUMBER function returns the sequential index of the output record being generated. This function can only appear in the SELECT and ORDER BY clauses.

```
QNTFLOOR_TO_DIGIT( value <INTEGER>, digits <INTEGER> )

QNTROUND_TO_DIGIT( value <INTEGER>, digits <INTEGER> )
```

The QNTFLOOR_TO_DIGIT and QNTROUND_TO_DIGIT functions return the first argument value truncated or rounded to the nearest power of ten having the specified number of significant digits. These functions are commonly used in GROUP BY clauses to group input records based on *categories* of numerical values.

The following example returns **12400**:

```
QNTFLOOR_TO_DIGIT( 12475, 3 )
```

The following example returns **10000**:

```
QNTFLOOR_TO_DIGIT( 12475, 1 )
```
The following example returns **12500**:
```
QNTROUND_TO_DIGIT( 12475, 3 )
```

```
QUANTIZE( argument <INTEGER | REAL | TIMESTAMP>,

        quantization <INTEGER | REAL> )
```

The QUANTIZE function returns the multiple of the specified quantization argument nearest to the value of the first argument. When used with an argument of the TIMESTAMP type, the function interprets the quantization argument as a number of seconds.

The following example returns **12460**:

```
QUANTIZE( 12475, 20 )
```

The following example returns **11:35:30**:

```
QUANTIZE( TO_TIMESTAMP( '11:35:47', 'hh:mm:ss' ), 30 )
```

REPLACE_CHR(string <STRING>, searchCharacters <STRING>,
replaceString <STRING>)

The REPLACE_CHR function returns its first argument after replacing each instance of any of the characters in the specified search string with an instance of the specified replace string.

REPLACE_IF_NOT_NULL(argument <any type>, replaceValue <any type>)

The REPLACE_IF_NOT_NULL function returns the second argument when the first argument is not NULL. If the first argument is NULL, the function returns NULL.

REPLACE_STR(string <STRING>, searchString <STRING>, replaceString <STRING>)

The REPLACE_STR function returns its first argument after replacing each instance of the specified search string with an instance of the specified replace string.

RESOLVE_SID(sid <STRING> [, computerName <STRING>])

The RESOLVE_SID function resolves the SID specified in the first argument and returns the full account name represented by the SID. The optional *computerName* argument specifies a remote computer where the account is defined.

REVERSEDNS(ipAddress <STRING>)

The REVERSEDNS function resolves the specified IP address returning the corresponding host name.

ROT13(string <STRING>)

The ROT13 function returns the ROT13 encoding or decoding of the specified value.

ROUND(argument <REAL>)

The ROUND function returns the integer nearest to the specified value.

RTRIM(string <STRING>)

The RTRIM function returns a right-trimmed version of the argument string.

SEQUENCE([startValue <INTEGER>])

The SEQUENCE function returns a new sequential integer for each input record. The optional *startValue* argument specifies the initial value of the sequence.

SQR(argument <INTEGER | REAL>)

The SQR function returns the square of its argument.

`SQRROOT( argument <INTEGER | REAL> )`
The SQRROOT function returns the square root of its argument.

`STRCAT( string1 <STRING>, string2 <STRING> )`
The STRCAT function returns the concatenation of the specified strings.

`STRCNT( string <STRING>, token <STRING> )`
The STRCNT function returns the number of times that the specified token appears in the first argument.

`STRLEN( string <STRING> )`
The STRLEN function returns the length of the specified string.

`STRREPEAT( string <STRING>, count <INTEGER> )`
The STRREPEAT function returns a string built by concatenating the first argument with itself for the number of times specified by the second argument.

`STRREV( string <STRING> )`
The STRREV function returns the argument string reversed.

`SUB( minuend <any type>, subtrahend <any type> )`
The SUB function returns the difference of the two arguments. When the arguments are of the STRING type, the value returned is the substring of the first argument that remains after removing the second argument from the beginning of the string.

`SUBSTR( string <STRING>, start <INTEGER> [ , length <INTEGER> ])`
The SUBSTR function returns the substring of the first argument that starts at the character with the specified index. The optional *length* argument specifies the length of the substring to return.

`SYSTEM_DATE()`
`SYSTEM_TIME()`
`SYSTEM_TIMESTAMP()`
These functions return the current date, the current time, and the current full date and time, respectively. The TIMESTAMP value returned is in Universal Time Coordinates (UTC).

`SYSTEM_UTCOFFSET()`
The SYSTEM_UTCOFFSET function returns a TIMESTAMP value representing the absolute bias of the local time zone.

`TO_DATE( timestamp <TIMESTAMP> )`

The TO_DATE function returns a TIMESTAMP value that contains the date portion only of the specified argument.

```
TO_HEX( argument <INTEGER | STRING> )
```

The TO_HEX function returns a string containing the hexadecimal representation of the specified integer, or of the characters in the specified string.

```
TO_INT( argument <any type> )
```

The TO_INT function returns its argument converted to an INTEGER value. If the type of its argument is a TIMESTAMP value, the value returned is the number of seconds elapsed since January 1, year 0.

```
TO_LOCALTIME( timestamp <TIMESTAMP> )
```

The TO_LOCALTIME function returns the result of converting the argument timestamp to local time coordinates.

```
TO_LOWERCASE( string <STRING> )
```
The TO_LOWERCASE function returns the argument string after converting its alphabetical characters to their corresponding lower-case characters.

```
TO_REAL( argument <any type> )
```

The TO_REAL function returns its argument converted to a REAL value. If the type of its argument is a TIMESTAMP value, the value returned is the fractional number of seconds elapsed since January 1, year 0.

```
TO_STRING( argument <INTEGER | REAL> )
TO_STRING( timestamp <TIMESTAMP>, format <STRING> )
```

When used with INTEGER or REAL arguments, the TO_STRING function returns a string representing the specified INTEGER or REAL value.
When used with a TIMESTAMP argument, the TO_STRING function returns a string containing the specified TIMESTAMP value formatted according to the specifiers described with the *format* argument.

```
TO_TIME( timestamp <TIMESTAMP> )
```

The TO_TIME function returns a TIMESTAMP value that contains the time portion only of the specified argument.

```
TO_TIMESTAMP( dateTime1 <TIMESTAMP>, dateTime2 <TIMESTAMP> )

TO_TIMESTAMP( string <STRING>, format <STRING> )

TO_TIMESTAMP( seconds <INTEGER | REAL> )
```
When used with TIMESTAMP arguments, the TO_TIMESTAMP function returns a TIMESTAMP value built after merging the data portion and the time portion of the specified arguments.

When used with STRING arguments, the TO_TIMESTAMP function parses the string representation of a date and/or time specified as the first argument according to the format specifiers described with the *format* argument, returning the resulting TIMESTAMP value. When used with INTEGER or REAL arguments, the TO_TIMESTAMP function returns the TIMESTAMP value of the instant of time corresponding to the specified number of seconds since January 1, year 0.

`TO_UPPERCASE( string <STRING> )`

The TO_UPPERCASE function returns the argument string after converting its alphabetical characters to their corresponding upper-case characters.

`TO_UTCTIME( timestamp <TIMESTAMP> )`

The TO_UTCTIME function returns the result of converting the argument timestamp to Universal Time Coordinates (UTC) time.

`TRIM( string <STRING> )`

The TRIM function returns a left-trimmed and right-trimmed version of the argument string.

`URLESCAPE( url <STRING> [ , codepage <INTEGER> ] )`

The URLESCAPE function returns a hex-encoded version of the argument string. The optional *codepage* argument specifies the target encoding codepage.

`URLUNESCAPE( url <STRING> [ , codepage <INTEGER> ] )`

The URLUNESCAPE function returns a decoded version of the hex-encoded argument string. The optional *codepage* argument specifies the source encoding codepage.

`WIN32_ERROR_DESCRIPTION( win32ErrorCode <INTEGER> )`

The WIN32_ERROR_DESCRIPTION function returns the Windows error message corresponding to the specified error code.

Appendix C

Input Format Reference

- ADS Input Format
- BIN Input Format
- COM Input Format
- CSV Input Format
- ETW Input Format
- EVT Input Format
- FS Input Format
- HTTPERR Input Format
- IIS Input Format
- IISODBC Input Format
- IISW3C Input Format
- NCSA Input Format
- NETMON Input Format
- REG Input Format
- TEXTLINE Input Format
- TEXTWORD Input Format
- TSV Input Format
- URLSCAN Input Format
- W3C Input Format
- XML Input Format

In This Toolbox

Log Parser 2.2 provides 20 input formats that can be used to parse a wide variety of text file formats (all the IIS log file formats, generic NCSA log files, CSV, TSV, and XML text files), to parse specialized binary files (NetMon files, ETW trace files), and to retrieve system information (Event Log, files and directories, registry keys, and Active Directory objects).

ADS Input Format

The Active Directory Services (ADS) input format returns properties of Active Directory objects. This input format works in two different modes. In *property mode*, the ADS input format returns an input record for each property of each Active Directory object enumerated under the Active Directory path specified in the query FROM clause. In *object mode*, users specify the name of an Active Directory object class, and the ADS input format returns an input record for each Active Directory object that is an instance of the specified class found under the Active Directory path specified in the query FROM clause.

From-Entity

The ADS input format accepts FROM clause values with the following syntax:

`[[provider:]//[username:password@]domain]/path [; ...]`

- **Provider** This is the name of the Active Directory provider, for example, LDAP (Lightweight Directory Access Protocol) or IIS. When not specified, IIS is assumed by default.

- **Username and password** This is optional authentication information for the connection to the AD provider. When not specified, the ADS input format uses the current user's credentials.

- **Domain** This is the name of the domain where the provider resides. When not specified, localhost is assumed by default.

- **Path** This is the Active Directory path containing the Active Directory objects that will be enumerated by the ADS input format.

Fields

When working in property mode, the ADS input format generates input records with the following fields:

- ObjectPath
- ObjectName
- ObjectClass

- PropertyName
- PropertyValue
- PropertyType

When working in object mode, the ADS input format generates input records with the following fields:

- ObjectPath
- A field for each property of the specified Active Directory object class

Parameters

- **objClass** Specifies the name of an Active Directory object class to be used in object mode. When this parameter is left unspecified, the ADS input format works in property mode.

- **username** Specifies the username to be used for the connection to the AD provider. If left unspecified, the ADS input format uses the current user's credentials.

- **password** Specifies the password for the user account specified for the **username** parameter.

- **recurse** Specifies the maximum directory depth reached while enumerating Active Directory objects.

- **multiValuedSep** Specifies the string to be used as a separator between the values of multi-valued object properties.

- **ignoreDSErrors** When set to **ON**, the ADS input format ignores errors occurring during the enumeration of Active Directory objects. When set to **OFF**, the ADS input format returns errors as *parse errors*.

- **parseBinary** When set to **ON**, the ADS input format returns object properties that contain binary data. When set to **OFF**, binary properties are not returned.

- **binaryFormat** Specifies the format of binary data as one of the ASC, HEX, or PRINT values.

BIN Input Format

The BIN input format parses the centralized binary log files generated by IIS version 6.0 and later.

From-Entity

The BIN input format accepts FROM clause values with the following syntax:

filename | siteID [, filename | siteID ...]

- **Filename** This is the path to an IIS binary log file; the path can contain wildcards and can be in UNC (universal naming convention) notation if specifying log files on a remote share.

- **SiteID** This is the Metabase path of an IIS virtual site, enclosed in angled brackets; the Metabase path can be a full path that includes a remote server name (for example, **<//Mycomputer/W3SVC/12>**), or it can simply be the site's numeric identifier or the site's **ServerComment** property value (for example, **<12>**, **<www.mysite.com>**), eventually including wildcards.

Fields

The BIN input format generates input records containing the following fields:

- LogFilename
- LogRow
- ComputerName
- SiteID
- DateTime
- ClientIpAddress
- ServerIpAddress
- ServerPort
- Method
- ProtocolVersion

- ProtocolStatus
- SubStatus
- TimeTaken
- BytesSent
- BytesReceived
- Win32Status
- UriStem
- UriQuery
- UserName

COM Input Format

The COM input format encapsulates custom input format plug-ins, making it possible for users to interact with these plug-ins through the Log Parser command-line executable.

From-Entity

The COM input format accepts any FROM clause value supported by the custom input format plug-in being used.

Parameters

- **iProgID** Specifies the progID of the COM object implementing the custom input format being used.

- **iCOMParams** Specifies values for the optional properties exposed by the custom input format plug-in. The value specified for this parameter has the following format:

     property_name=value[,property_name=value…]

- **iCOMServer** Specifies the computer name on which the COM object implementing the custom input format plug-in should be initiated.

CSV Input Format

The CSV input format parses comma-separated values text files. This input format works with a two-stage approach. During an initial *inspection stage*, the input format inspects a configurable number of lines in the CSV files to determine the number of fields, the field types, and the field names of the columns contained in the files. After the number of fields, their types, and their names has been determined, the real *parsing stage* begins, in which the files are parsed again from beginning to end, and input records are generated to be processed by the query.

From-Entity

The CSV input format accepts FROM clause values with the following syntax:

```
filename [, filename …] |
http://url              |
STDIN
```

- **Filename** This is the path to a CSV file; the path can contain wildcards and can be in UNC notation if specifying files on a remote share.

- **URL** This is the URL (uniform resource locator) of a resource formatted as CSV text.

- **STDIN** This special keyword specifies that the CSV input format should read the input data from the console input. This value is mostly used when piping commands and using the output of a command as the input of a Log Parser query.

Fields

The CSV input format generates input records containing the following fields:

- Filename
- RowNumber
- A field for each column in the input CSV file(s)

Parameters

- **headerRow** When set to **ON**, the CSV input format assumes that the file(s) being parsed contain a header line declaring the names of the columns in the file(s), and it extracts the column names from this line. When set to **OFF**, the CSV input format assumes that each file being parsed begins with the first line of data.

- **iHeaderFile** Specifies the path to a CSV text file containing a header line declaring the names of the columns in the file(s) being parsed. The column names found in the specified header file override the eventual column names declared by the header line in the file(s) being parsed.

- **fixedFields** When set to **ON**, the CSV input format assumes that all the lines in the CSV file(s) being parsed contain the same number of fields, and thus it determines the number of fields by inspecting the very first line in the file(s) being parsed. When set to **OFF**, lines can have a variable number of fields, and the CSV input format determines the number of fields by inspecting the number of initial lines specified by the value of the **dtLines** parameter.

- **nFields** This parameter can be used to specify directly the number of fields (columns) contained in the CSV file(s) being parsed. When this parameter is set to **-1** (the default value), the CSV input format determines the number of fields automatically during the initial inspection stage.

- **dtLines** Specifies the number of initial lines to be inspected during the initial inspection stage to determine the number of fields, the field types, and the field names of the columns contained in the file(s).

- **iDQuotes** When set to **AUTO**, the CSV input format properly processes field values enclosed in double-quote characters, ignoring spaces and comma characters within the values, and stripping the double-quote characters before returning the values; when set to **OFF**, the CSV input format returns field values as they appear in the file(s) being processed, ignoring the presence of eventual double-quote characters.

- **nSkipLines** This parameter specifies the number of lines that the CSV input format should skip in each file before it starts parsing its data.

- **comment** Specifies the prefix of comment lines that should not be parsed as data.

- **iCodepage** Specifies the numeric identifier of the codepage of the file(s) being parsed.

- **iTsFormat** Specifies the format of the timestamp values contained in the file(s) being parsed.

- **iCheckpoint** Specifies the path of the checkpoint file to use when parsing the input file(s) incrementally.

ETW Input Format

The ETW input format parses Enterprise Tracing for Windows trace log files and live tracing sessions. ETW traces contain debugging and performance information generated by one or more *providers*. This input format works in four different modes, selectable through the **fMode** parameter. In *compact* mode, the ETW input format returns an input record for each event found in the trace being parsed; the input record contains a few fields common to all the ETW events, and a single **UserData** field containing the values of all the event-specific properties concatenated with each other. In *fnames* mode, the ETW input format behaves exactly as in the compact mode, but each event-specific property value is prefixed by the name of the property. In *full* mode, the ETW input format returns the value of each event-specific property as a field of its own. Finally, in *meta* mode, the ETW input format returns meta-information about the events being parsed; in this mode, input records correspond to individual properties of events.

When the full or meta modes are selected, the ETW input format works with a two-stage approach. During an initial inspection stage, the input format inspects a configurable number of events in the trace files to determine the providers whose events are contained in the traces. After the providers have been identified, the real parsing stage begins, in which the traces are parsed again from beginning to end, and input records are generated to be processed by the query.

From-Entity

The ETW input format accepts FROM clause values with the following syntax:

```
filename [, filename …] |
session
```

- **Filename** This is the path to an ETW trace log file (.etl file). The path can contain wildcards and can be in UNC notation if specifying log files on a remote share.
- **Session** This is the name of a live ETW trace session.

Fields

In compact and fnames modes, the ETW input format generates input records containing the following fields:

- EventNumber
- EventName
- EventTypeName
- Timestamp
- UserData

In full mode, the ETW input format generates input records containing the following fields:

- TraceName
- EventNumber
- Timestamp
- InstanceID
- ParentInstanceID
- ParentGUID
- ProviderDescription
- ProviderGUID
- EventName
- EventDescription
- EventVersion
- EventGUID

- EventType
- EventTypeName
- EventTypeDescription
- EventTypeLevel
- ThreadID
- ProcessID
- KernelTime
- UserTime
- A field for each property of each event of each provided detected in the input trace(s)

In meta mode, the ETW input format generates input records containing the following fields:

- ProviderDescription
- ProviderClassName
- ProviderGUID
- EventName
- EventDescription
- EventVersion
- EventClassName
- EventGUID
- EventType

- EventTypeName
- EventTypeDescription
- EventTypeClassName
- EventTypeLevel
- FieldName
- FieldDescription
- FieldIndex
- FieldType

Parameters

- **fMode** Specifies one of the four possible ETW input format operation modes described above; possible values are compact, fnames, full, and meta.
- **providers** Specifies the providers whose events are contained in the trace(s) being parsed. This parameter can be specified as a comma-separated list of provider names or GUIDs, or as the path of a text file containing a provider GUID on each line. If this parameter is not specified, the ETW input format detects the providers automatically

by inspecting the first dtEventsLog or dtEventsLive events in the trace(s) being parsed. This parameter is used in the full or meta modes only.

- **dtEventsLog** Specifies the number of events to pre-process during the inspection stage in order to determine which providers have logged events in the trace log file(s) being parsed. This parameter is used in the full or meta modes only when the **providers** parameter is not specified.

- **dtEventsLive** Specifies the number of events to pre-process during the inspection stage in order to determine which providers have logged events in the live trace session being parsed. This parameter is used in the full or meta modes only when the **providers** parameter is not specified.

- **flushPeriod** Frequency of live session buffer flushes, in milliseconds.

- **ignoreEventTrace** When set to **ON**, the ETW input format ignores the **EventTrace** event that appears at the beginning of ETW trace files. When set to **OFF**, these **EventTrace** events are returned to the user instead.

- **compactModeSep** Separator to be used between the event property values returned in the **UserData** field when operating in compact or fnames modes.

- **expandEnums** When **ON**, the ETW input format expands enumeration values; when **OFF**, enumeration values are returned as unprocessed integer values.

- **ignoreLostEvents** When this parameter is set to **ON**, the number of lost events reported by the ETW infrastructure is ignored. When set to **OFF**, the ETW input format returns a final warning containing the total number of lost events reported by the ETW infrastructure while parsing the input trace(s).

- **schemaServer** Specifies the name of a remote computer whose Windows Management Instrumentation (WMI) repository contains the schema description of the events in the trace(s) being parsed. When this parameter is not specified, the ETW input format uses the WMI repository on the computer where the trace(s) are being parsed from.

EVT Input Format

The EVT input format parses the Windows Event Log and Event Log (.evt) backup files, returning an input record for each event being parsed.

From-Entity

The EVT input format accepts FROM clause values with the following syntax:

`[\\`*computername*`\]` *eventlogname* `|` *filename* `[,...]`

- **Computername** Optional, this is the name of the remote computer containing the event log to be parsed.

- **Eventlogname** Name of the event log to be parsed, such as standard Event Log names (System, Security, Application) or custom Event Log names.
- **Filename** Path to an .evt Event Log backup file; the path can contain wildcards and can be in UNC notation if specifying Event Log backup files on a remote share.

Fields

The EVT input format generates input records containing the following fields:

- EventLog
- EventNumber
- TimeGenerated
- TimeWritten
- EventID
- EventType
- EventTypeName
- EventCategory
- EventCategoryName
- SourceName
- Strings
- ComputerName
- SID
- Message
- Data

Parameters

- **fullText** When set to **ON** (the default), the EVT input format retrieves the text of the event log message; when set to **OFF**, the EVT input format does not retrieve the message text.
- **resolveSIDs** When set to **ON**, the EVT input format resolves the event log SID into a full account name. When set to **OFF** (the default), the EVT input format returns the SID in alphanumerical form.
- **formatMsg** When set to **ON**, the EVT input format removes multiple white space characters and carriage-return/line-feed characters from the event log message to preserve readability. When set to **OFF**, the event log message is returned as is.

- **msgErrorMode** Setting this parameter to **NULL** causes the **Message** or **EventCategoryName** fields to be returned as NULL when their text value cannot be retrieved. Setting this parameter to **ERROR** causes the EVT input format to return a *parse error* in these situations, and setting this parameter to **MSG** causes the EVT input format to return an error message as the value of the **Message** or **EventCategoryName** fields.

- **fullEventCode** When set to **ON**, the EVT input format returns the full 32-bit value of the EventID field. When set to **OFF** (the default), the EVT input format returns only the lower 16 bits of the **EventID** field, as displayed by the Windows Event Viewer.

- **direction** When set to **FW** (the default), events are returned from the oldest to the newest. When set to **BW**, events are returned from the newest to the oldest.

- **stringsSep** This parameter specifies the string used as a separator between the values of the **Strings** field. The default value is the pipe (|) character.

- **iCheckpoint** Specifies the path of the checkpoint file to use when parsing the input file(s) incrementally.

- **binaryFormat** Specifies the format of the binary data returned in the **Data** field as one of the **ASC**, **HEX**, or **PRINT** values.

FS Input Format

The FS input format returns properties of files and directories.

From-Entity

The FS input format accepts FROM clause values with the following syntax:

`path [, path ...]`

- **Path** Path to a file or to a directory, eventually containing wildcards.

Fields

The FS input format generates input records with the following fields:

- Path
- Name
- Size
- Attributes
- CreationTime
- LastAccessTime

- LastWriteTime
- FileVersion
- ProductVersion
- InternalName
- ProductName
- CompanyName
- LegalCopyright
- LegalTrademarks
- PrivateBuild
- SpecialBuild
- Comments
- FileDescription
- OriginalFilename

Parameters

- **recurse** Specifies the number of subdirectories to recurse into. The special **–1** value means *unlimited recursion*.

- **preserveLastAccTime** Specifying **ON** for this value causes the FS input format to restore the last access time attribute of each file visited during the enumeration. When this parameter is **OFF**, files that are visited by the FS input format will have their last access time attribute modified.

- **useLocalTime** Specifying **ON** for this value causes the FS input format to return timestamp values relative to the local time zone. When this parameter is **OFF**, timestamp values are returned in Universal Time Coordinates (UTC) time.

HTTPERR Input Format

The HTTPERR input format parses the HTTP Error log files generated by the Http.sys Windows HTTP driver. These log files contain entries for HTTP (Hypertext Transfer Protocol) requests that generated abnormal errors on the server computer, such as 400 errors, and connections that hit a timeout.

From-Entity

The HTTP input format accepts FROM clause values with the following syntax:

```
filename [, filename ...] |
HTTPERR
```

- **Filename** Path to an HTTP Error log file.
- **HTTPERR** This keyword specifies that the user wants to parse all the HTTP Error log files available on the local computer.

Fields

The HTTPERR input format generates input records with the following fields:

- LogFilename
- LogRow
- date
- time
- s-computername
- c-ip
- c-port
- s-ip
- s-port
- cs-version
- cs-method
- cs-uri

- cs(User-Agent)
- cs(Cookie)
- cs(Referer)
- cs-host
- sc-status
- sc-bytes
- cs-bytes
- time-taken
- s-siteid
- s-reason
- s-queuename

Parameters

- **iCodepage** Specifies the numeric identifier of the codepage of the file(s) being parsed.
- **minDateMod** Specifies the minimum value of the last date modified attribute of a log file for the file to be parsed.
- **dirTime** When set to **ON**, the HTTPERR input format fills in missing **date** and **time** field values with the value of the **#Fields** directive.
- **iCheckpoint** Specifies the path of the checkpoint file to use when parsing the input file(s) incrementally.

IIS Input Format

The IIS input format parses IIS log files in the Microsoft IIS Log File Format.

From-Entity

The IIS input format accepts FROM clause values with the following syntax:

filename | *siteID* [, *filename* | *siteID* ...]

- **Filename** This is the path to a log file in the Microsoft IIS Log File Format; the path can contain wildcards and can be in UNC notation if specifying log files on a remote share.

- **SiteID** This is the Metabase path of an IIS virtual site, enclosed in angled brackets; the Metabase path can be a full path that includes a remote server name (for example, **<//Mycomputer/W3SVC/12>**), or it can simply be the site's numeric identifier or the site's **ServerComment** property value (for example, **<12>**, **<www.mysite.com>**), eventually including wildcards.

Fields

The IIS input format generates input records containing the following fields:

- LogFilename
- LogRow
- UserIP
- UserName
- Date
- Time
- ServiceInstance
- HostName
- ServerIP

- TimeTaken
- BytesSent
- BytesReceived
- StatusCode
- Win32StatusCode
- RequestType
- Target
- Parameters

Parameters

- **iCodepage** Specifies the numeric identifier of the codepage of the file(s) being parsed. The special **-1** value means UNICODE, and the special **-2** value causes the IIS input format to automatically detect the codepage from the log file name and from the **LogInUTF8** property of the virtual site.

- **recurse** Specifies the number of subdirectories to recurse into. The special **-1** value means *unlimited recursion*.

- **minDateMod** Specifies the minimum value of the last date modified attribute of a log file for the file to be parsed.

- **locale** The 3-letter Locale ID whose date and time format has been used to generate values for the **Date** and **Time** fields.

- **iCheckpoint** Specifies the path of the checkpoint file to use when parsing the input file(s) incrementally.

IISODBC Input Format

The IISODBC input format returns records from the database tables to which Microsoft IIS logs Web requests when configured to log using the ODBC Log Format.

From-Entity

The IISODBC input format accepts FROM clause values with the following syntax:

```
siteID [,siteID …] |
table:tablename;username:username;password:password;dsn:dsn
```

- **SiteID** This is the Metabase path of an IIS virtual site, enclosed in angled brackets; the Metabase path can be a full path that includes a remote server name (for example, **<//Mycomputer/W3SVC/12>**), or it can simply be the site's numeric identifier or the site's **ServerComment** property value (for example, **<12>**, **<www.mysite.com>**), eventually including wildcards.

- **Tablename** Name of the table where the IIS Web server logs web requests.

- **Username** User account to be used when connecting to the database.

- **Password** Password for the database connection.

- **DSN** Data Source Name containing information about the database connection.

Fields

The IISODBC input format generates input records containing the following fields:

- ClientHost
- Username
- LogTime
- Service
- Machine
- ServerIP
- ProcessingTime

- BytesRecvd
- BytesSent
- ServiceStatus
- Win32Status
- Operation
- Target
- Parameters

IISW3C Input Format

The IISW3C input format parses IIS log files in the W3C Extended Log File Format.

From-Entity

The IISW3C input format accepts FROM clause values with the following syntax:

`filename | siteID [, filename | siteID ...]`

- **Filename** This is the path to an IIS log file in the W3C Extended Log File Format; the path can contain wildcards and can be in UNC notation if specifying log files on a remote share.

- **SiteID** This is the Metabase path of an IIS virtual site, enclosed in angled brackets; the Metabase path can be a full path that includes a remote server name (for example, **<//Mycomputer/W3SVC/12>**), or it can simply be the site's numeric identifier or the site's **ServerComment** property value (for example, **<12>**, **<www.mysite.com>**), eventually including wildcards.

Fields

The IISW3C input format generates input records containing the following fields:

- LogFilename
- LogRow
- date
- time
- c-ip
- cs-username
- s-sitename
- s-computername
- s-ip
- s-port
- cs-method
- cs-uri-stem
- cs-uri-query
- sc-status
- sc-substatus
- sc-win32-status

- sc-bytes
- cs-bytes
- time-taken
- cs-version
- cs-host
- cs(User-Agent)
- cs(Cookie)
- cs(Referer)
- s-event
- s-process-type
- s-user-time
- s-kernel-time
- s-page-faults
- s-total-procs
- s-active-procs
- s-stopped-procs

Parameters

- **iCodepage** Specifies the numeric identifier of the codepage of the file(s) being parsed. The special **-1** value means UNICODE, and the special **-2** value causes the IIS input format to automatically detect the codepage from the log file name and from the **LogInUTF8** property of the virtual site.

- **recurse** Specifies the number of subdirectories to recurse into. The special **-1** value means *unlimited recursion*.

- **minDateMod** Specifies the minimum value of the last date modified attribute of a log file for the file to be parsed.

- **dQuotes** When **ON**, the IISW3C input format expects string fields in the file(s) being parsed to be surrounded by double-quote characters.

- **dirTime** When set to **ON**, the IISW3C input format fills in missing **date** and **time** field values with the value of the #**Fields** directive.

- **consolidateLogs** When log files from multiple virtual sites are parsed in a single query, setting this parameter to **ON** causes the IISW3C input format to return log entries ordered by date and time across all the input files.

- **iCheckpoint** Specifies the path of the checkpoint file to use when parsing the input file(s) incrementally.

NCSA Input Format

The NCSA input format parses log files in the NCSA Common, Combined, and Extended Log File Formats.

From-Entity

The NCSA input format accepts FROM clause values with the following syntax:

filename | siteID [, filename | siteID ...]

- **Filename** This is the path to a log file in any of the supported NCSA Log File Formats; the path can contain wildcards and can be in UNC notation if specifying log files on a remote share.

- **SiteID** This is the Metabase path of an IIS virtual site, enclosed in angled brackets; the Metabase path can be a full path that includes a remote server name (for example, **<//Mycomputer/W3SVC/12>**), or it can simply be the site's numeric identifier or the site's **ServerComment** property value (for example, **<12>**, **<www.mysite.com>**), eventually including wildcards.

Fields

The NCSA input format generates input records containing the following fields:

- LogFilename
- LogRow
- RemoteHostName
- RemoteLogName
- UserName
- DateTime
- Request
- StatusCode
- BytesSent
- Referer
- User-Agent
- Cookie

Parameters

- **iCodepage** Specifies the numeric identifier of the codepage of the file(s) being parsed. The special **–1** value means UNICODE, and the special **–2** value causes the IIS input format to automatically detect the codepage from the log file name and from the **LogInUTF8** property of the virtual site.

- **recurse** Specifies the number of subdirectories to recurse into. The special **–1** value means *unlimited recursion*.

- **minDateMod** Specifies the minimum value of the last date modified attribute of a log file for the file to be parsed.

- **iCheckpoint** Specifies the path of the checkpoint file to use when parsing the input file(s) incrementally.

NETMON Input Format

The NETMON input format returns properties of TCP packets and connections from NetMon capture files (.cap files). This input format works in two different modes. In *TCPIP* mode, the NETMON input format returns an input record for each TCP/IP *packet* found in the capture file(s) being parsed. In *TCPConn* mode, the NETMON input format returns an input record for each TCP/IP *connection* found in the capture file(s) being parsed. In the latter mode, the NETMON input format reconstructs the whole TCP connection from the packets, returning

aggregate fields such as the total payloads exchanged during the connection, and the total duration of the connection.

From-Entity

The NETMON input format accepts FROM clause values with the following syntax:

`filename [, filename …]`

- **Filename** Path to a NetMon capture file (.cap file).

Fields

When working in TCPIP mode, the NETMON input format generates input records with the
following fields:

- CaptureFilename
- Frame
- DateTime
- FrameBytes
- SrcMAC
- SrcIP
- SrcPort
- DstMAC
- DstIP
- DstPort
- IPVersion
- TTL
- TCPFlags
- Seq
- Ack
- WindowSize
- PayloadBytes
- Payload
- Connection

When working in TCPConn mode, the NETMON input format generates input records
with the following fields:

- CaptureFilename
- StartFrame
- EndFrame
- Frames
- DateTime
- TimeTaken
- SrcMAC
- SrcIP
- SrcPort
- SrcPayloadBytes
- SrcPayload
- DstMAC
- DstIP
- DstPort
- DstPayloadBytes
- DstPayload

Parameters

■ **fMode** This parameter controls the operation mode of the NETMON input format; the possible values for this parameter are **TCPIP** and **TCPConn**.

■ **binaryFormat** Specifies the format of binary data as one of the **ASC**, **HEX**, or **PRINT** values.

REG Input Format

The REG input format returns properties of registry keys and values.

From-Entity

The REG input format accepts FROM clause values with the following syntax:

```
[\\computername]\[rootname[\subkeypath]]  [,…]
```

■ **Computername** Optional computer name; used when enumerating keys from a remote registry.

■ **Rootname** Name of the registry root; can be on the following values: **HKCR**, **HKCU**, **HKLM**, **HKCC**, or **HKU**.

■ **Subkeypath** Path to a registry key below the specified root.

Fields

The REG input format generates input records with the following fields:

■ ComputerName
■ Path
■ KeyName
■ ValueName
■ ValueType
■ Value
■ LastWriteTime

Parameters

■ **recurse** Specifies the number of subdirectories to recurse into. The special **-1** value means *unlimited recursion*.

- **multiSZSep** This parameter specifies the string used as a separator between the elements of MULTI_SZ key values. The default value is the pipe (|) character.

- **binaryFormat** Specifies the format of binary data as one of the **ASC**, **HEX**, or **PRINT** values.

TEXTLINE Input Format

The TEXTLINE input format parses generic text files returning whole lines as a single input record field.

From-Entity

The TEXTLINE input format accepts FROM clause values with the following syntax:

```
filename [, filename …] |
http://url             |
STDIN
```

- **Filename** This is the path to a text file; the path can contain wildcards and can be in UNC notation if specifying log files on a remote share.

- **URL** This is the URL of a resource formatted as a text file.

- **STDIN** This special keyword specifies that the TEXTLINE input format should read the input data from the console input. This value is mostly used when piping commands and using the output of a command as the input of a Log Parser query.

Fields

The TEXTLINE input format generates input records containing the following fields:

- LogFilename
- Index
- Text

Parameters

- **iCodepage** Specifies the numeric identifier of the codepage of the file(s) being parsed.

- **recurse** Specifies the number of subdirectories to recurse into. The special **–1** value means *unlimited recursion*.

- **splitLongLines** Setting this parameter to **ON** causes the TEXTLINE input format to return lines longer than the maximum allowed as multiple input records. Setting this parameter to **OFF** causes the TEXTLINE input format to truncate long lines, returning only their initial section.

- **iCheckpoint** Specifies the path of the checkpoint file to use when parsing the input file(s) incrementally.

TEXTWORD Input Format

The TEXTWORD input format parses generic text files returning each word as a single input record field.

From-Entity

The TEXTWORD input format accepts FROM clause values with the following syntax:

```
filename [, filename …] |
http://url              |
STDIN
```

- **Filename** This is the path to a text file; the path can contain wildcards and can be in UNC notation if specifying log files on a remote share.

- **URL** This is the URL of a resource formatted as a text file.

- **STDIN** This special keyword specifies that the TEXTWORD input format should read the input data from the console input. This value is mostly used when piping commands and using the output of a command as the input of a Log Parser query.

Fields

The TEXTWORD input format generates input records containing the following fields:

- LogFilename
- Index
- Text

Parameters

- **iCodepage** Specifies the numeric identifier of the codepage of the file(s) being parsed.

- **recurse** Specifies the number of subdirectories to recurse into. The special **-1** value means *unlimited recursion*.

- **iCheckpoint** Specifies the path of the checkpoint file to use when parsing the input file(s) incrementally.

TSV Input Format

The TSV input format parses tab-separated and space-separated values text files. This input format works with a two-stage approach. During an initial inspection stage, the input format inspects a configurable number of lines in the TSV files to determine the number of fields, the field types, and the field names of the columns contained in the files. After the number of fields, their types, and their names has been determined, the real parsing stage begins, in which the files are parsed again from beginning to end, and input records are generated to be processed by the query.

From-Entity

The TSV input format accepts FROM clause values with the following syntax:

```
filename [, filename ...] |
http://url              |
STDIN
```

- **Filename** This is the path to a TSV file; the path can contain wildcards and can be in UNC notation if specifying files on a remote share.
- **URL** This is the URL of a resource formatted as TSV text.
- **STDIN** This special keyword specifies that the TSV input format should read the input data from the console input. This value is mostly used when piping commands and using the output of a command as the input of a Log Parser query.

Fields

The TSV input format generates input records containing the following fields:

- Filename
- RowNumber
- A field for each column in the input TSV file(s)

Parameters

- **iSeparator** Specifies the separator character used in the text file being parsed. The parameter can be set to **tab**, **space**, or to a custom character.

- **nSep** Specifies the number of separator characters that must appear to signify a field separator. This parameter is usually set to a value greater than one when parsing text files that use multiple space characters as separators, and whose field values can contain a single space character, as is the case with the output of the netstat utility.

- **fixedSep** When set to **ON**, the TSV input format assumes that the number of separator characters between fields is fixed, and equal to the value specified for the **nSep** parameter. Setting this parameter to **OFF** causes the TSV input format to assume that the number of separator characters between fields is variable, in which case the **nSep** parameter is assumed to indicate the *minimum* number of separator characters between fields.

- **headerRow** When set to **ON**, the TSV input format assumes that the file(s) being parsed contain a header line declaring the names of the columns in the file(s), and it extracts the column names from this line. When set to **OFF**, the TSV input format assumes that each file being parsed begins with the first line of data.

- **iHeaderFile** Specifies the path to a TSV text file containing a header line declaring the names of the columns in the file(s) being parsed. The column names found in the specified header file override the eventual column names declared by the header line in the file(s) being parsed.

- **nFields** This parameter can be used to specify directly the number of fields (columns) contained in the TSV file(s) being parsed. When this parameter is set to **-1** (the default value), the TSV input format determines the number of fields automatically during the initial inspection stage.

- **dtLines** Specifies the number of initial lines to be inspected during the initial inspection stage to determine the number of fields, the field types, and the field names of the columns contained in the file(s).

- **nSkipLines** This parameter specifies the number of lines that the TSV input format should skip in each file before it starts parsing its data.

- **lineFilter** Specifies a comma-separated list of prefixes of lines to be considered or ignored when parsing the input file(s). If the value specified for this parameter starts with "+", the TSV input format only parses lines that begin with one of the specified prefixes; if the value starts with "-", the TSV input format ignores all the lines that begin with one of the specified prefixes.

- **iCodepage** Specifies the numeric identifier of the codepage of the file(s) being parsed.

- **iTsFormat** Specifies the format of the timestamp values contained in the file(s) being parsed.

- **iCheckpoint** Specifies the path of the checkpoint file to use when parsing the input file(s) incrementally.

URLSCAN Input Format

The URLSCAN input format parses the log files created by the URLScan IIS filter.

From-Entity

The URLSCAN input format accepts FROM clause values with the following syntax:

```
filename [, filename ...] |
URLSCAN
```

- **Filename** Path to a URLScan log file.

- **URLSCAN** This keyword specifies that the user wants to parse all the URLScan log files available on the local computer.

Fields

The URLSCAN input format generates input records with the following fields:

- LogFilename
- LogRow
- Date
- ClientIP
- Comment
- SiteInstance
- Url

Parameters

- **iCheckpoint** Specifies the path of the checkpoint file to use when parsing the input file(s) incrementally.

W3C Input Format

The W3C input format parses log files in the W3C Extended Log File Format. Examples of log files in this format include Exchange Tracking log files, Personal Firewall log files, and Windows Media Server log files.

This input format inspects the **#Fields** directive contained in the header of the W3C log files to determine the number of fields and the field names contained in the log. During this initial inspection stage, the input format also inspects a configurable number of lines in the W3C files to determine the field types. After the number of fields, their types, and their names has been determined, the real parsing stage begins, in which the files are parsed again from beginning to end, and input records are generated to be processed by the query.

From-Entity

The W3C input format accepts FROM clause values with the following syntax:

```
filename [, filename …] |
http://url                 |
STDIN
```

- **Filename** This is the path to a W3C file; the path can contain wildcards and can be in UNC notation if specifying files on a remote share.
- **URL** This is the URL of a resource formatted as a W3C log file.
- **STDIN** This special keyword specifies that the W3C input format should read the input data from the console input. This value is mostly used when piping commands and using the output of a command as the input of a Log Parser query.

Fields

The W3C input format generates input records containing the following fields:

- Filename
- RowNumber
- A field for each column in the input W3C file(s)

Parameters

- **dtLines** Specifies the number of initial lines to be inspected during the initial inspection stage to determine the types of the columns contained in the file(s).
- **dQuotes** When **ON**, the W3C input format expects string fields in the file(s) being parsed to be surrounded by double-quote characters.
- **iCodepage** Specifies the numeric identifier of the codepage of the file(s) being parsed.
- **separator** Specifies the separator character used in the text file being parsed. The parameter can be set to **tab**, **space**, to a custom character, or to **auto**, which causes the W3C input format to determine the separator character automatically.

XML Input Format

The XML input format parses XML documents, returning the values of elements and attributes. This input format works in three different modes. In *Branch* mode, the XML input format returns the values of the elements and attributes found along the paths that start at the document root node and end at the document leaf nodes. In *Tree* mode, the XML input format returns the values of the elements and attributes contained in entire subtrees that satisfy particular conditions. In *Node* mode, the XML input format only considers instances of a user-specified node, returning its value and its attributes. For more information on the difference operation modes, consult the Log Parser documentation.

The XML input format works with a two-stage approach. During an initial inspection stage, the input format inspects a configurable number of nodes in the XML documents to determine the number of nodes and attributes, their types, and their names; the different nodes and attributes names found during this stage become the fields contained in the XML input format records. After the number of fields, their types, and their names has been determined, the real parsing stage begins, in which the documents are parsed again from beginning to end, and input records are generated to be processed by the query.

From-Entity

The XML input format accepts FROM clause values with the following syntax:

```
filename[#XPath] | url[#XPath] [, ...]
```

- **Filename** Path to an XML document.
- **XPath** Optional XPath specifying which nodes in the document are to be considered root nodes.
- **URL** URL of an XML resource.

Fields

The XML input format generates input records with field names corresponding to the names of the elements and attributes found in the document(s) being parsed.

Parameters

- **rootXPath** XPath selecting the nodes in the document that should be considered root nodes. The value of this parameter is overridden by the optional XPath specified in the FROM clause.
- **fMode** This parameter controls the operation mode of the XML input format; the possible values for this parameter are **Branch**, **Tree**, **Node**, and **Auto**, which specifies that the XML input format should select the best operation mode suitable for the schema of the document being parsed.

- **iTsFormat** Specifies the format of the timestamp values contained in the document(s) being parsed.

- **dtNodes** Specifies the number of initial leaf nodes to be inspected during the inspection stage to determine the number, types, and names of the input record fields.

- **fNames** When this parameter is set to **Compact**, fields are named after the name of the element or attribute they represent. When this parameter is set to **XPath**, fields are named after the full XPath to the element or attribute they represent.

Appendix D

Output Format Reference

- CHART Output Format

- CSV Output Format

- DATAGRID Output Format

- IIS Output Format

- NAT Output Format

- SQL Output Format

- SYSLOG Output Format

- TPL Output Format

- TSV Output Format

- W3C Output Format

- XML Output Format

In This Toolbox

Log Parser 2.2 provides 11 output formats that can be used to format query output records in a wide variety of text file formats (CSV, TSV, XML, W3C, IIS, and custom formats), to display results to the screen (NAT and DATAGRID output formats), to create image files containing charts, to upload results to a SQL database, and to send results to a SysLog server.

CHART Output Format

The CHART output format creates GIF and JPG image files containing chart representations of the output records of a query. In order to use the CHART output format, the computer running the Log Parser query must have the Microsoft Office Web Components installed, which are distributed with Microsoft Office 2000 and later versions.

Into-Entity

The CHART output format accepts INTO clause values with the following syntax:

filename

- **Filename** This is the path to the output GIF or JPG filename.

Parameters

- **chartType** Specifies the type of the desired output chart. The available values depend on the version of the Office Web Components installed; for a comprehensive list of chart type available on your computer, type the following command:

  ```
  LogParser -h -o:CHART
  ```

- **categories** Setting this parameter to **ON** causes the CHART output format to utilize the values of the first output record field as the labels of the categories on the x-axis. Setting this parameter to **OFF** causes the CHART output format to not display category labels, and to process the first output record field as a series of the chart. Setting this parameter to **AUTO** causes the CHART output format to automatically assume an **ON** value when the first output record field contains values of the STRING data type.

- **maxCategoryLabels** This parameter helps reduce clutter in the output chart by specifying the maximum number of category labels displayed on the x-axis. Specifying **–1** causes the CHART output format to display as many category labels as the number of output records; specifying **0** causes the CHART output format to automatically adjust the number of displayed category labels based on the geometrical dimensions of the chart.

- **legend** Setting this parameter to **ON** causes the CHART output format to display a legend for each numerical series plotted on the chart. Setting this parameter to **AUTO** causes the CHART output format to display a legend only when there are more than one numerical series to be plotted. When this parameter is set to **OFF**, the chart legend is never displayed.

- **values** Specifying **ON** or **OFF** for this parameter causes the CHART output format to display or not display value labels on the chart. Specifying **AUTO** causes the CHART output format to display value labels depending on the chart type selected.

- **groupSize** Specifies the dimensions of the target image, in pixels. This parameter has the following syntax:

  ```
  widthXheight
  ```

- **fileType** Can be **GIF**, **JPG**, or **AUTO**, in which case the CHART output format selects the format based on the extension of the filename provided for the INTO clause.

- **config** This parameter can be used to specify a comma-separated list of JScript or VBScript scripts that are executed immediately before rendering the chart, allowing users to customize the chart as desired.

- **chartTitle** Specifies a title for the chart.

- **oTsFormat** Format in which output record fields of the TIMESTAMP type are formatted.

- **view** Setting this parameter to **ON** causes the CHART output format to display the chart image after it has been saved to disk.

CSV Output Format

The CSV output format creates text file formatted according to the CSV (Comma-Separated-Values) convention.

Into-Entity

The CSV output format accepts INTO clause values with the following syntax:

```
filename |
STDOUT
```

- **Filename** This is the path to the output CSV text file. Since the CSV output format supports the *multiplex* feature, users can specify asterisk (*) wildcards in the output filename, causing the CSV output format to write its output to different output files whose names are created after substituting the wildcards with the first values of the output records.

- **STDOUT** Specifying this keyword causes the CSV output format to write its output to the console.

Parameters

- **headers** Specifying **ON** causes the CSV output format to begin the output with a header line containing the names of the fields. Specifying **OFF** disables the header altogether, and specifying **AUTO** causes the CSV output format to write a header only when not appending output to an existing file.

- **oDQuotes** Specifying **ON** for this parameter causes the CSV output format to enclose each field value within double-quote characters. Specifying **OFF** disables double-quoting altogether, and specifying **AUTO** causes the CSV output format to only double-quote those fields that contain comma characters.

- **tabs** Specifying **ON** for this parameter causes the CSV output format to write a tab character immediately after each separator comma.

- **oTsFormat** Specifies how TIMESTAMP field values should be formatted in the output.

- **oCodepage** This parameter specifies the codepage of the output file. Specifying **-1** causes the CSV output format to write UNICODE text files.

- **fileMode** Setting this parameter to **0** causes the CSV output format to append its output to a file when the file already exists. Specifying **1** causes the CSV output format to overwrite existing files, and specifying **2** causes the CSV output format to not modify an existing file.

DATAGRID Output Format

The DATAGRID output format displays output records in a window, allowing users to browse through the records, and to copy selected records to the clipboard.

Into-Entity

The DATAGRID output format accepts INTO clause values with the following syntax:

```
DATAGRID
```

- **DATAGRID** This keyword identifies the DATAGRID output format.

Parameters

- **rtp** Specifies the number of output records that should be displayed before waiting for the user to press the **Next *N* rows** button. Specifying **–1** causes the DATAGRID output format to display all the output records without interruption.

- **autoScroll** Specifying **ON** causes the DATAGRID output format to automatically scroll the window when new output records are displayed. Specifying **OFF** causes the DATAGRID output format to display new output records without scrolling the window.

IIS Output Format

The IIS output format creates text file formatted according to the Microsoft IIS Log File Format.

Into-Entity

The IIS output format accepts INTO clause values with the following syntax:

```
filename |
STDOUT
```

- **Filename** This is the path to the output text file. Since the IIS output format supports the multiplex feature, users can specify asterisk (*) wildcards in the output filename, causing the IIS output format to write its output to different output files whose names are created after substituting the wildcards with the first values of the output records.

- **STDOUT** Specifying this keyword causes the IIS output format to write its output to the console.

Parameters

- **rtp** When the IIS output format is writing to STDOUT, this parameter specifies the number of output records that should be displayed before waiting for the user to press a key. Specifying **–1** causes the IIS output format to display all the output records without interruption.

- **oCodepage** This parameter specifies the codepage of the output file. Specifying **–1** causes the IIS output format to write UNICODE text files.

- **fileMode** Setting this parameter to **0** causes the IIS output format to append its output to a file when the file already exists. Specifying **1** causes the IIS output format to overwrite existing files, and specifying **2** causes the IIS output format to not modify an existing file.

NAT Output Format

The NAT output format displays output records to the console window in a tabulated readable format.

Into-Entity

The NAT output format accepts INTO clause values with the following syntax:

```
filename |
STDOUT
```

- **Filename** This is the path to an output text file. Since the NAT output format supports the multiplex feature, users can specify asterisk (★) wildcards in the output filename, causing the NAT output format to write its output to different output files whose names are created after substituting the wildcards with the first values of the output records.

- **STDOUT** Specifying this keyword causes the NAT output format to write its output to the console. When no INTO clause is specified, the NAT output format uses "STDOUT" by default.

Parameters

- **rtp** When the NAT output format is writing to STDOUT, this parameter specifies the number of output records that should be displayed before waiting for the user to press a key. Specifying **-1** causes the NAT output format to display all the output records without interruption.

- **headers** Specifying **ON** causes the NAT output format to begin each group of output lines with a header line containing the names of the fields. Specifying **OFF** disables the header altogether.

- **spaceCol** Specifying **ON** causes the NAT output format to space columns uniformly within each group of output lines. Specifying **OFF** causes the NAT output format to separate columns using a single space character.

- **rAlign** Specifying **ON** causes the NAT output format to right-justify values within their columns. Specifying **OFF** causes the NAT output format to left-justify the output values.

- **colSep** This parameter specifies the string to be used as a separator between the columns.

- **direct** When this parameter is set to **ON**, the NAT output format disables its internal buffering mechanism used to group rows together and to calculate the uniform spacing between columns.

- **oCodepage** This parameter specifies the codepage of the output file. Specifying **–1** causes the NAT output format to write UNICODE text files.

- **fileMode** Setting this parameter to **0** causes the NAT output format to append its output to a file when the file already exists. Specifying **1** causes the NAT output format to overwrite existing files, and specifying **2** causes the NAT output format to not modify an existing file.

SQL Output Format

The SQL output format uploads output records to a table in an ODBC-compliant database.

Into-Entity

The SQL output format accepts INTO clause values with the following syntax:

`tablename`

- **Tablename** This is the name of the target table.

Parameters

- **server** Specifies the name of the database server.

- **database** Specifies the database name.

- **driver** Specifies the ODBC driver to use.

- **dsn** Specifies a Data Source Name that contains information on the database connection.

- **username** Specifies the name of a SQL account to use for the connection. When this parameter is not specified, the SQL output format uses Integrated Windows Authentication utilizing the current user's credentials.

- **password** Specifies the password for the SQL account specified with the **username** parameter.

- **oConnString** This parameter can be used as an alternative to the previous parameters to specify a connection string containing the ODBC parameters for the database connection.

- **createTable** Setting this parameter to **ON** causes the SQL output format to create the target table in case it does not already exists in the database. When the SQL output format creates a table, the SQL column types are derived from the data types of the query output records. For more information on the mappings between the Log Parser data types and the SQL column types, see the Log Parser documentation.

- **clearTable** Setting this parameter to **ON** causes the SQL output format to delete all the existing entries from the target table before uploading the query output records.

- **fixColNames** Setting this parameter to **ON** causes the SQL output format to process the output record field names and remove illegal characters before creating column names for the target table.

- **maxStrFieldLen** This parameter specifies the maximum number of characters for the **string** SQL column types that are created when the target table does not already exist.

- **transactionRowCount** Specifies the number of output records to enclose in SQL transactions. Specifying **–1** causes the SQL output format to enclose *all* the output records in a single transaction, while specifying **0** causes the SQL output format to enable *auto commit* mode, in which each output record uploaded to the target table is individually committed.

- **ignoreMinWarns** Setting this parameter to **ON** causes the SQL output format to ignore minor warnings that might occur at run time. Specifying **OFF** causes the SQL output format to report these minor warnings when the command execution is complete.

- **ignoreIdCols** When uploading to an existing table, the SQL output requires that the number of fields in the output records match exactly the number of columns in the target table, and it uploads output record fields to each column in the target table. Setting this parameter to **ON** causes the SQL output format to ignore target table columns of the **identity** type, and it uploads output record fields only to those columns that are not of the **identity** type.

SYSLOG Output Format

The SYSLOG output format can be used to send output records to a SYSLOG server, to send SYSLOG messages to a user, or to create text files containing entries formatted according to the SYSLOG specifications.

Into-Entity

The SYSLOG output format accepts INTO clause values with the following syntax:

```
@server[:port] | filename | username [, ...]
```

- **Server** This is the name of the SYSLOG server.
- **Port** This is the optional port on which the SYSLOG server listens for messages.
- **Filename** This is the path to an output text file to which SYSLOG messages will be written to.
- **Username** This is the account name to which SYSLOG messages will be sent, using the Windows *net send* mechanism.

Parameters

- **conf** Specifies the path to a SYSLOG configuration file containing the actions to perform for different SYSLOG messages. For more information, consult the Log Parser documentation.
- **severity** Severity level of the message. Can be specified as a number, as a severity level name, or as the **$** character followed by the name of an output record field containing the severity value.
- **facility** Facility of the message. Can be specified as a number, as a facility name, or as the **$** character followed by the name of an output record field containing the facility value.
- **oTsFormat** Format of the SYSLOG message **timestamp** field.
- **hostname** Value of the SYSLOG message **hostname** field. Can also be specified as the **$** character followed by the name of an output record field containing the value of the **hostname** field.
- **processName** Value of the SYSLOG message **processname** or **TAG** field. Can also be specified as the **$** character followed by the name of an output record field containing the value of the **processname** field.
- **separator** Separator to be used between the SYSLOG message fields.
- **maxPacketSize** Maximum message size, in bytes.
- **protocol** Protocol to use when sending messages to a SYSLOG server; possible values are **TCP** and **UDP**.
- **sourcePort** Source port for messages sent to SYSLOG server. Specifying "★" causes the SYSLOG output format to use the first available port.
- **ignoreDspchErrs** Setting this parameter to **ON** causes the SYSLOG output format to buffer errors that occur while dispatching messages to their destination, reporting all of them as warnings when the execution is completed. Setting this parameter to **OFF** causes the SYSLOG output format to report errors when they occur, aborting the execution of the current query.

- **discardOversized** Setting this parameter to **ON** causes the SYSLOG output format to discard messages exceeding the maximum size specified with the **maxPacketSize** parameter. Setting this parameter to **OFF** causes the SYSLOG output format to truncate messages and dispatch them.

- **oCodepage** This parameter specifies the codepage of the messages. Specifying **–1** causes the SYSLOG output format to write UNICODE messages.

TPL Output Format

The TPL output format creates text file formatted according to user-defined templates. Template files specify the text that should be output once at the beginning (the *header*), repeatedly for each output record (the *body*), and once at the end (the *footer*).

Each of the three sections can contain variables that are substituted with output record values. The variables that can be specified in any section are:

- **%FIELDNAME_N%** Name of the specified output record field.

- **%FIELDS_NUM%** Number of fields in the output records.

- **%SYSTEM_TIMESTAMP%** Date and time at which the output is created.

- **%*environment_variable*%** Value of the specified environment variable.

The variables that can be specified in the body section only are:

- **%FIELD_N%** Value of the specified output record field.

- **%*field_name*%** Value of the specified output record field.

Template files can be specified as three different files (header, body, and footer), or as a single file containing tags delimiting the three sections. In the latter case, the tags are:

- \<LPHEADER>...\</LPHEADER>: delimits the header section.

- \<LPBODY>...\</LPBODY>: delimits the body section.

- \<LPFOOTER>...\</LPFOOTER>: delimits the footer section.

Into-Entity

The TPL output format accepts INTO clause values with the following syntax:

```
filename |
STDOUT
```

- **Filename** This is the path to the output text file. Since the TPL output format supports the multiplex feature, users can specify asterisk (*) wildcards in the output filename, causing the TPL output format to write its output to different output files whose names are created after substituting the wildcards with the first values of the output records.

- **STDOUT** Specifying this keyword causes the TPL output format to write its output to the console.

Parameters

- **tpl** This parameter specifies either the template file for the body section, or the single template file containing the three sections together, delimited by the <LPHEADER>, <LPBODY>, and <LPFOOTER> tags.

- **tplHeader** This parameter specifies the template file containing the header section.

- **tplFooter** This parameter specifies the template file containing the footer section.

- **noEmptyFile** When the query does not produce output records, setting this parameter to **ON** prevents the TPL output format from creating an empty file.

- **oCodepage** This parameter specifies the codepage of the output file. Specifying **-1** causes the TPL output format to write UNICODE text files.

- **fileMode** Setting this parameter to **0** causes the TPL output format to append its output to a file when the file already exists. Specifying **1** causes the TPL output format to overwrite existing files, and specifying **2** causes the TPL output format to not modify an existing file.

TSV Output Format

The TSV output format creates text file formatted according to the TSV (Tab-Separated-Values) convention.

Into-Entity

The TSV output format accepts INTO clause values with the following syntax:

```
filename |
STDOUT
```

- **Filename** This is the path to the output TSV text file. Since the TSV output format supports the multiplex feature, users can specify asterisk (*) wildcards in the output filename, causing the TSV output format to write its output to different output files whose names are created after substituting the wildcards with the first values of the output records.

- **STDOUT** Specifying this keyword causes the TSV output format to write its output to the console.

Parameters

- **headers** Specifying **ON** causes the TSV output format to begin the output with a header line containing the names of the fields. Specifying **OFF** disables the header altogether, and specifying **AUTO** causes the TSV output format to write a header only when not appending output to an existing file.

- **oSeparator** This parameter specifies the separator to use between the field values. Specifying **tab** causes the TSV output format to use a single tab character between the fields, while specifying **space** causes the TSV output format to use a single space character between the fields.

- **oTsFormat** Specifies how TIMESTAMP field values should be formatted in the output.

- **oCodepage** This parameter specifies the codepage of the output file. Specifying **-1** causes the TSV output format to write UNICODE text files.

- **fileMode** Setting this parameter to **0** causes the TSV output format to append its output to a file when the file already exists. Specifying **1** causes the TSV output format to overwrite existing files, and specifying **2** causes the TSV output format to not modify an existing file.

W3C Output Format

The W3C output format creates text file formatted according to the W3C Extended Log File Format.

Into-Entity

The W3C output format accepts INTO clause values with the following syntax:

```
filename |
STDOUT
```

- **Filename** This is the path to the output W3C text file. Since the W3C output format supports the multiplex feature, users can specify asterisk (*) wildcards in the output filename, causing the W3C output format to write its output to different output files whose names are created after substituting the wildcards with the first values of the output records.

- **STDOUT** Specifying this keyword causes the W3C output format to write its output to the console.

Parameters

- **rtp** When the W3C output format is writing to STDOUT, this parameter specifies the number of output records that should be displayed before waiting for the user to press a key. Specifying **–1** causes the W3C output format to display all the output records without interruption.

- **oDQuotes** Specifying **ON** for this parameter causes the W3C output format to enclose string field values within double-quote characters. Specifying **OFF** causes the W3C output format to never enclose fields within double-quote characters.

- **oDirTime** This parameter specifies the value that the W3C output format should use when writing the **#Date** directive at the beginning of the W3C output. When this parameter is not specified, the W3C output format uses the current date and time.

- **encodeDelim** Setting this parameter to **ON** causes the W3C output format to substitute space characters in field values with plus characters.

- **oCodepage** This parameter specifies the codepage of the output file. Specifying **–1** causes the W3C output format to write UNICODE text files.

- **fileMode** Setting this parameter to **0** causes the W3C output format to append its output to a file when the file already exists. Specifying **1** causes the W3C output format to overwrite existing files, and specifying **2** causes the W3C output format to not modify an existing file.

XML Output Format

The XML output format creates XML text files formatting the output record fields as XML nodes and attributes.

Into-Entity

The XML output format accepts INTO clause values with the following syntax:

```
filename |
STDOUT
```

- **Filename** This is the path to the output XML text file. Since the XML output format supports the multiplex feature, users can specify asterisk (*) wildcards in the output filename, causing the XML output format to write its output to different output files whose names are created after substituting the wildcards with the first values of the output records.

- **STDOUT** Specifying this keyword causes the XML output format to write its output to the console.

Parameters

- **structure** This parameter specifies the structure of the output XML document. Specifying **1** or **2** causes the XML output format to create nodes with the names of the output record fields, and to save the field values as values of these nodes. When **2** is specified, nodes contain a **TYPE** attribute with the data type of the field. Specifying **3** or **4** causes the XML output format to create nodes named **FIELD** having a **NAME** attribute with the name of the field, and to save the field values as values of these nodes; when **4** is specified, nodes contain an additional **TYPE** attribute with the data type of the field.

- **rootName** This parameter specifies the name of the document root node.

- **rowName** This parameter specifies the name of the node containing the field value nodes.

- **fieldName** This parameter specifies the name of the node containing the output record field values when the **structure** parameter is set to **3** or **4**.

- **xslLink** This parameter specifies the path to an XSL file a link to which is placed at the beginning of the XML document.

- **schemaType** Specifying **0** causes the XML output format to not write any schema in the XML document. Specifying **1** causes the XML output format to write an inline DTD schema in the XML document.

- **compact** Specifying **ON** for this parameter causes the XML output format to write compact XML output suppressing indentation space characters and carriage-return/line-feed characters.

- **noEmptyField** Specifying **ON** for this parameter prevents the XML output format from writing empty nodes when the corresponding output record field values are NULL.

- **standAlone** Specifying **ON** causes the XML output format to write an XML header and a root node that contains all the output record nodes. Specifying **OFF** causes the XML output format to write only the output record nodes.

- **oCodepage** This parameter specifies the codepage of the output file. Specifying **–1** causes the XML output format to write UNICODE text files.

- **fileMode** Setting this parameter to **0** causes the XML output format to append its output to a file when the file already exists. Specifying **1** causes the XML output format to overwrite existing files, and specifying **2** causes the XML output format to not modify an existing file.

Index